THE PRIME MINISTERS

THE
PRIME
MINISTERS

VOLUME THE SECOND

FROM LORD JOHN RUSSELL TO EDWARD HEATH

EDITED BY HERBERT VAN THAL

WITH AN INTRODUCTION BY ROBERT BLAKE

LONDON

GEORGE ALLEN & UNWIN LTD

RUSKIN HOUSE   MUSEUM STREET

First published in 1975

© George Allen & Unwin Ltd 1975

ISBN 0 04 942134 4

Printed in Great Britain
in 12 pt Barbou type
by W & J Mackay Limited
Chatham

CONTENTS

CONTENTS

ILLUSTRATIONS

The portraits numbered 1–7, 9, 11, 12, 14–16 and 18 were supplied by the National Portrait Gallery. The photographs numbered 17 and 19–23 were supplied by the photographer Vivienne, and portraits 8 and 13 by the Mansell Collection.

INTRODUCTION

THE PRIME MINISTER
1835–1974

BY

ROBERT BLAKE

THE PRIME MINISTER 1835-1974

In the period with which we are concerned the premiership became, more even than before, the goal on which politicians set their sights, the final object of their ambition. Melbourne was perhaps an exception. When sent for by the King he told his private secretary that 'he thought it a damned bore and was in many minds what he should do – be Minister or no'. His secretary ('a vulgar familiar impudent fellow', according to Greville, from whom the story comes) replied 'Why damn it, such a position never was occupied by any Greek or Roman, and, if it only lasts two months, it is well worth while to have been Prime Minister of England'. Melbourne decided to accept. A hundred and twenty-one years later Clement Attlee quoted the same expression in ironically congratulating Anthony Eden on his accession to office at a time when an election was generally regarded as imminent. Few people after Melbourne would have regarded the premiership as 'a damned bore'. Nearly all of them would have privately echoed the sentiments of his secretary.

Melbourne's own career symbolised and emphasised the most important single change which affected the post of prime minister since the days of Walpole – the change from the concept of government as the King's government to government as party government. Lord Liverpool, the Duke of Wellington, Grey, Melbourne himself, insofar as they reflected on the matter, would have thought of themselves primarily as servants of the Crown – and of course there is a sense in which prime ministers still rightly think of themselves in that light today. The difference is that until 1832 the Crown could within certain limits choose a prime minister who would be sure to win an ensuing general election. This was because of the 'influence' which automatically went to him by virtue of his position as First Lord of the Treasury. It is significant that from 1715 to 1835 no government actually lost a general election. Even in 1830 Wellington was not defeated at the polls. In such a situation, although the Prime Minister had to be able to manage Parliament and was liable to be pushed out if he was palpably incompetent to do so, it was even more vital for him to manage the monarch.

All this was changed – though not immediately – with the events of 1834–5. In November 1834 the death of Earl Spencer and the succession of his son Lord Althorp to the peerage created a vacancy in the leadership of the House of Commons. Rather than accept the nomination of Lord John Russell, William IV in effect dismissed Melbourne, making the same interpretation of his own constitutional role that his father had made when dismissing the Fox-North coalition half a century earlier. He assumed that Peel, after a few weeks in which to collect his forces together, would dissolve, and win the next general election even as the younger Pitt had done in 1784. But events did not work out that way, nor did either Wellington, or Peel who took office with reluctance, expect them to do so. The world of 1834 was very different from that of 1784, and not only because of the Reform Act. For many years past 'royal government' had been running down. By the 1820s there were signs that the supply of patronage – the oil that greased the moving parts of the old machine – was beginning to be insufficient. Successive Tory governments in 1818, 1820, 1826 and 1830 managed to win, but with increasing difficulty. The general election of January 1835, however, saw the first clear decision against a prime minister who had the avowed support of the King. Peel tried to carry on, but the Whigs were determined to force him out. After numerous defeats he resigned in April. The King was obliged to send for Melbourne and to accept Lord John Russell as Leader of the House. It was by the old standards a humiliating rebuff.

Never again was a monarch to dismiss a prime minister, although some monarchs continued to talk as if they could, and in the Ulster crisis of 1912–14 such a course was urged by the hotter headed Unionists. When once it was clear that the Crown could no longer ensure electoral success for its own nominee there was really no choice between the risk of open political partisanship which the Crown could not in the end survive, or withdrawal to the position of neutrality which prevails today.

Yet the logic of the situation was not at once apparent. The Bedchamber Crisis of May 1839 is one example. Neither Peel nor Melbourne would have behaved quite as they did if the Crown had been regarded as a neutral factor in politics, and the situation was made no easier by Melbourne's dual role as Prime Minister and Queen's Private Secretary – a combination which was ended soon after her marriage to Prince Albert who took on that task himself. But as late as 1841 the Prince was horrified to find that money from the Privy Purse had been used towards Whig expenses in the general election of that year. The Queen was, moreover, still sufficiently imbued with the notion that the government were 'her' servants to declare privately that she would not have agreed to a dissolution if she had expected Melbourne to lose.

Although the 1830s were marked by this important change from Crown government to party government, it would be a mistake to think that it was the sort of party government which we know today. The Prime Minister did, it is true, have to keep his party behind him if he was to survive, as Peel found to his cost in 1846. But parties were not the cohesive all embracing organisations familiar to us. They were ill disciplined groups, each with a fringe of those independent members whom Disraeli described as members who could not be depended upon. If power had passed from the Crown it had not yet moved to the electorate. In fact the period from 1835 to 1868 saw the heyday of the supremacy of the House of Commons – the situation so brilliantly described by Bagehot, at the very moment that it was on the verge of being transformed into something quite different. The Cabinet was a committee of the legislature. The House of Commons rather than the electorate made and unmade governments. Six parliaments were elected between 1841 and 1868. In the case of five of them the House of Commons had brought down at least one administration, sometimes two, before its dissolution. The only exception was the parliament of 1859 to 1865 which Palmerston controlled virtually from start to finish.

This period of governmental instability, more reminiscent of the French 3rd and 4th Republics than the British system of today, began to change in the 1870s. Whether or not it was a matter of cause and effect, the Reform Act of 1867 was followed by a series of general elections which gave far more decisive results in the House than anything since 1841 and this trend continued after further extensions of the franchise. It was symbolic of the new pattern of politics that in 1868 Disraeli resigned on the morrow of the general election without waiting to test the opinion of the House, so clear had been the verdict of the polls. Some people grumbled and said his conduct was unconstitutional, but Gladstone reluctantly followed the same course in 1874, and Disraeli repeated his action in 1880. Since then it has only been in highly exceptional circumstances (e.g. 1924 or 1974 when the election result was ambiguous), that a Prime Minister has failed to accept at once what appears to be the decision of the electorate. Even in 1964, despite one or two suggestions to the contrary, Sir Alec Douglas-Home resigned as soon as the results were in, though Labour's victory was by the narrowest margin ever known.

A corollary of this development has been the rareness since the 1880s of any government falling to an adverse vote in the House. Gladstone was defeated on a major bill (Irish Home Rule) in 1886. He promptly dissolved Parliament and lost the ensuing election. Rosebery resigned on an adverse vote in 1894, but he need not have done so, for the issue was a minor one. Ramsay MacDonald was defeated in 1924, and followed the same course with the same result as Gladstone thirty-eight years earlier. The last occasion on which the House can be said to have forced the Prime Minister to resign was the fall of Neville Chamberlain in 1940, but he was not actually defeated. It was a massive slump in his normally overwhelming parliamentary majority which decided him to go.

From the 1870s onwards party government in the modern sense has prevailed. It is during this period that the mass party organisations in the country established themselves – a recognition that power has shifted to the electorate. Gladstone appreciated the change when he wrote to Rosebery in the 1880s: 'What is outside Parliament seems to me to be fast mounting, nay to have already mounted to an importance much exceeding what is inside'. The Birmingham 'Caucus', the National Union of Conservative Associations – these were the typical institutions of the new era. Prime Ministers had become heads of one or other of two great political parties with electoral committees or associations in almost every constituency. Of course Peel and Melbourne, Russell and Derby had also been leaders of parties. The difference after 1867 was that Gladstone and Disraeli led parties which not only operated in Parliament but had spread their roots throughout the country.

By a natural process of development the leaders of these parties came to symbolise the cause or causes for which they stood. It is often alleged that this personification of politics is a new phenomenon, caused in part by the exposure to the mass media. It is no doubt true that every elector nowadays knows what Mr Heath and Mr Wilson look like. They would not be as lucky as Peel, who escaped assassination because the lunatic who intended to kill him shot his private secretary instead. But by the time of Gladstone and Disraeli most electors must from cartoons and other representations have had a fair idea of the appearance of the great rivals, and there can be no question that their personalities dominated the whole political scene, not merely, as for example in the case of Pitt and Fox, the House of Commons. Writing of the passions provoked by the Eastern crisis in 1878 Henry Loch, Governor of the Isle of Man commented.

'. . . when the questions are discussed, which they are morning, noon and night by all classes and by both sexes there is an intensity of excitement that frequently breaks out in the most violent language – and it is all *purely personal*, the divergence of opinion being not so much upon the merits of the questions which seem seldom understood, but upon the feelings that are entertained either towards Lord Beaconsfield or Mr Gladstone.'

There is nothing new during the last hundred years in this polarisation of personalities. It depends upon the personalities. There have been many times since the days of Disraeli and Gladstone when it did not apply – for example after Disraeli's death when Northcote and Salisbury opposed Gladstone. Again between 1902 and 1911 when on the one side Balfour and on the other Campbell-Bannerman and Asquith led their respective parties, one may well doubt whether personality was particularly relevant. Forty-five years later with Churchill and Attlee it was relevant, and also during the period when first Mr Macmillan confronted Hugh Gaitskell and later Sir Alec Douglas-Home and then Mr Heath confronted Mr Wilson. But there is no clear trend. We can go back to a time before the great duel between Disraeli and Gladstone and find Lord Shaftesbury writing after the election of 1857. 'There seems to be no measure, no principle, no cry, to influence men's minds and determine elections; it is simply, "Were you or were you not? Are you, or are you not, for Palmerston?"'

The question of personality leads to the question of power – one of the most keenly debated subjects in the historiography of the post of Prime Minister. Are Prime Ministers more powerful now than ever before? Has 'Prime Ministerial' Government replaced Cabinet Government? If so when has the change taken place? What are the reasons for it? Is it a good thing? How is it related to Presidential Government in the American mode? No one can deny that a great change has taken place since the era described by Bagehot. It is perhaps doubtful whether even in his day one could correctly describe the Cabinet as 'a board of control chosen by the legislature' or the Prime Minister as 'elected by the representatives of the people'. Certainly such descriptions would be inadequate in the 1970s. Indeed it could be argued that they have been inadequate for the last hundred years, although it was not until L. S. Amery's *Thoughts on the Constitution* (the Chichele Lectures delivered in Oxford soon after the end of the second World War), that the all-pervasive Bagehot myth was finally blown away.

Bagehot's picture of the working of the constitution does not correspond to modern reality. Nor did it correspond to reality as long ago as the era of Disraeli and Gladstone; the important question is what changes have taken place since then. The most interesting and controversial discussion of this matter is the late Mr R. H. S. Crossman's introduction to the new edition of Bagehot's *The English Constitution* published in 1963 just before Mr Crossman himself became a member of the Labour Cabinet. His theme is that the power of the Prime Minister has enormously increased during and since the second World War. Bagehot had described the Cabinet as 'the hyphen which joins, the buckle which fastens, the legislative part of the state to the executive'. According to Mr Crossman that role is now fulfilled by a single man. 'The post war epoch has seen the final transformation of Cabinet Government into Prime Ministerial Government.'

Mr Crossman discerns three causes for the change. There has been the growth of the power of party which has reduced that of the individual MP, diminished his chances of defying party orthodoxy and removed the real debate on political issues 'from the floor of the Commons to the secrecy of the Committee rooms upstairs'. This enhances the power of the Prime Minister in his capacity as the party leader. 'Politics is inevitably personified and simplified in the public mind into a battle between two super-leaders – appointed for life or until they are removed by an intra party *coup d'état*.' Secondly there was the ending of Cabinet informality by the creation of a secretariat to keep the minutes and circulate papers. This occurred soon after Lloyd George became Prime Minister, and inevitably enhanced the Prime Minister's powers by giving him what was tantamount to a department of his own.

Lloyd George was also involved in the third of Mr Crossman's suggested causes of change – the unification of the civil service, with the Permanent Under Secretary of the Treasury at its head. This occurred in September 1919 when Sir Warren Fisher persuaded the Prime Minister that the talents of civil servants would be better recognised and used if people could move from department to department, instead of staying for the whole career in the same one – the prevailing practice hitherto. A further regulation 'laid down that the consent of the Premier (which in practice meant the head of the civil service) would be required in all departments to the appointment of permanent heads and their deputies.' The upshot, so Mr Crossman argues, was the creation of a 'group of super-bureaucrats each confident that he can take charge at a few weeks' notice of a Ministry of which he has had no previous experience'. This has replaced the old system of a cluster of departments with their own traditions, styles and methods of recruitment.

Here Mr Crossman perhaps proves too much. The power of the Prime Minister over his Cabinet colleagues may well have been increased by the unification of the civil service, for Ministers no longer appoint to the permanent headships of their departments, but Mr Crossman agrees that it is not really the Prime Minister who takes over that role. In practice it is the head of the Civil Service. So, if the Prime Minister has gained power as regards Ministers, can it not be argued also that he has in some measure lost it to the 'super-bureaucrats'? This raises a wider question. Is it clear that Peel who was his own Secretary to the Cabinet and the Treasury and who supervised every department of state, had a less powerful position than Sir Alec Douglas-Home who was operating when the changes described by Mr Crossman should have had ample time to become fully effective? Prime Ministerial power is not a simple or straightforward concept. There is obviously one sense in which any modern prime minister has more power than Peel, Gladstone, Lloyd George or Neville Chamberlain, because government itself controls a far wider part of national life than it ever has before. The real question is the balance of power within the governmental system at this or that moment of time. It is doubtful whether the change has been as definite as Mr Crossman implies. In an illuminating study of the British constitution – *The Body Politic* (1969) – Mr Ian Gilmour who like Mr Crossman has come into office subsequently (though on the opposite political side) puts the point clearly.

'The writers of the Prime Ministerial school make the same mistake as the Whig historians made about George III and the monarchy: they overrate his power today and underrate the power he had in the past.

The development of the office has not been all one way. The progress towards Caesarism has been uneven and its starting point uncertain.'

Lord Morley in his *Walpole* (1889) said: 'The flexibility of the Cabinet system allows the Prime Minister to take upon himself a power not inferior to that of a dictator, provided always that the House of Commons will stand by him'. Morley was writing about the first prime minister, but he certainly had in mind the office as he knew it. He had been a member of Gladstone's Cabinet in 1886. He perceived the great power which lay in the hands of someone determined to use it, and also the limitations; the House of Commons did not stand by Gladstone in 1886 and he was defeated on the second reading of the Irish Home Rule Bill.

The truth is that the powers of the Prime Minister have varied with the personality of the Prime Minister or with the particular political circumstances of his tenure. No one has come nearer to Presidential government on the American model than Lloyd George. Yet none of the factors which Mr Crossman sees as causing this development in the second half of the twentieth century applied then. The cabinet secretariat and the unification of the civil service were indeed the results of decisions by Lloyd George but they cannot have had much effect before 1922. As for the position of the Prime Minister as leader of his party, Lloyd George was especially ill placed. He led no party, only a Liberal splinter group. In the end this weakness was fatal, but it did not handicap him at the height of his prestige when, after virtually abolishing the old Cabinet system, he said, perhaps half in jest, that he thought of doing without the Cabinet altogether, when he conducted foreign policy through a private office of his own, 'the garden suburb', by-passing the indignant Lord Curzon, and when he effortlessly dominated the House of Commons, carrying his way on almost every issue.

Lloyd George was not the first Prime Minister to treat his Cabinet in this cavalier way. Campbell-Bannerman never revealed to the full Cabinet the staff conversations with the French initiated in December 1905 by Sir Edward Grey. His latest biographer, Mr John Wilson, considers that this was a deliberate decision taken in order to avoid a row with the radical wing of the ministry. In 1877, during the Russo-Turkish war, an even more striking instance of Prime Ministerial secrecy occurred. Disraeli had tried to persuade the Cabinet to issue an ultimatum to Russia, threatening war in the event of a second campaign against Turkey in the spring of the following year. The Cabinet, as so often at that time, would neither agree nor disagree. Disraeli, accordingly, sent a secret emissary to St Petersburg to inform the Tsar that the

Cabinet was entirely united in its determination to go to war, if there was a second campaign. The other ministers, including the Foreign Secretary, were kept in ignorance of this démarche by their chief, and some of them would undoubtedly have raised the strongest objections had they known.

Modern Prime Ministers have been much more 'correct'. Oddly enough the two instances of Prime Ministerial indifference to Cabinet responsibility quoted by Mr Crossman do not really support his case. He makes much of Attlee's alleged by-passing of the Cabinet over the construction of the atomic bomb, but the facts do not substantiate the charge. The decision, it is true, was taken by the Defence sub-committee of the Cabinet, but the minutes were circulated to all members of the Cabinet. Moreover it was communicated to Parliament in answer to a question on 12 May 1948. He is possibly on better ground over the Suez crisis. The facts here are more obscure, but it seems on balance that, although some ministers may have felt that they had been 'bounced', the correct constitutional procedure was formally followed. No doubt much more was known by some than others, and the detailed planning was done by a group in close sympathy with Anthony Eden's aims. This, however, is common form. Neville Chamberlain constituted with himself, Lord Halifax, Sir John Simon and Sir Samuel Hoare just such a group at the time of Munich in 1938. In every Cabinet some ministers are more equal than others.

Of course Mr Crossman is quite right to point out some of the changes which have altered the constitutional framework within which the Prime Minister operated. The positions of the civil service, the political parties, the Crown, the legislature, are not the same as they were a hundred years ago, and they were not the same then as they had been fifty, let alone a hundred years before that. The enormous extension of the powers of government, in Britain as in all countries, in itself changes the role of the Prime Minister, just as it has changed that of the President of France or the President of the United States.

Nevertheless, the position of the Prime Minister in terms of an internal balance of power has not changed as fundamentally as all that. The differences are still largely between personalities – the way in which this or that occupant of 10 Downing Street in the light of his own circumstances feels that he should or can behave. Lord Liverpool was described some forty years after his death as the last prime minister to have governed Britain. He was succeeded by Goderich, 'a transient and embarrassed phantom' who lasted a few months and resigned before he met Parliament – one of the very few Prime Ministers in history to have escaped this not unimportant duty.

The study of Prime Ministers' lives is one of perpetual fascination. It is rash to lay down any hard and fast rules about the nature of the position. Perhaps in this respect one can echo the words Disraeli put into the mouth of one of the characters in a novel, 'Read no history, only biography, for that is life without theory.'

1

LORD JOHN RUSSELL

BY

JOHN PREST

Lord John Russell, created Earl Russell and Viscount Amberley 1861. KG 1862. Born 18 August 1792, the third son of the Sixth Duke of Bedford. Educated at Westminster School and Edinburgh University. MP (Whig) for Tavistock 1813, 1818, 1830; Huntingdonshire 1820, Bandon 1826, S. Devon 1831, Stroud 1835–41, City of London 1841–61. Married (1) 1835 Lady Ribblesdale (who died in 1838), four step-children, two daughters; (2) 1841 Lady Fanny Elliot, three sons and one daughter. Paymaster of the Forces 1830–34; drafted the Reform Bill 1830; entered the Cabinet 1831. Following his choice as Leader of the Commons in 1834, William IV dismissed his ministers. Home Secretary 1835–39, Colonial Secretary 1839–41; Prime Minister 1846–52; joined Aberdeen's ministry of 1852 as Leader of the Commons until 1855; Foreign Secretary 1859–65; Prime Minister 1865–66. Died 28 May 1878. Author of Memoirs of Affairs of Europe, *1824;* History of the English Government and Constitution, *1821; etc.*

LORD JOHN RUSSELL

Lord John Russell regarded Peel's fall as marking the end of an experiment. Politicians on all sides – and not least Lord John, who had drafted the Bill – expected the Reform Act of 1832 to diminish the influence of ministers, and to increase the pressures which public opinion and a majority in the House of Commons could exercise upon the government of the day. Melbourne accepted this, and in 1835 he allowed his administration to be committed to the appropriation of the surplus revenues of the Church of Ireland at the instance of Lord John and the coalition of advanced Whigs, Radicals and Irish by whom he was supported.

Peel, on the other hand, regarded 'weak' government as a great evil, and when he took office in 1841 he deliberately attempted to impose a 'strong' executive upon the reformed Parliament. Indeed, he aimed, Lord John thought, 'at a much greater agreement of opinion, and at a much greater identity of conduct on the part of the members of his Administration, and of his party generally' than had been achieved even by the most distinguished of his predecessors of pre-Reform Bill days, Pitt and Liverpool. Simultaneously he set his face against the Manchester manufacturers' campaign for the repeal of the Corn Laws, and brushed aside the Whigs' plea for a concession in season. 'For a time,' Lord John continued, 'from his great talents' and 'great power in conducting a ministry', Peel was successful. But the very unanimity of his Cabinet alarmed his supporters, who resented being whipped into line by threats of resignation and anticipated a *volte face* upon free trade, and in 1845 Disraeli spoke of having a commission issued 'to inquire into the tenure by which Downing Street is held'. When the disease of the potato made the demand for the repeal of the Corn Laws irresistible, Peel's failure was complete. 'Stout resistance' to extra-parliamentary agitation was followed by 'unqualified concession', and that in turn by the disintegration of the Conservative party. Peel had ridden on too tight a rein, and the crash of 1846 was proportioned to the over-confidence of the rider. As Lord John understated it, Peel's approach was not likely to be successful again, or to be advantageous to the country. His ministry had served, as many ministries do, not to solve the problem, but to eliminate one of the possible routes to its solution, and when Lord John took office it was apparent that there must be a new departure. 'Any government to be formed at present or in the future', and especially a Liberal one, must be conducted in a more responsive manner. Lord John would not attempt to stamp his own personality upon the affairs of every department, and he would tolerate wider divergences of opinion within his Cabinet than his predecessor had done.

Melbourne's administration had taken its policy from its majority in the House of Commons, Peel's from the aims of its chief. Lord John Russell's problem was that the attempt to rule Parliament through a strong executive having failed, it was impossible simply to fall back upon a party majority, because there was none. Lord John took office with about 250 supporters in a House of 658, and for a whole year, while he hoped that the general election in 1847 would do something to get the House back into two parties and give the Whigs a reliable majority, he was sustained in office by the mutual antipathies of the Protectionists and the Peelites. But the Peelites fought the election as a separate party, and the result was to weaken and fragment the Opposition still further. The Whigs, Liberals and Radicals came back about 330 strong, but parties take their cohesion from each other, and with disarray to the right of him, while the Irish famine of 1846 led on to the financial panic of 1847, the revival of Chartism in 1848, and a contest over all Europe between Jacobin and Absolutist principles, Lord John inevitably found himself cast as the defender of order. This meant that his ministry was bound, even more than Melbourne's after 1837, to fall out with its own left wing – the new generation of Radicals and 'Economists', about eighty strong, thrown up by the general election, and fanatically committed to the reduction of government expenditure. Far from having got the House back into two parties, it soon appeared that the election had further divided it into four. The consequence was that throughout his ministry from 1846 to 1852 Lord John was obliged to take account of the fact that any one of several possible combinations of opponents might lead to a defeat, and to calculate, occasion after occasion, much more carefully than any of his predecessors, where his majority was to come from. An open Cabinet faced an independent House of Commons, and the change from the Peel era was epitomised in 1849, when Lord John invited the Irish MPs to choose for themselves whether to support the insolvent Poor Law Unions by an income tax or a rate in aid.

[26]

Circumstances had not, however, reduced Lord John to the mere chairman of an open meeting of Parliament. The great issue of the day was free trade, and here conviction and opportunity coincided. Lord John had contested the general election of 1841 upon a free trade platform. He had since spent much of his time in opposition reading the works of the classical economists, and by the time he published his Edinburgh letter in November 1845 he was knowledgeably filled with the beneficent truths of the doctrines of *laissez-faire* and *laissez-passer*. In February 1846 he 'lent' Peel his supporters in order to carry the Bill to repeal the Corn Laws through the House of Commons, and in May he crushed a revolt among the Whig peers in favour of a Whig–Protectionist alignment. By the time he became Prime Minister free trade was a matter upon which he could not compromise if he was to retain credibility as a public figure.

Between 1846 and 1852 the immediate object of the free traders was to stand firm upon the repeal of the Corn Laws, and the prospective object was to carry the policy to its logical conclusion and to abolish the remaining protective duties. Two parties shared these objects, the Whigs and the Peelites, and between them they could command a majority – the one secure majority (apart from the Protestant one) in the entire period 1846 to 1868. Accordingly from the very first day of his ministry to the last Lord John used his authority to confirm his party in its free trade policy, and sought to attach the Peelites to him. Upon taking office he offered places to three of Peel's former ministers, and renewed his approaches upon no fewer than five occasions in 1847, 1849, 1851 (twice) and 1852, arguing each time that 'Whigs and Peelites ought to govern the country and not to quarrel about trifles'. But the Peelites did not recognise numbers as an argument for merging their identity in that of the Whigs; they did not accept that Lord John's title to the premiership lay in his having taken up the cause before Peel, who was a late convert; and they had not given up all hope of returning to the head of affairs themselves. They preferred their independence. Discouraged, but not deterred, Lord John continued to keep the Peelites apprised of his intentions while receiving no confidence in return, and strove to re-draw the lines of party politics with Free Traders on one side and Protectionists on the other. He bravely staked the existence of his ministry upon the passage of the Bill to repeal the Navigation Laws through the House of Lords, and upon that occasion, pocketing the Whig principles of his upbringing, he made such free use of the Queen's name and influence to ensure a favourable outcome that the Protectionists themselves, of all people, began to question the extent of royal power. If one is looking for consistency of purpose, and for 'strong' government in Lord John's career as Prime Minister, then this is the field in which to find it.

Lord John correctly identified the first objective of sound policy for the United Kingdom as being the maintenance of free trade, but the most urgent problem he was called upon to deal with was the famine in Ireland, where among a population of 10 millions, two persons in five were accustomed to living at subsistence level and were without their food.

Here Lord John had no regular majority in the House to guide him, but in 1846–7, at any rate, the gravity of the crisis was universally recognised, and there was a disposition among all parties not to embarrass the ministry and even to help it out. It was open to Lord John, therefore, to frame the measures he thought best, and in many ways he was well fitted for his task, for he was one of the handful of English statesmen who believed that Irishmen had a right to equal treatment under the Act of Union, and in the 1830s he had communicated his own crusading zeal to the regime in Dublin Castle. But a decade later, in her hour of need, Ireland cried out not for civil rights but for exceptional consideration. To some extent it was granted. Gigantic schemes of public works were put in hand under the Labour Rate Act of 1846, and throughout the spring and summer of 1847 the Government provided soup kitchens to keep the people alive. These measures cost £10 million, which was about one hundred times as much as any government had ever spent upon such an occasion before, and the worst that can be said of them is that they followed one step behind the course of the crisis (as one supposes any government's measures would have done).

But even at this early stage of the famine, which lasted until 1849, Lord John revealed an inflexible attachment to his newly assimilated rules of political economy, which his historical studies somehow failed to tell him were not as applicable to backward Ireland as they were to Britain. His refusal to allow the Government to purchase corn upon world markets can be defended on the ground that intervention would not have increased the amount of corn available and would have raised the price. But there seems to have been no satisfactory reason why the ministry should not have diverted corn from Britain to Ireland, and why it should not have stored and distributed more grain in the west of Ireland, where there was no retail trade, and death and disease struck hardest. Irish MPs coming to Lord John to represent the state of famine existing in their districts were referred (all too relevantly if the dogma alone is to be considered) to the fifth chapter of the fourth book of Adam Smith's *Wealth of Nations*.

Worse was to follow. The amount already being spent upon relief was bound to necessitate an increase in taxes, and the old Parliament itself would not, in any case, have been so lavish again. Then, at the general election in July 1847, the English and Scots constituencies revealed that they, like the Treasury, were determined to shift the burden of Irish paupers onto Irish landlords, who still enjoyed the privilege of paying no income tax. The country was passing through a financial panic, and the new Parliament was certain to parade a stony heart. Anticipating what was to follow, Lord John promptly terminated his programme of aid to Ireland in August and September. The decision was harsh, and it did not satisfy: when he came before the House of Commons in February 1848 to ask for an increase in the income tax, in order to pay for the expenditure incurred the year before, there was an outcry in the press, and a revolt among the economical Radicals who left the party and formed an organisation of their own. Lord John, fearing that a defeat would lead to a Protectionist administration and the revival of the Anti-Corn-Law League, gave way, and after that there was no possibility of the Government's being able to obtain any more money for the relief of Irish distress from the Parliament of 1847–52.

When we turn from the immediate problem of famine relief to survey the Government's long-term measures for the reconstruction of Irish society, we find a similar pattern. In many ways the ministry rose to the occasion: it was determined to turn the disaster to good use, and its proposals were startling in their magnitude. Through the agency of an Encumbered Estates Act, insolvent Protestant landlords were to be sold up and their estates transferred to Catholic merchants from the towns. Landlords being of the same religion as their tenants, land wars would then cease. Capital being made available for investment in agriculture, the process already begun by the Labour Rate Act of substituting wage labour for peasant farming would continue apace, productivity would rise, employment would be made more secure, and solvent landlords and tenants would be able to support their remaining poor, who would be given a right to relief, through the rates. Finally the priests would be attached to the new order by the provision of state stipends, and all would then be in harmony.

The ministry was not able to carry out this programme in its entirety, because the proposal to endow the priests excited the jealousy of the Irish hierarchy and must in any case have foundered in that most Protestant of nineteenth-century parliaments. But the main charge against it is not that it was guilty of taking up a proposal which it could not carry – rather that in its long-term plans as in its temporary relief measures, it was insensitive and dogmatic. And this time the dogma was the superiority of British society and institutions. Everything was to be rearranged after the British model, and Lord John completely mis-conceived the speed with which it would be possible, in his words, to change the habits of a whole people, and brushed aside the need for the Government to provide generous and even massive financial assistance in the transition period. He allowed himself to be overawed by the economical Radicals, took it for granted that it would be as difficult to obtain money for reconstruction as it was for relief, and when Peel spoke out in favour of appointing a commission to manage the distressed areas in the west, replied that that was the sort of proposal that could only have come from an opposition bench.

Irish affairs did not cause much friction between the executive and the House of Commons. The Irish MPs did not know what they wanted, and the Government willingly adjusted its course to the wishes of the English and Scottish MPs who did. But here, indeed, as we can now see, was a failure of the new system of open government. Prime Minister and Cabinet took their tone from the majority when it was wrong to do so, and were laxly doctrinaire when they ought to have been resolutely humane. It is difficult to resist the conclusion that Malthusian fears led both them and the Parliament of 1847–52 virtually to welcome the opportunity of clearing the surplus population of Ireland off the land and Anglicising the remainder. As the years passed and the survivors of the famine became aware of the extent of the disaster, which counted anything up to 1 million dead and 2 million emigrants, the conviction grew that more could have been done by the richest nation on earth to save the inhabitants of the most poverty-stricken province in Europe and to respect the native way of life. The legacy of bitterness, whose fruits included the rebellion of Young Ireland during Lord John's ministry, and the Fenian movement, founded and financed by the exiles in America, in his lifetime, was incalculable.

Lord John held staunchly to the free trade policy, and more timidly did what he could for Ireland within the Parliament of the day. It remains to be seen how his new course of 'low profile' government worked out in other fields of domestic policy. In his first few months he could afford, like any prime minister, to be bravely opportunistic. In 1846 he lowered the duties on sugar, and a majority voted for him rather than turn him out after one month. The next year he overhauled the English Poor Law to the indignation of the anti-centralisers, extended the scope of the State's provision for education in the face of virulent abuse from the Whigs' old allies the Dissenters, and went into the same lobby with the Protectionists in support of Fielden's Ten Hour Bill. 1847 was not a bad year for legislation, and it is doubtful whether any minority government before or since has ever left so deep a mark upon the statute book.

Lord John had taken his chance to do some good along a broad front while circumstances were favourable. But he must have wondered how long he could go on leaning first one way and then the other, and after the general election of 1847 it became clear that the honeymoon period was over. Thenceforth, the success of his measures would depend, as Disraeli put it, 'on a variety of small parties, who, in the aggregate, exceed in number and influence the party of the ministers'. In these circumstances ministers might have been forgiven if they had been content just to defend the free trade policy and to keep afloat. Instead they attempted more, and the first Health of Towns Act, passed in 1848, and the Act of 1850 establishing what was virtually a self-governing dominion in Australia, were both substantial reforms of a liberal character. But in order to achieve anything in that Parliament ministers were bound to expose themselves to the risk of being labelled bad work-men. Both the Health of Towns Bill and the Bill to repeal the Naviga-tion Laws were abandoned one year and reintroduced the next. The Encumbered Estates Act of 1848 was ineffective and had to be replaced (at Peel's suggestion) by a better one the following year. Time and again apparently settled questions like the sugar duties and the ten-hour day were reopened in response to outside pressures, the ministry en-countered unprecedented difficulties in continuing established policies like the maintenance of a naval squadron to suppress the slave trade, and even Bills which were eventually passed by large majorities en-countered an unusual degree of obstructive opposition on the way. The result was that when the Government's measures did receive the royal assent the impression left upon the public was, as Disraeli expressed it with mocking exaggeration, that they were 'so altered, remoulded, remodelled, patched, cobbled, painted, veneered, and varnished' that at last no trace was left of the original scope and scheme.

Within three years of taking office it appeared that Lord John's legislation could be amended at will by almost any and every little faction which chose to oppose it, and the Radicals then advanced beyond obstruction and began to take initiatives of their own, by proposing a reduction in official salaries, and limiting the income tax to one year. Graham thought the middle ground could have been more firmly held – Dunfermline, an ex-Speaker, blamed the forms of the House, and regarded Parliament as unworkable. The latter was nearer the mark, and it is scarcely to be wondered at that, as his Government wallowed in a sea of troubles caused by Peel's destruction of the party system, Lord John became ill, that he reminded himself ominously that Fox and Canning had both broken down at his age, that he contemplated reducing his labours by taking a peerage, that he became cross with his colleagues, and above all that he resented the contrast so often made between Peel's 'strong' Government and his 'weak' one.

The strain and the worry began to affect his judgement, so that when, in 1850, the Pope divided England into sees, Lord John reacted with a public letter to the Bishop of Durham in which he accused both the Roman Catholics and their fellow travellers within the Church of England, the Puseyites, of casuistry bordering upon a conspiracy to hand England over to Rome. His letter was the most popular thing he ever wrote, and the subsequent Ecclesiastical Titles Bill passed by an enormous majority. But the fact remained that Lord John had mistaken a piece of cheek in usurping the Queen's authority to confer territorial titles for an invasion by a hostile power, and that it was undignified for a nineteenth-century prime minister to put himself at the head of a Protestant hue and cry. Worst of all, however, from Lord John's point of view, was the fact that the Durham letter offended both the Irish MPs and the Peelites. There was no future for Lord John in the combination of Whig and Protectionist votes by which the Ecclesiastical Titles Bill passed the House of Commons (nor did he wish it), and he had by his own action forfeited an important part of his regular support, and made it certain that the union of Whigs and Peelites, which was his dearest political object, would not take place under his leadership.

From that moment Lord John was powerless and adrift, and the result was that the public generally began to agree with Brougham, who had argued as early as 1847 that 'a strong Government, which was not to be much liked . . . was, on the whole, to be preferred to a weak one. . . . Any Ministry was better than a Ministry without power.' So that Lord John's ministry in its turn seemed to have eliminated another possible approach to the problem of the relations between the executive and the legislature, and served to recreate a preference for a stronger form of government, without, however, pointing out any very obvious way in which one was to be obtained, though men looked increasingly to Peel, and after the Don Pacifico debate and Peel's death in 1850, to the claims of Palmerston. Simultaneously, the Government's majorities in the House of Commons fell away dramatically as it became increasingly difficult to persuade supporters to attend debates. No ministry with such a large paper strength ever went out upon such a small vote. In 1851 Lord John was defeated by 100 votes to 54, and although he was restored to office, his ministry was finished off the next year by a vote of 136 to 125. Rightly or wrongly open government now appeared futile, and *l'Angleterre s'ennuya*.

Lord John himself shared the public's increasing disillusionment with the work of the Parliament of 1847. But the problem, as he saw it, did not lie in any failing of his, and the answer was not simply to substitute a more powerful person at the head of the executive, but to obtain a solid party majority, either frankly Liberal or frankly Conservative, which would itself uphold a more effective government. Taking his inspiration from his own experience, his mind went back to the 1830s, which now appeared, in retrospect, as a golden age. Following the Reform Act of 1832 the executive had been conspicuous neither for its homogeneity (under Grey) nor for its capacity (under Melbourne), but the House of Commons had contained a Liberal majority, and for four years, from 1832 to 1836, Parliament had been visibly on the move, legislating in accordance with the spirit of the age. Not surprisingly Lord John Russell now began to wonder whether like causes might not produce like effects. For the first time since he took his stand upon 'Finality' in 1837, he began to consider reopening the whole question of parliamentary reform, and he at last acknowledged what eleven years of Chartist agitation, from 1838 to 1848, had never yet brought him to admit, that the Act of 1832 had shut out the working classes. It does not seem to have occurred to him that in the mid-century there might not be anything that could actually be identified as the spirit of the age at all, and that a Liberal majority, if one could be obtained, might not agree upon the objectives it wished to pursue. Nor did he ponder whether a working-class franchise was at that time more likely to add to or to diminish the forces of the economical Radicals, opposed to all legislation involving the action of government, who were the bane of the 1847 Parliament. He just took it for granted, until there was proof to the contrary, that the will to legislate was there, and that it was some fault in the existing arrangements that prevented him, as Prime Minister, from giving it expression.

Extending the franchise to the working classes might be expected to lead to a consolidation of party allegiances in the House of Commons and to a more firmly based Liberal administration with a clear line of policy. But this would be worse than useless, and might even be dangerous, if it subsequently led to a renewal of the deadlock between the two Houses which had taken place in 1836, when every measure of improvement for Ireland was blocked by the Orange peers. Admittedly the House of Lords had kept to the background since Lord John took office in 1846, but that was mainly because a landlord Cabinet and a minority government was apprised of and to some extent anticipated their wishes. The fact that the peers were still an obstructive force to be reckoned with was revealed by their opposition to the new Poor Law of 1847 in Ireland, by their coming within ten votes of throwing out the Bill to repeal the Navigation Laws in 1849, and by their vote of censure upon the Government's handling of foreign affairs the year after. Lord John decided, therefore, to try to reform the House of Lords at the same time that he extended the franchise, and in order to do this he returned to his favourite proposal, which Melbourne had snubbed in 1837, for the creation of life peers.

The facts are quickly told. Lord John began with his notion for life peers, and tried it out upon the Cabinet in 1849, in 1850, and again in 1851. The Queen and the Prince expressed cautious approval, and it was agreed that, if the experiment were to be made, it ought to be confined to eminent lawyers, and to Liberal Scots and Irish peers effectively excluded under the existing representative system. But when, early in 1851, Lord John invited Dr Lushington to become the first life peer, he declined to become a guinea pig, and the Cabinet, which had never been enthusiastic, thereupon slid backwards and concluded that life peers would lower the composition of the Upper House. So there was a divergence of opinion in his own Cabinet which Lord John could not overcome, and he had still not succeeded in creating a life peer by the time he left office.

Lord John would have preferred to have opened up the House of Lords before extending the franchise. But he did not make it an absolute condition, and in any case a second Reform Bill might turn out to be a prerequisite for the reform of the Upper House, so that each time he was thwarted in his wish to create life peers he turned instead to his argument in favour of a second Reform Bill. The Act of 1832 was interpreted by the working classes as an Act to enfranchise their employers, and in Lord John's view it would be better to make a reasonable and voluntary concession in time rather than to wait (like Peel) until he was obliged to yield more to agitation. This was the pure and even noble Whig doctrine with which he sought to persuade his Cabinet in 1849 and 1850. But his Cabinet, alas, knew less about Whig doctrine than he, and as long as the country was quiet, simply could not see the need. Their attitude left Lord John despondent and frustrated, and early in 1851, without consulting his colleagues, who then recalled that they had not been consulted about the Durham letter either, he committed the Government to bringing in a Bill the next year. In the autumn he drove his reluctant Cabinet into appointing a committee to draft Bills for England, Scotland and Ireland. The details were finalised in December, whereupon Palmerston, who had always been the most proudly wayward and mutinous member of the Cabinet, brought the ministry down in his own way, by acts of insubordination and revenge, which none of Lord John's colleagues approved of, and none regretted.

Thirteen years elapsed before Lord John became Prime Minister again. In the meantime the junction of Whigs and Peelites took place under Aberdeen, and the leadership of the Liberal party passed to Palmerston. Free trade budgets apart, the legislative record of those years of 'equipoise' was poor. But there was no popular cry for Reform; Lord John's Reform Bill of 1854 was abandoned upon the outbreak of war with Russia, and that of 1860 perished for want of interest in the House of Commons. While Palmerston lived Reform was dead, and in 1861 Lord John accepted a peerage and became Earl Russell.

Palmerston lived just long enough to hold a general election, so that when Russell succeeded him and became Prime Minister for the second time in October 1865, he was handicapped by a 'cave' of Palmerstonians, forty strong, in a House of Commons where the Liberals nominally enjoyed a majority of seventy. Russell did not hesitate: he was seventy-three, it was sixteen years since he had begun to advocate an extension to the franchise, and ten since Palmerston had brought politics back to 'the do-nothing days of Castlereagh'. But Gladstone had been converted to the cause in 1864, and now became the leader of the Liberal party in the House of Commons. Gladstone was at times dismayed by Russell's 'rapidity', but he scarcely attempted to check it, and at the very first Cabinet meeting after Palmerston's death it was agreed that there was to be a Reform Bill. The measure, lowering the county franchise from £50 to £14 and the borough franchise from £10 to £7, brought squawks from the more timid members of the Cabinet, the Cave duly rebelled, and in eight months all was over and Russell ceased to be Prime Minister and never held office again. But this time he had raised a question that must be answered – Bright saw to that, and a year later Disraeli's Reform Bill passed both Houses of Parliament.

And then was seen the foresight and sagacity of Lord John Russell. The second Reform Act, like the first, got Parliament on the move again. The general election of 1868 produced a revival of interest in party organisation, a clarification of party lines, and a Liberal majority large enough, for the time being, to overawe the House of Lords. Gladstone did not find the Liberal party subservient, and had Peel been alive to contemplate it he would not have classified Gladstone's first ministry as a 'strong' government. But Gladstone was at least able to carry on from the point at which the reforming impetus of the 1830s had come to a halt, to disestablish and disendow the Church of Ireland, and to take up great social questions like the relations of landlord and tenant, which had proved too much for the governments of the 1840s and 1850s. There had been no period of legislation to equal that of 1868–74 since the House of Lords put a stranglehold upon the reformers in 1836–7, and the fact that Lord John Russell's analysis turned out in the event to be correct means that our final view of him must be an appreciative one. As Prime Minister he held to his creed that governments have a responsibility to be active in the promotion of the public welfare, and when Parliament ceased to be up to its share of the work, he recognised the evil, and pointed to a remedy. He did not advocate democracy, but he did turn to the unenfranchised masses, who knew what the problems were, and looked to an infusion of popular votes and a better balance among the classes to reactivate the failing machinery of the State.

BIBLIOGRAPHY

Gooch, G. P. (ed.), *The Later Correspondence of Lord John Russell 1840–78* (2 vols London, 1925)

MacCarthy, D. and Russell, A. (eds), *Lady John Russell: A Memoir with Selections from her Diaries and Correspondence* (London, 1910)

Prest, John, *Lord John Russell* (London, 1972)

Reid, S. J., *Lord John Russell* (London, 1895)

Russell, Lord John, *Recollections and Suggestions 1813–73* (London, 1875)

Russell, Rollo (ed.), *Early Correspondence of Lord John Russell 1815–40* (2 vols, London, 1913)

Tilby, A. W., *Lord John Russell* (London, 1930)

Walpole, Spencer, *Life of Lord John Russell* (2 vols, London, 1889)

2

THE EARL OF DERBY

BY

DENYS FORREST

Edward George Geoffrey Smith Stanley, 14th Earl of Derby, born 29 March 1799, eldest son of the 13th Earl. Educated at Eton and Christ Church, Oxford. MP (Whig) for Stockbridge 1820, Preston 1826, Windsor 1830, North Lancashire 1832. Entered the House of Lords as Lord Stanley of Bickerstaffe 1844; succeeded as 14th Earl in 1851. Married 1825 the second daughter of Edward Bootle-Wilbraham; two sons and one daughter. Junior Lord of the Treasury under Canning 1827; Under-Secretary for War and Colonies under Canning and Goderich 1827–28; Chief Secretary for Ireland under Grey 1830–33; Secretary of State for War and the Colonies 1833. Resigned 1834 and joined the Conservative Party 1837. Reappointed under Peel 1841, but resigned over Corn Laws 1845 and became leader of the Protectionists. Prime Minister 1852, 1858–59, 1866–68; resigned through ill health. Died 23 October 1869.

THE EARL OF DERBY

In the little group of British statesmen who have had more than two separate terms as Prime Minister – Gladstone (four), Derby, Salisbury and Baldwin (three each) – Derby came first. But he remains the most difficult to know. The fact that each of his periods of office, though they became progressively longer, lasted less than two years, that each time he was in a minority, that there was a repetitive pattern of general elections which he just failed to win and that he never reached power except after a maze of negotiations with much the same people – all this creates a blur, even for the moderately assiduous political student. The common reader of Victorian history and biography is in worse case. Derby the statesman simply eludes him, and he makes do with Derby the collection of catch phrases – 'The Rupert of debate', 'Scorpion Stanley', 'The Derby Dilly', 'Dishing the Whigs', 'A leap in the dark'.[1] All are valid in their way, but they are inadequate signposts to a career which, although so little of it was spent in the supreme post, stretched over nearly half a century.

Edward Stanley was born and bred a Whig, *pur sang*. He wore the 'old Whig uniform of blue and buff' when at the age of twenty-one he entered Parliament for Stockbridge, a Rotten Borough bought for him from a Tory peer, who in turn had acquired it from a hard-up West Indian planter (politics unspecified). And when in 1826 he transferred to the family borough of Preston, he warned his constituents flatly that he was no Radical reformer, but 'an old constitutional Whig'. His acceptance of minor office under Canning and Goderich was an early hint of his future. In due course the old constitutional Whigs turned re-formers themselves, but the dashing young Stanley did not exactly leap into the front line. His reaction to the first Reform Bill was in fact incredulous laughter. He recovered himself, and delivered one of those speeches which sent a whisper along the benches, 'This is the man who should be our leader.' Yet the picture is of the trusty in-fighter who has received his instructions, rather than of the go-go reformer pawing the ground. What the talent-spotters divined in the heir of the Stanleys

[1] See Note pp. 51-2, for the origin and bearing of these phrases.

(then by no means one of the great political families) was a brilliant mind and a blossoming genius for debate.

Both qualities were tested when he became Grey's Chief Secretary for Ireland. Though he genuinely attempted to balance coercion with cautious reform, he was always, for his great antagonist O'Connell, the 'snappish, impertinent, High Church Stanley', graduating to 'Scorpion Stanley' in due course. It was probably wisdom in Grey to move him to the Colonial Secretaryship (then combined with War). Here he found waiting for him a great measure, the freeing of slaves throughout the British dominions, which chimed completely with his own religious convictions. Unfortunately, it was these convictions that forced him into the first of the two 'walk-outs' which were critical to his career. When in May 1834 he realised that the Cabinet was not behind him in his defence of that highly vulnerable body the Irish Church Establishment, he and a handful of colleagues resigned. Thus was formed the briefly famous 'Derby Dilly' or third party, the vehicle whereby Stanley passed over to the Conservative camp. Its life would have been even shorter had Stanley felt able to accept office during Peel's '100 days', but by early 1837 he had come to realise the futility of trying to wield the balance of power from somewhere near the middle of the road.[2] He had long been in the inner councils of Conservatism when he took his place as War and Colonial Secretary in Peel's Cabinet of 1841.

Colonial affairs, notably the winding up of the 'Opium Wars' with China and the dispute over Maori lands in New Zealand, gave scope for the pacific element always present in Stanley's make-up. Yet he felt he was being sidetracked as a front bench speaker, and at his own request he was called to the Upper House as Lord Stanley of Bickerstaffe. At least that is what the published correspondence between him and the Prime Minister implies, however Peel may not have been sorry to place a little more distance between himself and this rather careless, outspoken grandee, with his 'chaffing' ways.

The move turned out to be crucial. It meant that when the great Conservative schism came over the repeal of the Corn Laws, and Stanley emerged as the head of the Protectionist faction, the leadership of that faction in the Commons was thrown into the lap of Benjamin Disraeli.

The relationship between these two men is a fascinating study. The

[2] As W. D. Jones points out in his valuable study, *Lord Derby and Victorian Conservatism* (Oxford, 1956), p. 56, the middle of the road was then somewhat overcrowded with moderate Reformers.

truth about it lies in neither of the two opposing myths – of Stanley as Disraeli's aristocratic puppet or front man, and of Disraeli as Stanley's low-born hireling, who eventually took control. Fortuitous in its origins, their partnership was genuine and lasting. What they actually thought of each other is not so easy to say. Now and then Dizzy would work off his frustrations by petulant outbursts to his lady correspondents about what he regarded as the dilettantism of his chief, who nevertheless kept a highly professional eye on any Disraelian plotting in unsuitable quarters. Very rarely (at any rate in his published correspondence) Stanley would also advert to Disraeli's insecure personal and political standing. On the one notable occasion[3] when he described him as 'unpopular' and not seeing enough of the party in private, he seems to have been retorting complaints against himself for not entertaining the rank-and-file.

Stanley refused to join in the Disraeli–Bentinck witch-hunt against Peel, and no amount of rebuffs ever cured him of the belief that the Peelites, gently handled, might be lured into a reunited Conservative party. From the fall of Peel to his own first accession to power, he could only play a waiting game, pending a settlement of the Protection issue. He knew Disraeli had already ratted, and had decided in his own mind that free trade must be given time to vindicate or discredit itself. All this confirmed him in his lifelong stance as opposition leader – vigorous if intermittent in attacking the government of the day, resigned and even timorous about the prospect of regaining office himself.

When his first real chance did come, with Lord John Russell's fall in February 1851, Stanley set out briskly enough to find allies. But the Peelites failed him, some of his own followers proved chicken-hearted, and he abruptly abandoned the enterprise. It looked at first as though the pattern might be repeated when the next summons to Buckingham Palace came just a year later (21 February 1852). Conservatives were in a paper-thin majority in the House of Commons, but forty or fifty of them were Peelites. Failing once more to get help from outside, Stanley – or rather Derby, as he had now become through the death of the thirteenth Earl – managed to put together a Cabinet from among his own faction. Pakington, Henley, Herries, Spencer Walpole . . . even today one senses the lack of resonant names. However, the Peelites undertook to keep Derby in office for the time being, subject to a decision over Protection and an autumn Budget. Derby himself lay

3 In the course of the letter to Malmesbury quoted on p. 46.

very low about Protection, and even when a general election came on in July, merely reiterated that the voters must give their verdict. In fact, the issue was never put to them from the Government side – it was a common saying that a Derbyite was a Protectionist in the country, neutral in a small town and a Free Trader in the cities.

Finally, some twenty-five extra Derby supporters were returned – not enough to make their leader independent of the Peelites. So now he must rise to his feet and tell the House of Lords that the majority of the people were in favour of free trade and that the Corn Laws would not be revived. The old Anti-Corn Law Leaguers tried to insist on a more abject recantation, but a compromise motion by Palmerston in the Commons saved the day.

With this awkward corner turned, Derby attempted once again to broaden his base, and once again we find him in conclave with Peelites and with Palmerston. But the former would not swallow Disraeli and the Queen balked at Palmerston, under whose leadership in the Commons the Peelites might possibly have served. The next great obstacle, the Budget, had to be faced without allies.

Disraeli had been a doubtful choice as Chancellor of the Exchequer. He was no economic expert, as he admitted to his chief, who replied with a famous Derbyism – 'You know as much as Mr Canning – they give you the figures.' His task was to contrive a Budget which would appease the agricultural interest without infringing the sacred tenets of free trade. His devices to do this, the desperate straits into which he was subsequently driven, and the final foundering of his Budget before a Gladstonian typhoon which burst upon him in the early hours of 17 December 1852, belong essentially to Disraeli's own story. Derby, who knew, if anything, even less about finance, could do little to help him, and in any case was marooned in the wrong House of Parliament. The best he could offer was inspiriting noises at critical moments – 'Put a good face on it and we will pull through, *l'audace, l'audace, toujours l'audace!*'

And so the first Derby Government fell, amid more jeers than sympathy. Except that Lord Malmesbury proved a rather better Foreign Secretary than most people had expected, few of its members had time, or perhaps the capacity, to create a reputation. It is typical of the whole situation that though there were six Cabinet members in the Lords, the Prime Minister took charge of everything and answered for them all.

Derby went back into opposition still at the head of the strongest parliamentary group – certainly more united than Aberdeen's coalition of Whigs, Peelites and Radicals, which was wide open to disruption by an opposition leader out for blood. But Derby was in no hurry. Minority had scarred him, and while he realised that Aberdeen could be unseated, he did not give much for his own chances. This exasperated those who were keeping the party together in the Commons, particularly his own dour young son Edward Stanley, and of course Disraeli.

By now, certain uncomfortable traits in Derby's character were fully developed. As far back as the period after the fall of the 'Dilly', he had shown a tendency to retreat, at the more humdrum moments, to his great estate at Knowsley and to throw himself into sporting pursuits from which all but his most aristocratic cronies were necessarily excluded. Even Disraeli was not invited there until December 1853. To men for whom politics were their life – and in many cases their living – the spectacle of 'the Captain', as they called him, holed up for weeks or even months together in distant Lancashire, shooting pheasants when fit, or nursing his own agonising brand of gout, was only one better than hearing gossip of him at Newmarket or Doncaster, gambling and chaffing as though he had not a political care in the world. 'Boyish' was a pleasant enough epithet for that handsome young man in the Whig blue and buff; it did not sit so well on the middle-aged statesman who had grown a paunch.

The outbreak, and swift mismanagement, of the Crimean War brought Derby back into the arena, and in fact led to one of the most controversial episodes of his career. Aberdeen fell, and on 31 January 1855, Lord Derby drove once more to see the Queen. Overnight, Lord Ellenborough had warned him, *'Don't leave the room without kissing hands'*, but that is just what Derby did. He told the Queen that though public opinion was demanding Palmerston, the latter was too old, blind and deaf to be capable of carrying on the war, and that he himself must go away and talk to Peelites such as Gladstone and Sidney Herbert. Like all Derby's card houses, this one fell flat; the next day he informed the Queen that he could not go forward, and after further manoeuvres Palmerston came in.

Naturally, for the Conservative activists this was their worst disappointment yet; they believed, as many have since, that Derby threw away the finest prospect he ever had of taking office with the nation behind him, and in due course fighting and winning a general election. Yet it is impossible to feel much confidence in his chances as a war minister. The nation was not in fact behind him but behind Lord Palmerston, and that was the only thing that counted.

So – back to Knowsley, and more detachment than ever from day-to-day affairs at Westminster. Derby's reply to a despondent letter from Malmesbury (15 December 1856)[4] is the *locus classicus*. He has been, he says, too busy shooting to give time to politics (this may have been a mild tease) and appears surprised that the party has been able to keep together at all 'in the absence of any cry or leading question' to demarcate the two sides of the House. Palmerston has been 'a Conservative minister working with Radical tools'. For himself, he was never ambitious of office and is unlikely to become more so now, but will accept it if he sees a chance of not only gaining power but keeping it. That must depend on the Government committing a very gross blunder. The letter ends with a perfunctory reference to 'active exertions' at the forthcoming general election. Ice-cold cheer, this, from an opposition leader!

The 'gross blunder' came of course with Palmerston's ill-timed Conspiracy Bill. Pam resigned and Derby was sent for (20 February 1858). The Conservatives were in a heavier minority than ever, but this time Derby hardly hesitated. Within twenty-four hours he had kissed hands. Though Gladstone and Lord Grey refused their help, his Cabinet was strengthened by a couple of ex-Peelites, Sir Robert's brother General Peel (War Office) and Lord Ellenborough (Board of Control). The latter, as it turned out, was a doubtful asset.

In his ministerial statement to the Lords (1 March), Derby used a comparison which is the more significant since he was to repeat it almost word for word when taking office for the last time in 1866. This was to the effect that while it was easy enough to tell a High Tory from a Radical, the intermediate stages were as elusive as those between the various grades or ranks in society at large. 'There is a broad interval between the highest and the lowest, but the gradation whereby the one melts into the other is so impalpable that it is difficult . . . precisely to say where one commences and another ends.' There could be no greater mistake, he went on, than to suppose that 'a Conservative ministry means a stationary ministry'. Like those old country houses which successive generations had altered and improved, our institutions must be adapted to the needs of society. Finally, the Derby who in 1852

4 Earl of Malmesbury, *Memoirs of an Ex-Minister* (London, 1885), p. 385.

was talking of 'stemming the tide of democracy' now revealed that he was ready for a further instalment of electoral reform.

The Government's immediate preoccupation, however, was with Indian and European affairs. They pushed forward the plan (already adumbrated under the previous regime) to transfer political power in India from the East India Company to a Secretary of State, assisted by a Council, and though Ellenborough nearly wrecked the whole thing by trying to saddle the Council with an absurdly complicated structure, a simplified scheme went through. Ellenborough was to have been the first Secretary of State, but before the change could take effect he got the Government into further hot water. In the aftermath of the Indian Mutiny he sent the Governor-General, Lord Canning, a severe 'rocket' for his alleged confiscatory policy in Oudh, and allowed this to get into general circulation before Canning had even received it. There was a terrific outcry, and the administration was only saved by Ellenborough resigning and the Queen reluctantly authorising Derby to use the threat of a dissolution.

Happier episodes in the Government's first session were its swift and amicable settlement with France over the 'conspiracy to murder' affair which originally brought it to power, and the ending of the long contention that had kept Jews from sitting in Parliament. As a young Whig, Derby had regularly voted to remove Jewish disabilities, but the parliamentary oath 'on the true faith of a Christian' still remained, and one of the 'churchiest' of our prime ministers hesitated to scrap it. Yet he wanted the question settled, and finally agreed to a compromise whereby the House of Commons should be allowed to frame its own rules of admission. Derby was also following his lifelong principles when he opposed suggestions to open the trusteeship of schools to Dissenters and to abolish compulsory church rates.

Next came the first essay at a Conservative Reform Bill. Today it is chiefly remembered for its 'fancy franchises', giving special voting rights to professional men such as lawyers, doctors and teachers and to persons with various levels of savings, government pensions, investments in the Funds, and so on. Even this low-key measure was too much for two Cabinet members, who resigned, and in the House of Commons a critical amendment was carried by a majority of 39. On 4 April 1859, Derby announced a dissolution, and in the subsequent general election had once more the maddening experience of gaining about twenty-five seats but being left in an overall minority.

[47]

For the last time, an attempt was made to recruit the help of Palmerston, and when that failed of Gladstone – Gladstone, who had accepted the Ionian Islands High Commissionership from Derby the year before, Gladstone, who after speaking up for Rotten Boroughs in the Reform Bill debate had gone into the lobby alongside Disraeli, and was to do so again in the final Division which turned Lord Derby out. But as usual he ducked out of reach, only to surface again almost immediately as Palmerston's Chancellor of the Exchequer. Apart from his personal position as inevitable successor to the aged Pam, he certainly regarded the latter as sounder than Derby on the question which was obsessing him just then and which sealed the Government's doom – support for Cavour and the Italian Nationalists against Austria.

The next five years can be passed over swiftly. There were several occasions on which Derby's compact forces in the Commons could have made things distinctly awkward for Palmerston, but he preferred to give support, in almost formal terms, to a minister whose home policy was no less conservative than his own. While he continued to deliver his slashing speeches in the Lords, Knowsley claimed him more and more – not merely as sportsman now, but as Lancashire magnate deploying all his old administrative drive to fight the 'Cotton famine' of 1862–4, and as amateur poet and scholar amusing his leisure, and ever-longer interludes of gout, in translating the *Iliad*. His version, though not very exciting, at least stands up to those of his great predecessors, Dryden, Pope and Cowper.

Foreign affairs aroused Derby to a more critical attitude, but not until the Danish imbroglio of 1864 did he seize the headlines by condemning the Government for its worldwide policy of 'meddle and muddle'. This still gave the Conservatives little leverage in the election of the following year, and by one more gentle tilt of the seesaw they lost about the same number of seats they had gained in 1859.

Their eventual return to office arose therefore in a more striking degree than in 1852 or 1858 from dissensions in the enemy ranks – this time the split over yet another Reform Bill and the withdrawal of the anti-Reform Whigs into their 'Adullamite' cave. Lord Derby, who had declared time and time again that he would never resume office 'on sufferance', kissed hands once more. Only two years earlier he had still been lamenting to Malmesbury the lack of suitable office-holders if (as he characteristically put it) they were *doomed* to come in. Yet his third

Cabinet was his most impressive, and in spite of fierce strains and some resignations, proved his most durable. Apart from Disraeli and himself, Malmesbury (now Privy Seal), Sir John Pakington and Lord John Manners were survivors from 1852; Stanley (Foreign Secretary) and Peel (War) represented the best of the 1858 intake, while there were notable newcomers in Lord Carnarvon (Colonies), Viscount Cranborne – the future Lord Salisbury (India), Sir Stafford Northcote (Board of Trade) and Gathorne Hardy (Poor Law Board). Spencer Walpole – unfortunately as it happened[5] – returned to office as Home Secretary. Northcote had been sponsored by Disraeli, who also exerted strong influence over other appointments – in truth, the 1866 ministry compels attention more as the overture to the drama of Benjamin Disraeli, Prime Minister, than as Lord Derby's farewell performance.

Yet there is little doubt about which of them took the lead in committing their party to the great and central measure of their administration, the second Reform Bill. In his ministerial statement to the Lords (9 July) Derby declared that nothing would give him greater pleasure than to see 'a very considerable portion of the class now excluded' admitted to the franchise, though he reserved complete liberty not to introduce a Bill unless he saw a fair chance of passing it. By 16 September he was telling Disraeli that he had come 'reluctantly' to the conclusion that they must deal with the subject. He enclosed a sketch for a Bill; Disraeli demurred, but Derby continued to press him. His idea was that they might begin with a series of Resolutions. If these were carried they would be 'on velvet', but the defeat of one or two of them would not be fatal. By 1 November he produced the further concept of a Parliamentary Commission, or study group.

All this was broadly accepted by the Cabinet, but if a Commission were appointed, how was it to be kept busy? Something 'really sticky' would be needed, and after listing a few alternatives Derby concluded 'of all possible hares to start I do not know a better than Household Suffrage, coupled with plurality of voting'. Disraeli might remain lukewarm, but here was the grand selling message – Household Suffrage, however counterweighted with extra votes for the more substantial classes.

Then came a fantastic sequence of events. After a threatened Cabinet

[5] He brought the Government into ridicule by bursting into tears when confronted by a deputation after the 'Hyde Park Riots' of July 1866. Whether these riots helped to panic Derby and Disraeli in the direction of Reform is still disputed.

[49]

revolt (the newer men such as Cranborne and Carnarvon were more hostile than the old stagers), the Resolutions were put before Parliament in a vague and sketchy form. Disraeli, on his own initiative, met the 'needling' of the Opposition with a promise to produce a Bill on the day that the Resolutions were due to be voted upon (25 February). There were critical Cabinets on the 16th and 19th, and on Saturday the 23rd a hurried meeting accepted the leadership's draft. But after a weekend of studying the figures, Cranborne realised that Disraeli had concealed the fact that they would probably give the working-class voters a two-to-one majority, and this he could not stomach. Carnarvon and Peel joined him in revolt and on the Monday morning a compromise Bill, ditching Household Suffrage, was flung together. The meeting ended ten minutes before Derby was due to attend a party meeting; two hours later Disraeli was to introduce the Bill into the Commons. It went down very badly. With an unexpectedly large section of his own party joining with the Opposition to demand a more sweeping measure, Derby took the last great decision of his political career. In the teeth of the resignations of Cranborne, Peel and Carnarvon, a Household Suffrage measure was substituted for the 'Ten Minute' Bill.

Thereafter, Derby's influence on events in the Commons naturally diminished. It was left to Disraeli, by artifice, audacity and the supreme command of parliamentary tactics, to win the vital divisions and send up a much amended measure in triumph to the Lords. Derby introduced it there, and two phrases used in the subsequent debates powerfully helped to complete his historical image – his own description of the Bill as 'taking a leap into the dark' and Lord Granville's story of him telling Disraeli, 'Don't you see how it has dished the Whigs?' On 9 August 1867, the second Reform Bill received the Royal Assent. Six months later Derby, pleading ill health, relinquished the seals of office, and Disraeli became Prime Minister.

What is the student of Derby's career to make of all this? To many, he figures as a sort of lifelong latent reformer, fascinated, as Dr Asa Briggs puts it,[6] with the thought of comprehensive Reform for its own sake and more consistently concerned with social justice than ever appeared on the surface. The evidence is not strong. We saw that even in 1832, in the days of his impetuous, eloquent youth, he was the sword-arm rather than the spontaneous champion of Reform, and as middle age

[6] *Victorian People* (London, 1954), p. 288.

advanced empiricism gained on him in everything except the defence of the Established Church. Later still there was some widening of sympathies, especially after his contacts with the cotton operatives during the Famine had taught him how little revolutionary they were, even under the cruellest pressure.

Genuine reformer or not, when Derby died within twenty months of resigning office (23 October 1869), the obituarists were almost unanimous in writing down his career as a failure. They attributed this to his lack of consistent political theory and steady political action. Yet it is hard to imagine any other statesman, with only the least able segment of a broken party behind him, making a much better job of three minority premierships. His reputation as a 'gambler' is certainly misleading. Malmesbury, who knew him best, speaks of 'much reflection and calmness' before action. People who wanted to talk politics when he was up to his neck in racing or shooting could be exasperated by his indifference, but his mind operated on a two-way switch – it is Malmesbury again who records how, returning from covert-side, he could 'sit down at once to write the longest and most important paper right off, in a delicate hand and without a single erasure'.[7]

A word needs to be said about the parliamentary oratory of 'The Rupert of Debate'. The *Annual Register*, commenting on his speech on the Paper Duties in 1861, remarked that it was 'a wonder in its own way', but could give little idea of his old style – its music, its fire, its rapidity, its irresistible dash. Yet earlier Hansards hardly convey these qualities either; not surprisingly, since they are all attributes of delivery rather than composition. On the printed page, Derby's speeches are very much in the ponderous idiom of their time – utterly unlike Disraeli's best in that respect.

This brief essay is not claimed as a final verdict on Lord Derby. The time for that will presumably come when, at long last, somebody gets down to a full-length biography. But even then he seems likely to remain a somewhat shadowy, somewhat equivocal figure, moving in and out of the limelight of nineteenth-century British politics.

[7] Malmesbury, *Memoirs*, p. 32.

NOTE

'*The Rupert of Debate.*' First applied to Stanley by Disraeli, with satirical intention, during a privilege debate (24 April 1844), when the two men were still on opposite sides of the House: 'The noble lord in this case, as in so many others, is the Prince

Rupert of parliamentary discussion; his charge is resistless; but when he returns from pursuit he always finds his camp in the possession of the enemy.' Put to unforgettable use by Bulwer Lytton in his *New Timon* of 1845:

> 'One after one the Lords of time advance,
> Here Stanley meets – how Stanley scorns the glance!
> The brilliant chief, irregularly great,
> Frank, haughty, rash, the Rupert of Debate!'

'*Scorpion Stanley.*' Not coined by O'Connell, as is often thought, but joyously stolen by him from a leading article in the *Examiner* of 29 March 1840.

'*The Derby Dilly.*' In Canning's 'Loves of the Triangles', a 'mathematical and philosophical poem' of 1798, all about things that go in threes, there is the couplet:

> 'So down thy hill, romantic Ashbourne, glides
> The Derby Dilly, carrying three insides.'

O'Connell in February 1835 jokingly applied it to Stanley's 'third party', though apparently substituting 'six' for 'three', which made no better sense. 'Dilly', slang for *diligence* – cf. the 'Brighton Dilly' of Regency days.

'*Dishing the Whigs.*' Whether or not Derby used the phrase, 'dishing the Whigs' was a time-honoured sport. 'The Whigs are dished – dead,' wrote Disraeli to Lord John Manners, 8 March 1848.

'*A Leap in the Dark.*' In even wider currency than the preceding, long before Derby's remark of 1867 attached it permanently to his name. As early as 1841 Lord John Russell applied it to the Dissolution of that year, and Palmerston used it about the Reform proposals of 1860.

BIBLIOGRAPHY

As indicated in the text, Derby still awaits his biographer, and there has been only fragmentary publication of his papers. Towards the end of the Victorian period, and within a year of each other, appeared two short studies, *The Earl of Derby*, by George Saintsbury (Sampson Low, 'The Queen's Prime Ministers' series, 1892) and *The Life of the Earl of Derby*, by T. E. Kebbel (W. H. Allen, 'The Statesmen' series, 1893). Both worked on the assumption that a biography on the grand scale must soon follow. Of the two, Kebbel took more trouble to obtain first-hand information; Saintsbury was of course the better writer, and his outspoken Toryism is frequently amusing. Some of Derby's more important speeches are reprinted in a Lancashire publication, *Historical Sketches of the House of Stanley*, by Thomas Aspden (Preston, for the author, 1877). Second only to Malmesbury as a contemporary witness is Charles Greville – the fact that he was hostile to Derby in politics and suspicious of him on the Turf adds a special flavour to the numerous and oft-quoted comments in his *Diaries*.

3

THE EARL OF ABERDEEN

BY

NORMAN McCORD

George Hamilton-Gordon, 4th Earl of Aberdeen. Born 28 January 1784 and succeeded his grandfather, the 3rd Earl, in 1801, his father having died in 1791. Educated at Harrow and St John's College, Cambridge. Travelled in southern Europe and the Levant 1802–04, and carried out excavations at Athens and Ephesus. Married 1805, Catherine, daughter of the 1st Marquess of Abercorn. She died 1812 and no children survived. Appointed special ambassador to Austria 1813. Signed treaty of Töplitz 1813; present at the battle of Leipzig, and signed the treaty of Paris 1814. Remarried 1815, Harriet, dowager Viscountess Hamilton; five children. Chancellor of the Duchy of Lancaster, 1828; Foreign Secretary 1828; resigned 1830. Secretary for War and the Colonies under Peel 1834–35; Foreign Secretary 1841–46; resigned (with Peel) over the Corn Laws; became leader of the Peelites 1850; formed coalition cabinet 1852; ordered the fleet to Constantinople 1853 and declared war (the Crimean War) in March 1854; driven from office January 1855; retired and created KG 1855. Died 14 December 1860.

THE EARL OF ABERDEEN

George Hamilton Gordon, fourth Earl of Aberdeen, was born in 1784, five years before the outbreak of the French Revolution; he died in 1860, nine years after the Great Exhibition. His life therefore spanned a period of immense change in Britain. In 1784 Britain was still largely a decentralised rural society, even if industry was already embarked on its course of expansion. In 1860 an increasingly industrialised and urbanised society was justly proud of the role of 'workshop of the world'. In 1784 formal government played only a small role, but by 1860 rapid social and economic change, coupled with an unprecedentedly rapid increase of population, had necessitated considerable changes in the nature and activity of government. Aberdeen was one of the small ruling group who had to face the transformation of Britain in the space of a couple of generations. His part in this process was of less importance than that of Peel, for instance, yet his career was still one of considerable interest.

He was born into the landed aristocracy which continued to dominate Britain, as the eldest son of Lord Haddo, the heir to the third Earl of Aberdeen. The Gordon family was one of the most distinguished in the Scottish peerage, with a lineage traced, not without some doubt, to the man whose arrow had inflicted Richard I's fatal wound. The future Prime Minister's father died in 1791, his mother in 1795, and partly owing to friction with his grandfather the upbringing of the young orphan took him into the centre of late eighteenth-century political life, for the two men who played the most important parts in his guardianship in those years were Henry Dundas, Lord Melville, and William Pitt himself. He was therefore early attracted to the Tory side in politics. He succeeded his grandfather as the fourth Earl of Aberdeen in 1801, a few years before he came of age, and therefore never served a political apprenticeship in the House of Commons as so many young aristocrats did. In 1806 he became a Scottish representative peer, and remained a member of the House of Lords for the rest of his life. In the closing stages of the Napoleonic War he was employed in diplomatic tasks, mainly in helping to propel Austria into the Allied camp, and for his services here he received a United Kingdom viscountcy in 1814. He was present at some of the battles of the 1813–14 campaigns, and understandably derived from those experiences a sincere distaste for the bloodshed and waste of war.

Thereafter he was for some years engaged almost entirely in non-political activities. The estates he had inherited presented him with a considerable challenge, which he took up as a matter of duty, earning a place as an improving landlord. He spent a good deal of money and effort in such improvements as planting trees, and in providing better housing for those who lived on his property. As a territorial magnate he was much involved with the affairs of the Aberdeen district, and even when he was Prime Minister he did not relinquish his detailed concern with the local affairs of the district, finding time to attend not only to the business of his own estates, but also to the multifarious business of local societies and institutions in which his position had inevitably involved him.

In addition his intellectual interests were considerable. He had been educated at Harrow and Cambridge, and imbibed in those institutions a genuine interest in classical antiquity and art, which he retained throughout his life. Early visits to Greece stimulated these interests and turned him into an ardent philhellene. He was later to serve as an active trustee of the British Museum and the National Gallery, and he was for thirty-two years President of the Society of Antiquaries. He was not therefore a 'full-time' politician at any point, but, like many of his contemporaries active in public life, he combined a political career with the care of a substantial private estate and a variety of other non-political interests.

Aberdeen returned to active political life in 1828, on the formation of the Wellington Government. He entered that Cabinet at its inception as Chancellor of the Duchy of Lancaster, but with the departure of the Canningite ministers led by Huskisson a few months later he was promoted to the Foreign Secretaryship. This gave him a welcome opportunity to assist in the creation of the independent Greek kingdom in 1830. He was Secretary for War and Colonies in Peel's short-lived first Government of 1834–5. With Peel's triumph at the polls in 1841 Aberdeen returned to the Foreign Office, and at once inaugurated a more pacific policy than that which his predecessor, Palmerston, had introduced. A war with China was brought to an end, successive negotiations with the United States of America settled thorny boundary problems involving Canada's south-eastern and south-western frontiers, while in Europe Aberdeen brought about more friendly relations between Britain and France. Inevitably his official duties limited his interventions in domestic affairs, although he was a cordial supporter of Peel's general policies. The impending disruption in the Church of Scotland was the only domestic issue in which he took a major part, and here with the best will in the world he was unable to effect a peaceful solution to that tangled problem. During the Corn Law crisis Peel had his full support, and he left office with his leader in 1846. During the Russell Government which followed his interest in foreign affairs continued, and he pressed Peel to oppose Palmerston's aggressive policy towards Greece in the celebrated Don Pacifico crisis of 1850.

Peel's death later in 1850 left his followers in a difficult position. Peel himself had done little to preserve an independent political grouping, but many of the Peelites were anxious to retain their political cohesion, and Aberdeen emerged as the recognised head of this group, which included a formidable range of talent. Aberdeen and his associates courted unpopularity by their trenchant opposition to Russell's foolish, but immensely popular, Ecclesiastical Titles Act in 1851. That measure, designed to curb the Roman Catholic Church, was only one of a series of events which foreshadowed the fall of Russell's Government. Aberdeen was already spoken of as a possible premier at the head of a coalition of Whigs, Radicals and Peelites, and after the brief Conservative ministry which succeeded Russell in 1852 this coalition duly came into being, with Aberdeen at the head of a Cabinet which contained six Peelites, six Whigs and one very respectable Radical. The difficulties which accompanied the formation of the ministry were considerable, but largely confidential, so that at first sight the Aberdeen Government appeared strong and likely to enjoy a considerable tenure. Queen Victoria wrote of it as 'the realisation of the country's and our most ardent wishes . . . it deserves success, and will, I think command great support'.

Few Cabinets have seemed stronger in ministerial talent. The Peelites contributed Aberdeen himself, and men of acknowledged ability like Sir James Graham and Gladstone, whose first Budget in 1853 provided the new Government with a spectacular early success. Russell, Palmerston and Lansdowne were among the Whig ministers. If the nominal followings of the ministers could be relied on, the Government's majority seemed secure, while there seemed a very good chance of winning yet more support from Conservatives unhappy at the apparently arid politics of Derby and Disraeli. The session of 1853 saw a number of valuable if unspectacular reforms enacted, including a useful Factory Act, and if the deepening international crisis in the Near East was already worrying, it did not yet seem to threaten the security of the Government.

However, the way in which the Government drifted into the Crimean War seriously undermined its position in public opinion, and it was unable to withstand the mounting criticism that followed the revelations of mismanagement in the conduct of the war. The shift in public opinion was exemplified by *The Times*, then perhaps at the peak of its effective influence. That paper had given a general support to the Aberdeen Government in its early days, but in December 1854 it moved into a posture of vitriolic criticism of the shortcomings of the Government's administration of the campaign in the Crimea. However, the hostile public opinion was not something *The Times* created, but something it joined and encouraged. If the dispatches of its celebrated war correspondent, William Russell, were the most famous and among the most trenchant of the hostile reports, those reports were paralleled by scores of other scathing reports from members of the Army and visitors to the front. The mounting criticism out of doors was accompanied by a failing of the Government's parliamentary support. Early in 1855 the House of Commons inflicted on the Government one of the most stinging demonstrations of want of confidence by passing by 305 votes to 148 Roebuck's motion for a select committee to inquire into the condition of the Army in the Crimea, and the conduct of the government departments responsible for that condition. The Government at once resigned, and Aberdeen's career as a leading politician was over. For the remaining years of his life he played some part as an elder statesman, notably by trying his best by private urging to keep alive the Peelite/Whig coalition, which was not to be finally consolidated until the formation of Gladstone's first Government in 1868.

As prime minister Lord Aberdeen was not a great success. He was well aware of his own limitations, and at the formation of his Government regarded his appointment as something of a stop-gap. Events beyond his control, however, frustrated his intention to step down in Russell's favour at some convenient time, and he remained at the head of the Government until its fall. He was not a great leader of men, and failed to establish his authority and enforce his policies. It is possible that, but for the eruption of the Crimean War, the coalition he led might have established itself as a powerful ruling grouping, dedicated to 'free trade and moderate progress', concepts which could well have retained the support of the majority of politically influential elements in British society. This must remain, however, very much one of the 'ifs' of history, for the strains of the Crimean War shattered the Government's position and destroyed its hold on support in Parliament and in the country. For the Government's poor record in coping with this crisis in foreign affairs Aberdeen must bear much of the responsibility, and yet if some of the factors affecting his position are examined it may be possible to mitigate the condemnation.

Aberdeen's premiership took place in circumstances which would have posed difficulties to any executive. The period between the first and second Reform Acts was one in which the House of Commons enjoyed a greater independence than it had enjoyed in earlier periods or was to enjoy in future. The 1832 Reform Act had done something to clean up the electoral system, while leaving control of the constituencies in practice largely in the hands of minority ruling groups who could not easily be controlled by government. A man tended to sit in the mid-century House of Commons not so much because he was simply a good party man of ability, but because of his own status, wealth and influence. Increasingly the older methods by which governments had retained a hold on the Commons were being eroded; the use of government patronage as a cement of political support was increasingly limited and subject to criticism. Ironically enough, the Aberdeen Government itself, and especially its Peelite members like Gladstone and the Duke of Newcastle, played a part in the decline of the political use of patronage by their advocacy of open competition for Civil Service appointments.

If this older method of consolidating the Government's parliamentary influence was increasingly ineffective, the cohesion of party discipline was not yet strong enough to provide a government with a secure basis of parliamentary support. The Aberdeen Government held office at a period of especial uncertainty in party allegiances. Russell's failures of 1846-51 had greatly shaken his position as a leader of the Whig–Radical grouping, which had in any case never shown any very great unity. His conduct during the Aberdeen Government's tenure did nothing to strengthen the Whig ex-Premier's hold on his nominal following, and his resignation from Aberdeen's Government in face of Roebuck's hostile motion was widely, and not unjustifiably, interpreted as a disgraceful act of political desertion during a crisis. The aftermath of Aberdeen's resignation, when Russell could not find more than a handful of colleagues willing to serve under him, while Palmerston went on to form a government with relative ease, showed how far the nominal leader of the Whigs had sunk in influence. In these circumstances the Aberdeen Government was never in a position to rely confidently on the full support of the large Whig–Radical grouping in Parliament.

Since the split over the Corn Laws in 1846 the great Conservative party which Peel had led to victory in 1841 was irremediably broken. The Peelites certainly numbered in their ranks the majority of the very able ministerial group which had served in Peel's second Government, but their following in Parliament and in the country was smaller than their talents; they were to a large extent a notable group of political generals without an adequate army behind them. The Conservatives who had broken with Peel over the Corn Laws now followed Lord Derby with reasonably strong cohesion, but eyed their leader in the House of Commons, Disraeli, with markedly less cordial loyalty. On the whole the Peelites showed more capacity for union in these years than either Conservatives, Whigs or Radicals, but their basic numerical weakness in Parliament made this asset of limited value. Probably less than fifty Members of the House of Commons elected in 1852 could be counted as genuine Peelites, though from time to time their numbers were swelled by temporary support from other groupings.

In these confused and limited party situations the House of Commons itself was during the 1850s the principal agency in making and breaking governments. Party leaders and government ministers had no effective sanctions for bringing to heel recalcitrant followers, while the allegiance of many MPs was not at all clear – it was not unusual to find candidates describing themselves on the hustings in these years as Liberal Conservatives or Conservative Liberals. Members of Parliament enjoyed this independence and did not hesitate to use it with freedom. It was not a general election but the will of the House of Commons which brought down Russell's first Government and ejected its Conservative successor in favour of the Whig–Peelite–Radical Aberdeen coalition. It was the House of Commons which ignominiously ejected that coalition ministry, and installed Palmerston's first Government in its place. A fortuitous combination in the House of Commons defeated Palmerston over his

China policy in 1857, and if he returned triumphant from the general election of 1857 it was only to meet defeat in the House of Commons the following year on his policy towards France. A minority Conservative Government contrived to stay in office until 1859 when a further parliamentary combination ejected it. Governments were unable to rely on a solid basis of parliamentary support until the emergence of stronger party cohesion in the late 1860s improved matters for them. This basic political weakness of governments in the 1850s was one major factor behind the failure of the Aberdeen ministry.

There were other underlying factors too. The Aberdeen Government in its one way was undoubtedly a reforming administration in domestic affairs, and its ministers during the first peacetime months in office tackled a variety of reforming projects. Factory reform, Civil Service reform, law reform and even further parliamentary reform all had a place in the Government's programme. It might be thought that this should have won for that Government more support from Radical groups than it actually received. Yet the course of British Radicalism in the years after 1846 was not calculated to provide encouragement to a government trying to combine a policy of cautious improvement in domestic policies with a foreign policy which aimed at avoiding war. After the repeal of the Corn Laws Radicalism in Britain, which had never displayed any very high degree of unity, was very clearly divided. There were some prominent Radicals, such as Cobden and Bright, who strenuously advocated a pacific approach in foreign affairs, but there were other Radicals whose sympathy for oppressed nations abroad led them to advocate projects of intervention for purposes of liberation which far transcended anything Palmerston himself was ever prepared to contemplate seriously. The continental revolutions of 1848 had markedly accelerated that tendency, and the enthusiastic receptions accorded to refugees like Kossuth and Garibaldi emphasised the increased interest of British Radicalism in national crusades overseas. For Radicals of this school Russia was the arch-oppressor and the Crimean War a suitable occasion for the whole strength of Britain to be deployed in procuring the freedom of subject Poles, Hungarians or Italians. The moderation and vacillation of the Aberdeen Government in its relations with Russia, and then the woeful shortcomings in the management of the war, meant that the overwhelming bulk of Radical opinion in Britain moved to join the Opposition to Aberdeen's ministry. Up and down Britain Radicals denounced the Russian tyrant, and were even led to strange lengths of praise for the Government of Turkey. Aberdeen, more justly, thought that the Turkish system of government was 'vicious and abominable', but public opinion was so strongly anti-Russian that this kind of judicious assessment merely added to the Government's growing unpopularity. In these circumstances it is scarcely surprising that it was a Radical motion in the House of Commons that was to bring the Aberdeen Government down, and many Radical votes swelled the crushing majority by which Roebuck's motion was carried. If 102 Liberal votes of one kind or another supported Aberdeen in the crucial division another 84, including many Radicals, joined the official Conservative Opposition in ejecting the coalition Government which they had at first supported. The Aberdeen Government, however, could scarcely be blamed for failing to foresee how strong and determined the Radical swing to bellicose courses would be.

It is equally unreasonable that the Aberdeen Government should have borne all the obloquy derived from the patent shortcomings of British military administration in the Crimea. This was a situation they inherited, and many of the MPs who supported the Roebuck motion, and who joined in the anti-Russian outcry, had been adamant in the cause of cheap government in preceding decades. For most of the nineteenth century the armed forces of Britain were run on a financial shoestring, and successive parliaments had shown themselves much more concerned at reducing defence estimates than in equipping the country with operationally effective armed forces. The responsibility for the weaknesses of Army and Navy during the Crimean War did not in reality lie at the door of a government which had only taken office early in 1853, but rather in a long course of neglect and cheese-paring which had taken place since 1815, and was indeed to continue for long after the Crimean War had ended. The fact that the British armed forces were inefficient and unready when war came in March 1854 was not the fault of one government, but the result of a prolonged course of economy for which a whole succession of governments and parliaments, and indeed the general public insistence on cheap government, were in reality responsible. The Aberdeen Government was blamed and condemned, but its share of responsibility for this basic element in the situation was relatively small.

Yet when all allowances have been made, the Aberdeen Government still bears considerable responsibility for its undoubted failure as a national administration. The Prime Minister himself was not well qualified to undertake the task of managing a ministerial team which posed serious difficulties of personalities from the beginning. The most difficult member of the team from the beginning was Lord John Russell, who throughout resented his supersession in the premiership by Aberdeen. He held a key position as the nominal leader of the grouping which provided the bulk of the Government's parliamentary support, but he behaved as a very unsatisfactory ministerial colleague, to such an extent that by the time of his resignation from the Government he had succeeded in alienating even the Whig colleagues with whom he had entered the coalition. Russell would have presented serious difficulties to a premier of even tougher calibre than Aberdeen; as it was throughout the life of that Government the Prime Minister was perennially plagued by Russell's erratic attempts to assert himself and force his will on the Government. Aberdeen tried again and again to bring Russell around by sweet reasonableness, succeeding repeatedly but at the cost of his own increasing disillusionment at the task he had embarked upon, as he told Bright, 'sensible of his deficiencies'. The recurrent difficulties with his disloyal subordinate played a part in the decline of Aberdeen's energy and grip. From the Government's inception, however, Aberdeen's authority over his colleagues had been uncertain. He was not a man who could dominate a Cabinet as a Peel or even a Liverpool could do. Aberdeen was much more a conciliator, more concerned at securing agreement than in securing the adoption of policies which he himself felt to be right. He was prone to second and third thoughts about decisions already reached, and altogether showed an inability to present incisive leadership to his Government. It is fair to point out, however, that he was not alone in this Cabinet in that kind of vacillation and lack of clarity of vision.

Aberdeen himself must bear much of the responsibility for the Crimean catastrophe which overwhelmed his Government. As an ex-Foreign Secretary of considerable experience, he knew something of the tangled problems of the Turkish empire. While Foreign Secretary in Peel's second Government he had discussed Russo–Turkish problems with the Tsar himself only ten years before. It is perhaps typical of Aberdeen's personality that he apparently left the Russians under the impression that the two countries were more agreed on Eastern matters than was in fact the case. The one man in the Aberdeen Government who should have been able to give a decided lead as the crisis developed, and that the Prime Minister himself, failed to display the authority on this issue to which his experience and his position could have entitled him. It is probable that Russia could have been deterred, and a peaceful solution arrived at, if it had been made clear much earlier that Britain and France were prepared to go to war on the issues involved. As it was, prolonged and tortuous negotiations were allowed to drag on in conditions of uncertainty, while at home Russophobia mounted. A prime minister, anxious to avoid the horrors of war, allowed his administration to drift towards war – a phrase used with disastrous frankness by the Foreign Secretary on 14 February 1854. The lack of decisiveness on the part of the British Government was one important factor in bringing the war about. Aberdeen himself, propelled reluctantly into a war which he had feared and opposed, did not make a good war leader, and he patently failed to provide any great inspiration during the remainder of his ministry. The minister principally concerned in Army matters, the Duke of Newcastle, was not a success; he worked hard, but possessed no great insight or ability to rise above detail. It was true that by the time the Government fell much had been done or in-augurated to remedy the deficiencies which had brought about the dreadful death-rolls of the winter of 1854–4 in the Crimea, but there had not been the sense of urgency and clear grasp of essentials which alone could have reacted in time to save the Army and with it the life of the Government. Even when the individual abilities of many of the ministers are admitted, and their modest achievements in domestic and financial matters are considered, the members of the Aberdeen Govern-ment cannot be acquitted of all responsibilitiy for the tragedy of the Crimea. They continued to employ unsatisfactory men in key positions, and the undoubted fact that they did not know where to turn to find better men does not absolve them from their failure to replace key officers in whom they themselves had lost confidence. Britain has at times produced war leaders who could do a great deal better than this, though Britain has not always done so, and the failures of the Aberdeen Cabinet as war directors are not unique in modern British history.

Lord Aberdeen himself must remain something of a pathetic figure in the gallery of British prime ministers. As Foreign Secretary under a strong prime minister in 1841–6 he had acquitted himself competently, and it was his tragedy that he was induced to accept responsibilities which were beyond his abilities. Imbued with a strong sense of public duty, he accepted in difficult circumstances the responsibilities of the premiership for which he knew himself to be ill fitted, because he believed, and was repeatedly assured by others, that his leadership, if only on a temporary basis, was a prerequisite to the creation of a stable administration. His Government set off under apparently favourable auspices, and in its first months achieved some notable successes. The deterioration of international relations, and the drift of war, faced him with greater responsibilities still, and his limited abilities as head of government, and war minister, involved him in a political catastrophe which a stronger and more determined premier might have avoided. If his personal failures did exist, and they certainly did, responsibility lies also with his ministerial colleagues, and with those at whose pleading he consented to form a government and undertake responsibilities for which he was not well equipped. His career illustrates only too clearly that amiability and goodwill are not by any means the only qualities required in a successful prime minister.

BIBLIOGRAPHY

The best biography of Lord Aberdeen remains that by his son Arthur (Lord Stanmore), *The Earl of Aberdeen* (London, 1893). In recent years a good deal of interesting work on the Peelites as a political grouping has been published by J. B. Conacher; a number of earlier articles led in 1968 to the publication of a major study of Aberdeen's Government, *The Aberdeen Coalition, 1852–5* (Cambridge).

4

VISCOUNT PALMERSTON

BY

JASPER RIDLEY

*Henry John Temple, 3rd Viscount Palmerston. Born 20 October
1784, son of Henry, 2nd Viscount Palmerston. Succeeded 1802.
Educated at Harrow, Edinburgh, and St John's College Cambridge.
Elected MP for Newport, Isle of Wight, 1807. Junior Lord of the
Admiralty under Portland, 1807; offered the exchequer by Perceval
in 1809 but preferred the office of Secretary for War and held it
until 1828 under five prime ministers. MP for Cambridge University 1811–31; Bletchingley 1831; South Hampshire 1832;
Tiverton from 1835; Foreign Secretary 1830–41. Married 1839,
the widow of the 5th Earl Cowper. Foreign Secretary 1846–51;
Home Secretary under Aberdeen 1852–55; Prime Minister 1855–65
with one short interval in 1858–59. Died 18 October 1865.*

VISCOUNT PALMERSTON

If public opinion polls had been invented in 1860, they would probably have shown that 85 per cent of the British public approved of Palmerston as Prime Minister, though when he first took office as Foreign Secretary, thirty years before, less than 10 per cent would have had a good word to say for him. In his last years 'Old Pam' was so popular that both his supporters and opponents knew that he would win every general election until he died, whether he fought it on a Radical or on a Tory policy. The people loved him for his vitality. He could ride to hounds, consume enormous meals and pursue women when he was nearly eighty; but he could also sit for hours on the government front bench, with no refreshment except an occasional cup of tea in the Members' dining room, and then, after walking home from the House of Commons to his house in Piccadilly, work half the night writing reports to the Queen – standing, not sitting, at his desk in order to stop himself from falling asleep. The people loved him for the stoutness with which he defended British interests abroad, and equally, perhaps, for his willingness to give way, and abandon unpopular measures, in response to the pressure of public opinion at home.

When he first became Prime Minister in 1855, at the age of seventy, he had already achieved some of the greatest triumphs of his career. Since his entry into politics forty-eight years before, when family influence procured him a position in the Government even before he obtained a seat in the House of Commons, he had spent forty years in office in either a Tory or a Whig Government, and sixteen years as Foreign Secretary. It is as a Foreign Secretary, even more than as a Prime Minister, that he is remembered today; and when he became Prime Minister he inspired the foreign policy of his Government, though he was scrupulous in not interfering with his Foreign Secretaries in the day-to-day conduct of foreign affairs. Britain, with its powerful Navy and its prosperous economy, was the most powerful nation in the world in Palmerston's time; and Palmerston, holding excellent cards, played the hand supremely well. He laid down his guiding principle in foreign policy in a speech in the House of Commons in March 1848:

that the furtherance of British interests should be the only object of a British Foreign Secretary, and that Britain had no permanent friends or permanent enemies. Sometimes his view of British interests led him to support the cause of constitutional freedom, and he was then denounced as a revolutionary by the Conservatives and applauded as a champion of freedom by the Radicals; but on other occasions he believed that it would be in Britain's interest to support dictators and enemies of constitutional freedom.

In Portugal he supported the moderate Liberals, both against the autocratic Conservatives whom Metternich favoured, and against the Radicals and Democrats, who at one time were supported by France; but in Spain, where the French supported the moderate Liberals, Palmerston backed the extreme Radicals, and justified his action by the surprising argument that Spain, unlike Britain and every other country in Europe, was ripe for democracy. In Serbia, where the landowners were supported by Russia, Palmerston supported the peasant revolutionary, Milosh, who had established a military dictatorship and was refusing to grant the demand of the large landowners that he should govern with the assistance of a constitutional Council of Boyars; and the Tsar, the great protector of European autocracy, thereupon instigated a constitutional revolution against Milosh. On the River Plate, Palmerston supported General Rosas, the dictator of Buenos Aires, against the Liberal Government of Uruguay, because he feared that the French were trying to establish a foothold in South America by supporting the Liberals of Montevideo; and he persisted in his support of Rosas even after Rosas' *gauchos* had murdered a number of British settlers in Uruguay and Argentina. Despite his long campaign to suppress the international slave trade, and his reputation as an opponent of slavery, he supported the South and the cause of slavery in the early stages of the American Civil War.

In 1851, Palmerston supported the *coup d'état* by which Napoleon III overthrew the Constitution of the French Republic. While English Liberals were expressing their indignation at Napoleon III's action in arresting his political opponents in their beds and suppressing the Republican Constitution, Palmerston congratulated Napoleon on his action, and said that if the Liberals 'meant to strike a sudden blow at him, he was quite right . . . to knock them down first'. Palmerston also supported Napoleon III in 1861, when Napoleon sent an expeditionary force to invade Mexico and set up the Austrian Archduke

Maximilian as Emperor of Mexico. Palmerston preferred Maximilian to the Liberal leader, Juarez, because he thought that strong autocratic government in Mexico would be more likely to preserve law and order and establish the necessary conditions in which British traders could carry on their affairs. He had previously supported the Government of the military dictator General Santa Anna in Mexico for the same reason.

Palmerston's reputation as a Radical in foreign policy was undeserved. He had been a junior minister in the Government that signed the Treaty of Vienna of 1815, and his original idea, when he went to the Foreign Office, was to continue the system by which the affairs of smaller nations were settled by the Great Powers at international conferences. His first achievement on taking office was the settlement of the Belgian problem; but though a Belgian historian has called him '*le père de la Belgique*', he accepted the idea of an independent Belgian state as a second-best solution, after the revolution of 1830 had convinced him that Belgium could no longer remain as a part of Holland. He never thought of Belgium as anything other than a factor in Great Power relationships.

Palmerston originally drifted almost by chance into the position of a champion of constitutional freedom in Europe. In 1832 an outbreak of student unrest at some German universities caused the powers of the German Confederation, at the instigation of Metternich, to introduce censorship and other regulations restricting constitutional liberties in the German states. William IV, as King of Hanover, was a member of the German Confederation, and his representative in the Diet voted in favour of the autocratic decrees. In order to appease the indignation that the vote of the Hanoverian delegate had caused in Liberal circles in Britain and abroad, Palmerston made a speech in the House of Commons – in a debate that only eleven MPs troubled to attend – in which he mildly criticised the decrees of the German Diet, and uttered some vague platitudes in support of the principles of constitutional government. His speech was applauded by the German Liberals, and 200,000 copies of it were circulated in Germany. Metternich and the absolutist powers thereupon denounced Palmerston as a dangerous Radical revolutionary, and the Austrian, Russian and Prussian Governments concluded the Treaty of Münchengrätz, by which they agreed to suppress revolutionary outbreaks wherever they occurred. This threw Palmerston closer to France and the Liberal forces in Britain and on the

Continent. He replied to the Treaty of Münchengrätz by the Quadruple Alliance with France and the Liberal Governments of Spain and Portugal, whom he supported in their civil wars, first in Portugal and then in Spain, against the Conservative and autocratic forces under Dom Miguel and Don Carlos. Thanks to Palmerston's support, Liberalism triumphed termporarily in both countries.

In allying himself with France – which still preserved a revolutionary reputation even under the bourgeois monarchy of Louis Philippe – Palmerston had alarmed King William IV and the British Tories, defied the deep-rooted anti-French prejudices of the British people, and won the support of the Radicals; but in 1839 he made a complete reversal of policy, and, to the delight of the Tories and the dismay of the Radicals, united with Austria and Russia against France during the Middle Eastern crisis. His solution of the long-standing conflict between the Sultan of Turkey and Mehemet Ali, the vassal Pasha of Egypt, shows his boldness of conception, his ruthlessness in execution, and his disregard of all other considerations when British interests were involved. Mehemet Ali had conquered Syria in 1833, and had governed it for six years by a brutal military dictatorship, which was more resented than the corrupt and equally tyrannical regime of the Sultan. France supported Mehemet Ali in the hopes of extending her influence eastwards from Tunisia on the North African shore of the Mediterranean; Russia supported the Sultan out of fear of French designs in the Levant, and from a desire to uphold the authority of a lawful sovereign against a rebel leader. Palmerston wished to prevent a clash between France and Russia in the Middle East and the disintegration of the Turkish Empire. He came to the conclusion that the only way to achieve this was to require Mehemet Ali to evacuate Syria and return to Egypt – 'by such means the Desert would be interposed between the two parties'.

He put this forward as a solution after the Sultan's armies had ended the six-year truce by crossing the Turco-Syrian border and attacking Mehemet Ali's troops, and had been routed at the Battle of Nezib. Neither the Sultan's aggression, and his military defeat and incompetence, nor the claim made by Mehemet Ali's sympathisers in France that the Pasha was a civilising influence in the Middle East, could deter Palmerston from inflicting this humiliation on Mehemet Ali, and restoring Syria to the rule of the Sultan. He was convinced that 'Egyptian civilization must come from Constantinople, and not from Paris, to be durable or consistent with British interests of a most important kind'.

In view of this, 'no ideas therefore of fairness towards Mehemet ought to stand in the way of such great and paramount interests'.

As France refused to join the other Great Powers in imposing this solution on Mehemet Ali, Palmerston went ahead without France, and signed the Treaty of London of 15 July 1840, by which Britain, Russia, Austria and Prussia agreed to use whatever force was necessary to expel Mehemet Ali from Syria. This aroused the greatest indignation in France, and it seemed that a major European war was inevitable. But Palmerston, almost alone among his Cabinet colleagues, did not worry. He believed that France would be prepared, if necessary, to go to war with Britain, Russia, Prussia and Austria 'if those Powers were to threaten to invade France, to insult her honour, or to attack her Possessions; but France will not go to war with the other Great Powers of Europe to help Mehemet Ali'. His policy was completely successful. Mehemet Ali was expelled from Syria, and France did nothing to help him.

When Palmerston, after five years in opposition, returned to the Foreign Office in 1846, a series of events identified him more closely than ever with the Radicals in Europe. The foreign autocrats believed that he was the arch-revolutionary who was responsible for all the trouble in Europe in 1848; and he was called a 'Red' by a Conservative MP in the House of Commons. In fact, Palmerston's attitude to the revolutions of 1848, which he described as a struggle 'between those who have no property and those who have and wish to keep it', was mixed. He gave moral support to the revolutionary Government of Lamartine, which was established after the February revolution in Paris, because he believed, like Karl Marx, that it was the only bulwark between France and a Communist revolution. In Spain he supported the extreme Radicals, and suffered a defeat. But in Germany he successfully opposed the revolutionary threat to the rule of the Danish monarchy in Schleswig-Holstein. In Hungary, though he had some sympathy with the revolutionary nationalist movement, he refused to give it any support, or to make any official protest when Russian troops intervened to help Austria suppress the revolt. 'Much as Her Majesty's Government regret this interference of Russia, the causes which have led to it, and the Effects which it may produce,' he wrote to the Chargé d'Affaires in St Petersburg, 'they nevertheless have not considered the occasion to be one which at present calls for any formal expression of the opinions of Great Britain on the matter.' It was only after the rebels had been defeated that Palmerston, in response to British public opinion, protested against the hangings and floggings by which the victors were punishing the Hungarian patriots. But by supporting Turkey in her refusal, under a Russian threat of war, to extradite the Hungarian refugees, he won the undying gratitude of Radicals throughout the world.

Palmerston did not give any assistance to the Polish struggle for independence from Russia, although the friends of Polish freedom, under the leadership of Lord Dudley Stuart, had established a vociferous lobby in the House of Commons. Palmerston gave no active support to Poland in 1831, 1836, 1846 or 1863; and he refused to take up the Polish cause in 1856, when the peace treaty was being imposed on a defeated Russia after the Crimean War, though this was probably the only occasion when he would have been able to do something practical to help the Poles. The Polish poet Niemcewicz, who had an interview with Palmerston, found him 'colder than ice'; and the leader of the Poles in exile, Prince Czartoryski, was quite unable to get him to go to war to liberate Poland. 'The English nation is able to make war,' said Palmerston, 'but it will only do so where its own interests are concerned. We are a simple and practical nation, a commercial nation; we do not go in for chivalrous enterprises, or fight for others as the French do.'

But in Italy, Palmerston modified his usual policy of ignoring everything except British interests, because here he was influenced by British public opinion, to which he was always responsive. The traditional British policy in Italy had been to support Austria against French expansion; but the British people, because of their hostility to the Pope and Roman Catholicism and their romantic adoration of Garibaldi, were enthusiastically in favour of Italian unification and liberation. So Palmerston, after pursuing the traditional pro-Austrian policy during the revolution of 1831, became pro-Italian in later years. 'North of the Alps,' he wrote in 1848, he wished Austria 'all the prosperity and success in the world'; but south of the Alps she must give up Lombardy, and perhaps Venetia also. In 1859 he won a general election in Britain on a pro-Italian policy; and he was able to reconcile British interests and British public opinion by working for an independent united kingdom of Italy, which would be as effective a barrier to French expansion as the presence of the Austrian army in a disunited Italy.

In the Far East, Palmerston's policy involved Britain in three wars with China and a bombardment of Japan. His object here, as in other parts of the world, was not to acquire territory – he took 'the desert island of Hong Kong' reluctantly – but to secure the Chinese market for the British trader. 'The rivalship of European manufactures,' he wrote in 1841, 'is fast excluding our productions from the markets of Europe, and we must unremittingly endeavour to find in other parts of the world new vents for the produce of our industry. The world is large enough and the wants of the human race ample enough to afford a demand for all we can manufacture; but it is the business of the Government to open and to secure the roads for the merchant.' As China resisted the British trader, Palmerston used force to overcome this resistance.

There was no feeling of racial superiority in Palmerston's attitude to China. He once called the Chinese Mandarin Governor, Yeh, 'an insolent barbarian wielding authority at Canton'; but this was in an address to his constituents when he was electioneering on a chauvinist policy and successfully smearing his Conservative opponents as pro-Chinese and anti-British. He thought the Chinese were no better or worse than other races. 'Depend upon it,' he wrote, 'that the best way of keeping any men quiet is to let them see that you are able and determined to repel force by force; and the Chinese are not in the least different, in this respect, from the rest of mankind.'

In 1851 Palmerston was dismissed from the Foreign Office at the insistence of Queen Victoria, who disapproved of his policy of supporting revolutionary movements in Europe. He returned to the Government after only a year in opposition; but it was as Home Secretary, and not in the office with which the whole nation associated him. During the Middle Eastern crisis of 1853, when the Great Powers slowly drifted into the first major European war for forty years, Palmerston was not directly in charge of British foreign policy, though his influence in the Cabinet forced the pacific Premier, Lord Aberdeen, to stiffen his attitude towards Russia, and ultimately to declare war. After the first disasters at Sevastopol and Balaclava, popular indignation with military incompetence in the Crimea forced the Government to resign, and public opinion demanded that Palmerston should become Prime Minister. His colleagues in the Cabinet knew that he had been as much responsible as the rest of them for the mistakes which had been made; but no one else had the confidence of the nation. 'I am, for the moment, *l'inévitable*,' he wrote on 15 February 1855, ten days after he had formed a government.

Palmerston's appointment as Prime Minister did not lead to much improvement in the efficiency of the military command in the Crimea; but the war was won, and thanks to Palmerston's intransigence Russia was forced to accept harsh terms at the Peace Congress, and to relinquish the right to maintain warships in the Black Sea. Palmerston was very popular in Britain after the end of the Crimean War, and he won a great victory at the general election of 1857 when he appealed to the country to support his aggressive policy in China. Next year he suddenly fell from power when the House of Commons rejected his Conspiracy to Murder Bill, which placed restrictions on the freedom of foreign political refugees in Britain; but after less than eighteen months in opposition, he was again Prime Minister, this time at the head of a Liberal Government with Radical support. He and his party had won the general election of 1859 on a pledge to introduce new measures of parliamentary reform, which would give the vote to the working classes in the towns. But Palmerston, who had always opposed this proposal, succeeded in holding up the measure until after his death, in office, six years later, and it was not until 1867 that the second Reform Bill was passed.

In home affairs, the story of Palmerston's second premiership is of a Prime Minister who, by relying on his great personal popularity, his jovial temperament, and his skilful handling of his supporters, succeeded in thwarting, as far as possible, the political and social reforms which were favoured by the majority of his Cabinet, and especially by his Chancellor of the Exchequer, Gladstone. But Palmerston was in perfect harmony with the 'silent majority' of the period, though not at all with the ideas of the advanced intellectuals. He remained largely unaffected by the humanism of the nineteenth century. He moved forward along the lines of reform that the pioneers had indicated, but only when the majority of his contemporaries did the same; as his friend, Henry Bulwer, put it, 'in the march of his epoch he was behind the eager but before the slow'. He fought his first election in 1806, when he was a young man of twenty-one, as a supporter of the slave trade; thirty years later, as Foreign Secretary, he played the leading part in suppressing the slave trade of foreign nations by the use of the British Navy. As a young junior minister at the War Office, he strongly defended flogging in the Army; and though, some years later, he recommended that the maximum number of lashes that could be administered for a 'small' offence should be reduced from 300 to 200, he remained a believer in flogging all his life. In 1820 he played an active part in tracking down a young poacher, who had wounded his gamekeeper in Hampshire, for which the poacher was hanged, despite an agitation for a reprieve; and Palmerston's conduct in the case caused him to be attacked by Cobbett and the Radicals as a prototype of the oppressive landlord. But he ended his career, in Disraeli's words, as the Tory chief of a Radical Cabinet, and presided at the foundation of the modern Liberal Party in 1859.

He was out of sympathy with the new morality of the mid-nineteenth century, with its campaigns to redeem prostitutes, and said that he thought prostitutes fulfilled a useful function in society, because the existence of prostitutes prevented men from pursuing respectable women – a statement that did not apply in his own case. As Home Secretary he introduced some measures of penal reform, and took the first steps to establish a system of special treatment for young offenders; but when an outburst of violent crime aroused public indignation in 1862, when he was Prime Minister, he urged his Home Secretary to abolish most of the reforms which he himself had introduced nine years before. He believed ardently in free trade and the principles of complete economic freedom which he had learnt as a student from his Whig teachers at Edinburgh University, and insisted on applying them even when they meant allowing the export of food, and the denial of Poor Relief, in time of famine. He supported the new Poor Law of 1834, in the face of criticism from both Tories and Chartists, and reacted only with a jovial laugh when his Chartist opponent in his constituency at Tiverton asked him how he would like it if he and Lady Palmerston were confined in separate quarters in a workhouse and forbidden to see each other. But he helped Lady Palmerston's son-in-law, Lord Shaftesbury, in his campaigns to introduce social reforms, and he won the gratitude of the trade union movement by his support for the Ten Hours Bill.

Palmerston has been described as a Conservative at home and a Liberal abroad; but there was no real contradiction between his internal and foreign policy. He believed, like most Englishmen of his generation, that the British Constitution and social system of the early nineteenth century were the best in the world, and as near to perfection as any merely human institution could ever be. He believed in constitutional monarchy, with a sovereign who was by no means politically powerless, but who was subject to the law, respected the privileges of

Parliament, and acted on the advice of his ministers. He believed in a Parliament in which one House was composed of the wealthiest land-owners, and the other was elected on a franchise which gave the vote to only 5 per cent of the adult males in the country. He believed in the rule of law; but when the State was in danger, the rule of law included the Six Acts, which Lord Liverpool's Tory Government, in which Palmerston was a minister, passed in 1819 at the time of Peterloo, and which severely restricted the political freedom of the opposition parties. He believed in the freedom of the press, but of a press whose circulation was restricted to the wealthier classes by the stamp duties and the paper tax. He was a Conservative at home because he wished to preserve this system and prevent any developments in the direction of democracy. He was a Liberal abroad because he wished to see this system replace the absolutist monarchies of the Continent. In 1863, during the Polish revolt against Russia and the American Civil War, he told the House of Commons that peaceful England stood half-way, politically as well as geographically, between the two hateful extremes of royal despotism and Republican democracy.

This firm belief in English superiority was the chief cause of Palmerston's popularity in his later years as Foreign Secretary and as Prime Minister. The ordinary Englishman loved him because he sent gun-boats to protect the rights of any British subject who was injured or insulted abroad. In the debate in the House of Commons on the case of Don Pacifico in 1850, Roebuck declared that though the Tsar of Russia could send any of his own subjects to Siberia when he pleased, Palmerston would never permit him to do the same to a British subject. This was the Palmerston myth; but the reality was a little different. Palmerston used the Navy to blockade Greece to vindicate the rights of Don Pacifico, and to bombard Canton and Kagoshima to avenge an insult to the British flag or the murder of a British subject. But when Russian officers arrested an Ionian islander, who was a British subject, in Bucharest, Palmerston merely sent a protest; and he did nothing at all when a negro seaman, who was also a British subject, was dragged off his ship by the authorities at Charleston under a law that made it an offence for a free negro to be at large in the state of South Carolina. Russia and the United States were too powerful to be treated like Greece or Portugal.

There were only two occasions when Palmerston came near to using force against a great power to uphold the rights of a British subject or the honour of the British flag. Both times it was against the United States. The first occasion was in 1841, when a Canadian militiaman was put on trial for murder in New York because he had shot a United States citizen on the United States side of the frontier in the course of his official duties during the suppression of a rebellion. The case aroused strong feelings in both Britain and the United States, and the pressure of British public opinion drove a reluctant Palmerston to the brink of war. The other occasion was the case of the *Trent*, during the peculiar circumstances of the American Civil War, when a Northern warship stopped a British vessel on the high seas and removed two envoys of the Southern Confederacy who were travelling to Europe. In both cases, Palmerston's threat of war induced the United States to back down; but in the closing years of the Civil War, Palmerston developed a healthy respect for the power of the United States, and tolerated affronts to the British flag which were as flagrant as the case of the *Trent*. In 1858, he had stated that there were only three nations in the world who were strong enough to challenge British naval superiority – France, Russia and the United States. In the last months of his life, in 1865, he believed that it was the United States from which the threat to British power would come in the future.

Palmerston's policy of threatening weaker states with British power, and of conciliating stronger nations as much as possible, outraged the Nonconformist conscience and the sense of sportsmanship of some of the British people. Many Englishman saw him, as the cartoonists of *Punch* did, as a plucky boy who fought big bullies twice his size; but his critics, including such varied personages as Prince Albert, Cobden, Lord Cardigan and Marx, agreed with the Radical MP, Attwood, that Palmerston was 'a bully to the weak and a coward to the strong'. Palmerston's Cabinet colleague, Sidney Herbert, wrote: 'Palmerston can never resist shaking his fist in the face of anyone whom he is not afraid of. If they show fight, he runs away.' Palmerston replied to this accusation by pointing out that no one should accuse him of capitulating to powerful states, because he had been in favour of going to war with Russia in defence of Turkey in 1853.

When Palmerston was conducting British foreign policy, he did not act in the sporting spirit of a boys' public school, but in accordance with the harsh realities of international politics. He used British power to the full, in Britain's interests, against weaker opponents, and prevented Britain from clashing with powerful states in contests in which Britain might suffer damage. To have done less would, in his opinion, have been failing in his duty as a British Foreign Secretary. He had no faith in Cobden's ideal of international arbitration, and usually refused to submit to the arbitration of a third power in international disputes. He did not believe that any power could be an impartial arbitrator where Britain was concerned, because there was no state that did not have a conflict of interests with Britain in some part of the world. He thought that such conflicts were inevitable, because though he believed that there were many spheres, especially in trade, in which nations could co-operate for their mutual benefit, there were other areas in which interests were irreconcilable – for example in the Middle East, where Britain and France were like two men in love with the same woman. 'It would be very delightful if your Utopia could be realised,' he told Cobden, 'and if the nations of the earth would think of nothing but peace and commerce, and would give up quarrelling and fighting altogether. But unfortunately man is a fighting and quarrelling animal; and that this is human nature is proved by the fact that republics, where the masses govern, are far more quarrelsome, and more addicted to fighting, than monarchies, which are governed by comparatively few persons.'

It was therefore necessary to preserve British military strength. To have a powerful army and navy was like carrying an umbrella on a showery day; if you took it, you were sure not to need it, but if you did not take it, you would regret it. Unless Britain maintained her military superiority, she was lost, because though the anger of a weaker power did not matter, the anger of a stronger power meant national humiliation. Palmerston applied this rule to other nations, and expected them to apply it to Britain. When Bismarck ignored his bluff and invaded Schleswig-Holstein in 1864, after Palmerston had promised that in this case he would go to the assistance of Denmark, he did nothing to help the Danes, and announced, with a cheerfulness that shocked his Foreign Secretary, Lord Russell, that there was nothing he could do against 200,000 soldiers. But the British people did not lose faith in him. In 1865 he won another general election, but died before he could meet the new Parliament.

His humiliation at the hands of Bismarck was one of the few defeats of his career. In general, his handling of foreign policy was brilliant and successful. Cobden accused him of what would today be called 'brinkmanship'. 'Palmerston likes to drive the wheel close to the edge,' he wrote, 'and show how dexterously he can avoid falling over the precipice.' Only once during Palmerston's lifetime did the carriage go over the precipice. This was in 1853, during the months before the outbreak of the Crimean War, when Palmerston was in the Government, but not at the Foreign Office. If he had been in charge of Britain's foreign policy at the time, the carriage would probably just have managed to stay on the road.

BIBLIOGRAPHY

Biographies of Palmerston

Bell, H. C. F., *Lord Palmerston* (2 vols, London, 1936)
Dalling, Lord (Sir Henry Lytton Bulwer) and Ashley, Evelyn, *The Life of Henry John Temple, Viscount Palmerston* (5 vols, London, 1870–6)
Pemberton, W. B., *Lord Palmerston* (London, 1954)
Ridley, Jasper, *Lord Palmerston* (London, 1970)

Studies of Palmerston's policy

Connell, B., *Regina v. Palmerston* (London, 1962)
Douglas, George, Eighth Duke of Argyll, *Autobiography and Memoirs* (2 vols, London, 1906)
Guedalla, Philip, *Gladstone and Palmerston : being the correspondence of Lord Palmerston with Mr Gladstone 1851–65* (London, 1928)
Martin, Kingsley, *The Triumph of Lord Palmerston* (London, 1924) (for the Eastern Question in 1853, and the Crimean War)
Southgate, D., *'The Most English Minister . . .': The Policies and Politics of Palmerston* (London, 1966)
Vincent, J., *The Formation of the Liberal Party 1857–68* (London, 1966)
Webster, Sir Charles, *The Foreign Policy of Palmerston 1830–41* (2 vols, London, 1951)

5

BENJAMIN DISRAELI
EARL OF BEACONSFIELD

BY

JOHN VINCENT

Benjamin Disraeli, created Earl of Beaconsfield 1876. Born 21 December 1804, first son of Isaac D'Israeli, author, and Maria, daughter of Naphtali Basevi, merchant. Baptised into the Church of England 1817. Educated at the schools of Miss Roper (in Islington), the Rev. Potticany (Blackheath) and the Rev. Eli Cogan (Walthamstow), ending in 1819. Married, 1839, Mary Anne, widow of Wyndham Lewis, MP; she was created Viscountess Beaconsfield in 1868 and died in 1872. MP for Maidstone, 1837–41, Shrewsbury, 1841–47; Buckinghamshire, 1847–76. Chancellor of the Exchequer, 1852, 1858–59, 1866–68; First Lord of the Treasury and Prime Minister 1868 and 1874–80; Lord Privy Seal 1876–78; PC 1852; Trustee of the National Portrait Gallery (1856) and British Museum (1863–81); DCL (Oxford) 1873, LLD (Glasgow) 1873, FRS 1876, KG 1878. Died 19 April 1881. No issue. Author of numerous novels, Coningsby, Tancred, Sybil, Lothair, Endymion, *among them.*

BENJAMIN DISRAELI

Mr Gladstone once said to his son that 'Mr Disraeli was in the centre of three rings – his party, which he understood perfectly and governed completely; the House of Commons, of which his knowledge was good; the country, of which he was very ignorant.'[1] This judgement contains a core of truth: Disraeli was greater as leader of a parliamentary party than as Prime Minister and head of a government. With Fox, he was the greatest leader of an opposition this country has known. For most of his career a single-minded parliamentarian, his knowledge of the country at large was highly selective, and much limited by the peculiar background of his early life.

The evidence for Disraeli's early years is inevitably slight.[2] Three points stand out. Firstly, Disraeli was born and bred a town boy, nurtured in Holborn and Bloomsbury, without any knowledge of the rural pursuits that made an English gentleman: riding a horse was always a problem for him. Secondly, though his parents had at heart rejected most of Judaism, he was brought up in many ways as a Jew by religion, received lessons in Hebrew, and was not received into the Church of England until he was twelve. Thirdly, for reasons unknown, he was not educated as befitted the son of a rich and distinguished man of letters. He left school at about fifteen, thereafter engaging in only desultory study. After some time reading at home, he entered a solicitor's office for three years, then gave it up as unsuited to his requirements. Disraeli, aged 20, was already in 1825 a very ambitious youth of distinctive character and no prospects.

Disraeli's first attempt to take the world by storm occurred in 1824–6. He took part in an attempt to create a great newspaper, the *Representative*, to rival *The Times*, by using the money of the publisher Murray and the mind of Lockhart. The paper failed, and Murray lost £26,000. A brilliant novel of politics and society then appeared, anonymously, caricaturing poor Murray. Its initial success turned to disaster as

[1] Viscount Gladstone, *After Thirty Years* (London, 1928), p. 162.
[2] For his home background, see James Ogden, *Isaac D'Israeli* (Oxford, 1969): for Disraeli in the 1820s and 1830s, see B. R. Jerman, *The Young Disraeli* (London, 1960).

Disraeli's authorship leaked out. By 1826, Disraeli was *persona non grata* in the smart literary circles around Murray, access to which had been his only silver spoon. A failure at 21, Disraeli retorted upon the world with a prolonged breakdown or nervous illness. In addition, he had acquired Stock Exchange debts, a millstone round his neck for most of his life. The family moved, in 1829, to Bradenham in rural Buckinghamshire, with their son's illness very much in mind. In 1830, however, Disraeli was still an unemployed invalid of 25, apolitically nursing his constitution in country quiet, outside society.

In 1830-1, however, the pattern of his life was changed decisively by a tour in the Mediterranean and Near East, during which his nervous troubles virtually disappeared. He found aspects of Turkish life profoundly congenial: yet he never returned. It was a curious time for a future politician to be abroad, but when he returned, he was determined to cut a figure. Early in 1832 he took up residence in the West End. In 1832-4 he took his bearings, a minor mistress, and an idiosyncratic Radical line in politics. In 1834 he met and committed himself to Lord Lyndhurst, an ageing intriguer who became his mentor, and to the Conservatives. The years 1834-7 were ones of political and financial struggle, and of a considerable affair with Henrietta Sykes, mother of four and wife of a baronet: she died in 1846. Her feelings for him were intense: for his part, he felt able to pass her on to Lyndhurst, an act that was held against him in later years. Political success came in 1837, with election for Maidstone, and relative financial security with his marriage to Mrs Wyndham Lewis, a widow twelve years his senior, in 1839. Out of all his early precocity, his years of ill health, and his rakish adventures of the 1830s, he carried forward into middle life nothing more useful than an indifferent marriage (in the world's eyes), a bad name, and large debts.

In 1837-41 Disraeli was a loyal follower of Peel. In 1841 he begged Peel for office. In 1842 he remained loyal, though bitterly disappointed, conspicuously rejecting the opportunity to join the faction of agricultural malcontents who were the true opposition to Peel within the Tory ranks. With this section he had virtually no contact (or sympathy) before 1846. His course, instead, was to try to form a third force, neither wholly for nor wholly against Peel, but simply, in ideology, far above his prosy level-headedness, and in numbers capable of holding the balance. The numbers were a dream, for 'Young England', not originated by Disraeli but taken over by him, centred on three young men just down from university: Smythe, a Byronic cynic, Manners, a knight errant, and Baillie Cochrane, a fop. Pilgrimages were made northwards, and in 1843 Disraeli, opening the Manchester Athenaeum in company with Dickens and Cobden, declared Manchester to be as great a human enterprise as Athens. The mood was one of Tory democracy, in the sense that note was taken of the poor: the remedies were paternalistic. 'Young England' was a talking-point in 1843-4, but not an influence upon events, and by 1845 it belonged to the past. In one way at least it was not impeccable, for Disraeli sought to attach to it a scheme by which he and his comrades would exert influence on behalf of the French Government.[3] The real importance of Young England was not that it led Disraeli to break with Peel: it may, by distracting him, even have deferred such a break. Young England did, however, stimulate Disraeli to write novels far more remarkable than anything of which he had hitherto appeared capable: *Coningsby* (1844), *Sybil* (1845), and *Tancred* (1847).

Up to the end of 1845 there was little sign of Disraeli turning into an active parliamentary figure. He did not speak frequently before the crisis of 1846.

1845 saw the break-up of Young England, with its members disagreeing over the Maynooth grant, and Smythe, his leading ally, accepting office in Peel's last ministry. Early in 1845, Disraeli compared the situation to 'the third year of the Walpole administration'.[4] He spent most of summer and autumn 1845 abroad and out of touch with affairs, reaching Paris in December to hear of the ministerial crisis in London. Far from hurrying home, the Disraelis remained in Paris. 'I do not think I shall be tempted to quit this agreeable residence – especially as the great object of my political career is now achieved,' Disraeli told Palmerston on 14 December 1845.[5]

Disraeli's attacks on Peel, beginning on the first night of the Corn Laws debate, were a supreme rhetorical achievement, and no one at the time was unaware of the fact. The real question was how many ordinary

---

[3] For Disraeli's memorandum for the King of the French, 1842, offering to use 'a party of the youth of England' to manipulate the House of Commons and the press in French interests, see W. F. Monypenny and G. E. Buckle, *The Life of Benjamin Disraeli, Earl of Beaconsfield* (6 vols, London, 1910-20), ii, 409-13.

[4] Disraeli to his sister, 6 Feb. 1845. (*Lord Beaconsfield's Letters 1830 to 1852*, ed. R. Disraeli (London, 1887), pp. 204-5.)

[5] Monypenny and Buckle, op. cit., ii, 340.

Conservative MPs, having made their protest, really wanted to bring Peel down, and to create a separate Protectionist party. The formation of this latter body, early in 1846, decided nothing: even the partial acquisition of Stanley as leader and Bentinck as lieutenant decided nothing. In the end, under seventy Tory MPs[6] were able to bring themselves to vote Peel out of office on the Irish Coercion Bill on 25 June 1846. It remained for succeeding years to decide whether the Corn Law crisis had produced anything more than one more ephemeral splinter group on the right wing of the Conservative party.

The years 1847–8 showed how much Disraeli remained an outsider in the Protectionist party, and how little his achievement in 1846 had done to give him a permanent status in politics. Lord George Bentinck, hitherto a racing man who was not active in politics, had emerged in 1846 as the most forcible personality among the Protectionists in the Commons. It was to him, not to Lord Stanley, the party leader, that Disraeli attached himself. Indeed, until 1849 Disraeli and Stanley had little contact even for business purposes. Bentinck wanted his party to be a party of uncompromising principle where Peel and Protection were concerned, but to be reasonably tolerant on Irish, Catholic, and Jewish questions. His backbenchers were simple bigots, and Stanley, and the Commons whips under his control, felt bound to give way to their views. At the end of 1847 Bentinck resigned, after he and Disraeli had set the teeth of their party on edge by supporting Jewish rights. Disraeli remained on the front bench, to which his friend never returned: but he had no official position in the party. In 1848, a new leader, Lord Granby, was appointed by Stanley. His sole merit was that he was not Disraeli: and he resigned after four weeks, leaving the party in the Commons leaderless for the rest of 1848. Bentinck's sudden death, in September 1848, released Disraeli from loyalty to an impossible politician, and was to that extent an advantage, but it did not mean that Disraeli inherited the leadership by natural succession.

Disraeli had been relying on Bentinck and his brothers for a massive sum of money to purchase the Hughenden estate in Buckinghamshire. In the event Bentinck's brothers continued to provide finance, and in 1848 Disraeli finally became a country gentleman, having also acquired a safe seat for the county at the 1847 general election. Stanley still opposed Disraeli's advancement, as did the Whips, and it was only

[6] Robert Stewart, *The Politics of Protection: Lord Derby and the Protectionist Party 1841–52* (Cambridge, 1971), p. 74.

after many months of manoeuvre and confrontation that, early in 1849, a triumvirate of Disraeli, Lord Granby, and Herries, an aged bureaucrat, was chosen by Stanley to lead in the Commons. The triumvirate lasted on paper till early in 1852, but never existed in practice. Disraeli was in brilliant form in the 1849 session: in the three sessions from 1849 to 1851 his attacking tactics made the acrimonious little groups of 1846–8 into an effective alternative government. In 1851 the Whigs were defeated, but Stanley either could not or would not take their place. From the day Disraeli took over, however, it was only a matter of time before the Derbyites took office. Russell resigned over a trifle in February 1852, and Derby formed a minority government.

The 1852 ministry appeared laughably weak. It was a purely Tory ministry, without any accession of strength from Palmerston or from individual Peelites, such as the Protectionists had hoped for in 1849–51. For all that, the ministry managed its business creditably. There were very few embarrassing moments, and the new ministers emerged as conscientious and honest, if limited. Disraeli himself was highly pleased with affairs until the last few months of the ministry. Abroad, the aftermath of Louis Napoleon's *coup de 'état* was handled without incident. The business of the year, however, was of very little consequence save for the general election (July) and Disraeli's second Budget (December). The December Budget, designed essentially to compensate the landed interest by tax reductions for loss of protection, embodied Derbyite acceptance of the new situation. It came unstuck, partly for technical reasons, ultimately because the negotiations between Whigs and Peelites for coalition had been completed: but not before Disraeli had established himself as the indispensable leader of a united Derbyite party in the Commons.

The 1852 ministry, by abandoning Protection, left the Derbyites without a *raison d'être* for the rest of the 1850s, and out of office until 1858–9. Their prospects were at first felt to be grim, for Aberdeen's deep conservatism left little scope for providing what Derby wished, a party of resistance to Reform; while Disraeli's experiments with a Radical alliance, and his foundation of his own paper, *The Press*, in May 1853, excited much suspicion. In 1854, however, Russell's Reform Bill, widely regarded as an extreme measure, cheered Tory spirits and enabled them to look forward confidently to the break-up of the coalition. It is important to realise that the Tory leaders were very much not disheartened until the Crimean War. 'Disraeli is furious with the war, which he thinks keeps Government in,' Malmesbury wrote.[7] Despite a moment early in 1855 when a Derby government seemed possible, the Derbyites, unable to unite on a distinctive pro-war or anti-war policy, were completely overshadowed by Palmerston in 1855-8, years in which even Disraeli found little he could do.

The 1858-9 ministry was a success. Its Reform Bill, which did not pass, and its India Bill, which did, showed Tory ministers as capable of dealing with large schemes of legislation in a liberal spirit, in a way unknown in 1852. Ministers made no serious errors, though Malmesbury allowed himself to appear more opposed to Italian liberty than he was. Disraeli, now helped by the very able young Northcote, was able to appear a respectable, if not brilliant, Chancellor of the Exchequer. A start was also made on Tory social policy, with Disraeli carrying a major measure for the sewerage of London, and some legal reforms being carried. There were absurdities in Disraeli's Reform Bill, as in his Indian proposals, but the confidence of the Tory leaders and the unity of the party made a good impression compared with the discord amongst its opponents. This was reflected in the best election results for the Derbyites between 1841 and 1874. The 1858-9 ministry was very much a conscious preparation for an inevitable coming election. As such, it very nearly, but not quite, was a brilliant success, under its slogan of 'Conservative progress'.

The 1857 election was the first to bring into prominence the threat posed to the Church of England by an increasingly aggressive Dissent. Church Defence Associations sprang up in reply: and Disraeli was quick to spot the need to revive the rather latent connections of Church and Toryism. Disraeli also needed to take up a soundly reactionary policy on church questions for three reasons. Firstly, the line of 'Conservative progress' set out in 1858-9, while useful for making inroads into the Liberal consensus, needed balancing by a complementary traditionalist doctrine. Secondly, Disraeli wanted to commit his party to a reactionary line on church matters, so that it could remain flexible and uncommitted on Reform. Thirdly, Disraeli could and did win parliamentary victories on matters like Trelawny's Church Rates motions, without bringing the Government down (since they were Private Members' proposals). From the late 1850s, many senior Conservatives had plans for quietly conceding the main issues like church rates:

[7] Earl of Malmesbury, *Memoirs of an Ex-Minister: An Autobiography* (London, 1884), i, 434.

Disraeli, acting upon a higher strategy, saw to it that denominational controversy became the essence of party politics in the 1860s. From 1860 to 1868, Disraeli made defence of the Church the most conspicuous commitment of his party.

Between 1859 and 1865, a state of truce between the parties was a mixture of belief and fact. Disraeli, at least, accepted the party truce to the extent of being far less aggressive than in the 1850s. The truce meant different things at different times. In 1859–60, Tories wished to avoid a further election, although Palmerston's majority was only around a dozen. In 1861–2, the deaths, first of the Queen's mother, then of Prince Albert, were taken as grounds for subduing political strife. In 1863 and 1864, spirited challenges by the Opposition fell through partly because some Tory Dissidents preferred to keep Palmerston in power, partly because the Tory leaders' own strategy was to avoid coming to power until they could do so on their own terms, with a majority, and for a long period. In addition, Palmerston and the Tory squires were in real agreement on fundamentals, and this made the decade 1855–65 a period in which Disraeli could do little but mark time.

The Conservative position on Reform in the period 1850–66 was by no means one of simple dislike of a wide franchise. The party, and Disraeli, did at times take up a public posture of reaction, partly because (especially in Derby's case) they thought that the right role for the party, partly in order to lure away dissatisfied right-wing Whigs. This was most obviously the case in 1854 and 1866. In general, however, the Tories and Disraeli easily avoided any rigid commitment against Reform. Some leading Tories actually wanted Reform: young Lord Stanley wrote in 1853, 'It is the duty of statesmen . . . to bring within the pale of the Constitution everyone whose admission cannot be proved dangerous.'[8] Derby himself was not inclined to take the lowering of the franchise too seriously, provided that the political situation in the counties remained unaffected. As early as 1854, Disraeli and Derby had drawn up a Tory Reform Bill in case of need. Influenced by the conservatism of universal suffrage in France, important Conservatives came to believe that significant concessions could be made in the franchise without affecting the *status quo* in the counties, or the *status quo* in Parliament. In 1866, the general drift of Conservative opinion was towards compromise and a small reduction in the urban franchise, and but for Disraeli and Derby the question might well have been settled

[8] Monypenny and Buckle, op. cit., iii, 501.

quietly for a generation. Disraeli's tactics, however, were to split the Liberal party while also refusing coalition with Liberal anti-Reform Dissidents: thus, having wrecked Russell's Reform Bill of 1866, he and Derby again came to power, uncommitted to any policy, and unallied to any outside group, in June 1866.[9]

During the winter of 1866–7, a consensus emerged among Tory ministers in favour of action on the Reform question. Agitation out of doors may have determined this consensus: it did not decide whether such action was to be real or illusory, restrictive or inclusive. Disraeli naturally had many ideas, eventually coming out in favour of pure procrastination. In this respect he was decidedly less bold than his colleagues. Derby, however, was leader, and retained some of his rashness. The Tories decided to act, and Derby then fell ill. Throughout the 1867 session, the existence of both the party and the Bill rested on Disraeli's shoulders. He could not afford to fail. He tried, first, to create a restrictive measure designed to attract the support of all those who loathed Reform. Three right-wing ministers (Salisbury, Carnarvon, and General Peel) resigned over this, and the right-wing Whigs would not give support. This right-wing opposition to a moderate Bill made it certain that only an extremely Radical Bill could be passed. Unable to lure votes from the Whigs, Disraeli laid bait for the Radicals, who were happy to accept. The Bill eventually passed, altered out of all recognition from the Bill originally introduced: but this did not mar Disraeli's achievement. His party remained intact and in office, while the Liberals had disintegrated and Gladstone had been reduced to impotence. That, for Disraeli, was the meaning of the Bill.

The single provision of the Bill that really mattered was that the urban working class got the vote, subject to technical exceptions. It was not that this produced recognisable changes in political patterns in the short term: on the contrary, it simply gave existing middle-class Radical MPs in the big cities more constituents to canvass. On the other hand, omitting to enfranchise the politically conscious working class at such an early date might have led to a very different kind of politics. As it was, the 1868 election produced results little different from that of 1865: only in working-class Lancashire and suburban Middlesex

[9] See especially M. Cowling, 'Disraeli, Derby and Fusion, October 1865 to July 1866', *Historical Journal*, viii (1965): also F. B. Smith, *The Making of the Second Reform Bill* (Cambridge, 1966), and M. Cowling, *1867: Disraeli, Gladstone, and Revolution* (Cambridge, 1967).

did the Conservatives break new ground. The Conservatives probably benefited by controlling some of the details of the Bill, and also because the necessity of compiling a new register gave them grounds for remaining in office as long as possible. Finally, Disraeli benefited, by becoming the undisputed successor to Derby in February 1868, for a brief and unremarkable ministry of ten months.

Reform apart, Disraeli made no special mark in 1866–8. He conquered Abyssinia to rescue some missionaries, but gave it back to the Abyssinians. He allowed some progressive measures of social policy to pass, on subjects such as housing and London hospitals, but it was, after all, a Liberal majority that passed them. In his Budgets and in foreign and imperial policy, Disraeli maintained an economical, unadventurous, Little England approach, as befitted a Chancellor of the Exchequer. He did not take up the mantle of Palmerston by claiming to be the 'patriotic party': his choice of Stanley, a peaceful semi-Liberal, for the Foreign Office, stood in the way of that. The ministry was the youngest and ablest of the three Derby minority Governments. A new generation of politicians, including Northcote, Gathorne Hardy, Cranborne (Salisbury) and Carnarvon, sat in the Cabinet, and the Tories could no longer be called 'the stupid party' with any justice. In addition, Disraeli was, in 1868, beginning to form close ties with the Queen in a way that Derby never had.

For many traditional Tories, the one redeeming feature of the 1867 Reform Bill was that its enactment had reduced the Liberals to utter confusion. When confusion was speedily replaced, in 1868, by a Liberal electoral victory, the demand went up for Disraeli's head. Ineffective in office in 1868, Disraeli during the election campaign had created a mood of Anglican militancy, which found his pacific tactics over the Irish Church in 1869 distinctly feeble. In retrospect, he was simply waiting for the tide to turn: but in February 1872 his colleagues made their most serious attempt to ditch him. At a meeting of most Tory leaders, except for Salisbury and Derby, at Burghley House, the question of the leadership was talked over, and all except Manners and Northcote were against Disraeli. Nothing was done, but the danger was great, for there was always an unknown, but large, element of the Tory party that thought of Disraeli as 'that hellish Jew,'[10] as one senior backbencher put it. From 1867 onwards, Salisbury remained irreconcilable, and not on speaking terms with Disraeli, but was too obvious a focus for

[10] Sir R. Knightley, MP, to Lord Bath, 7 Mar. 1867 (Longleat MSS).

disaffection to be effective. There were, however, good grounds in 1867–72 for thinking that, as the leading Tory Duchess put it, 'We can never have a united party as long as Dizzy is the head of it.'[11]

What hold Disraeli had over his party was almost entirely due to his performance in Parliament. His speeches outside Parliament, 116 in all, only occasionally assumed general political significance. Some main themes can, however, be discerned. He took great pains to identify with the agricultural interest, and no fewer than twenty-five of his speeches are in some way related to this topic. There was no other body of interests that he cultivated assiduously, but whereas an appeal to the working class can be found at many points, any such appeal to the urban middle class is conspicuously absent. There were great gaps in his campaigning, too. He hardly spoke outside Parliament between the last of his Young England speeches in October 1844 and the 1847 election campaign: nor between the fall of the 1852 ministry and the 1857 election, save on local topics. (This latter period of repose was perhaps connected with his having *The Press* as mouthpiece.) It was not that he did not know how to 'stump', for in 1849 he had launched a Protectionist variant of the Midlothian campaign: but on the other hand, in the 1874 election campaign he made only two speeches. He had great talent for making the kind of speech that achieves a sweeping redefinition of the general situation, but he used it very sparingly.

The triumph of 1867 marked the beginning of a dark period in Disraeli's life. He lost the political initiative, and in 1872 nearly lost the Tory leadership. His health worsened. To complete the misery, his wife died, in December 1872. She had nearly died in 1868, and for some time before her death, though concealing her state and remaining socially active, she was in the grip of what both knew to be terminal illness. In 1872, the year of his greatest outdoor speeches, Disraeli was mainly concerned with cheering and nursing her. In the late summer of 1872, he took her 220 miles in drives around the suburbs of London. At her last party, at Hughenden a month before she died, Harcourt and Rosebery were guests. As the end approached, Disraeli wrote, 'I am totally unable to meet the catastrophe. . . .'[12] His losses were partly material, for his wife's income of £5,000 per annum, and their London home of half a lifetime, Grosvenor Gate, passed back to her first

[11] Duchess of Buccleuch to Lord Bath, 17 Dec. 1868 (Longleat MSS).
[12] Monypenny and Buckle, op. cit., v, 228.

husband's family, and Disraeli within weeks was living unhappily in a London hotel ('hotel life in the evening is a cave of despair').[13] This was a trifle, however, compared with the loss of the total devotion and approval which had sustained him throughout his political career.

The Conservatives in the years after 1867 were an unhappy party, and leading them was a thankless task. Nevertheless, as early as 1870 the light became visible at the end of the tunnel. A major conflict broke out within the Liberal ranks, with many of the Dissenters going into open opposition to the official party. In 1871 and 1872 the by-elections began to go seriously wrong. In 1873, Gladstone lost his major piece of legislation in the Commons (the Irish University Bill), while much of the rest was defeated in the Lords. After March 1873, when Disraeli refused to take office prematurely, the Liberals remained in office, but hardly in power: and the by-elections remained disastrous. In January 1874, with his hand forced by Cabinet and legal difficulties, Gladstone called a snap election. The only real issue was whether the country was tired of Gladstone, which it undoubtedly was. All that had to be done was for it to say so, which it did. The Tory majority in Britain was respectable, but it was enhanced by a landslide in Ireland, where the Home Rulers won nearly all the Liberal seats.

Of the innumerable reasons for the Liberal defeat, few had anything to do with Conservative merits. One cause for self-congratulation, however, lay in the field of party organisation. The Conservatives were much better organised in 1874 than before or later: and much better organised, again, than their opponents. Starting from scratch in 1846, the Conservatives had gradually built up a party machine. Up till 1852, the Chief Whip, Beresford, had done everything, with unhappy results. After his departure, the party in the fifties and sixties had relied on a large firm of London solicitors to manage its election business. In 1870 the agent, Spofforth, retired after a long career, and his work was transferred to a Conservative Central Office, with an ambitious young barrister called Gorst as Principal Agent.

Between 1870 and 1874, in very favourable circumstances, Gorst imparted zeal and system to the party machine. He was, however, not in close contact with Disraeli, who on the available evidence had not contemplated a new departure when Spofforth left. Gorst received no reward from the party for his services, and withdrew leaving Central Office to less able men. The Tory organisers in 1880 did nothing to

[13] Robert Blake, *Disraeli* (London, 1966), p. 527.

mitigate an unfavourable situation, but neither in 1874 nor in 1880 did the Tory chiefs see organisation as a matter of great concern.

Disraeli's new Cabinet was the smallest since 1832. It had twelve members, six of them peers, six commoners. The peers all went back to posts they had held during 1866–8, with the exception of Richmond, promoted to Lord President in recognition of his loyal leadership of the Lords, a position he continued to hold until Disraeli's ennoblement in 1876. None of the ministers of 1866–8 was obviously dropped, except for Marlborough, who later became Irish Viceroy, and Pakington, who lost his seat and was given a peerage and a lucrative Civil Service job. Disraeli, who consulted an inner group of Hardy, Northcote, Cairns, and Derby about appointments, clearly wished to heal old wounds, and attached much importance to wooing Salisbury and Carnarvon, whose return to the fold was in some doubt till the last moment. Salisbury, Carnarvon, Manners, Hardy, and to some extent Northcote, formed something of a High Church group within the Cabinet. The youngest minister was Carnarvon at 43. There were two weak appointments, Malmesbury, who was 67 and deaf, the oldest minister except Disraeli, and Ward Hunt, an archetypal country squire with an interest in subjects like cattle plague, who found the Admiralty heavy going. Malmesbury resigned in 1876, Disraeli taking his purely nominal office and, for a time, its £2,000 salary, while the unfortunate Hunt died in office in 1877, aged only 52. This led to a minor reshuffle, with Disraeli replacing Malmesbury in the Lords, Hicks Beach, the successful young Irish Secretary, staying at his post, but being admitted to the Cabinet, and W. H. Smith, the great newsagent in whose practical abilities Disraeli had complete confidence, replaced Hunt at the Admiralty, to the delight of Gilbert and Sullivan. This first reshuffle of 1876–7 had no political implications: that of 1878 had, for the resignations of Derby and Carnarvon were the product of eighteen months of tension. Salisbury took Derby's post; Gathorne Hardy replaced Salisbury at the India Office, with a peerage; Colonel F. A. Stanley, a quiet and homely country gentleman and Derby's brother, replaced Hardy at the War Office; the Duke of Northumberland took the Privy Seal; and Hicks Beach took over from Carnarvon. In addition, Lord Sandon was moved to the Board of Trade, previously outside the Cabinet. The front bench in the Lords gained Cranbrook, an ageing major figure, and Northumberland, a rich nonentity, in exchange for Carnarvon and Derby: while in the Commons Cranbrook's loss was hardly compensated by the gain of two minor figures like Stanley and Lord Sandon. The ministry was not getting stronger as time went by. Disraeli's only imaginative appointment, that of Derby's friend Cross to the Home Office without previous official experience, was to some extent balanced by his exclusion of Education, the Local Government Board, the Board of Trade (to 1878), and Ireland (except, for non-Irish reasons, in 1876–8) from the Cabinet.

The session of 1874 was a quiet one, partly through unpreparedness, partly because party and country alike wanted tranquillity. According to Cross, Disraeli had to rely entirely on the various suggestions of his colleagues,[14] contributing nothing definite of his own. A give-away budget was something of an anti-climax, and had little political effect. A political debt was paid to the publicans by a Licensing Act. Cross carried a Factory Act which the Liberals had in the pipeline. An Act was carried abolishing patronage in the Scottish Church, which awoke dormant church controversies in Scotland very much to the Government's future disadvantage. Foreign policy and imperial affairs were both conspicuously absent from the scene. The Ashanti war came neatly to an end, and the Tsar visited London for his daughter's wedding. The only strongly reactionary Bill, Sandon's Endowed Schools Bill, which sought to draw the grammar schools back to the Church, was dropped.

What excitement there was came from the Public Worship Regulation Bill, introduced not by the Government but by the Archbishop of Canterbury, in order to repress excessive ritualism among the clergy. The Bill was dangerous to Disraeli, for it divided the Cabinet and annoyed High Churchmen: it was also potentially advantageous, for it was broadly what the country wanted, and it divided Gladstone from the Liberal rank and file. Disraeli skilfully avoided most of the dangers, while gaining most of the advantages, and the Bill passed.

The session of 1875 opened with Gladstone's announcing his definite retirement, previously hinted at, from the Liberal leadership, though not from parliamentary life. Lord Hartington took his place, elected unanimously after Forster's withdrawal; Disraeli was more than ever master of the House. With neither the Irish, the Liberals, nor the foreign powers giving cause for anxiety, Disraeli embarked on the most impressive and attractive legislative programme of his career, though in few cases can his active involvement in any particular measure be shown. Cross carried an Artisans' Dwellings Bill, designed to allow local

14 Richard, Viscount Cross, *A Political History* (priv. pr. Eccle Riggs, 1903), p. 25.

authorities to pull down slums: not being compulsory, and being rather costly to ratepayers, its practical value was limited. Quite different in scope were two Bills, carried by Cross, which settled the basis of labour law for a generation. They were the Magna Carta of British trade unionism. Disraeli claimed that he, with Cross, pushed them through a reluctant Cabinet. Whatever the details, Disraeli clearly wanted good relations with the unions, and his efforts were warmly appreciated.

The above measures, perhaps accidentally, gave a sense of a ministry committed to vigorous social reform. A number of useful minor reforms completed the picture. There was no trace of reaction in the air, except for a famous fracas involving the Radical reformer Plimsoll over the Merchant Shipping Bill. The government Bill on this subject was un-contentious, but on 22 July Disraeli himself announced its withdrawal to make way for a Bill benefiting farmers. Plimsoll, in a famous scene, declared that hundreds of seamen would die as a result. Public opinion supported Plimsoll's wild behaviour, Disraeli backed down, and a temporary Bill was rushed through. Apart from this incident, Disraeli's handling of the House was faultless, and his reputation never stood higher.

In 1876 the situation changed, in domestic as much as in foreign matters. By-elections began to go seriously wrong. Disraeli's age and poor health appeared at last to be wresting from him his hold over Parliament. The session, a quiet one, comparatively undisturbed by foreign affairs, contained only two notable pieces of legislation: the Royal Titles Bill, making the Queen Empress of India, which received a bad press, and Sandon's Education Bill, which introduced the principle of compulsion into primary education. A Merchant Shipping Bill was carried, of no very drastic character. The shipowner was left free to paint his Plimsoll line where he thought fit. The theme of social reform which stood out in 1875 had fallen back to a routine level in 1876, not because of Irish or Eastern distractions, but because ministers had nothing much in mind. In August 1876, with himself and his party in poor shape even before the Bulgarian atrocities crisis broke, Disraeli decided to lead the party from the Lords. His prospects of remaining leader at the next election cannot have seemed good.

Ireland, which Disraeli never visited, played little part in his plans. At various times from 1846 to 1878 he sought parliamentary advantage from intrigues with Irish Catholic groups in the House of Commons. At the 1868 election he played the Orange card, but there was no love lost between him and Protestant Ulster. The actual government of Ireland did not cause him any anxiety, especially in 1874–80, when there was no real need to do anything, and able subordinates like Hicks Beach (Irish Secretary 1874–8) looked after the petty business. Disraeli carried no major Irish legislation, though in 1868 and 1877–8 he toyed with the Irish Universities question. Responsible Tories might even welcome the advent of the Home Rulers: 'Their humbug has a good deal to do with keeping Ireland quiet,' Beach wrote.[15] By 1878 the main group of Home Rulers under Butt, himself an old friend of Disraeli's in the 1850s, had come to prefer Tory rule. Butt thought, 'There are men in the present Cabinet more likely to deal fairly with Ireland than any we would be likely to find in a Whig Cabinet.'[16] More important to ministers than Home Rule was the obstruction carried on by a small minority of Irish Members, sporadically in 1875–6, systematically in 1877 and thereafter, except for a lull in 1878. This did not prevent major legislation, for there was little to prevent, but it did throw routine business into confusion, and more important, it meant that House of Commons ministers were extremely tired men by 1880.

Once Disraeli had satisfied himself, during the session of 1874, that he had healed the long-standing divisions in his party, his mind turned decisively to foreign policy. He had always been interested in the subject, although he had been abroad only once since 1845–6. He approached the topic with an open mind, especially where Turkey was concerned. He was fundamentally in sympathy with the Turks, and had in youth volunteered to fight for them, yet at the time of the Crimean War he had shown no flicker of war fever, and in the 1850s and 1860s his approach to foreign affairs had usually been that of an economising Chancellor intriguing against Palmerston for the 'Little England' Radical vote. True, the bias of his rhetoric was naturally towards patriotic declamation, and after the 1874 election Disraeli had every reason to continue a line of argument that had proved successful, namely that his party stood for a firm, and the Liberals for a weak, foreign policy. So far, so good: but Disraeli did not wish to extend this stance into thorough-going imperialism or annexationism, if only because he did not believe the electorate was imperialist. Peace with honour the country might want, if the alternative was peace with dishonour: but it did not, Disraeli considered, want war with honour. The

[15] David Thornley, *Isaac Butt and Home Rule* (London, 1964), p. 355.
[16] ibid., p. 367.

aggressive, and expensive, tendencies branded by Gladstone as 'Beaconsfieldism' were a mild and backward-looking attempt to take up the mantle of Palmerston, not a foretaste of Joseph Chamberlain.

Disraeli entered the fray with two chance successes. In May 1875 he intervened to prevent impending war between Germany and France. In November 1875 he acquired, not the Suez Canal Company, but a large minority shareholding therein. The purchase certainly proved a fruitful investment, but its political consequences in getting the British into, or the French out of, Egypt, were slight. Still, these events suggested to Disraeli that he had flair, and in autumn 1875, when the first revolts in Balkan Turkey broke out, it naturally occurred to him that he might solve the Eastern question. It certainly did not occur to him that the high-minded Victorian public which had thrown its weight so effectively behind Plimsoll in July 1875, and against the Fugitive Slave Circular in the winter of 1875–6, might also turn excitedly to what appeared a classical problem of diplomacy. During most of 1876, the key question was whether the Powers should and could impose far-reaching reforms on the Christian provinces of Turkey. The Powers, other than Britain, were ready to do this, whereas both British parties were opposed to this approach, and reluctant to give up their traditional protection of Turkey. On 9 May 1876, Hartington gave support to Disraeli's policy. On 24 May, the British Fleet was sent to Besika Bay, giving the Turks every reason to think that in the last resort Britain would protect them against any demand, however reasonable. Traditional Liberal criticism has centred on the way British policy in 1876 aimed at frustrating a moderate and peaceful settlement, and made inevitable the outbreak of hostilities between Turkey and Russia in April 1877.

During the summer of 1876, however, the Bulgarian atrocities made the question a central issue in British domestic politics in a wholly unexpected way. The first reports were published in the *Daily News* on 23 June. They did in fact exaggerate the numbers, if not the horrors. On 26 June, 10 July, and 31 July, Disraeli denied, minimised, or spoke with apparent jest in reply to questions about the massacres. His answers, partly due to poor staff work at the Foreign Office, were fuel on the flames. In August and September, as first-hand reports came in, a massive grass-roots agitation grew up amongst all classes outside Parliament, with Christian leaders unusually prominent amongst them. The agitation convinced Disraeli of the need to back down. On 3 September

1876 he told Salisbury, 'We must now dictate to Turkey.' On 5 September Gladstone, who though not in retirement had previously kept in the background, produced his famous pamphlet, *The Bulgarian Horrors and the Question of the East*. For Disraeli, the focus of the problem then shifted, from placating popular disquiet to discountenancing the Liberal party. He had, in addition, a crucial by-election to face on 22 September, defeat in which might even cost him the leadership. He turned again to a hard line: but this time the hard line was for domestic as well as diplomatic consumption.

Between September 1876 and April 1877, as war became inevitable, Disraeli's chances of winning British public opinion increased as his chances of maintaining the integrity of Turkey disappeared. In 1876 Disraeli had refused a settlement which at least appeared to maintain existing frontiers. In 1877, after Russian successes in the war, he was trying to secure not much more than the security of Constantinople, a very different matter. The success of Russian arms had to have its reward – that Disraeli did not and could not challenge. His main problem in 1877 lay in controlling his Cabinet. As the Russians marched south, the Cabinet wrangled bitterly. Salisbury, Disraeli's chief opponent, could muster enough support to prevent a war policy (or the bluff of war), but not enough to carry out his own policy of a negotiated settlement with large concessions. Both 'hawks' and 'doves', therefore, had in practice to acquiesce in the inertia of Derby, the Foreign Secretary. Disraeli's game throughout 1877 was to detach Salisbury from Derby and Carnarvon, the other main opponents of confrontation.

This was not a quick or easy business: as late as 12 January 1878 there was a threat of joint resignation by Derby and Salisbury. From then on, however, it was downhill. Derby resigned a first time on 23 January, returned, and finally resigned on 27 March. Disraeli rejected the Russian terms calling for a big Bulgaria (the Treaty of San Stefano) and set out to force Russia to the conference table. On 4 April the House of Commons voted 310–64 in favour of calling up the Reserves. At the end of May, Indian troops arrived in Malta. While the stage was thus being publicly set for another Crimean War, the diplomatic basis fo the Treaty of Berlin was being laid in direct Anglo-Russian and Anglo-Turkish negotiations. Finally, Disraeli and Salisbury set off to the Congress of Berlin (4 June–4 July), at which Britain gained public recognition of its main objectives, a 'small' Bulgaria, and a secure frontier for Asian Turkey. On his return, a majority of 143 ratified the Treaty of Berlin (3 August 1878), every Tory voting with the Government. Disraeli's complete failure to protect Turkey, as intended in 1876-7, was lost sight of in face of his evident success as a firm defender of British interests in 1878, an impression which Gladstone's opposition greatly enhanced.

The moral of the Eastern crisis was that a war policy that did not involve actual warfare was a useful way of reducing Turkish losses, though they still remained at a level that two years earlier had seemed unacceptable to both British parties. It was also useful in consolidating Disraeli's hold on his Cabinet, his party, and the British public, and for inflicting serious wounds on the Liberals. Unfortunately for Disraeli, his paper war in the Balkans was soon followed by very real wars in Afghanistan and Zululand, both of them involving massacre of British forces. Though there was no connection in fact between the three situations in the mind of Disraeli and his Cabinet, the Liberals said there was, and were widely believed. Disraeli's success in 1878 had made it plausible to say that he was a man for such adventures.

In the last stages of the Eastern crisis, the Russians had sent a mission to Kabul. Lytton, the Viceroy, reacted by preparing an armed column which was to march on Kabul to secure the reception of a British mission, and the expulsion of the Russians. It was not obvious that a diplomatic solution was impossible: senior ministers in London wished to try this, but, being tired and on holiday, got no immediate results, and failed to control Lytton, who, tired of waiting, marched to the frontier in clear disobedience of orders. His force was turned back, and London, until then quite innocent of aggressive intent, was faced with a question of prestige, and therefore, on current assumptions, a deliberate war became necessary. The British invasion, in winter 1878-9, went smoothly, there was no trouble with Russia, and a British mission was installed at Kabul. On 3 September, all members of the mission were murdered, and Roberts entered Kabul a second time on 13 October 1879, in good time to provide ammunition for Gladstone's Midlothian campaign, which began on 25 November. Though the soldiering went well, there was little glory for Disraeli in a conquest which he had not initially wanted, which he had not effectively sought to avoid, but to which he had twice fully committed himself, for very little obvious benefit.

The Zulu war was like the Afghan in that disobedience by the man on the spot was crucial, but unlike it in that the soldiering was badly done. Sir Bartle Frere, the High Commissioner, a man of simple expansionist views, wished to break the Zulu state, which was certainly a threat, but was causing no immediate trouble. Worse, he wished to do this in the autumn of 1878, when Disraeli had an Afghan campaign on his hands, and needed all his troops in readiness to make the Russians live up to their promises in European Turkey. The Cabinet expressly forbade a Zulu war. Frere, knowing this, started one. Almost the first Disraeli knew of the matter was on 12 February 1879, when news of the destruction of a British force of 1,200 men at Isandhlwana (22 January) reached London. Despite a final victory over the Zulus at Ulundi in July 1879, it was the initial defeat that mattered in its general effect on public opinion, although Disraeli at the time was probably more concerned with the effect of a remote colonial war on his ability to put pressure on Russia. Disraeli's rage over the folly of the war knew no bounds: but he failed to communicate this effectively to the British public, and Liberals were able to imply that the episode was representative of government policy.

The success or failure of Disraeli's foreign policy was all-important in the latter years of his ministry, for he had virtually ceased to have any home policy. The three sessions of 1877, 1878, and 1879 were remarkably barren in their legislative output, not primarily because of Irish obstruction, which was only intermittent. No major social reform was passed, while the weak state of the economy did not permit any exciting Budgets. Northcote, Disraeli's successor in the Commons, was thought to lack firmness and, still more, magic, in his handling of the House. Disraeli was unable to do much to mend matters. Pressure of foreign affairs apart, his health throughout 1877 left him 'prostrate with pain and debility'. 'Whether I can go on . . . I hardly know,' he wrote in April, and in October 1877 he was letting it be known that it was quite impossible for him to continue. This was, of course, partly another move in the game, but he must have been extremely unfit. He made few speeches in 1877, but the occasion when he told the Lords that railway accidents were 'the greatest subject that can come under your consideration' did not suggest a mind closely involved with domestic topics.

The 1878 session lasted seven months, the longest for many years, but proved equally sterile. In the Queen's Speech, ten out of thirteen paragraphs were directly related to the Eastern question, and against the background of the last stages of the Russian advance towards Constantinople, the Commons had little to debate other than Scottish roads and bridges. With distress in many industries, the Budget raised income tax by twopence, and made loans for social purposes to local authorities more difficult. The ministry passed only one reform of consequence, that of Irish intermediate education. This made a mark on the Irish secondary school system, and was the only Irish measure of interest carried during 1874–80. Gladstone gave Ireland good legislation and political excitement in 1868–74: Disraeli (and Beach) gave Ireland no legislation, good administration, and political quiet, in 1874–80. That Irish rural society began to fall to pieces in 1879, owing to climatic and economic changes beyond human control, should not be taken to mean that Disraeli's Irish policy was inappropriate at the time, or less meritorious than that of Gladstone.

The session of 1879 might have provided a fresh start. With Cabinet conflicts resolved, and relations with Russia now firmly in the hands of Salisbury, Beaconsfield had a year, or perhaps two, in hand in which to win the confidence of the country before going to an election. True, economic conditions were bleak, with unemployment in particular at record levels, and a crisis of low prices in agriculture. There was no question of the Government's taking any unorthodox step, except in Ireland, to remedy the distress, and the general feeling that taxes were too high inhibited any new departures in budgetary or social policy. Nevertheless, the chance to impress existed.

In fact, the main item in the meagre bill of fare promised was an Army Bill, the discussion on which turned into a debate on flogging. Beaconsfield did not care either way about the 'cat', but believed that abolition would split his party. After vehement opposition, and some concessions, the Bill passed, flogging was retained, and the Conservatives found they had spent most of the session on a measure that provided ideal propaganda for their opponents. The only other measure of consequence to pass was an Irish University Bill, which set up an examining body for Irish higher education, without establishing any new seats of learning. A very large number of minor measures, of the type of the Irish Dogs Regulation Bill and the Metropolis Carriage Bill, were introduced by ministers and then dropped for lack of time, energy, support, or interest. There was no theme, no co-ordination, simply departmentalism run riot and ministers obstructing each other's progress. In August 1879 ministers bade *au revoir* for the session by requiring a vote of £3,000,000 for the Zulu war. With extraordinary absence of artistry, Beaconsfield set the stage for the Midlothian campaign by letting his ministry appear without any redeeming features.

By autumn 1879 the Liberals, perhaps for the first time since 1873, looked the more credible government of the two parties, though few were confident of victory at the next election. The Liberals had had good by-election results earlier, when the party was in a state of torpor and decomposition. Now, with the party in full cry, they ran into two chance by-election reverses (February 1880), and the Government, which had planned to continue throughout 1880, decided at very short notice to hold a spring election. As with Gladstone in 1874, they left themselves with no time to make any impression in the campaign, which found their organisation in a state of weakness, their leaders ill or engaged in routine business, and the party with nothing to say. Disraeli tried, and failed, to start a scare about Irish Home Rule, and the tone of the campaign was dominated by Liberal criticism of the Government's record (the Liberals being no less without any policies or programme of their own than the Conservatives).

The election was a more serious reverse in terms of seats than in terms of a real rejection by the public. A few thousand votes the other way would have returned Disraeli to power. Nevertheless, despite the apparent arbitrariness of the overall statistics, there were some clear influences at work. Some of these were beyond Disraeli's control. The most important single change compared with 1874, the return of Dissent to the Liberal fold, was only partly of Tory making. The economic depression, which Disraeli saw as the main cause of defeat, was simply a bolt from the blue. Long-term social change in Wales also brought a Liberal advantage which just happened. The Liberal landslide in Scotland owed more to a serious Tory mistake, over the Patronage Bill of 1874, which had stirred up religious passions. The majority of Conservative losses, however, were widely spread through the English counties, the English large cities, and the English small or medium boroughs, all groups which responded fairly readily to the political situation in Parliament and on the platform. The Tories lost the 1880 election, not because they were doomed by structural factors to lose it, but because they did not fight it seriously at the level of general political utterance.

The general election of April 1880 was not seen by Disraeli, or anyone else, as the end of the road. He did take the opportunity to honour or reward the intimates of a lifetime: Baillie Cochrane and Manners, both survivors of Young England, received honours, as did Monty Corry, his perfect private secretary since 1866, while Lord Henry Lennox, his infatuation of the 1850s, received financial reward. There was, however, no question of Disraeli's retiring from the party leadership. If anything, the party felt it needed him more in bad times than in good.

The attacking skills that Disraeli had let rust in office now revived. Though his way of life might be that of an old man, his political strategy was that of his younger days. While dissuading the House of Lords from premature confrontations, Disraeli did his best to split up the Liberal majority. He spoke luridly of the great destructive powers of Gladstone and Radicalism, as instanced in the rather puny Irish land measure brought in by Gladstone in 1880. He may, in fact, have believed his own propaganda, for there is probably no period of his life when his mood was so alarmist, and when he was so inclined to make the Tories a party of resistance to Radicalism, pure and simple. When Disraeli last took stock of the political situation, his assessment was that the dominant fact for the Tory party must be the general alarm and despondency among the landed class.

Up to December 1880 there was every reason to think that Disraeli could continue to lead the party for years to come, and with singular ability. He even acquired a house in London during the winter to enable him to do so. He also began to write a novel about Gladstone,[17] the initial chapters of which show no decline in his powers. During the spring of 1881 his health declined, but he remained politically and socially active till a month before his death, from bronchitis, in April 1881.

We shall never know Disraeli well. His intimates did not Boswellise him. His inner thoughts, on the Jewish people for instance, could hardly hope for a sympathetic hearing. The real degree of his enthusiasm for, or distaste for, the English aristocracy and gentry, and their way of living, is unknowable. There were few people he felt at home with, and his apparent moments of self-revelation to female correspondents were no doubt carefully composed. Little is known, too, of what the Tory squires really thought of him. Except in the 1830s, he kept no diary, and he left no memoirs. His papers, though copious, may give a quite inadequate idea of his relations with the Queen, with Palmerston, and with the Rothschilds. There is some mystery as to how he died a rich man. He remains, despite the shadowiness, a sympathetically un-

17 Printed in Monypenny and Buckle, op. cit., v, 531–60.

orthodox figure: a man willing to sell his political position for use by a foreign power, an early advocate of a Zionist state, the first man to smoke 'pot' (for medical reasons) while Prime Minister, the only novelist to become a party leader, and a man who, though unusually chaste, was almost certainly attracted by both sexes. By any standards, past or present, he did not lack moral originality, conforming inwardly to no views but his own.

He left the Tory party very much as he found it. Below the surface, changes were taking place that were to turn the Tories from the 'country party' of the squires into the party of business, the residential suburbs, and the genteel south-east. Disraeli did little to hasten such changes, which gave him little pleasure, and in any case even by 1881 the process had not gone very far. So far as he looked for a new accession of support, it was (intermittently) in the direction of the working class that he hopefully turned his eyes. On the whole he preferred to keep the Tory party as it was, and to concentrate on the rearrangement of parliamentary factions. This, the technique of parliamentary opposition, was what he was superbly good at. As a Chancellor of the Exchequer he was entirely unremarkable, as a legislator negligible with the extraordinary exception of 1867. As a statesman, coming to foreign policy late, he faced a crisis partly of his own making, and came out of it better than could have been expected for a Power without allies or an army. His defeat in 1880 was a result of the short-term situation in 1879–80, and did not reflect generally on his hold on opinion after 1874. In particular, he was unlucky to be premier during seven lean years for the economy. The Conservative party he left behind was, as always, a not very competent body with an opposition mentality. In one respect – and this was perhaps his greatest achievement as a party leader – Disraeli had conferred a priceless and lasting advantage upon them. By an indefinable process, beginning about 1860, Disraeli made the Liberals look left-wing and dangerous to men of property, and thus ensured the future of his party.

BIBLIOGRAPHY

Blake, Robert (Lord Blake), *Disraeli* (London, 1966); *The Conservative Party from Peel to Churchill* (London, 1970)
Feuchtwanger, E. J., *Disraeli, Democracy, and the Tory Party* (1968)

Hanham, H. J., *Elections and Party Management; Politics in the Time of Disraeli and Gladstone* (London, 1959)

Monypenny, W. F., and Buckle, G. E., *The Life of Benjamin Disraeli, Earl of Beaconsfield* (6 vols, London, 1910–20)

Smith, Paul, *Disraelian Conservatism and Social Reform* (Cambridge, 1967)

6

W. E. GLADSTONE

BY

E. J. FEUCHTWANGER

William Ewart Gladstone, born 29 December 1809, youngest son of John Gladstone, a merchant of Liverpool, a supporter of Canning and member of Parliament from 1818–27. Educated at Eton and Christ Church, Oxford. Married Catherine, daughter of Sir Stephen Glynne, 1839; eight children. MP (Tory) for Newark 1832–45; under Peel held minor office 1834–35; was Vice-President, Board of Trade 1841, President 1843; resigned in 1845, but rejoined the same year as Secretary of State for the Colonies. MP for Oxford University 1847–65; Chancellor of the Exchequer in Aberdeen's Coalition 1853–55, under Palmerston briefly in 1855 and from 1859–65, under Russell 1865–66. MP for South Lancashire 1865–68; Leader of the House of Commons 1865–66. MP for Greenwich 1868–80; Prime Minister 1868–74. MP for Midlothian 1880–95; Prime Minister 1880–85 (1880–83 also Chancellor of the Exchequer), 1886 and 1892–94. Died 19 May 1898. Author of The State in its Relations with the Church, *1838;* Studies in Homer and the Homeric Age, *1858;* A Chapter of Autobiography, *1868;* The Bulgarian Horrors and the Question of the East, *1876; etc. Also editor of critical edition of the works of Bishop Butler, 1896.*

W. E. GLADSTONE

Gladstone's public life lasted sixty-one years and no other major political figure of the nineteenth century, except the Queen herself, equalled it in duration. During this time Gladstone traversed an exceptionally wide band of the political spectrum and developed from the Ultra-Conservative of the 1830s into the Liberal father-figure of the 1880s. Yet throughout his long life span he remained recognisably the same personality, of whom Balfour could say, after talking to him two years before his death, 'He is and always was, in everything except essentials, a tremendous Tory.' Gladstone's unusual political migration from right to left is the major theme of his career; and perhaps the most important clue to it is that to him politics always remained a second best to the priestly vocation which was his first love, and that his political path was a constant quest for God.

'Oxford on the surface, Liverpool underneath.' This was often said of Gladstone in Whig circles and it was true that he never lost the trace of a Lancashire accent. His father, John, was a Scotsman who made good in Liverpool and built up a fortune of three-quarters of a million pounds, a very large sum by early nineteenth-century standards. Much of the family wealth came from West Indian plantations and slaves; John Gladstone was a leading representative of the West Indian planter interest and opponent of the Abolitionists. This cast a shadow over his son's early political life, for filial piety and obedience were deeply ingrained in William. It was not without heart-searching and qualms of conscience that he detached himself from many of his father's convictions and causes. In politics John Gladstone was an ardent disciple of Canning and a prime mover in getting his mentor to represent Liverpool in Parliament for fifteen years. The Liberal Toryism of Canning was, therefore, the political tradition in which Gladstone was brought up and it remained alive in him throughout his long public life. Perhaps even more important than the Canningite heritage was the evangelicalism of his family background. Although Gladstone moved away from his evangelical roots in his early twenties they had left an indelible mark on his personality. Deep personal piety, an abiding sense of sin, a need to mortify and humble the self, an acute moral sensitivity, these were characteristics that remained an essential part of him throughout his life. They were transmitted to him by his mother, who spent much of her life being an invalid, and by his elder sister, Anne, who died at an early age of consumption. These two women also gave Gladstone a view of womanhood that was pure, saintly and idealised.

Gladstone passed through the traditional educational process of the upper class, Eton and Oxford. It was a big change to go from the self-contained, intensely religious middle-class life of Liverpool to the virtually pagan jungle of Eton. Already Gladstone had the self-control, the energy and ambition, the orderly habits and the great intellectual powers to enable him to survive. When he left Eton in 1827 his life there seemed to him to have been 'a time of very great and numerous delights'. Even deeper bonds of affection tied him to Oxford. He arrived there at a time of much intellectual vigour, but he had left before Keble's Assize Sermon of 1833 started the religious controversies of the Oxford Movement. The young Gladstone made his mark through his academic achievement and as a speaker in the recently established Union. His mind, supported by great energy and application, was a matchless instrument for the acquisition and marshalling of information, though perhaps the deepest levels of speculation were closed to him. His oratory, he soon found, gave him power over men; it was backed throughout his life by his fine physical presence and magnificent voice and as he grew older, by the increasing weight of his moral stature. Orator and statesman were indissoluble in him; he was fervent, zealous, a man of causes; but also impulsive and excitable. As he matured and amassed a vast store of political experience, he developed great powers of casuistry and an instinctive canniness which tempered and made viable his impetuous dynamism. While Gladstone was still at Oxford the great crisis over parliamentary reform swept the country. It was on the Reform Bill that he made the famous speech in the Union in May 1831, which first brought him to the notice of a wider public. By logical deduction from first principles, a mode of argument that always remained characteristic of him, but was as yet undisturbed by any trace of pragmatism, he had convinced himself that reform was the work of anti-Christ. It conjured up the spectre of revolution, Popery and utter ruin. From the Liberal Conservatism of Canning, Gladstone had now moved to an Ultra-Tory position; he had done so not by instinct, but by ratiocination, and he could by the same process move away from it again.

Towards the end of his time at Oxford Gladstone was much exercised by the choice of a career and strongly inclined towards the Church. His father persuaded him, after an intense and emotional correspondence, to go into politics. He left Oxford with a double first; completing his education with an Italian tour in 1832, he had the culminating experience that turned him from an evangelical into a High Anglican. The vision of Rome, renewed study of the Book of Common Prayer, these were some of the experiences that gave him an understanding of the Church as the community of believers and finally broke the narrow familial preoccupation with personal salvation. During the Italian tour the offer came to him of a parliamentary seat at Newark; the patron was the Ultra-Tory Duke of Newcastle whose son, Lord Lincoln, was Gladstone's friend at Eton and Oxford and for many years in later life his close political colleague. Thus Gladstone entered the House of Commons after the first election held on the reformed franchise, an earnest young man of 23, a High Anglican Tory with the most orthodox views on all major issues of the day. His main preoccupation was the future of the Church, at a moment when it was under attack as part of the established order in an era of reform.

Gladstone quickly established himself as a rising man on the Tory side of the House and held junior office in Peel's short-lived ministry of 1835. At this stage of his career, he was not so much an Ultra-Tory as a 'ministerial man'. Peel took him increasingly into the inner councils of the party and he was clearly marked out for promotion. He was well to the right of his master and of most Tories only in his view of the Church. He held that the Church was the spiritual aspect of the state and that, therefore, enjoyment of the full rights and duties of citizenship implied membership of the Church of England. Gladstone expressed these views, so much at variance with the tendencies of the age, in his first book, *The State in its Relations with the Church*, published in 1838. He wrote it in only two months under pressure of intense inner necessity. In reviewing it in the *Edinburgh Review* Macaulay used the phrase 'the rising hope of stern, unbending Tories,' which has clung to Gladstone ever since. The publication of such unfashionable opinions temporarily clouded the relations between the promising young politician and his leader; but when the Tories won the general election of 1841 Gladstone was again a strong candidate for office. He wanted to be Chief Secretary for Ireland, but Peel had the perspicacity to see that this impulsive and emotional young man, suspected of the 'romanising' tendencies of the Oxford Movement, would be disastrously out of place in Ireland. Instead he sent him 'to govern packages' at the Board of Trade, first as Vice-President and, from 1843, as President with a seat in the Cabinet. Here Gladstone's great industry, intellectual energy and capacity to learn found an ideal outlet.

Gladstone now learnt the lessons that established his economic liberalism. He was intimately associated with the economic and fiscal policies by which Peel's Government moved progressively towards free trade. Most of the detailed work on the revisions of the tariff carried out in 1842 and 1845 was done by him. He gained an unrivalled insight into the workings of commerce and industry, previously only known to him indirectly through his father, and into the operations of government departments. At the Board of Trade he received countless deputations from the multifarious interests affected by the tariff reform; he was closely involved in the consultations within the Government that led to Peel's reintroduction of the income tax in 1842. The regulation of the railways, which became an important issue in the 1840s, was another sphere in which he displayed his powers as a constructive administrator and statesman. His experiences at the Board of Trade convinced him that it was the duty of the State to create the conditions under which the economic initiative of the individual could flourish with the least possible interference; that the utmost economy of operation and the absence of any kind of corruption were the first pre-requisites of public administration. The removal of international barriers to trade would at the same time secure the greatest possible advance in wealth and well-being and make war and the waste of military expenditure increasingly impossible and unnecessary. To the end of his life Gladstone took great pride in the advance of prosperity of the ordinary people which his work as a public financier and administrator had made possible; but on the other hand he was never an egalitarian, nor was he ever interested in social change for its own sake. He firmly believed in the existing social order, in the beneficent role of aristocracy, and that it was the first duty of statesmanship to work for stability and social harmony. For those lowly in the social scale his prescription was self-help; he considered that no moral benefit would be derived from the State's doing for a man what he ought to do for himself.

Early in 1845 Gladstone resigned from Peel's Government over the Maynooth grant. The proposal to increase the government grant to this priests' seminary was meant as a gesture of peace towards Ireland.

Gladstone was in favour of it: even in the few years since the publication of his book his religious and ecclesiastical views had developed rapidly. The need for religious liberty had become much more real to him, not least because of the persecution at Oxford of Tractarians, with whom he had much in common. His acute sense of morality and justice had also made him much more aware of the wrongs and grievances under which the majority of the Irish population was suffering. Gladstone's sensitive conscience would not allow him to support the Maynooth grant as a member of the Government. The position he now took was so different from that with which he was associated in the public mind that he felt he could not give even the slightest appearance of clinging to office for its own sake. Thus he supported the Maynooth grant from the back benches; Cobden, after listening to his resignation speech, said that Gladstone's talent was marvellous but that after an hour of explanation he knew 'no more why he left the Government than before he began'.

Gladstone returned to Peel's Government as Colonial Secretary for the last six months of its existence, after the decision had been taken to repeal the Corn Laws. He went with Peel into the wilderness when the Government was defeated in the summer of 1846. Henceforth he was a Peelite, and the label Liberal-Conservative, often adopted by Peelites for electoral purposes, well describes his ideological position. From the point of view of practical politics, however, the situation of the Peelites was increasingly frustrating. Peel himself, until his death in 1850, refused to organise his followers; elections and the steady drift of back-benchers, mainly back to the Conservative fold, left only a small rump, mostly leaders and a few followers; and even the leading Peelites, of whom Gladstone was one, were not in the long run able to maintain their cohesion. Gladstone himself only held office for just over two years in the thirteen years between 1846 and 1859. His support for the repeal of the Corn Laws forced him to part company with the Duke of Newcastle and Newark, and he was without a seat in the House of Commons until the general election of 1847. Then he was elected as one of two Members for Oxford University, an honour he had greatly coveted. Politically it was a doubtful blessing because the Conservative High Anglicanism which was still predominant in the University and to which Gladstone owed his election tended to restrict his freedom of movement in national politics. Moreover, the complex political and religious cross-currents at Oxford forced Gladstone into a number of fiercely contested elections during the eighteen years in which he represented the University. Although Gladstone regarded Peel as his mentor in politics and was intensely loyal to him, he became increasingly irked by his leader's refusal to organise the Peelites as a parliamentary party and to use their bargaining power, which was much more formidable than their mere numbers would indicate.

It was perhaps fortunate for Gladstone that private preoccupations distracted him somewhat from politics during those years. Hawarden, the Flintshire estate of the Glynnes, his wife's family, was in dire financial straits and Gladstone had to use all his energy as well as the financial resources inherited from his father to prevent the loss of the estate. The experience was of great value to him when a few years later he came to deal with the nation's finances. Hawarden became his permanent country home, the backcloth to his public life and the scene of his happy family life. Catherine Glynne, whom he had married in 1839, thoroughly understood his intense, emotional, earnest nature and shared his fundamental simplicity; she was also the most discreet of political wives. Through her Gladstone was connected with many of the great Whig families, the Wyndhams, Grenvilles, Lytteltons, Spencers and many others. With her husband's support she was active in many charitable enterprises and the Gladstones knew at first hand something of the abject poverty of the Victorian age. William's own great charitable interest, in which he had his wife's support, was the rescue of prostitutes. From his idealised view of womanhood, which he shared with many Victorians, the fallen woman was seen as the ultimate in degradation and her rescue as a humbling office of piety. This work exposed Gladstone to countless rumours and calumnies and in his latter days as Prime Minister his entourage tried to persuade him to give up his 'night walks'. He did not do so until old age forced him to and it is a tribute to his radiant innocence that no scandal could ever touch him.

Soon after Peel's death in 1850 Gladstone and his family went on a prolonged visit to Naples. The first-hand experience of political oppression under the Bourbons, which he gained during this visit, forms another important milestone in his evolution towards political liberalism. Here was naked injustice, 'the negation of God erected into a system of government'; in the face of such evils Gladstone could not remain silent and the Conservative orthodoxies about the stability of Europe and the danger of revolution which he had hitherto taken for granted could not restrain him. His *Letters to Lord Aberdeen*, in which he publicly attacked the Neapolitan Government in 1851, caused an international sensation and clearly marked him out as a Liberal sympathiser, perhaps more so than he yet meant it.

In domestic politics there was still much talk of Conservative reunion and Lord Derby, the Tory leader, tried to bring Gladstone back into the fold when he attempted to form a government in 1851 and when he in fact formed a short-lived minority administration in 1852. The most obvious barrier to Gladstone's return to the Tory ranks was the continued inability of the Conservative leaders to turn their backs on Protection once and for all. Gladstone did not want to become separated from his closest Peelite colleagues, men like Sidney Herbert or New-castle, and between him and the Tory squirearchy on the back benches there was mutual antagonism. Increasingly Disraeli's growing influence on the Tory side became perhaps the most important obstacle to Glad-stone's return to his former moorings; to complete personal antipathy and mistrust there was added the calculation that a party had room for only one future leader. Gladstone played a leading part in the attack on Disraeli's Budget of 1852 which led to the fall of Derby's Government. The way was thus opened to a coalition of Whigs, Peelites and Radicals which foreshadowed the Liberal amalgamation a few years later. The Peelites, in spite of their small parliamentary following, had a large share of the offices, including the premiership in the person of Lord Aberdeen. Gladstone became Chancellor of the Exchequer. He held this office for two years in the Aberdeen Coalition and again for seven years from 1859 to 1866. During this time he established it as one of the key posts in any government and created new standards of financial policy and administration.

Gladstone's Budget of 1853 outlined a scheme by which the income tax was to be abolished gradually over the next seven years. Never before had a Chancellor looked ahead in this way, although in the event the heavy military expenditure of the Crimean War was to frustrate Gladstone's plan. Gladstone also introduced a general succession duty on all forms of property in this Budget, in place of the legacy duty up to then levied on personal property only. His Budget speech won him great acclaim, not only for the financial accomplishments it revealed but as an oratorical feat. The great power he had now attained as a parliamentarian made it impossible ever to disregard him in the shifting political combinations of the 1850s. Apart from his first Budget of 1853, that of 1860 was probably the most important he brought in.

In it he completed the establishment of free trade in conjunction with the Cobden Commercial Treaty with France; he also abolished the paper duties, for so long decried as 'taxes on knowledge' by all Radical movements. The obstruction of the House of Lords frustrated the abolition of the paper duties in 1860; in the following year Gladstone forced the peers to give way by putting all his proposals in one Finance Bill, which has become the modern custom. Gladstone's Budgets were based on the most rigid exercise of economy in the public service; in enforcing it the Treasury became the central department of state. Economy was a real passion with Gladstone and he carried his hatred of waste down to the paltriest detail. His work as a public financier did much to establish him in the minds of the middle classes of the mid-Victorian age as their champion, and in the 1860s the prosperous sections of the working classes also saw him as one of the chief architects of their well-being. This did much to pave the way for his assumption of the Liberal leadership in the future.

Militarism and war were forces plainly antagonistic to the policy of economy and peace which Gladstone had espoused as the disciple of Peel. Initially he supported the Crimean War, for it seemed to him that Russia had violated the code of conduct he felt should bind the nations of Europe together. The unity of European civilisation was very real to him, deepened by his extensive studies of the classics and the Christian religions and churches. By the beginning of 1855 he considered that the war was being carried on beyond the point where it was just and he resigned almost as soon as Palmerston took office as Prime Minister. The debonair jingoism of Palmerston became almost as repugnant to Gladstone as the brazen opportunism of Disraeli. His opposition to the war threw him into the political company of Cobden and Bright and this was significant for the future; but immediately it made him highly unpopular and for the next few years, in the prime of life, he was as isolated as he had ever been.

When in 1859, after the defeat of the second short-lived Derby–Disraeli Government, Palmerston returned to power, Gladstone at last found it possible to take office again. He approved of the support that Palmerston and Lord John Russell, his Foreign Secretary, intended to give to the Italian *risorgimento* while he had been affronted by the pro-Austrian policy of the Conservatives; in this way he found it compatible with his conscience to serve under Palmerston. The few remaining Peelite leaders, like Sidney Herbert, also joined, and cynics might say that a government led by two old men offered Gladstone the best chance of a rapid advance to the top. For the next six years he served under Palmerston, always carrying a letter of resignation in his pocket, as he put it. The two men clashed frequently, particularly on the recurring problem of military and naval expenditure. Palmerston, who did not know 'in theology Moses from Sydney Smith', was out of sympathy with Gladstone's High Anglicanism, while Gladstone had only contempt for Palmerston's aristocratic raffishness. There was, however, also an underlying respect, for Palmerston retained some liberal traits while his growing inclination to leave the *status quo* undisturbed did not unduly offend Gladstone's basically conservative attitude. Palmerston's Government, prodded by Russell, made a half-hearted effort to take up the question of electoral reform in 1860, but when this failed Gladstone was not perturbed. Four years later, however, he made the famous speech in which he said that 'every man who is not presumably incapacitated by some consideration of personal unfitness or of political danger is morally entitled to come within the pale of the Constitution.' What had changed in the meantime? Gladstone had become honestly convinced that the sober and prosperous working men of the 1860s could no longer be, in justice, excluded from the franchise. What had brought him among other things to this conviction was his own contact with the masses. He found that his great oratorical gifts were just as effective with the people at large as they were in the House of Commons. The high moral tone of his utterance struck a deep chord with the Victorian masses. The man in the street did not always understand Gladstone's meaning but he knew that he was on the side of the angels. Gladstone, in his turn, derived from this communion with the masses the certainty that he was walking in the path of righteousness. Among major political figures he more than any other bridged the gulf between the still aristocratic and exclusive parliamentary world and the great democracy waiting without. This process had only just begun in the early 1860s, but cynics might again say that by associating himself however cautiously with the cause of reform he was unmistakably staking out his claim to the succession to Palmerston and Russell.

In the general election of 1865 Gladstone was finally defeated at Oxford – his political and ecclesiastical views had become too Liberal. Instead he was returned for South Lancashire, whither he went 'unmuzzled' and amid scenes of great enthusiasm. After Palmerston's death in October 1865 he led the House of Commons under the premiership of Russell in the Whig attempt to pass a Reform Bill. It was a moderate Bill and indeed Gladstone's own views on the extension of the franchise were anything but radical, whatever the reform movement in the country at large had come to expect of him. Even the moderate Bill of 1866 frightened off a sufficient number of Whigs to bring about the fall of the Government, and Disraeli was given the chance of tackling the reform question from the Tory side. In the complex parliamentary situation of 1867 Gladstone was not at his best. He proved unable to bring together the Radical and moderate sections of the Liberal 'broad church' and Disraeli, with a party no less divided and in a minority, out-manoeuvred him. The management of men and of parliamentary groups was not Gladstone's forte.

It required a great moral cause to release Gladstone's dynamic energy and to make him fully effective as a leader. In 1868 he found his cause in the wrongs of Ireland, and the affairs of that unhappy country were henceforth to dominate most of his remaining career. The first Irish grievance to which he addressed himself was the anomaly that in a country three-quarters Roman Catholic the Established Church was Anglican. In moving his resolutions on the disestablishment of the Irish Church in May 1868 Gladstone welded the Liberal Coalition together again and paved the way for electoral victory and a Liberal Government led by himself. He had come a long way since the days when as the champion of the Established Church he had fought against the most meagre concessions on the temporalities of the Church of Ireland.

Gladstone's first Government was perhaps the greatest reforming administration of the nineteenth century. He did not dominate it in the way in which a modern prime minister would dominate his Cabinet and his party or even in the way in which Peel exercised a general control over the whole range of his administration. Gladstone took complete charge of the legislation connected with the cause that above all others he had at heart, Ireland. The other great reforms of this ministry, for example the Education Act of 1870, were in the main departmental measures, the concern of the relevant minister, in this case W. E. Forster. Gladstone played a full part in the preparation and Cabinet discussions of such proposals; but in the Cabinet he was no more than *primus inter pares*. It would have been repugnant to him to infringe the autonomy of departmental ministers. He lent to the agreed measures of his Government, such as the Education Act or Cardwell's Army reforms, the full weight of his parliamentary authority, where this was required. He led his party from a position of detachment. He took little interest in the small change of party management and electioneering. He was in politics for great causes and as long as the heterogeneous following of the Liberal party was prepared to support him in these he could give leadership of unrivalled power. When in the latter years of this administration the support began to crumble he felt the bond was broken and contemplated retirement. Gladstone's closest confidant among his colleagues was Granville who had a wide knowledge of the political world and of Court circles. When Granville became Foreign Secretary in 1870 he worked closely with the Prime Minister on the day-to-day conduct of foreign policy. He also helped Gladstone in his relations with the Queen, which began to be strained in the later years of this ministry.

Gladstonian Liberalism can be defined largely in terms of the reforms accomplished during this period in office between 1868 and 1874. These reforms were almost entirely concerned with abolishing existing hindrances and restraints to full individual self-expression. Where interest groups, like the trade unions, made demands that would have required more positive intervention by the law, Gladstone's Government would not fully meet them; the trade union legislation of 1871, therefore, disappointed organised labour. Many of the other major measures of the Government also caused as much disillusionment as they gave satisfaction: many Nonconformists were deeply offended by the Education Act, because it failed to create a universal system of secular education and instead seemed to perpetuate the predominance of the Church of England in the voluntary system. Bruce's Licensing Act of 1872 did not satisfy the temperance interest while turning the brewing industry into the staunchest of Tory supporters. Gladstone's own formidable energies were concentrated on the Irish Land Act of 1870, his first attempt to deal with the grievances of the Irish peasantry caused by an alien form of land tenure. In spite of the great labour Gladstone expended on it the Act was not very effective; there was a limit beyond which even he was not prepared to go in attacking the sacred property rights of landowners. In 1873 Gladstone tried to complete his Irish trilogy with a Bill to set up an Irish university to remove the disabilities from which the Catholics suffered in higher education. It was acceptable neither to the Irish hierarchy, nor to much of English opinion, particularly not to many Nonconformists. Gladstone's Government was defeated and only the refusal of Disraeli to take office compelled it to carry on. In January

1874 Gladstone rather unexpectedly dissolved Parliament: he hoped to recover the popularity his Government had clearly lost by forecasting a Budget based on economy and reduction of income tax. But this prescription, through which Gladstone had two decades earlier made his great reputation as a public financier, was no longer to the same extent the key to electoral success. Instead the disaffection of many Liberal activists and general apathy produced the first clear Tory victory since the days of Peel. For Gladstone it was the culmination of growing disillusionment with his followers and fatigue with the burdens of leadership. He had talked much of retirement and now declared his intention of resigning the Liberal leadership as from 1875. Hartington succeeded him as Liberal leader in the Commons and Granville in the Lords. Gladstone did not, however, resign his seat in Parliament.

For two years he was immersed in theological, literary and scholarly work. When the Vatican published its decree on papal infallibility in 1870 Gladstone had felt himself unable to speak out, although he had been kept fully informed of what went on in Rome, particularly by his two close Catholic friends, Lord Acton and Döllinger, the German theologian, both of them leading opponents of the decree. Now he went into the attack with a pamphlet which sold many thousands of copies within days. Gladstone admired the Catholic Church though he was never tempted to join it; he felt it had now deliberately cut itself off from the main currents of the age. Many were unable to give Gladstone credit for the honesty of his views and felt that the pamphlet was an attempt to mend fences with the Nonconformists and Protestant opinion in general. Another view was that such excursions into theological controversy were hardly appropriate in a leading politician.

In the summer of 1876 the Eastern question and Disraeli's pro-Turkish stance began to become matters of major political controversy. Gladstone was at first slow to commit himself to the rising agitation; but it soon became impossible for him to hold back. He became convinced that here was a cause he had to take up – the attack on the immorality and cynical opportunism of the Government's foreign policy, 'Beaconsfieldism', as he came to call it. It was a cause that re-established the rapport between himself and the moral consciousness of the masses, particularly those sections that made up the rank and file of the Liberal party. On the other side of the great divide there were the 'classes', the upper ten thousand, who in Gladstone's view had been increasingly corrupted by wealth and greed. Gladstone now became 'the People's

William', the man who in countless speeches aroused the fervour of large multitudes, and who, felling trees at Hawarden, became the centre of many pilgrimages. Nowhere was the difference between Gladstonian Liberalism and Disraelian Conservatism more clear-cut than in foreign policy. Gladstone stood for international justice, self-determination of peoples, peace and retrenchment, Disraeli for national interest, power and prestige.

Gladstone was unable to modify Beaconsfield's policy on the Eastern question to any extent and his rival had his moment of triumph in 1878 at the Congress of Berlin. Thereafter 'Beaconsfieldism' rapidly ran into trouble: economic slump at home was paired with foreign fiascos in the Zulu and Afghan wars. Gladstone was adopted as Liberal candidate for Midlothian and in November 1879, when the next general election could no longer be far away, he went to campaign in his new constituency. For a leading statesman such an appeal to the ordinary people of the land was unprecedented. Gladstone was the centre of immense popular enthusiasm; but he was also execrated more than ever before in the drawing-rooms of London society. It was a matter of some embarrassment to him that his whirlwind re-entry into the political arena had in practice undercut the leadership of his colleagues, Granville and Hartington. When the Liberals won a resounding electoral victory in the spring of 1880 it was inevitable that the Queen had in the end to send for the GOM, much as she would have preferred to have either of his two Whig colleagues as her first minister. By this time she was convinced that he was a wild and dangerous old man.

Gladstone may have sounded more and more Radical to the Queen's conservative ears, but in fact he had little sympathy for the Radicalism of which Joseph Chamberlain and Sir Charles Dilke were now the leading representatives. He found room for them in his Government with some reluctance, only Chamberlain initially obtaining Cabinet rank. The dominant place in Gladstone's Government went to his long-established Whig and moderate Liberal colleagues, who in his view had a prescriptive right to the leading ministerial posts.

Gladstone's second ministry had no more of a prearranged programme of legislation than his first, nor was there, this time, a backlog of domestic reform held up by previous inertia. The Prime Minister thought his own tenure of office was temporary; his task was to reverse the policies of 'Beaconsfieldism' and then to return to the retirement he had reluctantly left. One major reform was generally expected of this

Government and considered a *sine qua non* by the Radicals: the extension of household suffrage to the counties. As such a change would have to be followed fairly rapidly by fresh elections, Gladstone decided to postpone it until later in the life of that Parliament. As it turned out, domestic legislation was largely crowded out by a series of foreign crises, by the running sore of the Bradlaugh case and, above all, by Ireland. In spite of what his opponents said about him Gladstone had a lively sense of national dignity and an even stronger feeling for Britain's obligations as an imperial and colonial power. In some cases, for example Afghanistan, he was able to reverse the policy of his predecessors and reap advantage and credit for the nation; in other instances, such as South Africa, he was unable to bring about a clear-cut change of policy. Egypt above all highlighted the dilemma of Gladstonian Liberalism in an age of growing imperialist rivalry. The Prime Minister took the steps that led to the Battle of Tel-el-Khebir and virtual British control of Egypt with the greatest reluctance. His failure to face up to the consequences put a burden on the conduct of British foreign policy which he never fully grasped. The same half-heartedness led to the involvement in the Sudan and eventually to the death of Gordon, an episode that discredited his Government more than anything else.

Ireland was an even greater distraction from domestic legislation. Parnell now led a tightly-knit group of Irish Nationalists at Westminster and was prepared to use the manifold opportunities for obstruction available under the parliamentary procedure of those days with complete ruthlessness. Gladstone wanted to deal with the grievances of Ireland constructively and in the Irish Land Act of 1881 offered a much more far-reaching remedy for the problems of the Irish peasantry than he had been able to do eleven years earlier. He could not, however, escape from the need to use repression to cope with the disturbed state of Ireland and much of the impact of his constructive intentions was lost. At Westminister Parnellite obstruction produced a revolution in parliamentary procedure which facilitated the gradual departure from the individualistic Liberalism for which Gladstone stood.

It was not until 1884 that the Government was able to turn to the further extension of the franchise. The third Reform Bill and the Redistribution Bill that accompanied it produced, in the form in which they finally reached the statute book, universal male household suffrage and a system of single-member constituencies broadly as we now know it. It was, along with the Corrupt Practices Act of 1883, the most thorough revision of the electoral system accomplished during the nineteenth century. In the long-drawn-out reform battle of 1884, which involved a clash between the two Houses of Parliament, Gladstone showed that his domination of the House of Commons, of the political world and of public opinion at large was undiminished.

In 1885 Gladstone's Government, endlessly plagued by crises and internal dissensions, was defeated. It was, however, the very diversity and disunion of the Liberal party that convinced Gladstone that it was still his duty to remain as leader at least until the next election, to be held under the new franchise. The general election of 1885 returned over eighty more Liberals than Conservatives in Great Britain; but it also returned over eighty Nationalists in Ireland outside Ulster who under Parnell's leadership held the balance of power at Westminster. Gladstone had for some time recognised the force of Irish nationalism and the justice of its claims. It was the same generous and essentially liberal insight that had enabled him to sympathise with the national aspirations of the Balkan peoples. His diagnosis of the Irish problem was confirmed by the sweep of the Nationalists in Southern Ireland in November 1885, but he had refused to enter into an auction for Parnell's support before the election and the Irish leader had in fact given his backing to the Tories. After the election Gladstone hoped that Salisbury's Government would grasp the Irish nettle and he was prepared to give them his help. These hopes were disappointed, partly because Salisbury refused to take on so thankless a task, partly because Gladstone's own conversion to Home Rule was prematurely announced in the famous *Hawarden Kite*.

To some he was now 'an old man in a hurry', as Lord Randolph Churchill described him; a man who for the sake of holding on to power a little longer and in the egotistical blindness that only he had the solution was prepared to break the unity of the kingdom and Empire and of his own party. To others, and they included a majority of Liberals, he was the great and generous statesman who would replace the age-old Anglo-Irish feud with a 'union of hearts'. After the lapse of nearly a century Gladstone's scheme of Irish autonomy seems a conservative and balanced attempt to solve an intractable problem, perhaps one of the few opportunities to create a tolerable *modus vivendi* between England and Ireland. It required a man of Gladstone's greatness to recognise the problem, propose a solution and launch it into practical politics; but a much lesser man, more versed in the arts of political management, might have been able to get a Home Rule Bill of sorts through the House of Commons without too much damage to the cohesion of the Liberal party. The loss of Whigs and moderate Liberals had long been foreshadowed and might have mattered little in the longer run; but the loss of Chamberlain and his Radical Unionist followers was damaging. With the general election of 1886 the Liberal party, generally expected to be the majority party dedicated to reform, entered upon twenty years of virtual impotence. Gladstone, under whose mantle the divergent Liberal elements had gathered twenty years earlier, had come near to destroying the instrument he had once helped to create.

Gladstone, aged 76, was to remain Liberal leader for nearly eight years. He could still inspire popular enthusiasm, although others, for instance Chamberlain and Randolph Churchill, could now emulate him, though perhaps trading in a debased coinage. He was determined to keep Home Rule for Ireland in the forefront of the Liberal programme. There was in fact no other cause commanding sufficient support in the Liberal party to replace it. Gladstone had little interest in the many other reforms that were now proposed or in the preparation of elaborate reform programmes which he dismissed as 'constructionism'. What he called 'socialism' was repugnant to him; there seemed to him a growing danger that the moral sense of the masses, which had stood in such striking contrast to the selfishness of the classes, would itself be corrupted by the demand for material welfare. Gladstone was none the less prepared to support a list of reforms, such as were proposed in the Newcastle Programme of 1891, provided the cause of Irish Home Rule was kept alive.

The fall of Parnell in 1890, as a result of the divorce suit brought by Captain O'Shea, was a body blow to that cause and deprived Gladstone of an independent Liberal majority in the general election of 1892. Nevertheless he made a last heroic effort to do justice to Ireland. His second Home Rule Bill passed the House of Commons in 1893, but was rejected by the House of Lords. Even then he would have been prepared to continue the battle by going to the country over the powers of the Peers. His colleagues, however, were no longer prepared to support him. At heart he was still a Peelite Conservative committed to Peace, Retrenchment and Reform and he was increasingly at odds with his Cabinet over foreign and imperial policy and rising defence expenditure. He felt himself to be a 'survival' and in March 1894 he resigned for the last time, after over sixty years in the House of Commons. What hurt him most about his departure was the Queen's inability to disguise her relief. Often in his few remaining years he dreamt that she had invited him to breakfast, but the invitation never came.

Gladstone was a towering figure in the Victorian age. The shape and the content of politics would have been quite different without him. His range of interest and activity beyond politics was unusually wide and he wrote prolifically on religion, theology, the classics and literature. Only the natural sciences were a closed book to him. His Celtic ancestry was unmistakable and he was the greatest Scotsman who ever ruled England. Towards the end of his long public life there was a sense in which he had outlived himself, but the values he championed with such fervour have perennial validity.

BIBLIOGRAPHY

Biographies
Birrell, Francis, *Gladstone* (London, 1933)
Burdett, Osbert Henry, *W. E. Gladstone* (London, 1927)
Checkland, S. G., *The Gladstones: A Family Biography 1764–1851* (Cambridge, 1971)
Feuchtwanger, E. J., *Gladstone: A Political Biography* (London, in preparation for publication 1975)
Hamilton, Sir E. W., *Mr Gladstone* (London, 1898)
Magnus, Philip, *Gladstone: A Biography* (London, 1954)
Morley, John, *Life of William Ewart Gladstone* (3 vols, London, 1903)

Documents
Bahlman, Dudley W. R. (ed.), *The Diary of Sir Edward Hamilton* (2 vols, Oxford, 1972)
Bassett, A. T., *Gladstone's Speeches: Descriptive Index and Bibliography* (London, 1916); (ed.) *Gladstone to his Wife* (London, 1936)
Brooke, John and Sorensen, Mary (eds), *The Prime Ministers' Papers: W. E. Gladstone. I: Autobiographica. II: Autobiographical Memoranda* (London, 1971–2)
Foot, M. R. D. (ed.), *The Gladstone Diaries* (2 vols, Oxford, 1968)
Guedalla, P. (ed.), *Gladstone and Palmerston* (London, 1928); *The Queen and Mr Gladstone* (2 vols, London, 1933)
Lathbury, D. C. (ed.), *Correspondence on Church and Religion of W. E. Gladstone* (2 vols, London, 1910)
Ramm, Agatha (ed.), *The Political Correspondence of Mr Gladstone and Lord Granville 1868–76* (2 vols, London, 1952); *The Political Correspondence of Mr Gladstone and Lord Granville 1876–86* (2 vols, Oxford, 1962)

Other Works

Blake, R., *The Conservative Party from Peel to Churchill* (London, 1970)

Cooke, A. B. and Vincent, J. R., *The Governing Passion: Cabinet Government and Party Politics in Britain 1885–6* (Brighton, 1974)

Hamer, D. A., *Liberal Politics in the Age of Gladstone and Rosebery* (Oxford, 1972)

Hammond, J. L., *Gladstone and the Irish Nation.* New impression with an introduction by M. R. D. Foot (London, 1964)

Hammond, J. L. and Foot, M. R. D., *Gladstone and Liberalism* (London, 1952)

Hanham, H. J., *Elections and Party Management: Politics in the Time of Disraeli and Gladstone* (London, 1959)

Hirst, F. W., *Gladstone as Financier and Economist* (London, 1931)

Hyde, Francis Edwin, *Mr Gladstone at the Board of Trade* (London, 1934)

Schreuder, D. M., *Gladstone and Kruger. Liberal Government and Colonial 'Home Rule' 1880–5* (London, 1969)

Seton-Watson, R. W., *Disraeli, Gladstone and the Eastern Question* (London, 1935)

Shannon, R. T., *Gladstone and the Bulgarian Agitation 1876* (London, 1963)

Vincent, J. R., *The Formation of the Liberal Party, 1857–68* (London, 1966)

7

LORD SALISBURY

BY

ALAN PALMER

Robert Arthur Talbot Gascoyne-Cecil, 3rd Marquis of Salisbury,
second son of the 2nd Marquis by his first wife. Born 3 February
1830. Educated at Eton and Christ Church, Oxford. Voyaged round
the world 1851–53. MP for Stamford (Lincs.) 1853 and elected
Fellow of All Souls. Married, 1857, the elder daughter of Sir
Edward Hall Alderson. Wrote for the Saturday Review *and the*
Quarterly Review. *As Lord Cranborne entered Derby's cabinet in*
1866 as Secretary of State for India; resigned February 1867.
Succeeded as Marquis 1868. Chancellor of Oxford University
1870; Secretary of State for India 1874–78; Foreign Secretary
1878–80; represented Britain at the Berlin Congress 1878; Leader
of the House of Lords 1881; Prime Minister 1885, 1886–92,
1895–1902, (also Foreign Secretary 1886–92, 1895–1900). Died
August 1903.

LORD SALISBURY

Lord Salisbury was born fifteen years after Waterloo and died fifteen years before the German Armistice. Although detesting all soldiering he was in a curious way a link between the Napoleonic struggles and the wars of the twentieth century. For as a boy, young Robert Cecil walked beside his godfather, the Duke of Wellington, at Walmer Castle, listening to tales of Bonaparte and Marshal Soult; while as 'Prime Minister since God knew when', he was host to Lord Randolph Churchill's red-headed son, who was already experienced in a somewhat different type of warfare. In the year of Salisbury's birth Stephenson's *Rocket* first thundered from Liverpool to Manchester and in the year he died the Wright Brothers' aeroplane made its first flight. Salisbury's working habits depended as much on railways and steamships as do those of a modern politician on aircraft. We find him, for example, ordering his secretaries to make certain his red dispatch boxes are placed on the 4.20 from King's Cross to Hatfield; we read of him catching the night sleeper to confer with his sovereign in Scotland or the packet boat from Newhaven to take a holiday at his villa near Dieppe; and we hear of his delight in dodging importunate journalists by hiding in a third-class carriage – not for him the hurried sanctuary of a VIP lounge. The influence of steampower went even further: to a large extent, Salisbury's world map – increasingly tinted a patriotic red during his premiership – was shaped by the coaling capacity of warships and the projected routes of railways across Asia and Africa. He was, in Britain, the pre-eminent statesman of the Age of Steam, a time when political life was slower than today but infinitely more comprehensive than anything that had gone before.

The Cecils had risen to prominence in another age of expansion, the reign of Elizabeth I, but since the days of the great Burghley and his son an unduly long hiatus filled the family annals. Successive generations concentrated their interest on the county politics of Hertfordshire and Middlesex. The second Marquis, Robert's father, was however an exception: he took an active part in national government, sitting as Lord Privy Seal alongside Disraeli for ten months in the Derby Cabinet of

1852. At that time there seemed little prospect that either of his sons would achieve even this limited distinction: the elder, Lord Cranborne, had a pathetically deficient mentality; and Robert himself, the younger, was a sad disappointment. When fourteen he had been able to throw off Latin verses at school with effortless ease, but twelve months later he complained that life at Eton was 'insupportable'. To save him from further bullying his father took him away, entrusting his education to a private tutor in the family home at Hatfield. Achievement, too, fell far short of promise at Oxford. Lord Robert went up to Christ Church in the first weeks of 1848, Europe's 'Year of Revolutions'. He worked diligently, interested himself in politics and religion, and held office in the Oxford Union, though the prestige prize of the presidency eluded him. Unfortunately the strain of academic study week by week over-taxed his strength. He began to walk in his sleep, and before the end of his second year at the University he suffered what his physician termed 'a complete breakdown of his nervous system'. To be placed in the fourth class Honours list for Mathematics sadly mocked his intelligence, and it did not help him to recover his health. It began to seem as if the future Lord Salisbury might even become as mentally afflicted as his brother.

In desperation the second Marquis accepted the advice of his doctor and sent Lord Robert on a voyage around the world. He sailed for Australia by way of southern Africa in July 1851, eventually visiting Tasmania and New Zealand as well and returning across the Pacific and round Cape Horn. Travel was good for his health; it was also of in-estimable value to him educationally. When he arrived home in 1853 he was fit enough to stand as Tory candidate for Stamford, where he was returned to Parliament unopposed. Already he had a field of specialist study and experience. At twenty-three he knew more about the problems of a growing empire than most Members of the Commons: he had seen for himself the frustrations facing British officials as they sought to reconcile Boers and Kaffirs; he had visited the new goldfields in South Australia, incongruous among the diggers in his frock-coat and white top-hat, but noting with surprise that instead of murders and lynch-laws 'there is less crime than in a large English town'; and he had ridden from settlement to settlement across more than 200 miles of New Zealand, jotting down in his journal what he heard and what he observed of the colonists' difficulties. Although in 1853 the colonial question still aroused little interest in the Commons the world was narrowing with every steamship launched from the slipways, and the Member for Stamford's knowledge of what lay over the horizons soon began to mark him off from the High Tory squires around him.

So, indeed, did other matters. He married at twenty-six, a far younger age than most aspiring politicians among his contemporaries; his wife was a woman of intellect as well as of charm, daughter to a judge rather than a member of one of the party dynasties. Unfortunately Lord Robert's financial situation did not accord with the position in society he was expected to maintain, and the young couple had at first to live in Fitzroy Square (where one fashionable hostess complained it was impossible to call on them as 'she never left cards north of Oxford Street'). But this particular domestic problem indirectly had an important effect on Lord Robert's political career: to earn money he turned to political journalism, writing regular articles for two weeklies and, from April 1860 onwards, contributing to the famous *Quarterly Review*. It was these articles, some of them forty pages long, that made his reputation.

They were, as in most periodicals of the time, unsigned. But their authorship soon became known and Lord Robert's literary style easily recognisable. It showed a feeling for the trenchant phrase, a sense of the past, and a precision of argument refreshingly distinct from the measured pomposity of most Victorian periodical journalism. He did not pull his punches. The very first article he wrote for the *Quarterly* attacks Disraeli's flexibility of principles and Gladstone's quest for social equality in taxation, a false and foolish ideal ensuring that 'the rich will pay all the taxes and the poor will make all the laws'. Lord Robert's writing on domestic politics reveals an almost Aristotelian fear of democracy as the embodiment of mob rule transmitted into action by an elected demagogue. He was never afraid of the 'people' as such, only of their collective political judgement. It was a nice distinction, but to a generation still overshadowed by the revolutions of 1789 and 1848 a valid one.

Far more impressive were his articles on diplomatic questions and his biographical essays. He studied the intricacies of the Schleswig-Holstein dispute and the background to the Polish revolt in astonishing depth and he was thus one of the first English commentators to comprehend the character of Bismarck's diplomacy. What he saw of Prussian policy he did not like, but he cared still less for the badinage and bluster of Russell and Palmerston. His ideal British statesman was the much maligned Castlereagh: here, he insisted, was a man who had known how to maintain a judicious balance between committing his country to continental action and avoiding entanglement in alien concerns. 'A nation may uphold its honour without being Quixotic,' he wrote in April 1864, 'but no reputation can survive a display of Quixotism which falters at the sight of a drawn sword.' This was a sound principle of conduct for a rising politician who was already showing more interest than anyone else on the opposition benches in the changing power pattern of Europe. Salisbury's sense of imperial responsibility may have sprung from his travels; but his instinct for statecraft he perfected by reading, writing and reflection among his books at Hatfield or in the study of the house he acquired in Arlington Street.

Exactly fourteen years elapsed between Lord Robert's comments on Quixotic diplomacy and his first appointment as Foreign Secretary. For much of that time it still seemed likely that, despite his massive intellectual authority, he would never attain high office. He consistently refused to compromise his own beliefs for party advantage, for this seemed to him to make nonsense of the purpose of politics, and he was too strong a personality to follow meekly the lead Disraeli was giving to the country squirarchy. In July 1866, a year after he succeeded his unfortunate brother as Lord Cranborne, he was offered the India Office by Lord Derby and he accepted the post. For seven months he showed remarkable mastery of Indian affairs, but he was not happy in the Cabinet. He did not see how he could remain a member of a government prepared to extend the franchise, even though the original Derby–Disraeli proposals for the second Reform Bill had built-in safeguards against a surfeit of democracy in the form of plurality voting. In February 1867 Cranborne informed Derby he would have to resign. Disraeli complained he had been stabbed in the back (although he showed no rancour towards the assassin) and Cranborne seriously considered giving up politics altogether. The mood, however, soon passed; though out of the Government, his pen remained active and the articles in the *Quarterly* lost none of their bite.

In the following spring the second Marquis died and Cranborne became Lord Salisbury, master of Hatfield House in his own right and a member of what he later termed 'the dullest assembly in the world'. It was, once again, tempting to live in Hertfordshire, indulge his scientific curiosity with experiments on a grand scale at Hatfield, and allow politics to go to the Devil and Mr Gladstone. He did indeed begin a serious study of farming technique, painstakingly assessing the problems of the estates he had inherited; he refurbished the chapel at Hatfield and constructed a laboratory for himself; and on one occasion he surprised the editor of the *Quarterly* with an article in praise of photography rather than his customary survey of what mattered in Church and State. But he was not a man to vegetate for long, nor did he see any reason why he should not continue to amuse himself with science while speaking and writing against political changes he detested. In Ireland, in the Universities and in the Army the Gladstonian broom seemed to him to be sweeping away indiscriminately the chaff of ages and the seeds of security. By 1874 he was even willing to contemplate 'the nightmare' of serving in a government under Disraeli, and when the Tories won the general election that year he agreed to return to the India Office.

But the affairs of the subcontinent occupied him far less than he anticipated. Within a year revolts in Turkish Bulgaria and Turkish Herzegovina led to conflict between Muslims and Christians, with Russia backing the Balkan Slavs against their Ottoman rulers. Salisbury was involved in decision-making from the very start of the crisis, for quite apart from its strategic and religious implications for India, his understanding of foreign politics made his advice invaluable to the Cabinet. In November 1876 he was sent as British delegate to Constantinople, where it was hoped an international conference could induce the Turks to reform their system of government. The conference failed and the crisis worsened, but Salisbury's experience broadened still further his insight into the problems of diplomacy. He had travelled by way of Paris, Berlin, Vienna and Rome meeting the leading statesmen of the Continent and thus acquiring a personal knowledge of the workings of Europe's chancelleries such as no British Cabinet minister had possessed for half a century. When in the spring of 1878 it looked as if war would break out between Britain and Russia Lord Beaconsfield (as Disraeli had become) transferred Salisbury to the Foreign Office in the belief that an incisive and resolute policy would keep the peace of Europe. He was right.

Even before moving into the Foreign Secretary's room, Salisbury shut himself up in his study at Arlington Street and wrote a circular message to the principal European governments. He was accustomed to analysing and reviewing on paper the diplomatic questions of the day and the circular reads like one of his *Quarterly* articles with the argument made impersonal and the taunting phrases held in check. In the circular he proposed a basic settlement of all the disputes in the Eastern question, with preliminary agreements between the Powers to be amplified and confirmed in an international congress. It was in fulfilment of this policy that Salisbury accompanied Beaconsfield to Berlin later that summer, subsequently sharing popular adulation for having brought back 'peace with honour'. In retrospect, of course, the Berlin Treaty looks less impressive than it did to contemporaries for it created more problems than it solved, but at the time it prevented Russian dominance of the Balkans and the Straits; there was no major war in Europe for over a third of a century. For this achievement the author of the circular message deserved, and received, some credit.

Salisbury found this second experience of conference diplomacy even more stimulating than the month he had spent in Constantinople. Characteristically, however, he deplored the fuss and publicity and had to be coaxed by Beaconsfield before he would accept the great honour of the Garter. Privately he let it be known that he considered that the happiest consequence of his journey to Berlin was his meeting with the distinguished German physicist, Hermann Helmholtz, with whom he exchanged views on electro-magnetism. But the Berlin Congress had a double significance in his career: he lost the old antipathy for Beaconsfield once he became his partner in the diplomatic game; and he emerged, for the first time, as a likely contestant for the Tory succession should the Prime Minister's health finally give way. These two developments were, of course, closely connected. Salisbury much admired his chief's tenacity and resilience, while the Prime Minister himself was impressed by his Foreign Secretary's vigour and verbal courage. Both these qualities were certainly lacking in Sir Stafford Northcote, who as Chancellor of the Exchequer and leader in the Commons, was Beaconsfield's heir apparent. On the other hand Salisbury's essentially negative attitude to domestic reform, his contempt for popular enthusiasm, his dislike of social functions, his apparent disregard of the new mass organisation of the party, all counted against him. It was difficult to envisage someone so independent and aloof as Prime Minister of Jingo England.

Beaconsfield died in April 1881, having lost the previous year's election as much from party muddle and confusion as any other single cause. Salisbury duly succeeded his lost leader in the Lords; but had it been necessary to form a Conservative Government the Queen was firmly resolved to send for 'her old and kind friend' Northcote, chief opposition spokesman in the Commons. Salisbury, though respecting the Crown as the supreme symbol of Empire, never flattered his sovereign, nor did he even bother to hide a positive distaste for life in the Scottish Highlands. Why should he? He was without ambition. Had Northcote formed a ministry, he would inevitably have offered Salisbury the Foreign Office, and that was all he wanted.

Yet when Gladstone was defeated on the Budget in 1885 it was to Salisbury rather than to Northcote that Victoria turned, summoning him to Balmoral by a telegram which reached Hatfield when he was engaged in a particularly interesting experiment with a primitive telephone. For in opposition Northcote had shown himself unable to stand up to Gladstone over Ireland or to Lord Randolph Churchill's pressure group of Tory Democrats within his own party. The Queen, alarmed by the growth of Radicalism at home and by protracted unrest in Ireland, believed she needed 'strong and able and safe men' in her Government, and looked to Salisbury to find them. And the Conservative party – especially what Salisbury himself called the 'Villa Tories' in the middle classes – agreed with her. But that winter the electorate, following Joe Chamberlain rather than Gladstone, thought otherwise; and Salisbury after seven months of minority government returned to his laboratory at Hatfield.

Not, however, for long. Within eight weeks of Gladstone's return to Downing Street the Liberal Government was split down the middle over Home Rule, and a fresh election in midsummer gave the Conservatives a convincing majority. Salisbury formed his second ministry in the last week of July 1886 confident that this time he would exercise the reality of power. Though the Liberals were once more in office from 1892 to 1895, his was the decisive voice in British politics for the next sixteen years.

It was a voice that more and more of the electorate were hearing. For although Salisbury distrusted democratic government, he took pains to master its skills. He grew to respect the party machine and to listen as attentively to national agents as to diplomatic envoys, if only because they too were in a sense bearers of news foreign to him. Even before the 1885 and 1886 election campaigns, Salisbury had begun to address mass meetings in big cities and market towns throughout England, determined to counter the powerful influence of Gladstone's rhetoric; once he accustomed himself to this strange practice he stumped the country, at times positively enjoying the experience. He spoke slowly, emphatically, showing now and again an almost absent-minded informality, with none of Gladstone's sustained oratory or Disraeli's flights of imagery. It was an honest style, lit occasionally by a mordant phrase, free from humbug and condescension. Somehow it conveyed the presence of a magisterial authority easily assumed and kindly exercised, inviting trust and respect if not affection. No one expected a voice so reasonably sensible to promise heaven on earth; and no one was disappointed. Opponents outside the Conservative party, and carping critics within, consistently underestimated Salisbury's effectiveness as a public speaker.

At first, too, they underestimated him as a political manager. It was tempting to see Salisbury as the spokesman of a vanishing world, a patrician who would soon be swept from office by the irresistible force of Tory Democracy. That Salisbury stayed while Tory Democracy was swallowed up by the older tradition of the party was a consequence of two events which no observer would have predicted at the start of his second ministry: the appalling error by which Lord Randolph Churchill, the leader of the Tory Democrats, offered his resignation as Chancellor of the Exchequer over a relatively minor issue; and the willingness of Salisbury to allow the cautiously progressive members of his Cabinet to filch many of Lord Randolph's ideas of reform, especially where they benefited the agricultural interest. The legislative record of the Salisbury ministry is slight in comparison with the achievements of both Liberal and Conservative administrations in the previous decade, but enough was done to prove that the Prime Minister had at least a passing interest in domestic reform.

Most of the changes helped the farming community. This is hardly surprising; the countryside was hit by an agricultural depression, and the Tories were traditionally spokesmen 'for the country gentlemen of England'. Some reforms did, however, benefit the rural working classes (who had been enfranchised by the Liberals in 1884). Bills were introduced which modified the agricultural rating system, assisted smallholders, simplified the transfer of land, helped combat disease in livestock, adjusted the burden of tithes, and established local elected councils in the counties with powers similar to those enjoyed for half a century by the municipal corporations. As if to emphasise the priority of farming matters in Conservative thought, Salisbury established a department of agriculture, with a government minister at its head. His views were changing, sometimes with devastating logic: since Parliament insisted on making primary education compulsory, it seemed iniquitous to him that the poor should be expected to pay for their children's schooling, and thus the old defender of exclusiveness in the ancient universities introduced free elementary education for the mass population. Eager to stir the House of Lords from its torpor, he even proposed a measure to create life peerages for fifty men of distinction. But this reform, which was seventy years ahead of public thinking, was never enacted, partly through the pressure of other business.

Under Salisbury, as under his predecessors, much debating time at Westminster was occupied by the seemingly intractable problems of Ireland. He had always believed that (as he once wrote in the *Quarterly*) Home Rule by its very nature threatened 'the highest interests of the Empire'. Once he was in power he sought to check the continued lawlessness in Ireland by firm government, with his nephew Balfour – the Chief Secretary for Ireland – meeting violence with a combination of arbitrary pugnacity and ameliorative legislation. This was ultimately a policy that postponed decisions rather than patching up a solution; but at least Balfour's skill in the Commons guaranteed support for his uncle from Joe Chamberlain and his Liberal Unionists. This combination, originally forged over Irish affairs, was to have its greatest significance a decade later.

Salisbury's most distinguished achievements were concerned, in the broadest sense, with the well-being of the Empire. It was under his leadership that Britain acquired Kenya, Uganda, Nigeria and Rhodesia, as well as establishing control over the upper waters of the Nile and countering the ambitious plans of the French in Africa and the Russians in the Far East. These successes, to which might be added advantageous settlements with Germany and Portugal over African boundaries, mark off the second and third Salisbury ministries as peak periods of empire building. Yet the Prime Minister himself was never a conventional imperialist: he did not bother to read the fashionable publicists of the age; he had no use for theories of expansion; and he assumed every new colonial responsibility with reluctance, always conscious that annexation of territory created problems for a government instead of solving them. At heart he preferred an Africa of coastal settlements backed by a huge undeveloped hinterland where missionaries and agents of chartered companies fended for themselves. But if there was a danger of other European Powers trespassing on what had been a preserve of British traders, then Salisbury was willing to act in defence of British commercial rights and traditional interests. The great imperialists of the age

– Rhodes, Mackinnon, Goldie – saw the acquisition of a particular sphere of Africa as an end in itself: for Salisbury the scramble for Africa was only one aspect of a challenge being offered to British overseas supremacy by the other Great Powers. He had always believed that colonies should as soon as possible develop their own institutions and remain free from Whitehall's bureaucratic control, but he was convinced they could never survive unless their leaders recognised that the Empire was, above all, 'a combination for purposes of self-defence'. Hence he preached again and again the need for a powerful Navy and a flexible foreign policy if the work of the empire builders was to be consolidated.

For almost fourteen years Salisbury was Prime Minister: for more than eleven of them he served as Foreign Secretary as well as heading the Government. None of his predecessors had combined these offices, while among his successors the task was attempted only by Ramsay MacDonald (and then for a mere ten months). Critics inside and outside his party complained that he held on too long to the Foreign Office, speaking with increasing disparagement of his 'masterly inactivity'. But Salisbury had an understanding of diplomatic technique equalled among British statesmen only by Castlereagh, Palmerston in his first spell at the Foreign Office, and perhaps Curzon. He had no preconceived methods for dealing with diplomatic problems, preferring to meet each fresh challenge with an answer dependent on local conditions and the general balance of world forces. Thus he favoured partitioning regions beyond the reach of British naval or military expeditions into spheres of influence, supporting the creation if possible of buffer states between great power rivals, but elsewhere he would follow an almost Palmerstonian forward policy. For Salisbury there were no natural allies and no natural foes: he was prepared to co-operate with Italy and Austria-Hungary in the Mediterranean in the late 1880s, to police the troubled island of Crete jointly with Russia and France a decade later, and to work with Germany over the problems of China at the end of the century. He disliked long-term commitments, partly because they imposed limits on his freedom of action but also because he believed no government liable to be overthrown by popular vote should assume responsibilities that its successor might find morally difficult to honour. Though doubting at times the wisdom of the democratic process, he respected its conventions more conscientiously than many of its champions.

[140]

Popular legend has identified Salisbury with a policy of isolation, especially in the closing years of the old century. It is true that while Europe was divided into two rival camps (Germany, Austria-Hungary and Italy facing the Dual Alliance of France and Russia) Britain was able, through her massive preponderance of naval power, to remain without an ally. But Salisbury did not favour isolation under all circumstances. He used the famous phrase 'splendid isolation' sardonically in the first instance, gently rebuking in a speech at the Guildhall the patriotic self-righteousness of some of his own colleagues, notably Chamberlain. Since he believed passionately in the need for constant diplomatic exchanges, a policy of total isolation seemed to him completely wrong-headed. One of the ablest state papers he ever wrote, the circular dispatch of 20 October 1896, was an appeal to the other European Powers to solve the latest problems of the Eastern question by joint consultation rather than by a dangerous unilateral action; and, just as the circular of April 1878 had facilitated the summoning of the Berlin Congress, so this parallel document paved the way for an ambassadorial conference in Constantinople (though, on this occasion, with little success). More than half the work of the foreign service in his third ministry was concerned with finding common ground between London and the European chancelleries so that disputes could be thrashed out in negotiations. This was especially true of the British ambassadors to St Petersburg: Salisbury would have liked a comprehensive Anglo-Russian settlement since he feared that the quarrels of the two empires in Turkey, Persia and the Far East were a potential menace to the peace of the whole world.

There were, however, strict limits to the concessions he was prepared to make in any negotiations. He broke off talks with Russia when it seemed to him that the Tsar's proconsuls in Asia wished to absorb the northern provinces of China, where the British had considerable economic interests. Similarly, though willing to discuss African frontier problems with the French, he worked consistently to consolidate British influence in Egypt, refusing to acknowledge any French rights to establish a protectorate over the basin of the Upper Nile. No episode is so dramatic in Salisbury's premiership as the confrontation at Fashoda in 1898 when Kitchener, fresh from his victorious conquest of the Sudan, faced Colonel Marchand's expedition which was seeking to blaze for France a tricolour trail from west to east across Africa. Salisbury prepared for a general war with France rather than concede Marchand's claim to hold the Fashoda region in the name of the Republic. When, in the following spring, the French gave way and signed an agreement renouncing all ambitions to control the Nile Valley, Salisbury achieved a remarkable diplomatic victory. His understanding of the French political scene, a knowledge gained from long familiarity with the strains and stresses of the Third Republic, enabled him to ride out the crisis with iron nerves. The notion of an Anglo-French war was totally repugnant to him; he was rightly convinced that firmness and resolution would rule out any such disaster.

Unfortunately Salisbury did not show a similar understanding of South African problems. Ever since his visit to Cape Colony nearly half a century previously, he had distrusted the Boers, seeing in their narrow Calvinism an obstacle to his own ideal of racial harmony. He was, however, prepared to seek better relations with the militant Transvaalers, especially after the folly of Jameson's ill-conceived raid of 1895. But Salisbury left such matters to the Colonial Secretary, Chamberlain, in the first instance, and both men were more dependent than they realised on Milner, the Governor of Cape Colony. Bad advice and divided counsels led Salisbury's Government to treat Kruger's Boers with an obstinacy as uncompromising as that shown by the Prime Minister towards the French at Fashoda. But Pretoria was not Paris; and to his dismay Salisbury found in the autumn of 1899 that it was impossible to prevent Kruger from appealing to arms. 'Joe's War', as Salisbury privately called the conflict in South Africa, may have rallied popular feeling around his Government, but it lost him his mastery of the Cabinet and destroyed the freedom of action on which he based his diplomatic system. The effort to recover his ascendancy cost him his health.

By the autumn of 1900 Salisbury was rapidly ageing and his colleagues found him no longer willing to act decisively. The Conservative triumph at the polls in October – and, to some extent, the actual timing of this 'khaki election' – owed more to the political instincts of Chamberlain than to the Prime Minister. At last the old man agreed to leave the Foreign Office, handing over responsibilities to Lord Lansdowne. He headed the Government for another twenty months. Occasionally he intervened effectively in policy-making, notably in May 1901, when one masterly final memorandum rejected proposals that Britain might join the Triple Alliance of Germany, Austria-Hungary and Italy. But in the summer of 1902, very tired and very frail, he resigned and retired to

Hatfield. When he died thirteen months later people mourned the passing of a patriarchal figure whom the voters respected rather than revered. His natural shyness and reserve, his self-effacement and loathing of publicity had never captured the imagination. He remains the least known of the great prime ministers.

BIBLIOGRAPHY

Blake, Robert, *The Conservative Party from Peel to Churchill* (London, 1970)

Cecil, David, *The Cecils of Hatfield* (London, 1973)

Cecil, Lady Gwendolen, *Life of Robert, Marquis of Salisbury* (4 vols, London, 1921–32)

Cecil, Robert, Marquis of Salisbury, *Essays*, vol. 1, biographical, vol. 2, foreign politics (London, 1905)

Grenville, J. A. S., *Lord Salisbury and Foreign Policy: The Close of the Nineteenth Century* (London, 1964)

Kennedy, A. L., *Salisbury, 1830–1903: Portrait of a Statesman* (London, 1953)

Penson, Lillian, *Foreign Affairs under the Third Marquis of Salisbury* (London, 1962)

Pinto-Duschinsky, M., *The Political Thought of Lord Salisbury 1854–68* (Oxford, 1967)

8

THE EARL OF ROSEBERY

BY

ROBERT RHODES JAMES

Archibald Philip Primrose, 5th Earl of Rosebery. Born 7 May 1847, the son of Archibald, Lord Dalmeny, and Wilhelmina, daughter of the 4th Earl Stanhope. Educated at Brighton, Eton and Christ Church, Oxford. Succeeded his grandfather 1868. Married 1878, Hannah, daughter of Baron Meyer Amschel de Rothschild; two sons, two daughters. Lord Rector of Aberdeen University, 1878; of Edinburgh University, 1880. Under-Secretary, Home Office 1881; resigned 1883; First Commissioner of Works 1884; Foreign Secretary 1886; member of the first London County Council and Chairman 1889; resigned the same year, but resumed the office in 1892. KG 1892, Foreign Secretary 1892–94; Prime Minister 1894–95; resigned the Liberal leadership 1896. Chancellor of the University of Glasgow 1908; Lord Rector of St Andrew's 1911. Died 21 May 1929. Author of Pitt, *1891;* Appreciations and Addresses, *1925,* Peel, *1899;* Napoleon the Last Phase, *1900,* Lord Randolph Churchill, *1906,* and Chatham—His Early Life and Connections, *1910.*

THE EARL OF ROSEBERY

Archibald Philip Primrose, fifth Earl of Rosebery, was Prime Minister for only fifteen months, between March 1894 and June 1895. It was, as Winston Churchill has commented, 'a strangely-lit episode', in which Rosebery had 'a bleak, precarious, wasting inheritance'. When he thankfully resigned in June 1895 he was only forty-eight years of age. 'There are two supreme pleasures in life,' he subsequently wrote. 'One is ideal, the other real. The ideal is when a man receives the seals of office from his Sovereign. The real pleasure comes when he hands them back.' A year later he relinquished the leadership of the Liberal party. Although he lived until 1929, he never held public office of any kind again. Yet he remains one of the most perplexing and profoundly interesting men who have held the highest political office.

He was the elder son of Lord Dalmeny and the former Lady Wilhelmina Stanhope, and it is perhaps to the Stanhopes rather than the Primroses that we look for some explanation of his outstanding ability and introspective personality. 'She spoke with an exquisite precision, both of utterance and of diction,' G. W. E. Russell wrote of Lady Dalmeny. 'She hardly uttered a sentence without giving it a turn which one remembered: and her inclination to sarcasm was not unduly restrained. She was born in a learned home, and had lived all her life with clever and educated people.' She was also headstrong, and her intellect was brisk rather than profound. Lord Dalmeny, the heir to the Rosebery title and estates, is more remembered for his devotion to physical fitness than for his contribution as Liberal MP for Stirling Burghs, and his sole literary production was a pamphlet entitled *An Address to the Middle Classes upon the Subject of Gymnastic Exercises*. In January 1851, when his elder son was three and a half years of age, Lord Dalmeny died from a sudden heart attack, and Archibald succeeded to his title.

His mother married, in 1854, Lord Harry Vane, the heir to the very considerable Cleveland fortunes. Dalmeny was a reserved but precocious child. By the age of ten he was engrossed by Macaulay and had read Thiers' *History of the Consulate and the Empire* in its entirety. At Eton, where he was one of the pupils of William Johnson (later Cory), one of the greatest of all Etonian teachers and a poet in his own right, he was not outstanding. 'He was not remarkable for scholarship,' a contemporary remarked of him, 'but he possessed plenty of cool assurance', and Johnson wrote of him – in words that were to haunt Rosebery's reputation in his lifetime and subsequently – that 'he is one of those who like the palm without the dust'. Impatience with Dalmeny's lack of performance commensurate with his abilities was a persistent theme of Johnson's reports, but he also wrote of him, 'he has the finest combination of qualities I have ever seen.' One passage in particular from a letter from Johnson to Dalmeny's mother should be noted: 'He has in himself wonderful delicacy of mind, penetration, sympathy, flexibility, capacity for friendship – all, but the tenacious resolution of one that is to be great.'

From Eton, Dalmeny proceeded to Christ Church, Oxford. Already he was attracting attention as a gifted but somewhat enigmatic young man – 'very intelligent and formed,' Disraeli noted – but his period at Oxford had a comical flavour. Together with Lord Randolph Churchill, he and a few friends formed a coterie which, as he later admitted, 'saw regrettably little of the rest of the University'. He travelled a great deal, and his enjoyment of what he once called 'the noise, stench and villainy' of the Turf grew. Indeed, it was this latter fascination that brought his Oxford career to an abrupt end in 1869 when the college authorities gave him the choice of selling his racehorse – entered for the Derby, where it finished last – or remaining to take his degree. To the horror of his family, the dismay of his tutor – who had anticipated a first for his pupil – and the admiration of the Bullingdon Set, he chose the racehorse. It was not a decision he later viewed with much satisfaction.

By this stage, he had succeeded his grandfather as the fifth Earl of Rosebery and inherited the family estates. These brought him an income in excess of £30,000 a year, which was in those days a not inconsiderable fortune. He was eagerly courted by the Conservatives and the Liberals, but although he did not commit himself at this stage, it was evident that his sympathies lay with the latter.

It is difficult to be precise about the origins of Rosebery's Liberalism, but it is significant that although he was invited as an undergraduate to contest Darlington for the Conservatives, Disraeli had immediately realised that Rosebery was in the opposing camp. Family tradition may have had something to do with it, and certainly Rosebery had a Whig distaste for Tories from an early age. Despite his mode of life, he involved himself in working-class amelioration movements soon after leaving Oxford, and, despite his personal affection for Disraeli, was increasingly more attracted to Gladstonian Liberalism. In November 1871, in a speech in Edinburgh, he attacked class divisions with a spirit and a strength that disconcerted both his audience and his family. In the Lords, he began to emerge as by far the most talented of the younger Peers on the Liberal benches. He travelled a great deal – including three visits to America and one to Russia – and both his speeches and his letters emphasised the serious nature of a personality many observers had doubted.

Much of this can be subsequently understood. What is more difficult to comprehend is the aura – what we would now describe as 'charisma' – that he now began to convey to his contemporaries. His wealth, intelligence and superb speaking voice do not provide the full answer, although they were undoubtedly major factors. His management of Gladstone's Midlothian campaigns of 1879 and 1880 made him a national figure, but even before this he was being spoken of as a probable front-rank political personality.

He was clearly ambitious, although he affected a lack of interest in his own career, and was intensely sensitive to any charge of personal ambition. His wife – Hannah Rothschild, whom he married in 1878 – was more open than he, but his speeches in the 1874–80 Parliament were clearly designed to promote his position, and he was not the organiser of the Midlothian campaigns for nothing. This celebrated event was a turning-point for Rosebery, and he was well repaid for the £50,000 he said he spent on it (an estimate this commentator regards with scepticism). The campaigns – and particularly the first, in December 1879 – may have won the 1880 general election for the Liberals, but they certainly established Rosebery's position as a major national political figure.

Rosebery's complex relationship with Gladstone holds the key to his political career. In the Midlothian campaigns Gladstone was over seventy, and it would have been difficult to anticipate that he would remain the dominant figure in British politics for the next fourteen years. J. M. Barrie wrote that 'during the first Midlothian campaign Mr Gladstone and Lord Rosebery were the father and son of the Scottish people', and there were many who viewed the relationship thus. But it was an uncomfortable relationship from the outset. Immediately after

[149]

the Liberal triumph of 1880, and Gladstone's return to the premiership, Rosebery was offered a post in the Government, which he refused on the grounds, as Lord Granville told the Queen, that 'it would look as if Mr Gladstone had paid him for what he had done'. The offer was renewed shortly afterwards, and again rejected. Meanwhile, Rosebery had taken a keen interest in the situation whereby Scotland was administered, so far as the central government was concerned, by the Lord Advocate. Through a series of ludicruous but painful misunderstandings, Gladstone came to believe that Rosebery was thrusting himself forward and Rosebery became convinced that he was being neglected.

This pattern was destined to be repeated. Rosebery was always one of Gladstone's blind spots. At moments when a kind word or sympathetic understanding by the older man would have swept away all misunderstandings, Gladstone was silent. At moments when frankness by Rosebery would have been understood and appreciated, he sulked or despaired. The gulf between the two was never really closed. At the close of his life Gladstone regarded his promotion of Rosebery as one of his greatest mistakes; in his last recorded conversation Rosebery lamented that he had not followed Disraeli.

The gulf between Rosebery and Gladstone, opened by the latter's impatience with the performance of the younger man – first virtuously refusing office on two occasions and then apparently mortified by the absence of a third offer on his own terms – was perceptibly widened in 1881-2. An offer of the India Office under-secretaryship was declined in May, but an appointment to the Home Office with special responsibilities for Scotland was accepted in July. Rosebery was given to understand by Gladstone that the inferiority to the Lord Advocate would be purely temporary, but as the months passed and nothing happened his discontent grew. Gladstone was understandably obsessed by the Irish question, now in one of its most ugly and complex periods, and Scotland became discontented at her neglect. Rosebery contemplated resignation ('if I could find a pretext for leaving the Government without paining Mr Gladstone, I should go at once'), but when he received the news of the assassination in Dublin of the new Chief Secretary for Ireland, Lord Frederick Cavendish, it was a case of 'all hands are wanted at the pumps'. But within a few weeks he was discontented again, and in December 1882 the combination of lack of promotion and the continued neglect of Scotland resulted in a determination to resign which was only averted by intermediaries. 'The people who bother him at this moment more than all England are the Queen and Lord Rosebery.' Herbert Gladstone wrote of his father at this time. 'It is marvellous,' Gladstone wrote impatiently to Granville of Rosebery, 'how a man of such character and such gifts can be so silly.'

Rosebery did have solid grounds for grievance, but Gladstone's irritation is also comprehensible. The episode passed, but Rosebery was sore. 'It is incredible,' John Morley remarked, 'the want of *nous* which Mr Gladstone shows about Rosebery.' This comment was made in 1892, but has equal application to the earlier period. For his part, Rosebery had already demonstrated a weakness of character which has been accurately depicted by Winston Churchill:

'In times of crisis and responsibility his active, fertile mind and imagination preyed upon him. He was bereft of sleep. He magnified trifles. He failed to separate the awkward incidents of the hour from the long swing of events, which he so clearly understood. Toughness when nothing particular was happening was not the form of fortitude in which he excelled. He was unduly attracted by the dramatic, and by the pleasure of making a fine gesture.'

The issue on which Rosebery chose to resign was a statement in the Commons by the Home Secretary, Harcourt, which accepted the criticism that there was no under-secretary in the Commons. The real immediate cause was the continued failure to create a Scottish Department with Rosebery as its head, but the decisive element had been the collapse of Rosebery's relationship with Gladstone. Undoubtedly, Rosebery had expected special consideration; in the view of many of his colleagues and contemporaries, he had deserved it. This had been an ominous opening to Rosebery's ministerial relationship with Gladstone, and as a beginning to an official career represented something approaching a fiasco.

In several of Rosebery's earliest speeches he had emphasised the role of the British Empire, and his world voyage in the winter of 1883-4 was to have a profound impact upon Rosebery himself and upon the history of the Liberal party.

At this stage, the Liberals found themselves in a predicament that was to become increasingly serious. The 'imperial issue' had had hardly any domestic political significance in Britain until the 1870s, when its effects appeared to be negative. But the new interest in imperial questions in the 1860s, which Disraeli had discerned – perhaps prematurely – in the 1870s, became a major political factor in the early 1880s. The unexpected recrudescence of the Irish question and the bombardment of Alexandria, the Battle of Tel-el-Kebir, and the consequent 'temporary' British movement into Egypt had further aroused interest in, and high feelings on, these questions. Liberal thinking on the subject was confused and contradictory, whereas the Conservatives were increasingly regarding themselves as the Imperial party. The dichotomy within the Liberal party on this dilemma was to do more than any other single factor to lead to its impotence in the period 1886–1906.

Rosebery's interest in, and commitment to, what he subsequently called 'Imperialism, sane Imperialism, as distinguished from what I might call "wild cat" Imperialism' was greatly enlarged by his travels. In Adelaide, on 18 January 1883, he made the declaration that 'there is no need for any nation, however great, leaving the Empire, because the Empire is a Commonwealth of Nations', and on his return he publicly advocated the cause of Liberal imperialism, and became a strong supporter of the Imperial Federation League. His attitudes further separated him from Gladstone, who viewed the new movement with distaste and dismay. When offers were made to Rosebery to return to the Government, now in deep difficulties, he declined on the grounds of his opposition to its colonial policies.

The Gladstone Government, forced on by popular demand, had reluctantly dispatched a relieving force to Khartoum, where the adulated General Gordon was beleaguered. The enterprise was too little and too late, and a storm of obloquy descended upon ministers. The Government survived a motion of censure by only fourteen votes, and it was characteristic of Rosebery to use this hour of disaster to offer to rejoin the Government. It was a moment to 'swallow all my scruples and put my shoulder to the wheel'. Rosebery entered the Cabinet in February 1885 as First Commissioner of Works and Lord Privy Seal.

By this stage the much vaunted Liberal majority of 1880 had crumbled, and the Government Rosebery had dramatically joined perished quickly. Rosebery was disillusioned with his brief membership of the Cabinet. 'My experience of the present Cabinet,' he wrote in a personal memorandum, 'has convinced me that it cannot properly conduct the affairs of this country.'

The Liberal Government fell in June 1885, and was replaced by a Salisbury administration derided by Joseph Chamberlain as 'the Ministry of Caretakers'. The general election, held in November, gave Parnell's eighty-six Irish Nationalists the balance of power between the Liberals and Conservatives, and heralded the tumultous events of the next nine months. In this period, Gladstone committed himself to Irish Home Rule, Lord Randolph Churchill aroused Ulster, Lord Hartington and Joseph Chamberlain left the Liberals, and domestic politics were flung into total confusion. This extraordinary situation gave Rosebery his opportunity.

At the end of January 1886 the Salisbury Government, eagerly court-ing its own defeat on the Home Rule issue, was defeated in the House of Commons, and thankfully resigned. In the short-lived and grievously torn Liberal Government Gladstone then formed, Rosebery became Foreign Secretary. Granville was by now clearly unfitted for heavy official responsibilities, Sir Charles Dilke was involved in an unpleasant divorce case, and the Queen was hostile to the proposal for Lord Kimberley. It was already evident that it would be difficult to retain Hartington, Chamberlain, Sir Henry James and other Liberal leaders committed against Home Rule. Gladstone agreed to Rosebery's appointment without enthusiasm, on a *faute de mieux* basis.

The third Gladstone Government was short-lived and was dominated by Home Rule. The Bill was introduced in April, fervently debated throughout May, and was defeated on second reading on 8 June. The Government at once resigned, and was heavily defeated in the sub-sequent general election. The great Liberal majority of 1880 was now a shaken and disheartened minority. The combination of the defection of seventy-eight Liberal Unionists and the loss of so many of the major personalities in the party had been traumatic, and the party faced long years of Conservative rule in low morale.

In this crisis, Rosebery's star had risen remarkably. Almost alone among the Whigs, he had stood by Gladstone. 'The spectacle of this eloquent, magnificent personage separating himself from the bulk of his class, "biding by the Buff and the Blue", excited the hostility of the Unionist Party, and filled the Liberals in the shade with a sense of hope and expectancy for the future', as Churchill has written. His tenure of the Foreign Office, although brief, was principally characterised by his determination to maintain the continuity of foreign policy and his evident competence and knowledge. In particular, his calm handling of a potentially serious crisis in the Balkans won golden opinions, and impressed both the Queen and Gladstone – a formidable achievement. Speaking at Manchester on 25 June, Gladstone singled out Rosebery for special mention, describing him as 'the man of the future'. His reputation reached new heights when he was elected for the newly created London County Council in 1889, and then elected its first – and probably most distinguished – Chairman. His appeal to Londoners to 'do something for the people' and determination to achieve practical social improvement particularly attracted younger Liberals who were irritated by Gladstone's preoccupation with Home Rule and his neglect of domestic social reform.

By this stage, Rosebery was to many of his contemporaries the most fascinating man in public life. He was exceptionally well read, and his books – particularly his studies of Pitt and Lord Randolph Churchill – were characterised by wit, insight, and elegance. He was an ardent and knowledgeable bibliophile, and he created one of the great private collections in the country. John Buchan noted of the library at The Durdans that it was 'so full of rarities that the casual visitor could scarcely believe them genuine'.

The hospitality at his houses was always generous, although rarely lavish. His conversation, when he was in the mood, was memorable. After a dinner-table discussion on contemporary fiction a friend noted of Rosebery that 'one might think that he had never studied any other subject'. The young Winston Churchill later wrote that 'his voice was melodious and deep, and often, when listening, one felt in living contact with the centuries which are gone'.

His moods varied greatly, and already he was afflicted with the insomnia that was to plague him for the rest of his life. When out of humour his face would become a cold slab of boredom and distaste, and the chill of his displeasure could freeze the company. He constantly sought solitude, particularly in Barnbougle Castle, which he rebuilt in the early 1880s to house his treasures and where he could read, work, and meditate. Even his beloved sister Lady Leconfield never entered the Castle in Rosebery's lifetime, and it is in this strange building – and particularly in Rosebery's tiny bedroom at the top – that one feels closer to him than anywhere else.

As a public speaker he attracted and held the largest audiences in the country apart from Gladstone. His voice had a special quality that could stir and enthrall an audience, and every speech was meticulously prepared. 'Whenever there was a crowd in the streets or at the station, in either Glasgow or Edinburgh,' Margot Asquith wrote, 'and I inquired what it was all about, I always received the same reply: "Rozbury!"' Augustine Birrell later recorded of him that

'his melodious voice . . . his underlying strain of humour, his choice of words, never either staled by vulgar usage or tainted with foreign idiom, and above all his "out of the way" personality, and a certain nervousness of manner that suggested at times the possibility of a breakdown, kept his audience in a flutter of enjoyment and excitement. He was certainly the most "interesting" speaker I have ever heard.'

His passion for racing was an addiction that puzzled his more serious friends. His pleasure was centred on the peripheral delights, the friendship and *camaraderie* of the Turf, the excitements and frustrations of owning racehorses, the early morning matches on Epsom Downs, the gay dinner-parties, and the clatter, colour, and spirit of the meetings. He was a successful owner; between 1875 and 1925 his horses won every great race with the exception of the Ascot Gold Cup, and the Mentmore Stud was justly celebrated. 'Let not ambition mock these homely joys', as he himself once remarked.

Rosebery lived in a style that awed even Gladstone. Dalmeny, although beautifully situated on the Firth of Forth, is not a particularly large house, and at one point Rosebery commissioned plans for a much more imposing mansion. The Rothschild mansion, Mentmore, in contrast, is a very large house indeed, and was filled with treasures. The Rosebery house in Berkeley Square was not insignificant, and The Durdans was a large and imposing house hard by Epsom Downs. The Villa Rosebery near Naples was large, beautiful, and luxurious. Rosebery travelled a great deal, and never in discomfort. It was not surprising that the public regarded this Radical–grandee–scholar with such fascination. In Scotland he was revered, and in any company he stood out.

At this moment, with Rosebery's fortunes so high and his prospects so glittering, his wife died after a distressing and prolonged illness in 1890. The effect on Rosebery was devastating. He was plunged into a profound depression from which he was slow to recover. The melancholy aspect of his personality was greatly increased, and emphasised

[155]

his need for solitude. His insomnia became much worse, and was to remain with him all his life. He took no part at all in politics in 1891, and gave broad hints that he had abandoned public life. When the Liberals won a precarious victory in the 1892 general election it took all the energies of his colleagues and the intervention of the Prince of Wales to persuade him to become Foreign Secretary, and there is no doubt in the mind of this commentator that his reluctance was genuine. But the episode marked a sharp decline in Gladstone's estimation of him, and was an ominous beginning to the last Gladstone administration.

Rosebery became Foreign Secretary for the second time on his own terms, and he quickly made it clear what those terms were. 'He is absolute at the FO,' Reginald Brett noted. 'He informs his colleagues of very little and does as he pleases. If it offends them, he retires. We shall remain in Egypt and the continuity of Lord S[alisbury]'s policy will not be disturbed.'

The first difficulty arose over Uganda, and it emphasised the acute division on imperial and colonial issues between Rosebery and Edward Grey on the one side and Gladstone, Morley and Harcourt on the other. In the Liberal party as a whole there was a majority against further commitments in Africa, and particularly against a Liberal Government assuming responsibility for Uganda in place of the bankrupt East Africa Company. This was exactly Rosebery's objective, and a major Cabinet crisis was only averted by a compromise whereby the East Africa Company was given an interim subsidy. This enabled Rosebery to prepare opinion for his policy of annexation, which was eventually achieved in 1894.

This crisis emphasised that the ill feeling between Harcourt and Morley could be exploited by Rosebery on imperial issues, and also that the Government could hardly survive Rosebery's defection. When the issue of the British presence in Egypt erupted in January 1893, Rosebery – vehemently supported by the Queen – won the day with little difficulty. But the episode marked another dismal stage in the Gladstone–Rosebery relationship. A speech by Rosebery at the Royal Colonial Institute on 1 March, in which he said, 'We are engaged at the present moment, in the language of the mining camps, in "pegging out claims for the future,"' did not improve matters. Indeed, from this point the relationship moved from coolness to painful antipathy.

It is pointless to attempt to apportion blame for this situation. The division was as much ideological as it was personal, and it is understandable why Gladstone determined not to recommend Rosebery as his successor when, with deep reluctance, he resigned in March 1894. By this stage, however, Harcourt's overbearing manner had made him intolerable to his colleagues, and the Queen's selection of Rosebery – Gladstone not having been consulted – had the support of the majority of the Cabinet.

But the succession crisis was a bitter, rancorous affair. Harcourt eagerly sought the premiership, propelled forward by his devoted son Lewis (generally known by the unlovely nickname of 'Loulou'). When it was clear that their chance had gone, the Harcourts pressed severe conditions on Rosebery, of which the most important concerned foreign policy. He resisted strongly, and insisted that Lord Kimberley should succeed him at the Foreign Office. Rosebery believed that he had won his point. The Harcourts were convinced that Rosebery had bowed to their pressure to be consulted on all foreign policy matters.

Rosebery's position as a Liberal Prime Minister in the House of Lords would have been difficult in any event. In the circumstances of his accession it was virtually impossible. The third Home Rule Bill had been contemptuously rejected by the Lords, with hardly a ripple in the country. By-elections were sombre. The Government held office only with the support of the Irish. The Radical element in the Liberal party was impatient and hostile. The Cabinet itself was deeply riven on personal and political lines, with the Harcourts determined to cause trouble. The Queen exercised vigilant attention for any signs of 'flattering useless Radicals'. A poisoned chalice indeed!

The most serious aspect of all was that the Government had no policy at all. Home Rule had been so dominant that the collapse of the measure had exposed the barrenness of the Liberal planning. Gladstone's 'Newcastle Programme' of 1890 had contained virtually every proposal dear to every section of the party, but it could hardly be categorised as a coherent programme, and its all-embracing character contained its own destruction.

The Irish and the Radicals swiftly showed their hand. In his very first speech in the Lords as Prime Minister, Rosebery gave the clear impression that Home Rule would have to be held in abeyance until there was an English majority to support it. That evening an amendment to the Address moved by Labouchère, which virtually abolished the powers of the Lords, was carried by two votes. The vote was rescinded, and Rosebery's apologia averted a major crisis, but as a beginning to a premiership it could hardly have been worse. Rosebery's position never really recovered, and from this moment he was constantly under fire until he seized his opportunity for resignation in June 1895.

The relationship with Harcourt worsened over the 'death duties' Budget of 1894 and as a result of a series of battles over foreign policy. 'The fate of the present Government,' Harcourt wrote to the Prime Minister, 'and the issue of the next Election are temporary incidents which I view with philosophic indifference.' The rift was widely broadcast by the Harcourts, as was that over the abortive Anglo-Belgian Treaty relating to the Upper Nile. As Asquith subsequently wrote, Harcourt's 'lack of any sense of proportion, his incapacity for self-restraint, and his perverse delight in inflaming and embittering every controversy, made co-operation with him always difficult and often impossible. Cabinet life under such conditions was a weariness both to the flesh and the spirit.'

The impression was gradually being gained that Rosebery was a lightweight. The Queen urged him to take 'a more serious tone' in his speeches, 'and be, if she may say so, less *jocular* which is hardly befitting a Prime Minister.' Some of his public appointments – notably Professor Yorke Powell as Regius Professor of Modern History at Oxford – were so lamentable as to arouse widespread derision. When his horse *Ladas II* won the Derby in June[1] the Nonconformist conscience professed itself outraged. A close friend, Edward Hamilton, complained that Rosebery's speeches 'have been a little too flippant and make people think that, for a Prime Minister, he is not serious enough or sufficiently in earnest'. His colleagues found him difficult to see, and one described him as 'shy, huffy, and giving himself the airs of a little German king'.

The fact was that, faced with this situation, Rosebery – now plagued by persistent and debilitating insomnia – retreated into an isolation in which elements of self-pity were not entirely absent. The leadership a prime minister must give to a Cabinet was not forthcoming, and his obsession with reform of the House of Lords was not shared by his colleagues, who in effect disavowed him. His conduct, in short, illuminated his principal political defects of impatience, lack of proportion, excessive sensitiveness to criticism, and indecision which had been apparent since he had first held office.

[1] *Sir Visto* won in the following year, thus giving Rosebery the unique distinction of winning the Derby twice while Prime Minister.

On 19 February, after vehement attacks on him in the Commons which Harcourt had flagrantly ignored, Rosebery delivered an ultimatum to his Cabinet in a desperate attempt to restore his authority. The device succeeded, temporarily, but almost immediately afterwards he suffered what appears to have been a nervous breakdown. The immediate cause was severe influenza, but behind this lay the insomnia, and beyond that lay causes that cannot be precisely defined. 'I cannot forget 1895,' he subsequently wrote. 'To lie night after night, staring wide awake, hopeless of sleep, tormented in nerves, and to realise all that was going on, at which I was present, so to speak, like a disembodied spirit; to watch one's corpse, as it were, day after day, is an experience which no sane man with a conscience would repeat.' On 8 May, while making a short speech in London, he lost the thread of his remarks, and recovered himself with difficulty in a shocked silence.

The Government drifted dismally towards inevitable disaster, its councils acrimonious, its leaders divided, its supporters dispirited or violently disillusioned, its stature at home and abroad visibly disintegrating. On 21 June, in a snap vote, the Government was defeated on the issue of the supply of cordite to the Army. Rosebery eagerly argued for resignation, and for once was supported by Harcourt. The urgings of the party officials, that a sudden resignation with no comprehensible electoral policy would be suicidal, were overruled by a Cabinet sick of office.

The subsequent general election exposed these schisms cruelly. No coherent Liberal policy was presented, and in the Unionist triumph – the most considerable victory won by any political party since 1832 – Harcourt and Morley were in the ranks of the defeated. 'I do not need consolation with regard to this election,' Rosebery wrote on the morrow of the Liberal disaster. 'It was inevitable, and can scarcely fail to do good. The Liberal Party had become all legs and wings, a daddy-long-legs fluttering among a thousand flames; it had to be consumed in order that something more sane, more consistent, and more coherent could take its place.'

Although this marked the end of Rosebery's ministerial career – at the age of forty-seven – he remained a major political figure for another decade. For more than a year after the fall of his Government he was leader of the Liberal party in name – but in name alone. 'There was nothing very definite in the position taken up by Lord Rosebery,' the

Annual Register commented with tartness but with truth. He was, in fact, seeking an opportunity to escape from this last thraldom, and the occasion came when Gladstone emerged from his retirement for the last time to declaim against the Turks for the Armenian massacres and to urge a European crusade against 'the great assassin'. Rosebery's public line had been more cautious, and he eagerly seized his opportunity. On 8 October 1896 he announced his resignation from the leadership. To Gladstone he wrote, characteristically, 'I wish you to know from myself that I have resigned the leadership of the Liberal Party – that is, if I ever held it, of which I am not quite sure.'

But in spite of everything, his followers remained devout. As E. T. Raymond wrote, 'Dalmeny became a St Germain, and it was long before the dream of a Rosebery restoration was quite banished.' The Harcourt–Morley combination proved flaccid, and the feeling that Rosebery had been grossly ill used gained ground. His independent aloofness became attractive, and as the reputations of Harcourt and Morley declined, the party began to regard its former leader with greater enthusiasm. When the obscure Campbell-Bannerman succeeded Harcourt at the beginning of 1899 there were many who regarded him as a *locum tenens*. H. W. Massingham described Rosebery as 'the veiled prophet'; Morley compared him to 'a dark horse in a loose box'; his rare speeches commanded more attention and interest than any he had made as Prime Minister. Such are the swings of public interest.

What were Rosebery's intentions? His own statements are so contradictory that it would be possible to prove either that he was intent upon a serious return to the Liberal leadership on his own terms, or that he had lost all taste for politics. Perhaps the correct estimate is that of Edward Hamilton: 'What he likes (at least this is my belief) is to figure largely in the mind of the public, and at the same time to be independent and thus not over-weighted with responsibility.'

In the South African war Rosebery vehemently and with high eloquence supported the policies of the Unionist Government. In this he was supported by Asquith, Grey, Haldane, and other rising young Liberals, but found himself opposed by the bulk of the Parliamentary party. When the underestimated Campbell-Bannerman joined the ranks of those Liberals opposed to the war, the battle was joined. The Liberal League was the open forum of the Liberal imperialists, and as long as the war lasted it had a potent influence. But when Chamberlain raised the flag of Imperial Preference in May 1903 the situation was transformed. The war was over, and general Liberal sentiment was now markedly in favour of those who had opposed it; now, the magic banner of free trade could cover all the warring elements in the party. Furthermore, the Liberal Leaguers were becoming exasperated by Rosebery's vagueness and refusal to lead. His position was, accordingly, weak before he dramatically cut himself off from Campbell-Bannerman on the issue of Home Rule just before the resignation of the Balfour Government in December 1905 – and the subsequent Liberal triumph. He was offered the post of Ambassador to Washington, but curtly refused. This was the end.

The last years were melancholy. Rosebery's political attitudes became more markedly Conservative, and his alienation from the Liberals became most evident in his violent opposition to Lloyd George's 'People's Budget' of 1909, which he attacked as 'the end of all, the negation of faith, of family, of property, of monarchy, of Empire'. This last foray was the final death knell of the Liberal League.

As the First World War approached, Rosebery viewed politics and international affairs with increasing dismay and revulsion. He had opposed the *entente* with France, and had been universally derided. He had no political position. He wrote in 1910,

'The secret of my life, which seems to me sufficiently obvious, is that I always detested politics. I had been landed in them accidentally by the Midlothian election, which was nothing but a chivalrous adventure. When I found myself in this evil-smelling bog I was always trying to extricate myself. That is the secret of what people used to call my lost opportunities, and so forth.'

No doubt, he believed it.

His hopes for the future were concentrated on his younger son, Neil Primrose, whose political career was prospering greatly. Neil's death in action in Palestine in 1917 was a virtually mortal blow to his father. Early in November 1918 Rosebery was prostrated by a stroke, and although he lived for another ten years it was a forlorn, sad, and lonely aftermath. 'It was a melancholy experience for me,' John Buchan wrote, 'to see this former Prime Minister of Britain crushed by bodily weakness, sorrowing over the departing world, and contemptuous of the new. . . . I went for a drive with him, I remember, at The Durdans on an April day in 1929. I had never seen Surrey more green and flowery, but he was unconscious of the spring glories, and was sunk in sad and silent meditations.'

He died in the early hours of the morning of 21 May 1929, and was buried at Dalmeny. It was thirty-four years since he had relinquished the premiership.

Of course, those who regard politics in swift and simplistic terms can easily dismiss Rosebery. It is not difficult to categorise his deficiencies and describe his failures. But of all modern prime ministers since Disraeli, he remains one of the most fascinating and remarkable. Intellectually, he was at least the equal of Salisbury, and superior to Balfour or Asquith. As a public speaker, he was comparable to Gladstone in his prime. But fortune, which had smiled on him so long, withdrew her favours abruptly in 1890. One is presented with the sad picture of a prime minister who was acutely intelligent, but politically and personally utterly alone, ravaged by insomnia and by indecision. But so strong was the impact of his personality, and so high were his talents, that for another decade he was eagerly courted by his admirers and feared by his opponents. As Churchill wrote of his adherents: 'At first they said "He will come." Then for years "If only he could come." And finally, long after he had renounced politics for ever, "If only he would come back"'.

Tragedy and high political attainment are often closely linked. But there have been few prime ministers who aroused comparable emotions of admiration and sympathy as Rosebery did and still does. The tragedy of his career was not simply a personal one. It involved the division of the Liberal party, and the loss to the service of the nation of a man of the most exceptional calibre. It is not the task of the historian to apportion blame. He may be permitted, however, to lament the perverse Fate which raises men to the highest posts and then casts them brutally down, to be replaced – as in Rosebery's case – by inferiors.

BIBLIOGRAPHY

Buchan, John, *Lord Rosebery* (London, 1930)
Crewe, 1st Marquis of, *Lord Rosebery*, 2 vols. (London, 1931)
James, R. Rhodes, *Rosebery* (London, 1963)

9

ARTHUR JAMES BALFOUR

BY

KENNETH YOUNG

Arthur James Balfour, created 1st Earl of Balfour 1922. Born 25
July 1848, son of James Maitland Balfour and Lady Blanche
Gascoigne Cecil, sister of the 3rd Marquess of Salisbury. Educated at
Eton and Trinity College, Cambridge. Elected MP for Hertford
1874 (retained the same seat until 1885). Private secretary to Lord
Salisbury (Foreign Minister) in 1878; President of the Local
Government Board under Salisbury 1885–86: Secretary for Scotland
1886; Chief Secretary for Ireland 1887–91; FRS 1888; First
Lord of the Treasury and leader of the House of Commons 1891;
Leader of the Opposition 1892–95; MP for East Manchester
1895–1905; Leader of the House 1895–1902. During Salisbury's
absence abroad and from illness in charge of the Foreign office,
1898–1902. Succeeded Salisbury as Prime Minister 1902;
President of the British Association 1904; defeated in the election
of 1906; elected MP for the City of London (1906–22) and leader
of the Conservative Party until 1911; joined the first Coalition
ministry of May 1915 as First Lord of the Admiralty; OM 1916;
Foreign Minister (1916–19); second British plenipotentiary at the
Paris Peace Conference 1919 and signed the Treaty of Versailles;
Lord President of the Council (1919–22 and 1925–29); chief
representative at the League of Nations 1920, and the Washington
Conference 1921–22. KG 1922. Died 19 March 1930. Author of
A Defence of Philosophic Doubt, *1889;* Essays and Addresses,
1893; The Foundations of Belief, *1895;* Theism and Thought,
1923; etc.

ARTHUR JAMES BALFOUR

The political world fell about laughing in January 1887 when Prime Minister Salisbury announced that the new Chief Secretary for Ireland was to be Arthur James Balfour. After a moment of utter disbelief the Irish MPs chortled with anticipatory glee: 'We have killed Forster, we have blinded Beach.[1] What shall we do with Balfour?' And one paper justified its incredulity by asserting that Balfour was 'a silk-skinned sybarite whose rest a crumpled rose-leaf would disturb'.

In this less than flattering way Balfour, the future Prime Minister, came to the notice of the public at large. He had been in the House for thirteen years, since 1874 but had not even exerted himself sufficiently to venture upon his maiden speech until two years later when he spoke on, of all subjects, Indian silver currency. Subsequently he somewhat desultorily joined with Randolph Churchill and two others (the 'Fourth Party') in sniping at his own leaders; then held minor offices in Salisbury's Governments in the 1880s.

The 'great' Lord Salisbury was his uncle. Balfour's father, a rich Scottish laird and MP, died when he was six; and Arthur Balfour was brought up by a clever but tyrannical mother, becoming in the process what was called 'delicate'.[2] But he survived Eton and enjoyed Trinity College, Cambridge, where he was known as 'Pretty Fanny', not, it seems, because of any dubious sexual proclivities but because he collected blue porcelain rather than riding to hounds, preferred listening to music to shooting birds, royal tennis (later golf) to rowing, and intellectual conversation to almost anything else. Hunting, shooting, drinking and whoring he despised.

At Cambridge he became a professionally adept philosopher, though caring 'not a jot' for the history of philosophy but only about 'the clash of benefits held by modern men about the universe'. Henry Sidgwick was his philosophical mentor; John Strutt, the brilliant physicist,

[1] Former Chief Secretaries for Ireland, one Liberal, one Tory.
[2] The psychological aspects of this are well brought out in Lucille Iremonger's *The Fiery Chariot: a study of British Prime Ministers and the search for Love* (London, 1970), pp. 159–174.

gave him an insight into the practicalities of science and its ramifications; and the don F. W. H. Myers inspired an interest in psychical research. These matters kindled his ardent intellect throughout his life.

He was certainly the only British prime minister to have a genuine reputation among philosophers as a philosopher, based on such works as *A Defence of Philosophic Doubt* (1879), *The Foundations of Belief* (1895) and the Gifford lectures on 'Theism and Humanism'. He desired in his early manhood to become a professional philosopher, but his mother gave him 'a tremendous rating' for, as she saw it, seeking to shirk the responsibilities of his position in society; shrewdly, she insisted: 'Do it and you will find that you have nothing to write about by the time you are forty.' He did not do it. Philosophy became a hobby only.

All his days he loved Society – not the rough-and-tumble, hard-drinking, horsey society of many of his contemporaries but the graceful, sometimes intellectual, sometimes frivolous, often speculative conversation of the so-called 'Souls', a group of beautiful, usually aristocratic women, and clever men such as Oliver Lodge and H. G. Wells, who met in London drawing-rooms and country houses. Here his distinction of mind, his discriminating judgement, his wit and his bachelordom made him the cynosure of all eyes, the adored of many women.

The Duchess of Marlborough (Consuelo Vanderbilt) saw him as 'some fine and disembodied spirit. . . . When he spoke in philosophic vein it was like listening to Bach. His way of holding his head gave him the appearance of searching the heavens and his blue eyes were absent, and yet intent, as if busy in some abstract world. Both mentally and physically he gave the impression of immense distinction and of a transcendent spirituality.'

So in 1887 the public was right: what on earth could this pampered exquisite, this charming idler, this sceptical-seeming logician, this dilettante, drifting as the young Asquith saw him 'with lazy grace in a metaphysical cloud land',[3] do with an Ireland half aflame as usual with planned resistance to law and order, dark murders and famine?

Salisbury knew his nephew better. True, he had not been greatly impressed by some of Balfour's parliamentary performances, causing his nephew disconsolately to confide that 'he had quite come to the

---

[3] J. A. Spender and C. Asquith, *Life of Lord Oxford and Asquith* (London, 1932), pp. 102–3.

conclusion that he had no aptitude for politics and that as a public man he was a failure'.[4] But Salisbury guessed that behind the soft paw was a feline claw – when for example Balfour, referring to Gladstone's *volte face* over Irish Home Rule, sneered at the GOM: 'Mr Gladstone was formerly as ready to blacken the Irish Members' characters, as he is now ready to blacken their boots.' And in Balfour his uncle discerned something of his own younger self – deep interest in science, a sense of humour, an ability to write excellent English, a distaste for crude sports, a gift for shrewd if often undetectable management of politicians: Balfour, as someone later said, could tread across snow without leaving any tracks. Both kept the vulgar at arm's length. Both, too, had a profound belief in God – and this, Margot Asquith believed, was the deepest moving force in Balfour's life.

In 1887 politics was Ireland. Ireland, which had broken so many, built Balfour. Cool, utterly unafraid for his personal safety, he travelled his willowy way, offering a policy of stick-and-carrot, through that unhappy country; and the only mishap he had there was when his brougham was run into from behind by the jaunting-car of escorting detectives. He not only pacified the country ('bloody Balfour', the *enragés* called him) but gave it the means to attain prosperity through development schemes, drainage, Land Purchase and Congested Districts Acts. He settled Ireland for almost twenty years. He was as successful when he visited the precincts of St Stephen's from his headquarters in Dublin Castle. Accurately did Lord George Hamilton state in his memoirs: 'The history of the House of Commons for the next four years [i.e. from 1887] is really a record of Balfour's marvellous Parliamentary performances.'[5] The former Commons understrapper became the Cabinet kingpin, a power feared by his less agile opponents for his polished raillery and intellectual satire, for he could sting as well as cajole.

Balfour was on the way up. His love affair with Mary Elcho (later Lady Wemyss) was at its height. Salisbury appointed him Leader of the House and in 1895 (after the collapse of the Rosebery Government) First Lord of the Treasury, in short the spokesman, as well as the confidant, of Prime Minister Salisbury in the Lords. Such was his prestige that cartoonists and gossip writers made him a 'personality'.

The public fancy was caught by the contrast between langour and

[4] op. cit., pp. 102–3.
[5] *Parliamentary Reminiscences and Reflections, 1886–1906.*

toughness; they saw him as a sort of Sir Percy Blakeney.[6] They rejoiced in the long-legged, tennis-playing, golfer aristocrat who cycled – a habit that greatly shocked Gladstone – to Downing Street wearing pince-nez. They savoured his celebrated forgetfulness, his *insouciant* muddling of regiments with corps, thousands with hundreds, one Member with another. Newspapers he professed not to read and when Winston Churchill suggested that press comments were sometimes of value, he remarked (or so the story went): 'I have never put myself to the trouble of rummaging through an immense rubbish heap on the problematical chance of discovering a cigar end.'[7]

This was the *persona* – with its apocrypha – the public enjoyed. In private he was rather different. He could be haughtily cold to women who loved him and of whom he tired, and the intimacies of marriage he avoided. He spoke of himself as a self-indulgent bachelor with expensive tastes. Yet his nephews and nieces loved him dearly and he indulged them like a fond parent. He was soft-hearted, too, which he mostly concealed. Yet on at least three occasions – on the death of his first love, May Lyttelton, of his brilliant young brother Frank and of his dearest friend Alfred Lyttelton – he burst into tears in public.

Neither public nor private *persona* was allowed to interfere with the pursuit of politics, in which he could be ruthless, abandoning both causes and personalities when it seemed expedient,[8] nor with his conduct of ministerial business which was severely practical. 'In [political] business,' wrote John Morley, 'he is absolutely without atmosphere.' To Balfour, as to his uncle, politics was always 'the art of the possible'. True that, when in doubt, he was capable of treating a Cabinet meeting as a seminar[9] – no bad way of eliciting opinion, at least from those as mentally dexterous as himself – and at the end taking no decision at all.

Such in essence was his attitude to the hysterically debated topic of tariff reform. Of its practicality and value he was as sceptical as in *A Defence of Philosophic Doubt* he was of the excessive claims of science. But Balfour's boredom with the protectionist doctrine in the face of

[6] The apparently effete Englishman who rescued French aristocrats from the guillotine in Baroness Orczy's 'Scarlet Pimpernel' novels.
[7] Cynthia Asquith, *Remember and Be Glad* (London, 1952), p. 31.
[8] On his own initiative as acting Prime Minister he telegraphed Buller: 'If you cannot relieve Ladysmith, hand your command over to Sir Francis Clery and return home.'
[9] Denis Judd's phrase in *Balfour and the British Empire* (London, 1965).

Joseph Chamberlain's tenacity in propagating it smashed the Cabinet over which Balfour presided from 1902–5 into diffractive smithereens affecting many issues with which he was profoundly concerned.

Balfour in reality was effectively Prime Minister for longer than the official three and a half years. Salisbury was often ill. So Balfour often found himself in charge, and as until 1900 Salisbury was also his own Foreign Minister he gained great experience in that then most important office which he took over for lengthy periods. Between uncle and nephew there were but 'rare and occasional differences'.[10] From Salisbury, one of the greatest Foreign Secretaries, Balfour learnt never to be precipitate, never to expect too much, to play his cards close to the chest, above all never to be self-deceiving whoever else had to be deceived. In short, to be diplomatic.

The tutelage prepared him for dealing with matters about which his colleague, Joseph Chamberlain, showed the fervid enthusiasm that would have been approved by the Nonconformist preachers at whose feet he and his family sat – but not by Lord Salisbury. One was the question of a formal alliance with Germany. Since the Crimean war Britain had remained splendidly isolated: what did her Imperial Majesty need with allies? However, in the latter years of the century there had been ominous signs of ganging up against her. Chamberlain believed that the proper response was a treaty with Germany. Balfour was not totally opposed to this and indeed took part in some of the tortuous negotiations. Salisbury, however, regarded the Kaiser as unstable, thought his one object was to lure Britain into war with France and was unwilling to be connected with the decaying Austro-Hungarian Empire. Balfour, learning fast, wrote his uncle on 14 April 1898, 'Of this loving couple I should wish to be the one that lent the cheek, not that imprinted the kiss.' From Germany neither cheek nor kiss was forthcoming; and by 1900 negotiations tailed off – for ever. The wisdom of allowing this to happen has been much debated. The truth is that the Kaiser, aware of the new-found industrial strength of his country, simply lost interest, turning not the cheek but a rather less dignified part of the anatomy to his grandmother's country.[11]

---

[10] As Balfour said in his sorrowing letter to King Edward VII after Salisbury's death. See Kenneth Young, *Arthur James Balfour* (London, 1963), p. 195.
[11] A detailed study, using French and German as well as British official papers, is Steven C. Hause's as yet unpublished *The Realignment of European Alliances, 1898–1901.*

Chamberlain's other great passion was for a closer knitting of the Empire – an Imperial Parliament and an Imperial *zollverein* with the motherland. A vision indeed and one that, after the embarrassments of the South African war, appealed to many not only on the Tory side.

Balfour thought the scheme, as elaborated by Chamberlain, to be impracticable. The Empire was too diverse, too heterogeneous, too unequal in the capabilities of its several parts and too centrifugal in its ambitions. He saw little natural harmony in it. As for the Dominions, they were big boys now and must be allowed to go their own way. He hoped – and worked hard – for their co-operation but it could, he believed, come about only by their free will. Imperial evolution would happen, was happening, and could not be prevented. It was Balfour himself, many years later, who presided over the Empire's legal emancipation – or dissolution – enshrined in the Statute of Westminster which was ratified in 1932 after his death.

Balfour, like Salisbury, was happy with the Empire as it was; certainly they did not want it bigger. Salisbury had criticised Disraeli for allowing officials to take over Transvaal in 1877; he was furious with Lord Randolph Churchill for annexing Upper Burma. As grasping imperialists intent on painting ever more bits of territory red on the map, the Tories generally were far less credible than such Liberals as Rosebery. It was an expense in both men and money from which the material return was almost as speculative as the South Sea Bubble. 'For my part,' said Balfour in 1906, 'the last thing I want to see is an extension of the British Empire. I want to see its strengthening and consolidation.'

Exactly. We must hold what we have. Expansion could be permitted only where it clearly served existing British interests, for instance safeguarding the route to India, that biggest jewel in the British crown, belief in whose supreme importance was axiomatic with Tories – perhaps, it occurs to me, because, like Balfour himself, whose grandfather in the early nineteenth century had returned thence a millionaire, their fortunes came from that country. So on this principle Balfour was ready to blockade Algeciras in 1898 unless Britain was allowed to inspect naval works there, such works being a potential threat to Gibraltar,[12] the keyhole to the Mediterranean, to Suez, to India.

It followed that, if what was had must be held, some organisation for co-ordinating the military defence of the Empire in case of war was

[12] British Museum Additional MS. 49706.

essential. There must, too, be systematised preparation to defend the Empire's heart, Britain herself. Balfour saw that, ally-less, she was more vulnerable to invasion than she had been even during the Napoleonic wars. From the mid-1890s Balfour did not doubt that war, igniting one country after another, was a distinct possibility.

The incompetence of British military leadership during the war against the Boers had startled him. He, as a senior minister, knew in full the incompetence, even though he could not admit it in public. The cunning of the Boer fighters had come as a surprise. Salisbury (backed by the Treasury) had always been lukewarm about military precautions. 'His mind didn't work on those questions, they didn't bite on it,' Balfour told his niece.[13] Not so Balfour who in the 1890s had backed the raising of twelve new battalions for the Army, an increase in artillery and £5 million for military works and stores. Still, he was dismayed when the Royal Commission on the South African war revealed: 'No plan of campaign ever existed for operations in South Africa.' Privately he complained that 'the mistakes that have occurred are entirely due to the advice of experts respecting matters on which experts alone have the right to form an authoritative opinion.' 'The chief blunders have been made, in my private opinion, by our generals in the field.' Nor was he much better pleased with the Navy; in fact, 'I am extremely indignant with the Admiralty for their want of foresight in connection with the detention of neutral vessels', that is German ships suspected of gun-running to the Boers.[14] And in addition, as Balfour saw, 'there was no co-ordination, no co-operation between the people in charge of land and sea war and defence'.[15] Not only that: Navy and Army were at loggerheads over their division of responsibility for defence, even of the British islands. The Navy maintained that its function was to seek out and destroy the enemy's navy; the Army, disbelieving in the Navy's invincibility, urged that large garrisons be maintained in Britain as well as throughout the Empire. 'Our safety against invasion was a subject of bitter controversy between the Services,' he told Mrs Dugdale.

Balfour could not tolerate either his own dismay or the perilous situation of his country. When in July 1902 he succeeded his uncle as Prime Minister, he set about remedying matters. Remedy them he did and I do not doubt that this was his greatest achievement. St John

[13] Blanche E. C. Dugdale, *Arthur James Balfour* (London, 1936), i, 365.
[14] Young, *A. J. Balfour*, pp. 107-8.
[15] Dugdale, op. cit., i, 365.

Brodrick (later the Earl of Midletōn) wrote to Curzon: 'Arthur Balfour is the first Prime Minister who has given real consideration to national defence.'[16]

First of all, within weeks of becoming Prime Minister in July 1902, Balfour reconstituted the old Defence Committee of the Cabinet. He had every right to claim many years later (talking to his niece and biographer), 'I had the idea, which was really original. I don't say that out of conceit – I mean simply that the Defence Committee had no precedent.'[17] Its originality lay in the fact that the old Defence Committee, which met infrequently, could merely take up points referred to it by the Cabinet, which seldom did so because it forgot the Committee's existence. Balfour's creation could independently survey in detail all the strategical military needs of the Empire. The Prime Minister himself would normally take the chair; defence chiefs, as well as the appropriate Cabinet ministers, would form a permanent nucleus with others called in as required. Additionally, the CID, as it came to be known, had a permanent secretariat, modestly staffed, so that for the first time its transactions were fully recorded. The Committee was flexible enough to include on occasion Dominions defence ministers: 'A new precedent of great imperial significance,' Balfour informed King Edward.[18]

Under Balfour's powerful urging, the War Office agreed that all important defence papers should reach the Cabinet only via the CID, and the fiery black-a-vised Admiral Fisher agreed on close co-operation between Navy and Army and even suggested an amalgamation into one service.

The CID, Balfour emphasised, remained a consultative not an executive body; but once the Prime Minister and the War and Navy ministers had agreed in committee, the 'advice' would usually be activated. Balfour 'deserves every credit not only for devising this scheme [the CID] but also for giving his time and energy to it after calling it into being.' So said the Liberal Haldane, later to be Secretary of State for War. Indeed not only did Balfour chair all the CID meetings – which were fortnightly – but himself submitted numbers of papers for its consideration. Defence of Britain, defence of India (against Russia) were his main themes. This led among other things to the crea-

[16] Quoted Judd, *Balfour and the British Empire*, p. 73.
[17] Dugdale, op. cit., p. 365.
[18] Young, *A. J. Balfour*, pp. 224–5.

tion of the Territorial Army in 1907; but little escaped the attentions of the CID.[19]

Parallel with the re-creation of the CID was the War Office (Reconstitution) Committee set up by Balfour in November 1903. Lord Esher was its chairman. He had a passion for military affairs and his recommendations – for an Army Council and a general staff system, among others, were accepted. Balfour, fearful of what a Liberal regime might do when his Government fell (he had little doubt it would), placed Esher on the CID as a permanent member to ensure that even out of office he would know what was afoot. Happily the succeeding Liberal Governments made full use of the CID, and Asquith went so far as to put his fallen opponent back on it before the outbreak of war, so that Austen Chamberlain would write thirty years later:

'It is impossible to overrate the service thus rendered by Balfour to the Country and Empire. Without this Committee and the work done by it under him and his successors, the outbreak of the Great War would have found us wholly unprepared for the problems with which it at once confronted the Government and, humanly speaking, victory would have been impossible.'

Just how fervidly Balfour felt about defence may be judged by the fact that, with his Cabinet shot, as it were, from under him, and resignation politically desirable, he hung on to office to ensure that, of all things, the Field Artillery should be rearmed with eighteen-pounders. A small matter? He did not so regard it and told his niece that he delayed resigning because of this matter of which none of his colleagues were aware. 'The rearming of the Field Artillery I considered vital for the safety of the Empire and worth risking a *débacle* in the Unionist party and I was determined not to go out of office until we were so far committed to the expenditure that no Liberal Government could withdraw from the position.'[20] These eighteen-pounders were fired with effect in Flanders in 1914.

Nor, it should be added, did Balfour neglect the Navy. Fisher, the

[19] See F. A. Johnson, *Defence by Committee: The British Committee of Imperial Defence, 1885–1959* (Princeton, 1960).
[20] Young, op. cit., p. 232. Mrs Dugdale made this note but did not use it in her biography.

bluff First Sea Lord, scrapped obsolescent ships, built the Dreadnoughts,[21] expanded from two fleets to three and established a Navy
War Council. Estimates rocketed and the Liberals howled in close
harmony with the Treasury. Unperturbed, Balfour backed Fisher to the
hilt. When in 1912 Churchill gave Asquith's First Lord (McKenna) the
credit, Fisher wrote, 'He ought to have gone further back than
McKenna for the credit. *It was Balfour!* He saw me through – no one
else would allow 160 ships to be scrapped, etc. etc. etc.'[22] In this case,
Balfour's misgivings about the Liberals were justified. The Campbell-
Bannerman Government, which succeeded Balfour's, abandoned the
naval programme and so encouraged Germany to draw level again.

Let us be quite clear what Balfour was about: with measured tread
and a logician's ingenuity he was preparing for war, diplomatically as
well as militarily. But against whom? As late as 1904 the secret war
plans envisaged the enemy as France plus Russia. In that same year,
however, Balfour's trusty and perceptive friend, Lord Esher, wrote that
because Germany contemplated the absorption of Holland 'there must
come a day when France and England will have to fight Germany in
order to neutralise the Dutch Kingdom, and this day may not be very
far off'. Esher did no more than formulate what Balfour had for some
time felt in his bones.

He had worked hard for the Anglo-French Convention, which was
signed in 1904. Lansdowne did most of the negotiation; but the driving
force was Balfour's. The Convention – *entente cordiale* – ended Britain's
long policy of isolation and gave her serious commitments in Europe.
Militarily, at first, it meant little. Though secret staff talks with the
French began, France's military deficiencies were glaring, and the
French were terrified by Germany, which had forced the resignation of
Foreign Minister Delcassé, negotiator of the Convention with Britain.

Balfour next turned his attention to neutralising France's ally,
Russia, which had advanced into Manchuria and China and was regarded as the prime potential threat to India. Fortunately, Russia was
also a certain threat to Japan, as the Japanese well knew. British and
Japanese interests coincided. They signed a limited alliance for five

---

[21] Unfortunately the war when it came was not one where such battleships could be
deployed. The only line-of-battle contest was Jutland (when Balfour was First
Lord). Hindsight makes clear that Fisher should have spent on convoy vessels, not
Dreadnoughts, many of which never fired a shot in action.
[22] Fisher to Esher. See Young, *A. J. Balfour*, p. 233.

years in 1902 – limited because Britain pledged to go to Japan's help only if she were to be attacked simultaneously by two countries. Balfour decided to go further – and for excellent reasons. 'A war between Japan and Russia, in which we were not actively concerned and in which Japan did not suffer serious defeat, would not be an unmixed curse,'[23] he suggested to the King (December 1903). If Russia won she would be seriously weakened because she would have to maintain long lines of communication and financially burdensome forces in the area.

The following year (1904) Russia fought Japan and lost. Her rebuff in the Far East she took as final. She also made known her desire for an understanding with Britain, which was concluded in 1907. During the Russo-Japanese war the British public, with whom the Russians were unpopular, and who applauded every Japanese success, thought their Prime Minister acted timidly. It was, however, tightrope-walking not timidity. A Russian fleet fired on some Hull trawlers (believing them to be disguised Japanese torpedo boats); there was uproar in the British press and demands for reprisals which would have meant war. War, military and naval involvement, were no part of Balfour's plans. He made some threatening noises, a little diplomatic blackmail. It worked. As Admiral Fisher told his wife: 'It has nearly been war again. *Very near indeed*, but the Russians have climbed down. Balfour is a splendid man to work with.' In August 1905 Balfour, encouraged by Japanese military prowess, concluded a firmer treaty with her. Now Britain was to go to her aid if only one enemy assailed her. In return Japan was to help Britain defend her interests on the Indian Frontier.[24]

So the dogs of war ambled to the kennels prepared for them. It was nine years yet to Armageddon. As yet, no arrangement was irreversible. The Kaiser, though by now he could scarcely be blamed for feeling encircled, could still have broken the circle if he had sought to do so. But he had appreciatively tasted the nectar of power – and Germany *was* powerful, even merely counting heads. She had a population of 80 million, compared with France's 40 million and Britain's 40 million.

How far can we ascribe these new diplomatic dispositions to Balfour himself? According to Austen Chamberlain, totally:

'No Prime Minister ever took a closer interest or . . . more active part

[23] Young, op. cit., p. 234.
[24] Balfour saw the snag here. As he told the King, this might provide an excuse for a 'Radical government' to reduce our Army in India on the grounds that there would be an unlimited supply of men from Japan.

in the conduct of foreign policy. . . . It does not detract from Lansdowne's services as Foreign Secretary to say that his chief accomplishments would never have been achieved but for the constructive mind of Balfour and the constant support he gave him, not only in executing his foreign policy, but in conceiving and shaping it.'[25]

British statesmen by tradition looked eastward. Prophetically Balfour looked to the West as well. At first he found the westward land far less bright than did A. H. Clough in his famous hymn.[26] In 1895 United States President Grover Cleveland took it upon himself to warn Britain that his country would resist 'by every means' any appropriation of Venezuelan territory Such would be 'wilful aggression'. He referred to the dispute between British Guiana and Venezuela, which had recently seized British territory and fired on a British gun-boat.

The dispute came to nothing – or rather to arbitration. But Balfour declared, against the tut-tutting of most Tories, 'The time will come, the time must come, when some statesman of authority will lay down the doctrine that between English-speaking people war is impossible.'[27] From this moment he pressed for close co-operation between Britain and America and foresaw, hopefully, that such co-operation would become the cornerstone in a new international balance of power. This is why, among other reasons, he supported the United States in its war against Spain in 1898.

His aspiration was not dashed. Gradually American politicians forgot to think about 'Britain, our historical foe'. By 1905 Choate, United States ambassador in London, did not demur when Balfour asserted his belief that 'the two great co-heirs of Anglo-Saxon freedom and civilisation have a common mission'. This aim Balfour himself did much to encourage during visits to the United States in the First World War – even afterwards, to the point of undoing the Japanese treaty because of American fears, subsequently justified, of rivalry across the Pacific, upon which they stared 'with eagle eyes'.

Of course Balfour was not affected by any English-speaking union sentimentality. He dealt only (in politics) with the realm of realities. He knew that by the turn of the century, perhaps before, Britain was falling behind industrially. Her steel production, for example, was al-

[25] Quoted Young, *A. J. Balfour*, p. 236.
[26] 'Say not the struggle naught availeth.'
[27] Quoted Young, op. cit., p. 172.

ready third to that of Germany and the United States, textiles stagnated, and she was becoming ever more dependent on imports to feed her people: Britain's wheatfields were diminished by another half million acres between 1890 and 1900, which meant trouble in case of war and in fact – because German submarines sank so many supply ships in the Atlantic – almost caused Britain to surrender in the first world war. Warm friendship with the future all-powerful Uncle Sam was, therefore, a *sine qua non*.

It was not just industry and wheat. Britain, once the leader in technological invention, was lagging there too. Yet Balfour was sure, long before most politicians, that while the future doubtless should be left to Providence, progress – whatever that implied – would depend on the faster, ever faster, application of science to industry. Technology! He had not in his youth mixed with scientists such as Strutt (later Lord Rayleigh, his brother-in-law) for nothing. As Prime Minister, he was intellectually stimulated by contact, official and social, with J. J. Thomson, Ernest Rutherford, John Larmor, Oliver Lodge. It is noteworthy, says Professor A. S. Eve, that Balfour, the philosopher, quickly understood the work of the physicist. Did he hear and if so did he ponder Rutherford's apparently jesting remark of 1904 that 'some fool in a laboratory might blow up the universe unawares'? Certainly in the 1920s, as an elder statesman and Baldwin's Lord President of the Council, he used his influence to see that public money went into the Department of Scientific and Industrial Research, into atomic experiments at Cambridge and elsewhere. As Prime Minister he gave the presidential address in 1904 to the British Association for the Advancement of Science and received the rare praise of Rutherford himself.

The future, Balfour was sure, lay in 'the modern alliance between pure science and industry', and he said in his lecture on 'Decadence' in 1908:

'On this we must mainly rely for the improvement of the material conditions under which societies live . . . although no one would conjecture it from a historic survey of political controversy . . . science is the great instrument of social change . . . the most vital of all revolutions which have marked the development of modern civilisation.'

There lay the hope for the poor, not in the levelling down preached by Lloyd George and the Socialists.

[177]

Dark thoughts, however, broke through, for he knew that in technical education and training Britain had fallen far behind Germany and even France.

'Turning scientific discoveries to practical account – technical instruction – there is nothing of which England is at this moment in greater need. There is nothing which, if she in her folly determines to neglect, will more conduce to the success of her rivals in the markets of the world, and to her inevitable abdication of the position of commercial supremacy which she has hitherto held.'[28]

Polytechnics existed, but too few.

Education in general preoccupied Balfour. 'There is probably no more serious waste in the world than the waste of brains, of intellect', . . . and the wastage in Britain was horrifying.[29] This is why he persisted, in the teeth of every kind of discouragement and at the risk, as Chamberlain repeatedly warned him, of bringing down the Government, in pushing forward the Education Bill in 1902. It differed little from the failed Bill of 1896: it proposed to unify primary education, then composed partly of rate-aided Board Schools and partly of voluntary schools, managed by the Church of England or other denominations, which often had little money for teachers or equipment. The proposal was to give them state aid and at once the Nonconformists – who were mainly Liberal voters – raised an outcry against the State's subsidising Anglican schools. The 1896 Bill was then withdrawn.

Balfour's second attempt was no less a tussle and he himself drafted every line of the Bill with the able assistance of Robert Morant, an official in the Education Office. Eventually it was passed: both secondary and elementary education were placed on the rates and brought firmly under county and county borough councils. The Act ensured that teachers should be properly paid and that all children should have an equal standard of education wherever they might live. Grants (that is state aid) to secondary schools – grammar and the like – resulted in an increase in pupils; and there was a spate of university foundations – Manchester, Liverpool, Leeds and Sheffield. Thus Balfour built the

28 Speech to Chemical Society, London, 27 March 1895 (*The Times*).
29 In 1885 there were, proportionately to population, two and a half times more students in the German states than in Britain.

substructure of an educational system which proved its worth over and over and lasted almost unchanged into recent times.

There is no doubt that when Balfour was determined, he would fight for his progeny like a cornered animal. Usually his causes were good. Certainly it was so in education; and in this case his Liberal and Non-conformist opponents were revealed as putting petty sectarian issues before better education for all – about which some of them had often prated. Ironically, some Conservatives have dubbed Balfour's Act 'state Socialism' (whatever that means), and have claimed that in after years Balfour himself said, 'I did not realise that this Act would have as its consequence more expense and more bureaucracy.'[30]

Balfour's outlook on education was not narrowly practical: 'Industrial work unbalanced by literary work, literary and industrial work unbalanced by speculative work are unfit to form the mental sustenance and substance of academic training,' he told the Convocation of Victoria University,[31] Manchester, in 1891. 'Science knows no country and is moved by no passion – not even the noblest passion of patriotism.'

Balfour had more than a little of the Radical in him. He was not Radical in the contemporary authoritarian sense: neo-Rousseauian generalisations never influenced him and usually bored him. Consider, however, his attitude to King Edward VII. That monarch he constantly, and with *insouciance*, baulked, not, as some have said, because he was Whiggish towards the monarchy or Tory towards the 'upstart' Hanoverians, and certainly not because he disapproved of the monarch's private life if he bothered even to listen to the gossip. Of course he would not belong to the raffish circle around the throne; where Edward was gross, Balfour was discriminating. But censoriousness was not in his nature.

No, it was simply that from time to time Edward wanted to do things that cut across Balfour's policies; and Balfour blandly, politely, would not have it. True, on the death of Queen Victoria he had written to his mistress, Lady Elcho: 'The King will take up a good deal more of his Ministers' time than did the Queen . . . I think he is in the

[30] The remark is quoted in Elie Halévy's *A History of the British People*, vol. i, Epilogue, p. 207; but contrary to his custom, Halévy gives no source for the quotation.
[31] This was a collection of university colleges that preceded the grant of charters to the constituent colleges.

right.'[32] Well, perhaps; but even when Edward was still Prince of Wales and Balfour merely First Lord of the Treasury he had vetoed the Prince's proposed contribution to a newspaper: the Prince was known to be an intimate of such Liberals as Campbell-Bannerman.

He insisted in 1901, against the King's express interdiction, that the Duke and Duchess of Cornwall – later King George V and Queen Mary – should tour Australia, New Zealand, South Africa and Canada. He had his way. In 1902 Balfour's Foreign Secretary, Lansdowne, desired that the Shah of Persia be given the Garter in return for certain benefits to Britain. The King disliked the Shah and refused. Balfour insisted and Balfour won.

He refused to allow the King to see Cabinet papers 'as of right' before decisions were taken. He prevailed; as usually he did when the King wished to give peerages to persons Balfour thought unworthy; and he contradicted those who credited Edward with the *entente cordiale*: 'We must not think of him as a dexterous diplomatist,' he said, though graciously granting that the King, 'by his personality alone', impressed the French with 'the friendly feeling'[33] of Britons towards them. Privately he wrote to Lansdowne: 'So far as I can remember, during the years which you and I were his Ministers, he never made an important suggestion of any sort as to large questions of policy.'

After the catastrophic defeat of his party and himself in January 1906, Balfour returned to lead the Opposition. Not all Tories were happy with this leadership; their dissatisfaction came to a head when Balfour and a majority of the shadow Cabinet decided not to oppose the Liberal Government's Bill to reduce the Lords power of veto, particularly over finance Bills. If the Lords, the bulk of whom were Tories, refused to pass the veto-reducing Bill, Asquith threatened to create some 400 Liberal peers to ensure its passage. This would have caused a tremendous constitutional crisis; it might even have shaken the throne. Balfour and Lansdowne, the Tory leader in the Lords, refused to take the risk. Some of the Tories accused them of cowardice, of giving way on a matter of principle. A slogan was invented: 'Balfour must go.' Balfour, though he thought himself ill used, did not wait long. He resigned the leadership on 8 November 1911.

That – and a peerage – should have been the end. Instead it was a new beginning. When the war was about to breakout, Asquith sought

[32] Young, *A. J. Balfour*, p. 201.
[33] Young, op. cit., p. 247.

Balfour's advice. He made him a permanent member of the Committee of Imperial Defence. When Asquith was forced to form a coalition, the only Conservative to get a key post was Balfour, who succeeded Churchill as First Lord of the Admiralty, an office in which he did not shine. His subsequent role as Foreign Secretary was much more his *métier*.

Today Balfour's name, if mentioned in non-political company, evokes the 'Balfour Declaration'. The Declaration, made on 2 November 1917, was, of course, a Cabinet decision; as Foreign Secretary Balfour happened to sign it. Not that he disagreed with 'the establishment in Palestine of a national home for the Jews'; indeed, after his meeting and subsequent friendship with Chaim Weizmann in 1905, he was strongly in favour of it. Thus Balfour's death in 1930 was lamented by Jews all over the world.

Strangely enough, Balfour was no Semitophile; he once said, after a long talk with Cosima Wagner at Bayreuth, that he 'shared many of her anti-Semitic postulates'. As Prime Minister he had spoken strongly against alien (in those days almost entirely Jewish) immigration into Britain. And the Aliens Bill, restricting immigration, passed into law in the last year of his premiership. As long ago as 1899 he had remarked in a private letter: 'I believe the Hebrews were in an actual majority – and tho' I have no prejudices against the race (quite the contrary) I began to understand the point of view of those who object to alien immigration!'

These attitudes would not, of course, preclude his support for a Jewish national home; on the contrary it was a natural if somewhat cynical corollary. Better the Jews in Palestine than in Britain. At the same time he was fascinated by the uniqueness of the Jewish race and its history and by such paradoxes as the fact that the founder of Christendom, himself a Jew, had been rejected by his own people. He appreciated the enormous Jewish contribution to science, the arts and civilisation in general.

What he helped to do for the Jews, Balfour pondered late in life, was the most worth-while thing in his political career. He was almost certainly wrong. Although the Declaration specifically stated that 'nothing shall be done which may prejudice the civil and religious rights of existing non-Jewish communities in Palestine' (90 per cent then of the population), it was clear that this could never be assured. Balfour either knew and ignored it or had been rendered so starry-eyed (a most unusual condition for him) by wizard Weizmann that he allowed his optimism too free a rein. He should perhaps have listened more carefully to the sole Jew in the Cabinet, Edwin Montagu, who in a memorandum to his colleagues forecast that Zionism would cause suffering by encouraging anti-Semitic countries to expel their Jews and would then put the Jews in a position where they in turn would expel the present inhabitants from Palestine and take all the best lands.

Gradually during and after the war, Balfour drifted from *moyen âge* into *doyen âge*, from politician to statesman, from 'Mr' (via Sir Arthur) to the first Earl. He remained almost continuously in high office until a year before his death at eighty in 1930. He liked office – even to the point of switching allegiance from Asquith to Lloyd George during the war, and then from the Conservative party to the post-war Coalition; and when the Coalition collapsed he was soon back as a Conservative minister. As Churchill once said, he was 'like a powerful cat walking delicately and unsoiled across a rather muddy street'. This liking for office was not, however, quite as one contemporary commentator saw it: 'A man who would make almost any sacrifice to remain in office. He loves office more than anything this world can offer. . . . So restless, so dissatisfied, even in old age, outside the doors of public life.'[34] This is too naive a view of a maze-like character. He was not ambitious in the vulgar sense. He gave a clue to his attitude to politics when he remarked to John Morley: 'When I am at work on politics I long to be in literature and vice versa.' In him the desire for action and the desire for contemplation were mixed about fifty-fifty. Or, put another way, he wanted to avoid the tedium inseparable from unrelieved politics and no less, as every writer knows, from unrelieved 'literature'. Desmond MacCarthy puts it exactly: 'There were moments throughout his career when it was apparently with relief that he felt again beneath him the firm ground of abstraction. . . . Then again he would throw off the robe of the philosopher . . . and put on his ruffles and rapier to fight for his side.'[35]

In politics he followed Sydney Smith's terse maxim, 'Take short views', because, as Balfour said in a Rectorial address at Glasgow, the wise man will have 'a full consciousness of his feeble powers of foresight. He will be content to deal as they arise with the problems of his own generation.' Visions of 'some millennial paradise' were no substitute for 'the private virtues of citizens, their love of knowledge, the

[34] Harold Begbie, *The Mirrors of Downing Street* (London, 1917).
[35] *Portraits* (London, 1931), p. 24.

energy and disinterestedness of their civil life, their reverence for the past, their caution, their capacity for safely working free institutions. . . .' There indeed he spoke with the voice of true Conservatism. At the same time he knew that change was inevitable and that the best safeguard against too rapid change was to preserve the flexibility of Britain's political customs and institutions.

In philosophy, it is true, his speculations – and without doubt his intuitive, almost mystical nature – opened up to him curious immeasurable vistas: 'Metaphysicians,' he wrote, 'are poets who deal with the abstract and the super-sensible instead of the concrete and the sensuous.' Yet in philosophy, too, short views prevailed. As he told his biographer-niece, 'Don't worry your head about what need be said about my philosophy. . . . All that any man's thought is, is a contribution greater or lesser to the stream of thought of his own time which flows on and turns into the thought of the next generation.' (He was latterly much affected by Henri Bergson's 'flux' philosophy.)

He continued to believe in God – 'a personal God to whom men may pray'. As for death he said once, 'I do not think, so far as I can judge in the absence of actual experience, that I am at all afraid of dying.' He did not doubt personal survival beyond the grave whatever his final conclusions about communication between the living and the dead.

His own death on 19 March 1930 was undramatic and at eighty-two in the fullness of time. But it had an ironical prelude. As though to strengthen his thesis of man's feeble powers of foresight, he had long ignored the warnings given by his accountants of his diminishing fortune. With a recklessness elsewhere foreign to him he had since before the war poured thousands upon hundreds of thousands of pounds into schemes for making powdered peat into an industrial fuel. On his deathbed he asked his nephew, later the third Earl, whether there would be enough left for him to live on. It was not quite as bad as that. Nevertheless after his death his magnificent library was broken up and sold; Whittingehame House was let and the house in Carlton Gardens sold. Balfour died a comparatively poor man.

BIBLIOGRAPHY

Dugdale, Blanche E., *A. J. Balfour*, vols i and ii (London, 1936)

Esher, Viscount, *Journals and Letters of Viscount Esher*, edited M. V. Brett (London, 1934)
Gollin, A., *Balfour's Burden* (London, 1965)
Johnson, F. A., *Defence by Committee* (London, 1960)
Judd, Denis, *Balfour and the British Empire* (London, 1968)
Young, Kenneth, *Arthur James Balfour* (London, 1963)

10

SIR HENRY CAMPBELL-BANNERMAN

BY

JOHN WILSON

Sir Henry Campbell-Bannerman, born Glasgow 1836, younger son of Sir James Campbell, business man and Lord Provost. Educated Glasgow High School, Glasgow University and Trinity College, Cambridge. Joined the firm of J. & W. Campbell in 1858; married, 1860, Charlotte, daughter of Major-General Sir Charles Bruce. MP for Stirling Burghs, 1868, and represented this constituency for forty years. Assumed the additional surname of Bannerman in 1871. Financial Secretary, War Office 1871–74 and 1880–82; Parliamentary Secretary, Admiralty 1882–84; Chief Secretary for Ireland, 1884–85; Secretary of State for War 1886. Member of the Hartington Commission, 1888–90. Again Secretary of State for War 1892–95; secured the resignation of the Duke of Cambridge as C.-in-C. 1895. Resigned office same year, when the Rosebery government was defeated on a motion to reduce his salary. GCB 1895. Leader of the Liberal Party in the House of Commons 1899; leader of the Opposition, 1900; Prime Minister 1905–08. Resigned owing to illness, 3 April 1908. Died at No. 10 Downing Street on 22 April 1908.

SIR HENRY CAMPBELL-BANNERMAN

———

Henry Campbell-Bannerman, the first man to be given the official title of Prime Minister, was an unusual sort of man to hold that office. He was easy-going, indolent, devoid of great ambition and devoted to his own comfort. He put the interests of his ailing wife before those of public affairs and nothing was allowed to interfere with his annual autumn holiday at the spa of Marienbad in Bohemia. Yet his period at 10 Downing Street – a mere two years – was one of the most successful of any modern Prime Minister.

He was in politics all his life, and was MP for the Stirling Burghs for forty years, but it took him a long time to reach the top, and until the splendid sunset of his last two years he was consistently underrated.

He was a lowland Scot, a Presbyterian, son of a self-made business-man who had become a Knight, a Tory and Lord Provost of Glasgow. His elder brother, who inherited the running of the family business, became a Tory MP. Although he had a conventional education at the High School and University of Glasgow and at Trinity College, Cambridge, his father sent him as a boy to the Continent, and he grew up speaking fluent French, good German (which he spoke with a 'smart Viennese accent') and some Italian. He was not in the least insular and was thoroughly at home in Europe, but he never visited the United States, India or other parts of the British Empire. His wife Charlotte, another Scot, shared his tastes and also spoke fluent French. She was a diabetic, for which there was then no cure, so she became enormously fat and suffered dreadful pain in her last years. But they were extraordinarily devoted to each other.

Henry Campbell (the Bannerman was added, reluctantly, in 1871 when he inherited property from an uncle) was a Liberal MP from 1868. He and his wife lived a comfortable, spacious life in enormous London houses during the session. That in which they spent most of their time, 6 Grosvenor Place, still stands and was sold in 1972 for more than £2½ million. They had a large country house called Belmont near Meigle in Forfarshire (Angus) which they loved. Both of them were thorough Scots and much preferred living on 'the best side of the Tweed'. They entertained a great deal and kept a fine table. Every autumn they went off for six weeks or so to Marienbad, which became in their time a social mecca. Campbell-Bannerman's colleagues, indeed, often tried, and usually failed, to get him back from Marienbad or down from Scotland. He liked an unhurried way of life and said once, 'Personally I am an immense believer in bed, in constantly keeping horizontal', an unusual sentiment for an active politician.

Campbell-Bannerman, or C.B. as he was always called, spent a good deal of his official career at the War Office in the first years under Edward Cardwell, a reforming minister whom he greatly admired and made his pattern in life. He was twice Financial Secretary and twice Secretary of State for War, and was much concerned all his life with Army affairs and War Office reform. He was opposed to the conception of a general staff as leading to foreign entanglements and consisting of officers who would 'sit apart and cogitate' and thus get up to mischief. His most notable achievement was bringing about the resignation of the Duke of Cambridge, a portly Hanoverian who was resolutely opposed to what he called 'pwogwess', after thirty-eight years as Commander-in-Chief; a task that needed all his resources of tact, patience and ingenuity. He achieved it with the help of Queen Victoria, with whom his relations were invariably sunny. At the War Office he was much liked by both soldiers and civilians, but detail bored him and he was sometimes found in his office reading a French novel.

In the House of Commons he was universally popular but for most of his career he made no great mark. He was not a brilliant speaker, though his speeches were always lucid and well written, and he did not have the quickness needed to deal with unexpected attacks, though he answered questions with gaiety and sparkle. His qualities were not those that make the best show in a noisy debate. They were those that caused Mr Gladstone to describe him as 'cantie' and 'couthie'.

Early in his career he had had a short spell as Chief Secretary for Ireland, and his imperturbability in the face of the furious assaults of Irish Members in the House greatly increased his reputation. It was said of him that he treated the Irish party 'like one of the mists of his native land – a tiresome phenomenon, but not one to be overcome by indignation or denunciation', and that he had 'unfathomable, unreachable depths of imperturbability'. When the Liberals split over Gladstone's conversion to Home Rule for Ireland in 1886, C.B., after some agonising doubts, stuck to his leader. He had come to believe that there was no alternative to a separate Irish Parliament and to self-government for Ireland, and he remained a Home Ruler for the rest of his life. He thought that Home Rule all round – for Scotland, England and Wales as well as for Ireland – would be a good solution, but realised that it was politically unattainable at that time.

He became leader of the Liberals almost by accident: because Rosebery, Harcourt and Morley had successively eliminated themselves from what seemed a thankless task and because Asquith, at forty-six, was regarded as too young and doubted if he could afford to take on a full-time job.

C.B. was regarded by many Liberals as a mere *locum tenens*, who would keep the seat warm until Rosebery elected to return. He himself had only modest ambitions, and when he was a member of the Rosebery Government in 1895 he had made a determined effort to have himself nominated for the Speakership, an aim that was frustrated by Rosebery and Harcourt, who regarded him as an indispensable member of that most unhappy of administrations. In the party he was looked on by the brighter spirits as an amiable but undistinguished old war horse who could not hold a candle to the brilliant and dashing Rosebery. The contrast could not have been greater – Rosebery a patrician, a glamorous public figure, the darling of the press; C.B. plain, predictable, unexciting. Yet Rosebery failed because he lacked common sense and was so aloof and enigmatic that people became exasperated. C.B. succeeded precisely because he had common sense in ample measure.

No sooner had C.B. become leader of the Opposition than his party faced the crisis of the Boer War. Rosebery, Asquith, Haldane and Grey – the Liberal Imperialists – supported the war. Other Liberals like Lloyd George, Bryce, Courtney and C. P. Scott strongly opposed it. The party seemed certain to split and then disintegrate. But, vilified and abused by both sides, C.B. held his party together, though in big debates, with only lukewarm support or open mutiny behind him, he was often worsted by Balfour, who led the Conservatives, and who mocked him unmercifully. He himself took a middle position. He voted supplies to the Government, but from the first disliked Chamberlain's policy of bluff, which failed, and the subsequent ineffectual efforts to force the Boers to submit. He also regarded Milner's policy in South Africa as disastrous. In June 1901, influenced by what he had been told by Miss Emily Hobhouse, just back from South Africa, he defied the whole weight of patriotic emotion when he spoke out against farm-burning and the herding of Boer women and children into concentration camps and described these as 'methods of barbarism'. He was denounced with unparalleled fury – a clergyman wrote to him saying, 'Sir, you are a cad, a coward & a murderer, & I hope you will meet a traitor's or a murderer's doom' – but in the end he was seen to be a man of courage, absolute integrity and unwavering principles, and the British public came to respect a man who had been right and had refused to trim his sails to the storm.

The end of the Boer War and Chamberlain's call for protectionist policies in May 1903 helped C.B. to reunite the Liberals. On the issue raised by Chamberlain he had no doubts. 'To dispute free trade, after fifty years' experience of it,' he said, 'is like disputing the law of gravitation.' Chamberlain's proposals he described as wild and reckless. Politically they helped him greatly, for not only did the Liberals unite in opposing them, but the Conservatives were split. C.B., therefore, was able, by patience and skill, to put together a political coalition of the left, the greatest ever constructed in this country. It included Free Trade defectors from the Conservative benches, of whom the most notable was Winston Churchill, the Liberal Imperialists like Asquith and Grey, the radicals like Lloyd George, and the new Labour party. Soon after Balfour had resigned in December 1905 and C.B. was asked to form the first Liberal Government for ten years, Asquith, Grey and Haldane, acting on a plan worked out three months earlier with the connivance of King Edward's private secretary, tried to force C.B. into the Lords, where he would have been Prime Minister in name only. But, supported by Charlotte, he stood firm, and the conspiracy collapsed. All shades of Liberals were represented in the new Government, one of exceptional ability, and in January 1906 C.B. led the Liberals to their greatest electoral triumph, a landslide victory. They won 229 seats from their opponents – Balfour and many of his colleagues lost their seats – and ended with a majority of 222 over the Conservatives and 88 over all other parties combined.

C.B. was in power at last. W. T. Stead now wrote of him:

'He is the hub of the Cabinet. All the spokes centre in him . . . he is the solidest, most seasoned, best balanced of all the Liberals. Sir Henry Campbell-Bannerman is not a flighty rhetorician, neither is he an artful dodger. Still less is he a haughty patrician. He is a plain, honest, respectable, good-humoured Scot, wary and canny beyond most of his countrymen . . . with a cool head and a warm heart. . . .'

But he was sixty-nine, and he was an ailing man with only two years to live. Charlotte, too, was at the end of the road, and after many sufferings she died in 1906. Nevertheless, as Prime Minister C.B. achieved more than many who have been much longer in No. 10. He it was who held his party together when it had achieved power. When Balfour returned to the House he began speaking in the same ironic, supercilious style he had employed so successfully before, but C.B. angrily rebuked him with the words, 'Enough of this foolery', in a four-minute speech which crushed Balfour and was described by Balfour's own sister-in-law as the greatest parliamentary triumph she had ever witnessed. Balfour never baited him again. C.B.'s authority became immense, and it was said of him that 'his premiership was common sense enthroned'.

But it was more than this. As Sir Robert Ensor wrote:

'Radicalism and socialism alike . . . were radiant with sudden hopes of a new heaven and a new earth. No leader not alive to that morning glory could have carried the house with him: and that was where Campbell-Bannerman in his kindly and generous old age gave the parliament an incomparably better start than the efficient but earthbound Asquith could have done.'

In his Cabinet, made up of Imperialists and anti-Imperialists, Home-Rulers and anti-Home-Rulers, Feminists and anti-Feminists, moderate Liberals and extreme Radicals, differences melted away under his benign influence, and he controlled it very effectively. He was much better than his successor, Asquith, at preventing differences between colleagues from getting out of hand. And it was the same story in the House of Commons, where his ascendancy was unchallenged. Grey, who had been one of his fiercest critics, and had despised C.B. as second-rate and intellectually inferior, admitted later that he had not realised that the House of Commons needed to be 'grasped by the heart, and not by the head'. It was said of C.B. that when he got up in the House 'the discontented became reconciled; the rancorous were transformed into geniality; the rebels came back to the fold'.

C.B.'s greatest achievement was the settlement with South Africa, under which the defeated Boer states – the Transvaal and the Orange

Free State – were given full self-government and allowed to elect Boer governments. This was a wise, large-minded and imaginative solution which turned Botha and Smuts into lifelong friends of Britain and resulted in South Africa's coming to Britain's help in two world wars. It also undid the harm done to British standing by the Jameson Raid and the hectoring, aggressive policies of Milner and Joseph Chamberlain in South Africa. It won for Britain a reputation for generosity and magnanimity. Winston Churchill and Lloyd George testified that the inspiration for this settlement came from C.B. himself. He also put an end to Milner's scheme for bringing in Chinese coolie labour to work in the Transvaal mines.

As Prime Minister, C.B. did not hesitate to take his own line, even against his chief colleagues, as he did when he accepted the Labour version of the Trades Disputes Bill, giving trade unions immunity from legal damages, and over the inclusion of domestic servants in the Workmen's Compensation Bill. He helped the first working-class MP's to find their place in the House of Commons. For him, Labour held no terrors.

He was, as Prime Minister, under pressure from his supporters, who had suffered for long years in the wilderness of opposition, to push through with the greatest possible speed a massive programme of social reform. But it soon became apparent that this could not be done while the House of Lords, in which the Conservatives had an overwhelming majority, retained intact its power to block legislation. The clash came when C.B.'s Government introduced an Education Bill designed to rectify the clerical bias of Balfour's 1902 Act, and to abolish religious tests. This was strongly supported by the Nonconformists and as strongly opposed by the Church of England and by Roman Catholics. Balfour, powerless in the House of Commons in face of the great Liberal majority there, said bluntly, when this came to be debated in the House of Commons, that the real discussion must be elsewhere – meaning in the Lords – and did not hesitate to use Conservative power in the Lords to destroy C.B.'s Bill and other Liberal legislation. C.B. described this as 'the treachery of openly calling in the other House to override this House', and said of Balfour's tactics:

'There is one thing I have learned in my parliamentary experience . . . it is not cleverness that pays in the long run. The people of this country are a straightforward people. They like honesty and straightforward-

Lord John Russell, by F. Grant

Edward Stanley, 14th Earl of Derby, by F. R. Say

George Hamilton Gordon, 4th Earl of Aberdeen, by J. Partridge

Henry John Temple, 3rd Viscount Palmerston, by F. Cruickshank

Benjamin Disraeli, Earl of Beaconsfield, by J. E. Millais

Sir Henry Campbell-Bannerman

Herbert Henry Asquith, 1st Earl of Oxford and Asquith, by A. Cluysenaar

David Lloyd George, 1st Earl of Dwyfor, by W. Orpen

Andrew Bonar Law

Stanley Baldwin, 1st Earl of Bewdley, by R. G. Eves

James Ramsay MacDonald, by J. Lavery

(Arthur) Neville Chamberlain, by H. Lamb

Sir Winston Churchill. Photo by Vivienne

Clement Richard, 1st Earl Attlee, by G. Harcourt

Robert Anthony Eden, 1st Earl Avon. Photo by Vivienne.

Maurice Harold Macmillan. Photo by Vivienne

Sir Alec Douglas-Home. Photo by Vivienne

James Harold Wilson. Photo by Vivienne

Edward Richard George Heath. Photo by Vivienne

ness of purpose. They may laugh at it and they may be amused by it, and they may in a sense admire it, but they do not like cleverness. You may be too clever by half. . . .'

Inevitably the two Houses came into conflict. Though it was to be left to Asquith to tackle this constitutional issue, it was C.B. who suggested the way out – a version of the suspensory veto.

As Prime Minister C.B. introduced four Land Bills and was active in the cause of land reform, seeking to arrest the depopulation of the countryside and to increase the number of smallholdings. But on this economics were against him.

In foreign affairs he agreed, though with some apprehension, to the opening of staff talks with the French. He spoke out for parliamentary democracy in Russia after the dissolution of the Duma by the Tsar, approved a tough line against Turkish pretensions in Sinai but supported efforts to achieve international disarmament. Sir Charles Hardinge, Permanent Under-Secretary at the Foreign Office, described him as 'the best Prime Minister that this Office has ever had to deal with'.

He was one of the first to concern himself with the problems of the quality of life, particularly in large cities like his native Glasgow. 'What', he said, 'is all our wealth and learning and the fine flowers of our civilisation and our Constitution and our political theories – what are all these but dust and ashes, if the men and women, on whose labour the whole social fabric is maintained, are doomed to live and die in darkness and misery in the recesses of our great cities?'

C.B. held to the principles of Cobden and Gladstone. He himself defined Liberalism as

'the acknowledgement in practical life of the truth that men are best governed who govern themselves; that the general sense of mankind, if left alone, will make for righteousness; that artificial privileges and restraints upon freedom . . . are hurtful; and that the laws . . . ought to have for their object the securing to every man the best chance he can have of a good and useful life.'

He believed absolutely in free trade and in self-government for those who wanted it, whether they were the Irish or the Boers in South Africa. He had a sure touch when dealing with the difficult problems of relationships between different peoples. He was a moderate on social

[193]

reform and disliked too much state interference, but he greatly preferred small yeomen proprietors to big landowners and he worked all his life to improve the lot of humble people.

Above all, he was one of the nicest and most sensible men ever to lead a political party or to be prime minister. No prime minister was ever more loved by his followers. He was a modest man, who disliked fuss and over-exertion, but he had the wisdom and sagacity of a good family solicitor or of an old shepherd, and he was afraid of no one and nothing.

BIBLIOGRAPHY

Harris, Jose F. and Hazelhurst, Cameron, 'Campbell-Bannerman as Prime Minister', *History* (October, 1970), 360–83

Mackie, J. B., *The Model Member. Sir Henry Campbell-Bannerman, Fifty Years Representative of the Stirling Burghs* (1914)

O'Connor, T. P., *Sir Henry Campbell-Bannerman* (London, 1908)

Spender, J. A., *Life of Rt Hon Sir Henry Campbell-Bannerman G.C.B.* (London, 1923)

Wilson, John, *C.B.: A Life of Sir Henry Campbell-Bannerman* (London, 1973) (contains a full bibliography)

11

H. H. ASQUITH

BY

JOSEPH GRIMOND

Herbert Henry Asquith, 1st Earl of Oxford and Asquith (created 1924), son of Joseph Dixon Asquith, cloth manufacturer of Morley, Yorks. Born 12 September 1852. Educated at the City of London School and Balliol College, Oxford. Married 1887, Helen, who died 1892; four sons and one daughter. Called to the Bar. Entered Parliament as member for East Fife in 1886 and appointed Home Secretary in Gladstone's Government 1892. Married 1894, Margot Tennant, daughter of Sir Charles Tennant, one son and one daughter. Chancellor of the Exchequer under Campbell-Bannerman 1905; Prime Minister on Campbell-Bannerman's resignation 1908. Continued as Prime Minister until 1916, when succeeded by Lloyd George. Leader of the Opposition 1916–18. Defeated in election of 1918, but returned as MP for Paisley 1920, till defeated in 1924, when he accepted an earldom. KG, FRS 1924. Retired from party politics 1926. Died 15 February 1928. Author of The Genesis of War, *1923;* Fifty Years of Parliament, *1926;* Memoirs and Reflection, 1852–1927, *1928;* Occasional Addresses 1893–1916, *1918;* Speeches, *1927.*

H. H. ASQUITH

Asquith was a comparatively poor member of the northern middle class. He was in some measure the leader in a shift of political power from the aristocratic or upper-middle, rather rich, classes to a new stratum. Campbell-Bannerman was from a similar stable but richer. Disraeli was a joker in the prime ministerial pack. Mr Gladstone was Eton. But Mr Asquith was at the City of London School.

If there is any truth in the conventional view of northern Englishmen as hard-headed, hard-working, stalwart and somewhat unimaginative, Mr Asquith was typical. Overlaid with the supposed graces of London and Oxford, yoked to the extravagances of the Scottish Miss Tennant, Asquith's Yorkshireness was apt to be forgotten. He never had much contact with the county of his birth but there must have been some residue of Morley left in the family when D. H. Lawrence after his only meeting with his daughter, Violet, could remark, 'You could see at once she is a Yorkshire lass.'

Equipped with an excellent mind, undistracted by too much curiosity, he sailed from school to Balliol and from Balliol to the Bar, collecting first classes and prizes as he went. The ease with which he dominated the House of Commons, his social life with Margot, the fact that he was Prime Minister longer than anyone in the last 200 years and his disdain of publicity and gimmicks have given him a certain aloof, self-sufficient air in the history books – 'The Last of the Romans', proud, cold and cautious. This seems far from true. He never shrank from risks. He had a difficult start at the Bar. He did not in fact earn much of an income until after his cross-examination of the Manager of *The Times*, before the Parnell inquiry, an incident full of drama in the classical legal tradition. It was indeed a risk to stand for Parliament for a Scottish seat in 1886 when MPs got no salary or expenses. And in later life it was he who sometimes kept Lloyd George's head to the wind when Lloyd George showed signs of quavering before attack. Nor was he cold. He formed deep friendships which were of much importance to him. In his early days he saw much of Haldane, already looking like a character out of Lear, and Grey. Later he had a varied social life and his attachment to Miss Venetia Stanley has attracted a good deal of comment. He was certainly no calculating politician. From his early days his intellect was governed by a warm conviction of the importance of reform, improvement and the maintenance of political standards.

When he first entered Parliament Mr Gladstone was engaged in his titanic struggle to achieve Home Rule for Ireland. The folly and selfishness of his Unionist opponents are almost unbelievable. And the cost of denying Home Rule to Ireland has been heavy. A terrible responsibility lies upon the Tory party. Mr Asquith, as one would expect, was a Home Ruler. He was indeed a deep admirer of Gladstone. And he held his first Cabinet appointment as Home Secretary in Mr Gladstone's Cabinet of 1892. If we are to assess Asquith's place in political history it is worth considering his early days in office. For his political life was all of one piece. He held the view of the conduct of politics with which he started until he finished, and that view owed a considerable amount to Mr Gladstone. But Mr Gladstone was a passionate man, absorbed in various designs from theology to Home Rule. Mr Asquith was never quite so absorbed. Mr Gladstone, however, also had a wide view of the many sides of politics. He had political imagination. He believed in the power and responsibility of politicians. He held to the tradition that politics is more than administration: more than office: more than a career: that it is an education as well as the management of life in all its aspects. The public service is a service to the public and not an opportunity to manipulate their affairs. He certainly believed that politics was about the quality of life – that phrase which has become hackneyed and indeed rather odious by being mouthed by all sorts of publicists who never seek to put it into practice. He was a meticulous administrator. These were also Asquith's qualities. What is not always realised about Mr Gladstone was his astringency. The stories of his final Cabinet when tears flowed freely illustrate this side of his character. He looked round with much disdain and ever afterwards referred to it as the 'blubbering' Cabinet. Asquith too lacked the superficial emotions. Asquith regarded Gladstone as a survivor of the heroic age in English politics. And no summing up of Asquith should forget that he carried on the Gladstone tradition of politics as a heroic and endless engagement in trying to translate moral attitude into practice and raise the standards of aesthetic and intellectual as well as economic life.

The Home Secretary's position in any government is fraught with danger. The House of Commons quickly latches on to personal cases. The issues of the Home Office too are avidly seized on by the press. They are often of genuine difficulty: the Home Secretary is the minister who has to face at first hand moral claims and counter claims. Cases blow up from a clear sky. Further, the Home Secretary now has to temper adherence to the dogma of his party with a regard for what is generally acceptable. Asquith can claim some credit for this development. Politics is an art of complexity and many facets. The reconciliation of claims by reference to some system of values is the essence of the politician's task and in no office is it more difficult or more necessary than in the Home Office. Sometimes a Home Secretary must risk putting his colleagues in political jeopardy. Sometimes he has to ensure that he does not seem to browbeat the public against its own judgement. Asquith was adept in finding the right course. He has left behind a tradition which persists to this day.

The political events of the decade between the fall of Lord Rosebery's Government in 1894 and his accession to office again as Chancellor of the Exchequer in Campbell-Bannerman's Government of 1905 – Ireland, the House of Lords, the South African war – helped to form the statesman from the politician in Asquith. Were this a biography, Asquith's attitude to these problems would need to be dealt with at some length. But as the main theme of this book is the contribution of our prime ministers to British political history these topics can largely be discussed in relation to his tenure of office. A non-political event that took place while Rosebery was still Prime Minister on 10 May 1894 must however be mentioned. In a scene of some splendour Asquith married Margot Tennant. The register was signed by four prime ministers, past, present or to be. The streets were crowded. Whether one thinks that Asquith's advent to Downing Street opened a new age or was the crowning achievement of the old regime – I myself will argue that he was one of the crucial links in our history ensuring continuity but sowing the seeds which are still flowering today – certainly Margot was a new type of prime minister's wife. Lady Melbourne had glamour, Lady Campbell-Bannerman had influence. Margot contributed new extrovert qualities. Above all, she had vitality which had a streak of Edwardian vulgarity but was felt directly and pervasively by everyone she met. Hunting, smart Edwardian life, its corollary of fundamental religion (had she not prayed in a railway carriage with General Booth?) and an originality of mind which made her a successful hostess to all sorts of writers, painters and playwrights, combined to make her a personality of her own. Downing Street under the Asquiths was the centre of a blend of official and personal entertaining hardly seen again until the White House under Kennedy. How much Margot affected Asquith's political judgement I find it difficult to tell. Little, I think. I doubt if she had fixed political opinions. Her likes and dislikes were strong and strikingly expressed – of Lloyd George, 'cannot see a belt without hitting below it'; or, in a less biting moment, 'I saw Linky Cecil in the Park this morning riding his horse like a string of opinions'. But she was mercurial and generous and whether the wounds their repetition must have inflicted went on to fester I do not know.

Her style of life cannot have made relations with some wings of the Liberal tradition at all easy. On the other hand, warm and appreciative letters from her to Lloyd George exist. However, there she was to remain, extravagant ('I hope to leave nothing but debts'), exhausting (appalling accounts have come down of the deafening noise in the dining-room of the Wharf at Sutton Courtney), uninhibited, not beautiful ('I have no face, only two profiles clapped together'), but tigerishly loyal and a powerful influence on all near her.

It is a great temptation to write about Campbell-Bannerman, one of the most attractive British politicians. Nor indeed would it be wholly irrelevant to an assessment of Asquith, for though they were never close friends, indeed had serious political disagreements and differed in social and political style, yet it was Campbell-Bannerman who started the great Liberal era of 1905–14 which must be associated for ever with Asquith's name.

Asquith became Chancellor in Campbell-Bannerman's Government of 1905. In Asquith's case the importance of the Chancellorship was enhanced as he was deputy leader to a prime minister who was ill, idolent, and in any case had no Oxford Union inclination to make speeches in the House of Commons.

Asquith's Budgets are important in fiscal history. He first differentiated between earned and unearned income. And it was under him that super-tax was first accepted in principle though implemented when Lloyd George was Chancellor. I have said that I regard Asquith as a crucial and seminal link in political history. As Home Secretary this had been more in changing the style of that office than in legislation (though he introduced a moderately important Factory Act), but as Chancellor he started a substantive move forward. He took an initiative that projected the State into what was for Britain an entirely new role. I refer of course to the foundation of the social services. Never again after Asquith could any government disclaim responsibility for the troubles of the poor or unfortunate. The notion that the business of the State was to hold the ring so that individuals would make their own way and provide for their old age by their own exertions was killed. So was the belief that the *laissez-faire* system could meet all economic needs except for a small area such as refuse collection where the profit motive was hardly enough. And indeed a great breach was made in the intellectual boundaries that surrounded the nineteenth-century State. This took many forms. It led to a new conception of the State as a positive instrument changing society and going far beyond law and order, defence and the pursuit of national interests. It led to a new view of the wealth and capabilities of the State. It challenged the rights of the upper classes. And it stimulated a new type of democracy. As the State became more and more involved in their pensions, unemployment pay, the support of their constituency industries and the provision of funds for their local authorities, MPs could no longer even pretend with J. S. Mill that constituency or private interests were not their affair. In the long term Asquith's initiative changed the focus of government. It slanted it away from foreign affairs and the aggrandisement of the state in the eighteenth-century sense. It slanted it away even from personal liberty, the maintenance of the Constitution and the extension of the franchise which had occupied the nineteenth century.

Asquith started these moves. I am not saying that this leap forward was unique to Britain. Bismarck might well claim to be the world founder of the Welfare State. But in Britain it was started not as an extension of a paternalist or collectivist philosophy, but within the democratic framework by someone who never doubted that framework. Asquith gave this new development its particularly British qualities. The legitimacy of British democratic progress was never questioned or broken by Asquith. No political changes can be pinpointed to one year, one event, or one man. The Factory Acts had already breached the doctrine of *laissez-faire*. They imposed state intervention in new fields. But they were negative. In a sense they were still 'holding the ring' – an extension of the legal framework. The whole conception of the joint stock company was an interference in economic affairs, but again not a positive use of the State's wealth and power to help certain individuals. Nor, finally, am I saying that the changes for which Asquith was primarily responsible happened all at once. Far from it. They have been continued by the Health Service, by the family incomes supplement. They are still happening, that is what makes them so important.

As with many great reforms the actual change now seems very small. It was a non-contributory old age pension of 5 shillings a week for those over seventy whose total income did not exceed 10 shillings. Even allowing for the fact that the pound was perhaps ten times as valuable as it is today, it does not seem now an act of cataclysmic extravagance. But it did to Asquith's conservative contemporaries. And it is one of the few legislative changes long remembered with gratitude by several generations of recipients. Even now someone occasionally remembers that the Liberals brought in the old age pension.

This first step towards the Welfare State was to be followed by unemployment insurance and the employment exchanges when Lloyd George was Chancellor and Asquith Prime Minister.

The next great matter with which Asquith had to deal was the constitutional question of the relationship between the Commons and the Lords. Here too so accustomed have we grown to a surviving but impotent House of Lords, so astonishingly indefensible and indeed disastrous does the behaviour of the Tories of Asquith's day now appear, that perhaps we fail to appreciate what a difficult matter it was at the time. We also fail to appreciate how well Asquith handled it. Great damage was done to Ireland and to Britain by the rejection of useful Bills such as the Education Bill of 1906 and the Licensing Bill of 1908. But if the Lords had had their way the situation might have been much worse. Or if more radical solutions had been found, though I personally believe they would have been justified, we might have lost both a second chamber and that 'legitimacy' which alone of major European governments the government of Britain can now claim. On balance I believe Asquith was too tolerant. But I do not underestimate the dangers and threats of active treason which he faced. Nor do I believe that the majority even of liberal opinion would then or now have welcomed the more drastic solution of abolition of the second chamber.

The obstruction of the House of Lords had started long before Asquith became Prime Minister. As has been said, the Lords had thrown out Gladstone's Home Rule Bills. Their motives were a mixture of obscurantism, selfishness and political expediency. For anxiety about the general good there was little evidence. They threw out the Education Bill, but not the Trades Disputes Bill because to have done so might have harmed the Tory party. The bigoted stupidity of the Tory Lords reached its apex when they threw out Lloyd George's Budget of 1909.

Britain has no written Constitution. But her wisest statesmen have had a strong constitutional sense. The strongest element in this sense has been that British government is an affair of limits and balances. The minister as well as the subject is under an impartial law. Not only must the Government respect the law as it stands at any moment; in changing it they must have regard to prescriptive rights and the organic nature of British society as well as natural justice or moral imperatives. Further, British parliamentary government is not a fully-fledged system of positive participatory democracy. Indeed it is now and was more so in Asquith's day a system dependent upon the leadership of an executive, not directly elected but subject to criticism and control by a House of Commons and a House of Lords with a largely negative but important role. These Houses had to be argued with and convinced. In Asquith's day they contained many more men of independence with a position of their own in politics not dependent on the party machine. More MPs were less concerned to achieve some office. Ministers remained much longer in the Commons listening to debates than they do now. Roy Jenkins quotes Harcourt as saying, 'When I am ill I am in bed, when I am well I am in the House of Commons.' The constitutional doctrine was strong: stronger and more pervasive perhaps than in a country where it is laid down in a document and protected only by a court of law or a two-thirds majority. It was imbedded in the hearts and heads of the best of those who ran the system. Asquith knew that populism was not the British type of democracy. And he consciously approved of the British way of doing things as giving stability and guaranteeing change with protection of personal freedom and the rights of minorities.

The breaking-point came over the Budget of 1909. It was against every constitutional convention for the peers to reject the Finance Bill. But they did. Parliament, or rather the non-elected wing of Parliament, refused the Government the financial means to run the country. The Government could not carry on in these circumstances. Parliament was dissolved. At the general election the Liberals gained a small majority over the Tories alone and a large one counting Labour and the Irish Nationalists. The issue was now threefold. The need to pass the Budget. The need to curb the House of Lords. The possibility of reforming it.

All these issues concerned the position of the Crown. It is not my business to write a history of this matter. Asquith, showing consummate diplomacy both towards the King and the Irish, who were in some respects restive, forced the Tories to accept the Budget. But the need to curb the Lords remained. Democratic government could not continue so long as the Lords behaved as they had behaved for the last twenty years. But at this point Edward VII died and these most trying constitutional matters came before a new and inexperienced king. Again Asquith showed almost too much forbearance. He negotiated with the Tory leaders. He made every effort to keep the King out of the controversy. But in the last resort he was firm. The creation of peers was promised and the House of Lords lost its powers to frustrate a Commons majority.

Not only was this a constitutional crisis important in itself in the history of our country; it established the powers of the Lords for fifty years. And it set a precedent in how in Britain constitutional crises should be tackled. It was not a precedent always followed. It was not followed by Lloyd George's Government over Ireland. But it has to some extent, and allowing for different circumstances, been followed by Baldwin over the Abdication and Mr Whitelaw over Ulster. Both showed a reluctance to use the steam-roller of a Commons majority: both negotiated patiently: each had a clear purpose to which he adhered.

It may be convenient at this point to look at Asquith's treatment of the Labour party. The Liberal party in the early years of the century deliberately made room for the Labour party. An attitude very different from that of late taken by the present Labour party to the Liberals. The small and insecure Labour party of the first decade of the century could probably have been strangled at birth by the Liberals. But Liberals such as Asquith believed that all shades of opinion had their rights to representation. The Labour vote represented a part, be it a small part, of the electorate. It should be represented in the House of Commons. His own son, Raymond, was running in harness with a Labour candidate for the double member constituency of Derby when he was killed. It is interesting to compare Asquith's attitude with that of Lloyd George. From 1910 Lloyd George from time to time toyed with the idea of a coalition with the Tories – and of course never achieved office without seeking most of his support from the Tories. There was nothing particularly secret in his moves. But it is interesting that he never seems to have sensed the value of close co-operation with Labour or the value of close Liberal-Labour co-operation.

It was Asquith who in 1923 decided that there should be the first Labour Government. He held the balance of power with the considerable number of 158 Liberal seats as against 191 Labour and 285 Tories. He could have kept the Tories in office, taken office himself or forced some sort of coalition. But to him it seemed clear that once the Tories retired the next call must go to Labour. Their advent was viewed with horror by many people who appealed to Asquith for succour. As usual he was neither frightened nor unsure. He saw all too well that constitutional propriety demanded that the King should call upon Ramsay MacDonald. He believed too that nothing would be more likely to embitter Labour supporters and do irremediable damage to the Constitution and the nation than the feeling that they had been excluded from office by a coalition of the old guard. Asquith had seen Ireland lost by the fear and short-sightedness of the Tories, he was not to repeat their mistake.

Ireland was indeed another of the great issues of the 1910 Parliament. It was an issue that Asquith failed to bring to a successful conclusion owing to the outbreak of war. But again he showed his patience, his firmness and his determination to stick to the rational and radical course. Howled down by the Tories led by Hugh Cecil, faced with treason in the Army, encouraged by the ineffably treacherous Sir Henry Wilson and rebellion in Ulster, he drove steadily to the conclusion he reached in 1914, which could have saved Ireland from the disasters and tragedies that continue to this day.

By 1914 Asquith and Redmond had a firm agreement which would have given Ireland all she wanted including in the longer term unity with Ulster. The Tories and the IRA, the two evil geniuses of Irish history, made that impossible. When the Treaty came the Irish got less than Asquith had won for them. And they got it in circumstances that have left a fatal residue to this day.

The other activity in Asquith's political career which I have left to the last, for it is the one aim upon which his reputation has largely suffered, is the 1914–18 war. His conduct of military affairs has not the seminal importance of the founding of the Welfare State which, as I have claimed, along with other developments of policy led to long-term results in the conduct of British affairs. But it was of course of immense importance in the history of Britain.

The reputation of wartime leaders is always subject to prejudice. Ultimate success ensures praise. Reputations are founded on the most curious premises. Some people seem to believe that we should have surrendered in the last war had it not been for Churchill. To me it is inconceivable that Britain would have folded up without a fight in 1940 whoever led us. It is even more inconceivable that once America and Russia were in the war the allies could have lost. This does not mean that Churchill was not a great war leader. But it does mean that we should not have lost the war without him.

Churchill started with the advantage of clean hands. He was not responsible for the lack of preparation for a war. In Asquith's case the curious thing is that he was not driven from office because he took the country into war unprepared as Chamberlain did. On the contrary, it has never gone better prepared into a war. If the direct credit for this belongs to Haldane, Asquith is certainly entitled to some share in it and the ultimate responsibility for it was his.

Asquith was not guilty of bad timing and indecision as Chamberlain was over Norway. Nor indeed was he forced into coalition and then out of office through conspicuous military failings or lack of munitions. The Dardanelles failure certainly was a main cause of the coalition. But the prime author was of course Churchill.

As for the aftermath of his resignation, the great mistakes and disasters of the war such as the appointment of Nivelle and the disaster of the Chemin des Dames and Passchendaele took place when Lloyd George was Prime Minister. The evidence shows that Asquith was a competent, steadfast war Prime Minister who on many occasions showed his qualities of loyalty, good judgement and determination. Why was he evicted?

Perhaps whoever is in the saddle at the beginning of a war is unlikely to last it out. But to me the qualities that led to his undoing had little to do with the war. He was intellectually somewhat arrogant. He neither appreciated such men as Bonar Law nor made much effort to understand them. He had curious flaws in his judgements about people. Though he sometimes realised his superficiality, to the end he liked and admired Balfour, a disastrous politician and frequently devious in his dealings with Asquith. However dedicated he was to his duties as Prime Minister, Asquith seems to have given the impression of not being sufficiently involved. This impression crops up again and again in letters. His own letters to Venetia Stanley show by modern standards a curious commentary on his outlook. He was no hypocrite and no showman. He despised the despicable press that hounded him. No doubt too he was tired. It is difficult for anyone today to appreciate the appalling strain of the First World War. Asquith lost one son and had one badly wounded. Bonar Law lost two sons.

Asquith was at once a link and a new departure. He carried in his respect for reason, the Constitution and Parliament the great nineteenth-century traditions of Gladstone. He had a traditional distrust of demagogy. He loathed the type of administration made up of political adventurers and 'hard-faced men who had done well out of the war', such as Lloyd George was content to lead. Had he been there, the peace treaty would have been more far-sighted. He would never have engaged in Lloyd George's Eastern Mediterranean goings-on. Yet, as I have said, he started a major new political departure which set Britain on a new course into the twentieth century. That our parliamentary system survived the aftermath of the First World War and absorbed the rise of the Labour party, that Liberal values still dominate us and discussions, however distorted by appeals to self-interest and the mass media, are still guides of the political system, is largely due to the Asquith tradition.

I have mentioned that under the Asquiths 10 Downing Street became a centre for official and unofficial entertaining of artists and all sorts of people distinguished outside politics. It is true that most of these came from one social set. But it was a wide and talented set. Asquith was subjected to a campaign of vilification and slander unequalled in our history. The main protagonists were such Tories as the Duchess of Sutherland, the top of the so-called aristocracy and the press. He was also accused of all manner of perversion by Lord Alfred Douglas because he befriended the friends of Oscar Wilde. This should be recalled not only to show the incredible behaviour of the British Conservative upper classes and the difficulties under which the left operates in this country (a far higher standard is expected of it than of the right) but also because an important part of Asquith's style as Prime Minister was his contact with circles outside politics. He continued the Gladstonian tradition of addressing public meetings. In his constituency he would explain government policies to meetings in towns as small as Ladybank. And, as he himself said, he found his audiences of railwaymen and farm labourers well informed, appreciative and critical. (A good point would be greeted with murmurs of 'Weel turned, Asquith, weel turned'.)

As Prime Minister he continued to see people who were neither in search of favours, nor his hosts nor guests in an official capacity. He never, I think, had a government car. He could, therefore, at least see the taximeter ticking up the cost. Part of the present yawning gap between politicians and the public is due to the insulation of ministers from ordinary life. They do not notice rising prices or the breakdown of public services as they are wafted in their official cars from their official residences to their well-appointed offices. They lunch and dine in the company of their kind or their clients. It is no matter for wonder, therefore, that the gap between the government and the governed is a major feature of our time. One cannot imagine Asquith tape-recording conversations or employing a personal bodyguard of public relations officers like a renaissance bravo. Nor would he have tolerated the bureaucratic outlook. Too many of those in charge of our affairs seem primarily concerned with their professional advancement. More and more is the public service associated with the reduction of individuality to a uniformity of methods and outlook. Bureaucracy aims at the lowest common denominator. Asquith viewed politics as essentially bound up with some pursuit of individuality and excellence. Democracy to him was not the grey imposition of bureaucratic fashion from above.

For eight and a half years Asquith presided with complete authority over the most brilliant Cabinet of all time. He was an accomplished chairman, a masterly expositor and loyal to the point of rashness. In all this, in his contact with a fairly large slice of ordinary life, in his loyalty and steadfastness and his respect for the proprieties of the Constitution, the seeds sown by his premiership did not immediately bear fruit. But in the long run they have done. We face new dangers today from faceless men and the worship of technology but the endurance of our standards of public life for half a century is a continuing reminder of Asquith's service to the British people.

BIBLIOGRAPHY

Asquith, H. H., *Memories and Reflections*, 1852–1927, 2 vols. (London, 1928); *Speeches*, 1887–1926 (London, 1927)
Jenkins, Roy, *Asquith* (London, 1964)
Spender, J. A., and Asquith, C., *Life of Lord Oxford & Asquith*, 2 vols. (London, 1932)

12

DAVID LLOYD GEORGE

BY

PETER LOWE

David Lloyd George, created (1945) Earl Lloyd-George of Dwyfor
and Viscount Gwynedd of Dwyfor. Born 17 January 1863.
Educated Llanystumdwy, near Criccieth, by his uncle. Articled to a
solicitor at Portmadoc, 1879. Married (1) 1888 Margaret Owen;
two sons, three daughters, (2) 1943 Frances Louise Stevenson.
MP (Caernarvon Boroughs) 1890–1945. Identified with Welsh
nationalism 1894–96. Opposed Joseph Chamberlain and Unionist
Government 1899–1902. President of the Board of Trade under
Campbell-Bannerman 1905; Chancellor of the Exchequer under
Asquith 1908; introduced the 'Peoples Budget' 1909; introduced
the National Insurance Act 1911; Minister of Munitions 1915;
Secretary of State for War 1916; Prime Minister, Coalition
Government 1916–18 and 1918–22; Representation of the People
Act 1918; Fisher Education Act 1918; participated in the Paris
Peace Conference 1919; Irish settlement 1921; resigned the
Premiership 1922 and rejoined the Liberal Party 1923; Liberal
leader 1926 (resigned 1931); leader of the Independent Liberals
1931–45; resigned as MP 1945 and died 26 March same year.
Author of War Memoirs *(6 vols), 1933–36;* The Truth about
the Peace Treaties, *1938.*

DAVID LLOYD GEORGE

David Lloyd George was perhaps the most unconventional of all British prime ministers in his background, character, outlook and policies. There was a highly adventurous, buccaneering quality about his six years in the premiership, between December 1916 and October 1922. Contemporaries were entranced, dazzled, astounded, impressed, alarmed and shocked by his behaviour and attitudes. One feature was certain: Lloyd George could never be ignored. He had emerged as a prominent and vociferous politician at the time of the South African war and continued to be respected or feared until the Second World War. Although he was born in Manchester, Lloyd George was brought up in rural Wales in humble circumstances and his Welsh background was vitally important in his life; he always spoke Welsh in his family circle and would even discuss high policy in Welsh on occasion, as with the deputy secretary of the Cabinet, Thomas Jones. Lloyd George was devoted to Wales; while he rose to become a statesman of world stature, he never forgot his homeland and frequently returned there for relaxation. The deep influence of his early years in rural, Nonconformist Wales was revealed in his radicalism, which was conditioned by his dislike of landowners and inherited wealth; he did not fully comprehend urban radicalism and the more extreme manifestations of socialism. As a young man, he was ruthlessly determined to advance his career. His attitude is illustrated in one of his early letters to his future wife:

'My supreme idea is to get on. To this idea I shall sacrifice everything – except I trust honesty. I am prepared to thrust even love itself under the wheels of my Juggernaut, if it obstructs the way. . . . Believe me – & may Heaven attest the truth of my statement – my love for you is sincere & strong. In this I never waver. But I must not forget that I have a purpose in life. And however painful the sacrifice I may have to make to attain this ambition I must not flinch – otherwise success will be remote indeed. . . .'[1]

[1] K. O. Morgan (ed.), *Lloyd George: Family Letters 1885–1936* (Cardiff and London, 1973), p. 14, undated letter, probably 1885, Lloyd George to Margaret Owen.

He was elected to Parliament in 1890 as Liberal Member for Caernarvon Boroughs, the constituency he represented continuously until shortly before his death in 1945. As a politician Lloyd George was motivated by a fierce concern for ordinary people and a determination to do all he could to assist them in improving the conditions of their lives. He emerged as the leader of the Radical wing of the Liberal party before 1914 and gave a powerful stimulus to the social policies of the Liberal governments. In the practice of politics, Lloyd George was mercurial, vocal, tenacious and flexible. While he believed that confrontation was sometimes necessary, he was concerned with making tangible progress and would exploit any opportunity to secure a realistic compromise.[2] He earned a reputation for brilliance as a political tactician including an extreme deviousness; he was undeniably devious but the extent was often exaggerated.

Lloyd George's personal life was as complex as his political career. He married Margaret Owen, daughter of a Welsh farmer, in 1888; they had five children and remained married until her death in 1941. Publicly he preserved the image of the respectable family man; he had numerous affairs with women, however, and from 1912 a permanent mistress, his attractive and intelligent private secretary, Frances Stevenson, with whom he lived whenever he could and by whom he had a daughter. Yet he regarded his wife with genuine affection and she helped him in his political campaigns, on occasion undertaking a heavy programme of speeches, as in the 1918 general election and in the important Cardiganshire by-election in 1921. Understandably she resented his affairs but Lloyd George wrote to his wife, in a revealing passage, that this was a facet of his nature which had to be accepted:

You say I have my weakness. So has anyone that ever lived & the greater the man the greater the weakness. It is only insipid, wishy washy fellows that have no weaknesses. . . .

You must make allowances for the waywardness & wildness of a man of my type. What if I were drunk as well? I can give you two samples you know of both the weaknesses in one man & the wives do their best under those conditions. What about Asquith & Birkenhead? I

2 Two examples before 1914 being his attempts to settle the conflict involving the Welsh Church in 1895 and his proposal for a coalition government with the Unionists during the constitutional crisis in 1910, as noted by K. O. Morgan, 'Lloyd George's Premiership: A Study in Prime Ministerial Government', *Historical Journal* xiii, 1 (1970), 131–2.

could tell you stories of both – women & wine. Believe me hen gariad [old darling]. I am at bottom as fond of you as ever. . . .[3]

Frances Stevenson's deep feeling for Lloyd George is revealed in the following extract from her diary:

'We went down to Walton H. on Saturday afternoon (21 April) & had a perfect weekend. I do not think that we have ever loved each other so much. D. says that ours is a love that comes to very few people and I wonder more & more at the beauty & happiness of it. It is a thing that nothing but death can harm, and even death has no terrors for me now, for D. asked me yesterday if I would come with him when he went. He begged me not to stay behind, but for both of us to go together, and I promised him to do so, unless I have any children of his to claim me. So, I am not afraid now of the misery if D. is taken away, for then I shall go too & his end will be my end, and until then everything is happiness, if our love stays. I hope by any chance I shall not go first, for I know his misery would be great, and he could not leave his work, which is a great one. I am so happy now that we have decided this, for sometimes my heart would stop beating with terror at the thought of life without D.'[4]

It is in some respects surprising that his personal life did not result in a major scandal, given the number of his enemies and the extent to which the British public expected moral rectitude in its leaders.

Lloyd George became Prime Minister at the end of 1916 owing to the lack of success in Britain's war effort and to the bankruptcy of the Asquith Coalition. While Asquith had some achievements to his credit, notably in helping to create the relative unity with which Great Britain entered the war in 1914, he had failed in all essentials as a war leader. He did not inspire confidence or provide decisive leadership; by the latter months of 1916 it was widely felt in Parliament and in the country that change was necessary. Lloyd George was the one member of the Coalition whose standing in the country had risen steadily, principally because of his outstanding success in developing the ministry of munitions in 1915–16. As Frances Stevenson noted in her diary in early

[3] Morgan, p. 203, Lloyd George to his wife, 24 July 1924.
[4] A. J. P. Taylor (ed.), *Lloyd George: A Diary by Frances Stevenson* (London, 1971), p. 153, diary entry for 23 April 1917.

December 1916, there was a widespread faith in Lloyd George throughout the country and the nation would accept him as a virtual dictator.[5] Many politicians disliked and distrusted him but they, too, were forced to admit that the Government could not continue as it was. Lloyd George challenged Asquith directly by demanding a drastic reform of the Government's war-making machinery so as to eliminate the unwieldy large Cabinet, substituting a small committee in its place, and aiming to relegate Asquith to a subordinate position, although he would remain Prime Minister. After initial vacillation, Asquith declined to accept Lloyd George's conditions and resigned as Prime Minister; he most probably but mistakenly believed that Lloyd George would be unable to form a government.[6]

The major political difficulty facing Lloyd George when he assumed office was that he did not lead a political party. It is true that MacDonald in 1931 and Churchill in 1940 were in a similar position but MacDonald had led the Labour party for a considerable period and Churchill soon inherited the Conservative leadership after Neville Chamberlain's resignation. Throughout his premiership, Lloyd George lacked the support of a powerful political party of his own; he possessed the allegiance of the amorphous Coalition Liberals but depended for survival on the loyalty of the Unionists (Conservatives), as was made brutally clear by the circumstances of his fall from power in 1922. He appealed to many Unionist backbenchers, if not their leaders, in 1916 because he exemplified a ruthless, determined approach to waging war, in itself a recognition of the importance of mobilising all the resources of the country regardless of the infringements on individual liberty. Of the situation when he formed his Government he wrote in his memoirs:

'Had there been a united party behind me which, with dependable allies, would have commanded in the House of Commons a majority solid and large enough to carry me through the inevitable vicissitudes of evil as well as good tidings for a period of two years and more, I should have had a freer, a wider and a more promising choice. I could then have secured a more homogeneous form of Government and a Government

[5] Taylor, op. cit., p. 132, diary entry of 5 December 1916.
[6] For a discussion of Lloyd George's record in the war before he became Prime Minister, including an assessment of the complicated events in November–December 1916, see P. Lowe, 'The Rise to the Premiership, 1914–16', in A. J. P. Taylor (ed.), *Lloyd George: Twelve Essays* (London, 1971), pp. 95–133.

more sympathetic to the War policy in which I believed. I was anxious to change the men and methods which were too much associated with old war direction.'[7]

He at once abolished the old full Cabinet and set up a small War Cabinet of five members, which met almost daily and continued to function until late in 1919. In addition, he established a Cabinet secretariat to service the numerous requirements of the War Cabinet. This was a development of fundamental importance constitutionally and, more immediately, it achieved much improved efficiency in the political organisation of war. Previously there had been no official minutes of Cabinet meetings, the only record being the prime minister's frequently cursory letters to the monarch. The haphazard growth of the Committee of Imperial Defence provided the nucleus of a secretariat. The secretary of the CID, Sir Maurice Hankey, who kept the minutes of the War Committee which had functioned under Asquith, took command of the Cabinet secretariat and built it into a formidable body.[8] Lloyd George set up a complementary personal secretariat of his own, known or derided as the 'Garden suburb'. Unlike the Cabinet secretariat, which survived as an autonomous body as a result of Hankey's strenuous efforts after Lloyd George's resignation, the 'Garden suburb' disappeared in 1922. The value of the War Cabinet and the Cabinet secretariat was that they constituted an efficient means of formulating high policy; sub-committees of the War Cabinet were often formed to examine various issues. The Prime Minister was not particularly consistent or predictable in his handling of the War Cabinet. He summoned meetings whenever he desired them, sometimes with inadequate notice, or arbitrarily altered the schedule; this annoyed Hankey, who disliked having to change his meticulous arrangements.[9] Lloyd George also held meetings at breakfast, which did not suit some who attended. His actions reflected his dislike of convention and his preference for discussing issues verbally rather than in writing. Despite Lloyd George's erratic

[7] D. Lloyd George, *War Memoirs of David Lloyd George* (2 vols, London, 1938), i, 620.

[8] For the development of the secretariat and Hankey's role see the admirable biography by S. Roskill, *Hankey: Man of Secrets*, vols i–ii (London, 1970–2).

[9] For the views of Lloyd George's colleagues and officials on the functioning of the War Cabinet, see T. Wilson (ed.), *The Political Diaries of C. P. Scott, 1911–28* (London, 1971), pp. 277–9; K. Middlemas (ed.), *Thomas Jones: Whitehall Diary* (3 vols, 1969–71), i, 31; and Roskill, op. cit., i, 371, 618, 621 and ii, 32–4, 148.

behaviour, there was no doubt that the Government was infinitely more dynamic and efficient. Business was conducted more thoroughly and information reached the War Cabinet more rapidly. Lloyd George possessed immense energy and stimulated the entire governmental machine. Unlike Asquith, he was not afraid to take decisions; the calibre of leadership was radically different. After the war, the pressure from his colleagues eventually brought about a reversion to the traditional Cabinet in October 1919; Lloyd George pondered the possibility of having a medium-size Cabinet of twelve members but Hankey emphasised the need to retain the loyalty of all his colleagues, which could only be attained through a large Cabinet.[10] The full Cabinet returned but brief minutes, essentially comprising conclusions, were kept.[11] Lloyd George's premiership was, therefore, of fundamental significance in constitutional terms for the adoption of new methods of organising the central conduct of government business. As in other respects, he gave the powerful impetus that led British politics and government away from the lingering connections with the nineteenth century into the twentieth century.

When it came to the wider issue of waging the war, Lloyd George's achievements are best revealed in his innovatory policy of bringing new blood into Whitehall and in the reform of the Navy; he was conspicuously unsuccessful at gaining effective control of the Army. As Minister of Munitions, he had persuaded various businessmen to enter Whitehall and contribute their specialised knowledge to improving production; as Prime Minister, he extended this trend to other areas. The appointment of Sir Joseph Maclay as Shipping Controller was the earliest example, Maclay being appointed before his ministry had been created.[12] The appointment of Sir Eric Geddes as Controller of the Navy (and later First Lord of the Admiralty) and of Lord Rhondda as Food Controller were other examples.[13] These appointments were sometimes resented, not least by military and naval personnel, but were usually successful, the one notable disappointment being Neville Chamberlain in the admittedly difficult role of Director of National Service.[14]

[10] Roskill, ii, 127.
[11] Roskill, ii, 106.
[12] Lloyd George, *War Memoirs*, i, 726.
[13] ibid., i, 734, 791. Rhondda (D. A. Thomas) was a former politician and colleague of the Prime Minister.
[14] ibid., i, 809–12.

Within the armed forces, Lloyd George's difficulties in securing changes in strategy stemmed from the independent authority enjoyed by the commanders and from his own tenuous position as Prime Minister. He had long been critical of the British military leaders in particular and of their obstinate belief in a breakthrough on the Western Front, despite the futility of their previous tactics. In 1915–16 he had advocated a campaign in the East, designed to help Russia and eliminate Austria-Hungary or Turkey. While the concept was not simple to implement successfully, as the misfortunes in the Dardanelles demonstrated, the generals were not in the least inclined to favour such ideas: they felt that civilian politicians were not properly equipped to assess strategical matters and regarded the more vociferous of them, such as Lloyd George, with thinly disguised contempt. Lloyd George believed that it was essential to attain improved co-ordination between the allied armies and to avoid further huge casualties in pointless bloody offensives. It was tragically ironic that his chief failure lay in this sphere and that the horrors of the offensive in Flanders in 1917 occurred while he was Prime Minister. He disliked Sir Douglas Haig, the Commander-in-Chief in France, but could not remove him. Haig was popular with King George V: more significantly, he was popular with the Unionists, so that it was politically impossible to remove him provided Haig kept his political nerve and continued to resist Lloyd George's attempts to undermine his power. Sir William Robertson, Chief of the Imperial General Staff, was another implacable opponent of the Prime Minister. While Lloyd George would dearly have liked to replace Haig, he ruefully conceded in his memoirs that there was probably no one who was superior to Haig.[15] He was, however, successful in removing Robertson in February 1918 and replaced him with Sir Henry Wilson. The alternative to replacing Haig was to improve co-operation with the French and subordinate him to the French generals, whom Lloyd George believed to be more capable. This was the policy he pursued, with limited success, in 1917 and 1918. Lloyd George was captivated by General Nivelle early in 1917 and thought he had the solution that would produce a victorious offensive in France. Nivelle's offensive proved a miserable failure and allowed Haig the opportunity to urge his own ideas for an attack in Flanders in consequence. Haig was extraordinarily optimistic on the chances of success; Lloyd George reluctantly

[15] *War Memoirs*, ii, 1366. On reflection, he thought that the Australian, Sir John Monash, might have been superior (ibid., ii, 2016).

assented, since he was unable to enforce an alternative strategy.[16] The campaign to which the name 'Passchendaele' is attached became a nightmare of carnage and mud, ending as a battle of attrition that failed at tremendous cost. To a large extent, Lloyd George was a prisoner of the military. There were no dramatic new initiatives in military policy. His most concrete advance was in securing the appointment of Foch as Supreme Allied Commander in April 1918 but Foch's power was limited; Haig survived as British Commander until the end of the war. Lloyd George did not seemingly possess any profound strategical insight but had he possessed a freer hand he would certainly have terminated the policy of attrition, for he was never one to adhere to policies that had manifestly failed.

With the Navy, Lloyd George imposed his authority to greater effect. The gravest problem at sea was the extent of merchant shipping losses in 1916–17 resulting from the German submarine onslaught in the Atlantic. Neither the Admiralty nor the Board of Trade had any solution to the problem. Unless the situation was speedily remedied in 1917, Britain would be driven to surrender by starvation and shortage of raw materials. The First Lord of the Admiralty, Sir Edward Carson, had been a close political ally of Lloyd George in 1916; once in office, he became extremely negative and supported the Admirals without question. The obvious solutions to the vast shipping losses were to organise shipping more tightly, so as to eliminate the carrying of commodities that were not urgently required, and arrange for ships to travel in convoys. Sir Joseph Maclay worked to secure the former objective. The Admiralty was at first hostile to convoys, holding that they would multiply and not reduce losses owing to the difficulty of ensuring necessary co-operation from merchant captains and because of the volume of shipping involved. Lloyd George descended on the Admiralty in person in April 1917 and, according to his own account, insisted on the adoption of convoys. This account has been challenged as too colourful and exaggerated: the Admiralty had reluctantly come round to the view that convoys were necessary and were apparently prepared to adopt them before Lloyd George's famous visit.[17] However, it can-

---

[16] ibid., ii, 1247–1364 for Lloyd George's acrid discussion of the Flanders offensive and his mordant criticisms of the British commanders in France.

[17] For Lloyd George's account, see *War Memoirs*, i, 691–2. For the revisionist view, see A. J. Marder, *From the Dreadnought to Scapa Flow* (5 vols, London, 1961–70), iv, 152–66.

not be doubted that his deep concern and sympathy for the younger, more imaginative naval officers galvanised the Admiralty into more vigorous action than it would otherwise have adopted. The use of convoys soon proved the answer to the submarine depredations. Lloyd George was very critical of the naval chiefs, particularly of Jellicoe who seemed too defensively minded as First Sea Lord. It was first necessary to remove the obdurate Carson, which was achieved by promoting him to membership of the War Cabinet; Geddes replaced him as First Lord and in December 1917 Jellicoe was replaced by Wemyss. By this time the worst of the naval crisis was over. Lloyd George had contributed forcefully to the reforms within the Admiralty and he possessed effective control over the Navy by the end of 1917. One of the outstanding successes of his administration by 1918 was the war at sea. To cite his own words:

'The great Allied triumph of 1917 was the gradual beating off of the submarine attack. This was the real decision of the War, for the sea turned out to be the decisive flank in the gigantic battlefield. Here victory rested with the Allies, or rather with Britain. The moment the War became a struggle, not to beat the foe in a fight, but first to exhaust his strength and then to beat his defences down, the sea became inevitably the determining factor.'[18]

While Lloyd George has gone down in history as 'the man who won the war', as the extreme advocate of complete victory and maximum mobilisation of resources, he did not always think in terms of fighting on until Germany and her allies surrendered. Late in 1917 and early in 1918, he seriously considered making a compromise peace with Germany at the expense of Russia. The two revolutions of 1917 crippled and then terminated Russia's active role in the war. Milner, a member of the War Cabinet, was an enthusiastic advocate of encouraging German expansion in eastern Europe at Russia's expense.[19] Lloyd George's position is still shadowy but it appears certain that he did contemplate such a compromise peace.[20] There was no likelihood of such a peace materialising, however, for the simple reason that Germany

---

[18] *War Memoirs*, i, 711.

[19] See A. M. Gollin, *Proconsul in Politics: A Study of Lord Milner in Opposition and in Power* (London, 1964), chap. 20.

[20] Wilson, *The Political Diaries of C. P. Scott*, pp. 303–4, 329.

did not desire it. The matter is of interest primarily since it illustrates again the flexibility of Lloyd George's thinking and his desire to utilise the opportunity of escaping from a situation of stalemate.

The general election of December 1918 was an astonishing personal victory for Lloyd George. He had decided several months in advance that he would fight an election under the auspices of the Coalition as soon as the war ended. Sidney Webb, and perhaps others, had reflected on the possibility of Lloyd George's becoming leader of the Labour party, but the Prime Minister felt that his fortunes, at any rate for the foreseeable future, were linked with the Unionist party of which he might become leader.[21] As soon as Germany sought an armistice, Lloyd George determined to hold the election and campaign on the dual platform of the victorious war leader of the past and the man who would guide the nation through the reconstruction of 'normalcy' afterwards. Hankey, the secretary of the Cabinet, described him as he appeared immediately after the election campaign and before the votes had been counted:

'Ll.G. has brought the country through the war, but is very anxious lest he should not get the big majority in the election on which his supporters count. Consequently he is in a nervous, irritable and difficult frame of mind. The mistake he is making is to try and absorb too much into his hands. He seems to have a sort of lust for power; ignores his colleagues, or tolerates them in an almost dictatorial way, and seems more and more to assume the attitude of a dictator. . . .'[22]

When the results came in, the extent of his triumph was clear: candidates pledged to support the Coalition secured 478 seats and the rest 229 seats. The latter figure included some who supported Lloyd George, although they had not received the 'coupon', and the 73 Sinn Fein Members who refused to take their seats. The Opposition in the House of Commons was reduced to a weakly led Labour party dominated by worthy trade union stalwarts and to the Asquithian Liberal rump.[23] Hankey observed that Lloyd George was 'almost stunned' by

[21] Wilson, p. 320, diary entry of 16–19 December 1917, and Taylor (ed.), *Lloyd George: A Diary by Frances Stevenson*, p. 144, diary entry of 14 February 1917.
[22] Roskill, *Hankey*, ii, 39.
[23] Asquith lost his seat but was returned in a by-election at Paisley in February 1920. In the intervening period, the Independent Liberals were led by Sir Donald Maclean.

the magnitude of his victory.[24] The general election of 1918 was the most personalised of any election in the twentieth century and the victor did not lead a strong political party of his own. While the huge victory was encouraging in one respect, it was alarming in another: Lloyd George was the prisoner of the Unionist masses who were opposed to conciliatory policies at home and abroad. He hoped to persuade his Coalition Liberals and the Unionists to agree to fusion in a new Centre party under his leadership, which he made strenuous efforts to secure in 1920. Neither party was prepared to assent: the Coalition Liberals prided themselves on their Liberalism and they were indeed an appreciably larger band than the Independent Liberals, while the Unionist rank and file as distinct from their leaders now distrusted Lloyd George.[25]

The issue of making peace and of dealing with the numerous concomitants occupied the largest proportion of Lloyd George's time between the end of the war and his resignation: his international activities brought some praise but more criticism. As a generalisation, it might be said that the law of diminishing returns operated and that his role in foreign affairs resulted in steadily fewer benefits: in the end it contributed significantly to his fall. In the 1918 election, he had promised appropriate punishment for Germany's misdeeds. He neither supported nor favoured a lenient peace for Germany. Equally he did not wish to punish her too severely and obviate any possibility of reconciling her to the peace terms. The tasks facing Lloyd George, Clemenceau and Wilson were immense and complex. Given all the relevant circumstances – chronic instability in Europe, the looming menace of Bolshevism, the clamour for harsh treatment of Germany, the pressures of time, apart from clashes of personality – it was sanguine in the extreme to expect a lasting settlement to emerge in Paris.[26] Lloyd George's achievement was that the Treaty of Versailles was less severe as a result of his efforts than it would have been otherwise. He showed a

[24] Roskill, ii, 40.

[25] On the Coalition Liberals, see the cogent survey by K. O. Morgan, 'Lloyd George's Stage Army: The Coalition Liberals', in Taylor (ed.), *Lloyd George: Twelve Essays*, pp. 225–54. For the Unionists, see Lord Beaverbrook, *The Decline and Fall of Lloyd George* (London, 1963), *passim*.

[26] For a full discussion of the background to the Paris peace conference, see A. J. Mayer, *Politics and Diplomacy of Peacemaking: Revolution and Counter-Revolution in Europe* (London, 1968).

willingness to stand up to Clemenceau, Foch and Wilson and, in particular, warned them of the danger of Bolshevism spreading to Germany in his Fontainebleau memorandum. Simultaneously he had to out-manoeuvre both his own Secretary of State for War, Winston Churchill, and the French in their desire to intervene more actively in Russia.[27] He shrewdly realised that large-scale intervention in Russia against Bolshevism would be the most effective way of encouraging revolution in western Europe itself, which was war-weary. In addition, the labour movement in Britain was becoming more bellicose and disliked the Government's anti-Bolshevik policy. The Treaty of Versailles was accepted with extreme reluctance by Germany in June 1919. Lloyd George bore his share of responsibility for the unwise features of the treaty, especially reparations and the attempt, about which he was curiously enthusiastic, to try the ex-Kaiser.[28] Yet it has to be remembered that, harsh as it was, Germany was left virtually intact with the resources to become a formidable power again in the near future. The aspect of the treaty most distasteful to Lloyd George was the eastern frontier assigned to Germany and the existence of the Polish corridor: it seems all the more ironic that the occasion of Great Britain's entry into the Second World War in 1939 was to defend Poland.

His role on the diplomatic stage at Paris had filled Lloyd George with a desire to extend his participation in international diplomacy. His Foreign Secretary, Curzon, was willing to submit to Lloyd George's outrageously arrogant behaviour towards him and to accept the Prime Minister and the 'Garden suburb' assuming many of the functions of the Foreign Office. Lloyd George believed that personal diplomacy at the summit was the answer to pressing problems; it was preferable to the 'old diplomacy' which had culminated in the war of 1914. It was a mistaken and unfortunate conclusion. Summit diplomacy requires careful preparation if it is to succeed: frequent meetings of leaders endeavouring to resolve thorny issues in a hurried atmosphere cannot succeed. Unfortunately Lloyd George had succumbed to the meretricious glamour of foreign travel. His preoccupation with foreign policy distracted him from the domestic scene in Britain and meant that he failed to give the consistently decisive leadership in the reconstruction

[27] Roskill, ii, 45, 47, 62, 69, 70-1.
[28] D. Lloyd George, *The Truth About the Peace Treaties* (2 vols, London, 1938), i, 142.

of the country which was required and expected when he was so triumphantly re-elected. This is not to maintain that his domestic record was one of failure but rather to emphasise that he did not achieve all he could have done had he not been so preoccupied abroad. Towards the Russo-Polish war of 1919–20 his policy was muddled and uncertain but implemented with his customary tactical astuteness. Lloyd George detested the Poles and had a sneaking admiration for the Bolsheviks, which was however combined with suspicion. His policy was saved from ruins by the obstinacy and determination of Pilsudski in the battle of Warsaw, for which Lloyd George and the French claimed the credit subsequently.[29] One of the principal short-term successes of his Government lay in its contribution to the Washington conference of 1921–2; the conference agreed on the termination of the Anglo-Japanese alliance and on the adoption of ratios for capital ships to minimise dangerous naval rivalry in the Pacific. Lloyd George had originally hoped to attend the conference but the gravity of the Irish crisis precluded it. Instead the British delegation was ably led by the veteran Lord Balfour, aided by the ubiquitous Hankey.[30]

Of the domestic problems Lloyd George faced, the growing belligerence of the labour movement and the deteriorating situation in Ireland were the most serious. A new feeling of unity and common identity with an accompanying resolution to assert the latent power of the working class had swept through the labour movement in the years immediately preceding the First World War. It was in part diverted by the coming of the war, since much of the labour movement responded to the appeal of patriotism. However, in certain industries and geographical areas, notably in industrial Clydeside and in the mining valleys of south Wales, industrial discontent manifested itself in a number of conflicts. Lloyd George did not properly understand the mood of militance; he was impatient with industrial discontent during the war and tended to attribute it to pacifist or subversive elements. The war was a profound stimulus to change in every respect within British society, as in Europe as a whole. The trade unions expanded greatly in size during the war and after down to 1920. The new generation of union leaders, such as Ernest Bevin, were adamant that the conditions

[29] N. Davies, *White Eagle, Red Star: the Polish-Soviet War 1919–20* (London, 1972), pp. 167–77, 224.
[30] See I. H. Nish, *Alliance In Decline: a Study in Anglo-Japanese Relations, 1908–1923* (London, 1972), chs. xix–xxii.

[223]

of work and the wages of their members must be improved.[31] Between the spring of 1919 and the spring of 1921 the industrial situation was extremely dangerous, more so fundamentally than at the time of the General Strike in 1926. The desire for sweeping reform, the inspiration of the Russian Revolution before the ideals had begun to turn sour and the atmosphere of instability throughout Europe coalesced to confront Lloyd George with a series of crises that tested his skill and deviousness to the full. Thomas Jones, the deputy secretary of the Cabinet, wrote to him early in 1919:

'Bolshevik propaganda in this country is only dangerous in so far as it can lodge itself in the soil of genuine grievances. There is no doubt that large numbers of work-people are expecting a big and rapid improvement in their social and industrial conditions. . . .'

A definite reiteration by yourself of the Government's determination to push forward with an advanced social programme is the best antidote, and this should be followed up by instructions from you to the Departments concerned to get on with the necessary Bills at top speed. . . .[32]

Lloyd George was preoccupied with the deliberations in Paris but when he visited London was, according to Jones, 'full of schemes of dealing with the miners and the railwaymen should they come out during the next week or two'.[33] Lloyd George had promised, in his election campaign, a vigorous administration which would implement a thorough, imaginative programme of reconstruction. His promises were by no means broken: his Government extended unemployment insurance to all industries and made progress with educational and housing reforms. Nevertheless, there was no carefully directed, ambitious policy of social reform.

The major industrial confrontations occurred with the unions comprising the so-called 'Triple Alliance' of miners, railwaymen and transport workers. The triple alliance was far less formidable in practice than

[31] For a useful discussion of Bevin's attitude and of the post-war Labour movement, see A. Bullock, *The Life and Times of Ernest Bevin* (2 vols, London, 1960–7), i, 98–179. Trade union membership totalled more than 8 million in 1920, of which nearly $6\frac{1}{2}$ million were affiliated to the TUC (Bullock, i, 100, n.).

[32] Middlemas, *Thomas Jones: Whitehall Diary*, i, 73–4, Jones to Lloyd George, 8 February 1919.

[33] ibid., i, 76, Jones to Hankey, 10 February 1919.

it was on paper because there was no machinery for prior discussion and unified co-ordination between the three unions concerned; each put its own interests first and the miners in particular were truculent. However, the failure of the triple alliance did not become obvious until 1921. The miners demanded nationalisation of the coalmines in 1919 and improved wages: they declared their willingness to strike to secure their objectives. Lloyd George shrewdly offered a Commission of Inquiry, headed by a progressive judge, Sir John Sankey, and stated that the Government would be bound by the report. The miners accepted the inquiry. Evidence was given by the coal owners and miners; the miners emerged creditably. The Commission was divided in its ultimate report: Sankey favoured nationalisation but Lloyd George used the lack of unanimity as a pretext to postpone action, appreciating that his political position would not allow him to contemplate nationalisation. One victory had been won by Lloyd George. The railwaymen were also belligerent, if less so than the miners. The Government was helped by the personality of J. H. Thomas, General Secretary of the National Union of Railwaymen, who was an astute moderate disinclined to embark on conflict if he could avoid it or to maintain it once it had started. Periodic crises continued in 1920–1 and the Cabinet was most alarmed at the trend.[34] Planning developed to meet the contingency of a general strike but time was needed to prepare adequately. The most serious industrial challenge came in April 1921, when the miners decided to strike to defend the principle of national, as opposed to local, wage agreements and to prevent reductions in wages. The railwaymen and transport workers agreed to support them. Just as the strike appeared inevitable, Lloyd George cleverly exploited an equivocal statement made by the General Secretary of the Miners Federation, Frank Hodges, to open a rift within the miners' Executive and between the miners and the other two unions. Faced with a situation where the miners did not seem to know whether to accept Lloyd George's compromise proposal, the railwaymen and the transport workers reluctantly withdrew their support. 'Black Friday', as 21 April 1921 was mordantly referred to in militant labour circles, was, in the words of Thomas Jones, 'the most exciting day since the Armistice'.[35] Thereafter, the self-confidence of the unions was undermined, although militance was still pronounced

[34] Middlemas, op. cit., i, 99–103.
[35] ibid., i, 153, Jones to Bonar Law, 24 April 1921. For Bevin's view, see Bullock, *The Life and Times of Ernest Bevin*, i, 173–4.

until 1926. Equally important was the fact that economic depression had set in after the post-war boom and trade union membership declined, as the unemployment figures rose to the high level that persisted for the rest of the inter-war years. Lloyd George's achievement was that he succeeded in manoeuvring between those who wanted a confrontation: the reactionaries in his Cabinet and in the Unionist party, on the one hand, and the vociferous trade union militants, on the other. He discerned the revolutionary potential and defused the situation on critical occasions through his consummate tactical ability.

Of all the post-war problems Lloyd George handled, the one in which he faced the most bitter censure, and paradoxically also enjoyed outstanding ultimate success, was Ireland. During his premiership, he had to grapple with the climax to the long struggle for self-government in Ireland. He had striven hard to reach a settlement after the Easter Rising in 1916, when Asquith had entrusted him with the task of negotiating a solution: the attempt had foundered, as previous and subsequent attempts were to founder, over the difficulty of reconciling Ulster to Irish independence. As Prime Minister, between 1916 and 1921, Lloyd George was too preoccupied with the urgent demands of war and peace to give Ireland the concentrated attention it merited. Conditions in Ireland steadily worsened in 1916–18 as a result of the growing popularity of Sinn Fein and hostility towards England stemming from the drastic military suppression of the Easter Rising. John Redmond had courageously staked the future of the Irish parliamentary party on English sympathy for Irish Home Rule in return for his generous support of the war. The gamble had failed and the parliamentary party's authority was progressively diminished.[36] In 1917 the Government sponsored the gathering of the Irish Convention, modelled on the earlier body in South Africa which had produced the Union. The Convention fully indulged the Irish love of interminable debate but sadly failed in its mission. In March–April 1918 the war was causing such grave anxiety that Lloyd George proposed an understanding whereby the Home Rule Bill would be applied, except in Ulster, in return for the enforcement of conscription in Ireland. This was logical in view of the pressure on Lloyd George from the Unionists but was politically maladroit: it caused profound indignation and temporarily united the rising star of Sinn Fein with the declining force of the Irish

[36] For a lucid discussion of the Irish question during Lloyd George's premiership see F. S. L. Lyons, *Ireland Since the Famine* (London, 1971), pp. 380–463.

parliamentary party in a concerted campaign against the proposal.[37] It was not pursued further but the damage had been done.

In the general election of 1918 the Government pledged itself to do all possible to obtain a just and equitable solution. The prospects of attaining it were not enhanced by the return of the seventy-three Sinn Fein Members who refused to attend Westminster and of a dismal rump of six Members representing the vanished supremacy of the parliamentary party. Sinn Fein already constituted an embryo administration: in 1919–20 power increasingly fell into its hands and the grip of Dublin Castle correspondingly slackened. Opinion in England had advanced during the war: as *The Times* remarked, 'We are all Home Rulers today.'[38] Even right-wing Unionists who had trenchantly opposed Home Rule in 1912–14 were prepared to envisage its appearance so long as Ulster was not compelled to be a part of a united Ireland against its wishes. The bulk of Irish opinion was, however, no longer satisfied with Home Rule and desired full independence. Lloyd George's policy in 1919–21 was designed to persuade and then coerce Ireland into accepting a settlement. When this failed, he adroitly switched to a conciliatory policy, pursued with brilliant tactical astuteness in the negotiations with the Sinn Fein representatives between October and December 1921.

In 1920 the Government introduced the Government of Ireland Act, which set up two parliaments in Dublin and Belfast: the latter was intended to reduce the Ulster fear of subjugation to Dublin, although it was hoped that Ulster might later agree to accept unity provided reasonable autonomy was permitted. It was, ironically enough in the light of developments after 1969, accepted reluctantly by Northern Ireland; Sinn Fein contemptuously rejected it. Thereafter followed the rapid collapse of law and order in 1920–1 and the use of extreme violence by both sides in enforcing their respective policies. Lloyd George was entirely willing to envisage the use of force in Ireland. By so doing he exposed himself to severe criticism from a variety of opponents which contributed to the decline in his personal standing.[39] The rise in mutual atrocities and the sanctioning of the activities of the notorious 'Black

[37] See F. S. L. Lyons, *John Dillon: A Biography* (London, 1968), chap. 15.
[38] *The Times*, 26 March 1919, cited in D. G. Boyce, *Englishmen and Irish Troubles: British Public Opinion and the Making of Irish Policy, 1918–22* (London, 1972), p. 25.
[39] See Boyce, chapters 2–8, for a discussion of English reactions and of the activities of the Peace with Ireland Council, formed in the summer of 1920.

and Tans' offered no remedy and accentuated the weariness of British public opinion. While Lloyd George publicly defended his policy, his shrewd grasp of reality is shown by his private warning to the commander of the 'Black and Tans', General Tudor, against unnecessary coercion and by his encouragement of Archbishop Clune's unofficial mediation in 1920–1.[40] By the summer of 1921 Lloyd George recognised that the policy of coercion was bankrupt but, for political reasons, he could not proceed too swiftly in the other direction. He was dependent on the Unionists for survival and, while they were certainly more progressive than formerly, it would be impossible to expect them to accept Sinn Fein's terms. For its part, Sinn Fein was ready to negotiate: unknown to the Government, the IRA's resources were gravely depleted and Michael Collins was not optimistic about the chances of continuing the struggle.

In the new conciliatory chapter opening in July 1921, following the first discussions with de Valera, Lloyd George relied heavily on Thomas Jones and on Alfred Cope, a progressive official at Dublin Castle, to foster contacts with Sinn Fein. He revealed the whole range of his negotiating skills in the talks held in London between October and December 1921. He was conciliatory or tenacious, as the moment required, but always flexible and dynamic: the Irish delegates were no match for him. The crux of the problem was, as always, Irish unity. Sinn Fein was committed to independence for the whole of Ireland; Northern Ireland was vehemently opposed to the idea. Lloyd George had to discover some means of bridging the gap. He soon discerned that there were differences among the Sinn Fein leaders, particularly between Arthur Griffith and Michael Collins in London and de Valera in Ireland: he put pressure on Griffith especially to adhere to an undertaking he had given accepting a boundary commission to determine the frontier between the rest of Ireland and the newly defined Ulster. The alternative was a resumption of the struggle. James Craig, the Prime Minister of Northern Ireland, was intensely suspicious of the negotiations and inspired much anxiety. Lloyd George spoke of resignation if the Ulster Unionists prevented a settlement. Austen Chamberlain and his colleagues stood firm in support of Lloyd George. After heated debates among themselves, the Sinn Fein representatives signed the agreement with Lloyd George on 6 December 1921: the Irish Free State came into existence, within the British Empire as Lloyd George

[40] Boyce, pp. 55–6 and Middlemas, *Thomas Jones* . . ., iii, 44.

had insisted and contrary to the wishes of much Irish opinion. By any criteria, it was an outstanding triumph for Lloyd George.[41] However, it had come after a singularly unpleasant and distasteful period for which he bore a large share of responsibility. The stark memory of the events of 1920–1 robbed him of comprehensive appreciation of his success. It is currently and understandably fashionable to look more critically at the settlement of 1921 in the light of the breakdown of the Stormont regime in 1969–72 and of the British Government's recognition in 1972 of the need for a lasting solution to the Irish question. However, settlements should be appraised ultimately by the exigencies of the contemporary situation: there can be little doubt that Lloyd George in 1921 achieved the most satisfactory settlement feasible at that time. The failure of Stormont was arguably not inevitable; it was ensured nevertheless by the reactionary character of Ulster Unionism.[42]

Lloyd George was brought to power as a result of a major crisis in wartime necessitating new leadership; his fall from office was occasioned by fear of his leading Britain into war in the Middle East against the resurgent Turkey of Kemal Ataturk. Lloyd George had proved surprisingly successful in attracting the leaders of the Unionist party and in preserving their loyalty. Indeed attitudes within the Unionist party by 1922 were the reverse of 1916: in 1916 mass support for Lloyd George had come from the backbenchers longing for dynamic leadership and the leaders had been hesitant – in 1922 the backbenchers had had enough of dynamism but the leaders were under the magician's spell. The famous Carlton Club meeting, on 19 October 1922, reflected the extent of the disenchantment with Lloyd George; the success of the meeting was guaranteed by the contributions of two prominent Unionists who changed sides, one former colleague, Bonar Law, and one member of the Cabinet, the relatively insignificant Stanley Baldwin. The Chanak crisis symbolised rather than explained Lloyd George's fall. The decline in his standing and the growth of opposition stemmed from a combination of circumstances. He had based his appeal on vigorous,

[41] In the words of a recent historian, 'Only a negotiator as wily and indefatigable as David Lloyd George could have turned the unfavourable situation which had arisen by early November 1921 to his advantage' (Boyce, *Englishmen and Irish Troubles* . . ., pp. 167–8).

[42] See Lyons, *Ireland Since the Famine*, pp. 682–755, for an account of Northern Ireland between 1921 and 1970. For a personal view by a reforming leader, see Lord O'Neill of the Maine, *The Autobiography of Terence O'Neill* (London, 1972), pp. 40–3, 110–54.

efficient government and on the successful solution of complex problems. To many people, by 1922, the record of the Government did not
seem impressive. The Paris peace conference was a disappointment
and had not produced the stable Europe which had been hoped for. The
concatenation of other conferences engendered cynicism. When the
post-war boom broke, the economy declined with large-scale unemployment. There was chronic discontent among labour. The Irish
crisis had considerably damaged the Government. It was unfair to
blame Lloyd George personally for the disappointments and, as has
been seen, there was a positive side to most of the above issues. But
Lloyd George's record was tarnished. In addition, there was the sale of
honours and the formation of the Lloyd George political fund. Previous
governments, whether Conservative or Liberal, had sold honours for
political purposes. Lloyd George did so on a more blatant scale and
established his own fund to finance his future campaigns. In a conversation with J. C. C. Davidson, after he had left office, Lloyd George
defended his actions. According to Davidson:

I dropped the remark that Mr Lloyd George was fortunate in being
much better situated than the Conservative Party. He laughed at the
remark and, which [sic] his characteristic flair for altering his ground,
burst into an enthusiastic defence of the system of raising Party funds
by the sale of honours. 'You and I,' he said, 'know perfectly well it is a
far cleaner method of filling the Party chest than the methods used in
the United States or the Socialist Party.' He complained that the
Socialist Party was a trade union party solely because of the power of
the trade unions to withhold funds. 'In America the steel trusts supported one political party, and the cotton people supported another.
This placed political parties under the domination of great financial
interests and trusts.' 'Here,' said Mr Lloyd George, 'a man gives
£40,000 to the Party and gets a baronetcy. If he comes to the Leader
of the Party and says I subscribe largely to the Party funds, you must
do this or that, you can tell him to go to the devil.' 'The attachment of
the brewers to the Conservative Party was the closest approach.' said
Mr Lloyd George, 'to political corruption in this country. The worst
of it is you cannot defend it in public but it keeps politics far cleaner
than any other method of raising funds.'[43]

[43] R. Rhodes James, *Memoirs of a Conservative: J. C. C. Davidson's Memoirs and
Papers, 1910–37* (London, 1969), p. 279.

There was a certain robust frankness in Lloyd George's attitude, but while in office he had failed to give adequate consideration to the feeling of many people that the distribution of honours should not be abused.

Lloyd George's caution rapidly deserted him after the 1918 election. As both Hankey and Lloyd George's newspaper friend, Lord Riddell, noted he had become more arrogant, dictatorial and complacent after several years as Prime Minister and a total of seventeen years continuously as a Cabinet minister between 1905 and 1922.[44] Lloyd George had to some extent succumbed to the occupational hazard of all politicians – a belief in his own indispensability. When he surrendered the seals of office to King George V, he left Downing Street and the world of high politics for ever. He could not engineer a return to office because he did not possess a strong party of his own; he was a great leader with a dwindling band of supporters. After the Unionists rejected him, the logical answer was to join the Labour party and aim, within a short time, to become its leader. Lloyd George was undoubtedly a Radical by temperament and belonged naturally to the left rather than the right. However, he was disliked and distrusted by the most prominent Labour politicians and trade union leaders, not least by Ramsay MacDonald. The Lloyd George political fund was a further obstacle. So he remained a Liberal, nominally at any rate, until his death. Throughout the middle and later 1920s and 1930s he remained out of office, amidst all the setbacks at home and abroad, to his country's immense loss.

David Lloyd George was the most independently minded prime minister of modern times. Handicapped by the absence of a powerful party to support him, he more than made the most of the opportunities fate allowed him. This is the paradox of his leadership. It has rightly been said of him that he was a 'presidential' prime minister, 'the nearest thing England has known to a Napoleon'.[45] When his policies succeeded, he took the credit and reaped the reward, as in 1918. By 1922 the policies appeared in a more murky light; the credit balance had been used up. The future down to 1940 lay with Baldwin, MacDonald and Neville Chamberlain, men of a very different outlook.

[44] Roskill, *Hankey*, ii, 148, 215, and Lord Riddell, *Lord Riddell's Intimate Diary of the Peace Conference and After 1918–23* (London, 1933), pp. 48–9, 67.
[45] A. J. P. Taylor, *English History 1914–45* (Oxford, 1965), p. 73.

BIBLIOGRAPHY

There is no satisfactory biography of Lloyd George at present but the following works are helpful to varying degrees.

Grigg, J., *The Young Lloyd George* (London, 1973)

Jones, T., *Lloyd George* (London, 1951)

Morgan, K. O., *Lloyd George – Welsh Radical as World Statesman* (Cardiff, 1963)

Owen, F., *Tempestuous Journey: Lloyd George, his Life and Times* (London, 1954)

The diaries and memoirs of Frances Stevenson, later the Countess Lloyd-George, are valuable, particularly the former.

Lloyd George, F., *The Years That Are Past* (London, 1967)

Taylor, A. J. P. (ed.), *Lloyd George: A Diary by Frances Stevenson* (London, 1971)

On Lloyd George's premiership the following should be noted.

Blake, R., *The Unknown Prime Minister: The Life and Times of Andrew Bonar Law 1858–1923* (London, 1955); (ed.), *The Private Papers of Douglas Haig, 1914–19* (London, 1952)

Beaverbrook, Lord, *Men and Power* (London, 1956); *The Decline and Fall of Lloyd George* (London, 1963)

Boyce, D. G., *Englishmen and Irish Troubles* (London, 1972)

Bullock, A., *The Life and Times of Ernest Bevin*, vol. i (London, 1960)

Davies, N., *White Eagle, Red Star: The Polish-Soviet War, 1917–20* (London, 1972)

Kinnear, M., *The Fall of Lloyd George: The Political Crisis of 1922* (London, 1973)

Lloyd George, D. *War Memoirs* (either 6 vols, London, 1933-6 or 2 vols, London, 1938); *The Truth About the Peace Treaties* (2 vols, London, 1938)

Lyons, F. S. L., *Ireland Since the Famine* (London, 1971)

Lyons, F. S. L., *John Dillon: A Biography* (London, 1968)

Marder, A. J., *From the Dreadnought to Scapa Flow*, vols iv–v (London, 1969–70)

Mayer, A. J., *Politics and Diplomacy of Peacemaking* (London, 1968)

Middlemas, K. (ed.) *Thomas Jones: Whitehall Diary*, vols i, iii (London, 1969–71)

Morgan, K. O., *Wales in British Politics 1868–1922* (Cardiff, 1963); (ed.) *Lloyd George: Family Letters 1885–1936* (Cardiff, 1973); 'Lloyd George's Premiership: A Study in "Prime Ministerial" Government', *Historical Journal* xiii, 1 (1970), 130–57

Nish, I. H., *Alliance in Decline: Anglo-Japanese Relations 1908–23* (London, 1972)

Pakenham, F., *Peace By Ordeal* (London, 1935)

Taylor, A. J. P., *English History 1914–45* (Oxford, 1965); *Beaverbroork* (London, 1972); (ed.) *Lloyd George: Twelve Essays* (London, 1971)

Ullman, R., *Anglo-Soviet Relations 1917–21* (3 vols, London, 1961–73)

Wilson, T., *The Downfall of the Liberal Party 1914–35* (London, 1966); (ed.) *The Political Diaries of C. P. Scott 1911–28* (London, 1970)

13

ANDREW BONAR LAW

BY

JOHN RAMSDEN

*Andrew Bonar Law. PC (1911), LLD (Glasgow). Born in
Canada 16 September 1858 and later moved to Glasgow. Educated
in Canada, then at Gilbertsfield School (Hamilton) and Glasgow
High School. In business in Glasgow 1885–1900. Married 1891
Annie Pitcairn Robley; two sons, two daughters. MP for Glasgow
(Blackfriars) 1900–06; Parliamentary Secretary to the Board of
Trade 1902; MP for Dulwich 1906–10, Bootle 1911–18; PC and
leader of the Conservative Party 1911; Colonial Secretary under
Asquith 1915–16; Chancellor of the Exchequer and Leader of the
Commons under Lloyd George 1916–18; MP for Glasgow Central
1918–23; Lord Privy Seal 1919; resigned for reasons of ill-health
1921; Prime Minister 1922; resigned and died 1923. Member of
the War Cabinet 1916–19; Leader of the Unionist Party 1912–21.*

ANDREW BONAR LAW

Bonar Law was Prime Minister for a shorter term than any other modern premier: becoming Prime Minister on 23 October 1922, he was obliged to retire through ill health on 20 May 1923, and died in October 1923. However, before this he had been leader of the Conservative party for ten years and had been Leader of the House of Commons and *de facto* deputy Prime Minister to Lloyd George from 1916 to 1921. Thus, although Prime Minister for such a short time, Law had already been at the summit of British politics for a decade. Moreover, his seven months as Prime Minister were filled with serious problems and decisions, the importance of which were only grasped later. It was during this period that British politics returned to 'normalcy' after the hot house years of Lloyd George's rule. It was therefore necessary for the new Government to decide how far to proceed with the dismantling of the coalition system of government, both in terms of institutions and policies, and in terms of political style. An equivalent tidying-up problem in foreign affairs concerned the settlement of debts incurred during the World War. In all of these affairs, Law exerted an important influence; it was perhaps only because of the shortness of his premiership that he was able to make such a small impact on the popular mind, but a further explanation of his political obscurity must be found.

When leaving Law's funeral service at Westminster Abbey, Herbert Asquith is reputed to have remarked, 'It is fitting that we should have buried the Unknown Prime Minister by the side of the Unknown Soldier'. The anecdote circulated widely and became the title of Robert Blake's biography of Law.[1] As a book, *The Unknown Prime Minister* did a great deal to rescue Law from oblivion, but its title perhaps did even more to bury him. Many who know nothing else about Law, now know that he was unknown; but this is to miss the real point of Asquith's remark, which contained a certain element of truth as well as an intention to denigrate. Law was in fact no less well known than any other Prime Minister in the sense of being known to be Prime Minister.

[1] Robert Blake, *The Unknown Prime Minister* (London, 1955), p. 13 and *passim*.

Where Law differed from a man like Asquith himself was in the depth of knowledge the public was allowed to share, the depth of personal and private feelings that was exposed. In this more limited sense, it cannot be denied that Law always remained a shadowy figure to those outside his immediate circle of colleagues. Famous he may have been but familiar he never was, and this is perhaps the most interesting aspect of his entire career. He was the first *ordinary* man to hold the highest political office in Britain – the first Prime Minister who asked the public to identify with him as an equal rather than to admire him as a hero figure.

Law was in no sense a brilliant man and, like Baldwin after him, he was able to make a virtue out of his lack of brilliance. In so far as Law had a public image at all it must have been as a rather pedestrian figure, a man with no warmth of character, with a narrow mind, and with no small-talk. Politically, he was seen as near the extreme right of his party and tinged with a reactionary bigotry. Very little of this public image had any foundation in fact and to those few who knew him well, Law gave an exactly opposite impression. The men who became personal friends were not men likely to enjoy the company of a narrow-minded boor, and both Lloyd George and Beaverbrook relied heavily on him.[2] His greatest advantage, which explains his attraction to the brilliant men of his day, was his ability to listen and then to make sound commonsense criticisms of the high-flown schemes suggested to him. Outsiders saw him as hard and brutal but his friends saw him as all too indecisive and unassuming. As for his reputation for bigotry, this can be explained entirely in terms of what he did for political advantage. In 1913 and 1914, Law had encouraged Protestant Ulster to the point of civil war against the British Government, but behind the scenes he had been working strenuously for a compromise settlement.[3] Without Law's inflammatory speeches, the Unionists could never have got such a good deal out of Asquith's Liberal Government as they were getting by 1914. In effect, Law was tough-minded enough to risk more than the Government over Ireland and because of this he gained more. To a liberal intellectual like Asquith, Law's tough but realistic Irish policy was not only repugnant but also incomprehensible. Law defied political conventions further by the direct and unaffected style of his public speeches and by his refusal to get involved in the normal Westminster round of

[2] A. J. P. Taylor, *Beaverbrook* (London, 1972), pp. 46–7 and p. 211.
[3] Blake, op. cit., p. 149.

dinners, parties and receptions.[4] In this sense too, Asquith was speaking truly when he said that he did not know Law. However, by 1922, Law's past career had furnished him with considerable experience of power politics, and the way in which he finally achieved the premiership provided a further lesson.

Law had retired because of his health in 1921 and remained on the touchline of politics for the last eighteen months of the Lloyd George Coalition. As that Government sank deeper into crisis in 1922, it was to Law that the dissident Conservatives turned for a lead.[5] Normally loyal, Conservatives found it difficult to justify a rebellion and so the presence of an ex-leader in the wings provided an important legitimating factor for rebellion against Austen Chamberlain, Law's successor in the party leadership. At this supreme crisis of his career, with the highest prize his for the taking, Law was tortured by doubts. He was being dragged back into politics despite continued bad health and he could only return over the political corpse of Austen Chamberlain, for many years his loyal supporter. Torn by loyalty and duty on one side and friendship on the other, Law wrote a letter to his constituency chairman, announcing his retirement from politics; he then showed the letter to Beaverbrook, who converted him, as he was probably intended to do.[6] As so often at moments of crisis, Law needed reassurance before taking crucial decisions, but he was incapable of refusing his party's call. He therefore attended the Carlton Club meeting to vote against a continuance of the Coalition and his very presence helped to secure the Coalition's fall. Law thus became Conservative leader again and was almost automatically asked to form a government, for the Conservatives already had an overall majority. Here Law demonstrated his weakness by refusing the King's commission until he had been formally elected as leader of his party.[7] He was elected unanimously – for his coalitionist rivals were not prepared to push the disagreement so far as actually to permit a contested election for the party leadership. Once elected, Law immediately accepted the King's invitation and was able to draw on all the reserves of party loyalty to the leader in forming his Government. It was thus that Law became Prime Minister by a sort of legal rebellion, legal in that it was quite obviously the right of the Conservative party

[4] Blake, op. cit., p. 87.
[5] Maurice Cowling, *The Impact of Labour* (Cambridge, 1971), p. 206.
[6] Taylor, *Beaverbrook*, p. 197.
[7] Blake, *The Unknown Prime Minister*, p. 459.

to change its leader if it wished to do so, and yet still a rebellion which left a legacy of mistrust and opposition.

Law's great problem in forming his Government was the refusal of most of the late Cabinet to join the new one; Austen Chamberlain had suggested that if the party had no confidence in its leaders then they must find new leaders, and it was to Law that the task fell. Success was made more likely by the fact that not all of the late ministers shared Austen Chamberlain's views: Lord Curzon, Stanley Baldwin and Sir Arthur Griffith-Boscawen from the Lloyd George Cabinet agreed to serve with Law, and most of the junior ministers agreed to serve. What was lacking was the whole group of experienced coalitionist ministers – Austen Chamberlain, Lord Birkenhead, Arthur Balfour, Winston Churchill, Sir Robert Horne and Sir Laming Worthington-Evans.[8] No government could ignore such men and there is no doubt that they were missed, for what the new Government lacked was not so much ability as experience. Into the Cabinet for the first time in 1922–3 came Neville Chamberlain, Sir Philip Lloyd-Graeme, L. S. Amery, Edward Wood; Sir Douglas Hogg and Sir Samuel Hoare became junior ministers and Stanley Baldwin became Chancellor of the Exchequer after little over a year in the Cabinet. Like Pitt's first Government in 1783, the Law Cabinet had to stagger on with a surfeit of peers, shunned by most big political names, but finally vindicated by the electorate. The new ministry was dismissed contemptuously by Birkenhead as 'a government of the second eleven', but if the first team were all sulking in the pavilion, where else was Law to find his players? From the talent available to him, Law chose wisely, although the care lavished on the senior posts was not always repeated at the next level, as Sir Robert Sanders noted:

Yesterday I was offered & accepted Ministry of Agriculture. The manner of it was quaint. Stanley Baldwin dashed in about 7 p.m. 'Peter will you take Agriculture?' 'Yes, love to' I said. 'All right that's settled' and off he went. Went to the Palace this morning & kissed hands as PC & then took oath as Minister . . .. So far it is a real old Tory Cabinet. Of the H. of C. members most of us are intimate friends. It is curious that Peel, Baldwin & I were all in the Upper Sixth at Harrow together.[9]

[8] Cowling, *The Impact of Labour*, p. 214.
[9] Diary of Sir Robert Sanders, 25 October 1922. I am grateful to Hon. Mrs V. E. Butler for permission to quote from the diary.

This description includes almost all of the characteristics of the Law Cabinet, its easy informality, its 'real Old Tory' complexion, and the importance of Baldwin. The Carlton Club meeting, called not by the rebels but by the then leader Austen Chamberlain, had been attacked as a 'reactionary intrigue', and so by extension the new Government was soon labelled as 'reactionary'. If it was reactionary at all, it was only in its composition and this of course was forced on Law; it did in any case include several members like Hoare and Wood who were well to the left of the party. The only other problem of composition occurred when Griffith-Boscawen lost his seat at the general election; after a frenzied search, Griffith-Boscawen fought a by-election at Mitcham but when that too was lost he retired from politics. This further loss of experience was partially mitigated by the promotion of Neville Chamberlain to the Cabinet.

It might have been expected, in view of the Cabinet's lack of political experience and its dependence on Law for its very existence, that it would have been under his close control. That would be to misjudge Law, who preferred not to dominate his Cabinet but to leave ministers free to run their own departments. This policy was to be subjected to severe strain with Baldwin's settlement of war debts, but it also resulted in Chamberlain's 1923 Housing Act, a major piece of social reforming legislation. It was in the Cabinet itself that the Law Government made its most important decision, when it decided to prune but not to abolish the apparatus of Cabinet secretarial assistance which it had inherited from the Coalition Government. No secretariat had existed before the First World War, and only military necessity had changed the practice, but in the years after the war the whole system became tied up with Lloyd George's personal style of government. The teams of policy- and press-advisers who were imported into Downing Street by Lloyd George were regarded as a serious constitutional impropriety and this 'garden suburb' was further discredited by its connection with the honours scandals of 1921 and 1922. As usual, Law took a realistic line and decided to retain the secretariat itself while removing most of the rest of the apparatus.[10]

However, before the Government could begin its term, it was plunged into an immediate general election. Law decided on a general election in order to establish the new Government, and it was announced three days after his appointment as Prime Minister. An election victory

10 H. Daalder, *Cabinet Reform in Great Britain* (London, 1964), p. 60.

would not only give a full five years of office, but it would also discredit those Conservatives who had stayed outside the Government and who would be greatly embarrassed by an election campaign. The keynote of Law's election campaign was therefore the apostolic line of Conservative succession whereby he himself was the practising heir of Disraeli and Lord Salisbury. Law also made a clear distinction between his new Government and the last one; in speeches and in his manifesto, he defined his policy as 'tranquillity', and his picture appeared on pamphlets with the slogan 'Safety First'. A contrast was to be made between the 'dynamic force' of the Lloyd George Government and the peaceful tranquillity of Law's Conservatism. Taunts about the new Government's 'second-class brains' can only have helped, for the reputation of clever politicians stood rather low after the Lloyd George Government. Law reaffirmed pre-war Conservative policy in its negative as well as its positive forms.[11] Thus he gave a pledge that tariffs would not be introduced without a further general election – identical to the pledge he had given in 1913. He also reaffirmed the determination of the Conservatives to get on with the reform of the House of Lords, left unfinished by the Liberals in 1911 and shirked by all subsequent governments. (In the event, the Law Government too failed to grasp this nettle.) The most important issue of all, Ireland, had been implicitly settled by the decision to call an election in November 1922; such urgency was only necessary if Parliament was to meet again before the end of 1922 in order to pass legislation within the time-table of the Government of Ireland Act. Despite pressure from extremists in his own party, Law refused to go back on the Irish Treaty negotiated by Lloyd George in 1921; Ulster had won a good bargain from the prolonged struggle over Home Rule and it was not in Law's nature to fight for abstract principles. In this as in all other areas, Law sought to present a picture of a party that would avoid confrontations and antagonisms. Above all, his Government would return politics to the conditions of peace which had not prevailed since 1914. Law's personal message to the electors concluded:

There are many measures of legislative and administrative importance which, in themselves, would be desirable . . . but I do not feel that they can, at this moment, claim precedence over the nation's first need,

[11] F. W. S. Craig (ed), *British General Election Manifestos* (Chichester, 1970), pp. 10–12.

which is, in every walk of life, to get on with its own work with the minimum of interference at home and of disturbance abroad.[12]

Law seems to have grasped intuitively the electorate's deep feeling of nostalgia for the years before the war; more than anything, what was wanted was a period of rest and recovery, of no crises and no great changes. Perhaps that was merely what Law himself wanted, but apparently his view was shared by those who voted in 1922.

The Conservative party won in 1922 its first election victory since 1900 and secured the overall parliamentary majority that Law and his party managers had expected. In fact, the victory was based heavily on the splitting of the anti-Conservative vote in many constituencies, but surprise at the result itself gave the Government a good deal of new confidence. Law now seemed set for five years of Conservative government in the traditional style. This moment of triumph would perhaps have come, but for the war, in 1916, but now it was too late, for Law himself had less than a year to live.

The one major Cabinet crisis that occurred between the election victory of November 1922 and Law's resignation in May 1923 found Law in conflict with the whole of his Cabinet. In January, Baldwin returned from Washington, where he had been seeking a final settlement of all outstanding loans.[13] In relation to the United States, Britain was a net debtor to a considerable extent and the only argument was about the rate of repayment and the rate of interest. It was felt that a quick settlement would help to steady the international credit system and would encourage other countries to settle outstanding debts. However, Baldwin unfortunately leaked details of his proposals to the press on his return and thereby precipitated an international political crisis. Once the proposals were known in the United States, it became impossible to expect any further improvement in what many regarded as a highly disadvantageous settlement. Instead of considering proposals to which it was in no way committed, the Cabinet found itself instead faced with a choice between the proposals and the Chancellor of the Exchequer. Many of the Cabinet disliked the proposals, but only Law wished to turn them down and thereby to challenge the American Government to a showdown. Isolated in his own Cabinet, Law considered resignation, but great pressure was exerted on him and he

[12] Craig, op. cit., p. 12.
[13] K. Middlemas and J. Barnes, *Baldwin* (London, 1969), p. 143.

finally agreed to stay on and accept the majority decision. It was unprecedented for a Prime Minister to take up an issue, find it rejected by his own Cabinet and yet not resign. There was however at least one exact precedent in the past career of Law himself, when he had announced a change in the party's tariff policy in 1912. After much pressure he had finally given way, and after further persuasion he had agreed to stay on as leader.[14] As Prime Minister, Law continued to place the unity of the party as of higher value than any matter of policy. 'I must follow them, I am their leader,' he is reputed to have said. There is no better case than the US debt settlement of 1923 to illustrate the weakness of a prime minister who is concerned to preserve party unity. On the merits of the case, however, Law was probably right; other countries which were not so keen to settle their debts quickly were able to secure much better terms later. At the time though, Law was in a minority of one, and he was not assertive enough to press his views against such odds.[15]

At the end of April, Law was advised to go on a sea voyage because of a further illness, and in May he collapsed and resigned. He was then found to be suffering from an incurable throat cancer, which can only have been worsened by the strains of the previous six months. His last political action was a curiously ambiguous one, concerning the choice of Baldwin as his successor.[16] Law certainly refused to give formal advice to the King but equally certainly he favoured Baldwin for the succession. Eventually, a memorandum by his former secretary, J. C. C. Davidson, was shown to the King as if it did represent Law's view and this document was an important influence towards the selection of Baldwin rather than Curzon. Perhaps Law could simply not bring himself to face the prospect of thwarting the hopes of Curzon, the only one of the party's old guard who had stood by him in the last six months. It was not so surprising, however, that Law really favoured Baldwin, for after all Baldwin was his protégé and was a politician made in his own image. Law had been Conservative leader during most of Baldwin's career in politics, and Baldwin was PPS to Law in 1916; in many ways, Baldwin's public image as a politician was made up of Law's private virtues, and like Law he prized honesty more than brilliance. However, as well as a political style, Law also handed on to Baldwin a whole new

[14] Blake, *The Unknown Prime Minister*, p. 115.
[15] Blake, op. cit., p. 494.
[16] R. Rhodes James, *Memoirs of a Conservative* (London, 1969), p. 154.

generation of party leaders. The men promoted ahead of their time into Law's Cabinet of 1922 were, with very few exceptions, to remain at the head of British politics for the rest of the inter-war years.

Law died on 30 October 1923, and typically his will asked that he should be buried quietly. His friends and colleagues refused this last request and so Law became the first Prime Minister to be buried in Westminster Abbey since Gladstone in 1898. Appropriately, Baldwin spoke about the death of Law to the House of Commons; he spoke of the personal and national loss which had been sustained, but most of all he spoke of the gentle and considerate man that the public and even many politicians had never known.[17]

BIBLIOGRAPHY

Blake, R., *The Unknown Prime Minister: The Life and Times of Andrew Bonar Law 1858-1923* (London, 1955); *The Conservative Party from Peel to Churchill* (London, 1970)
Cowling, M., *The Impact of Labour, 1920-24* (London, 1971)
James, R. Rhodes (ed.), *Memoirs of a Conservative: J. C. C. Davidson's Letters and Papers* (London, 1969)
Taylor, A. J. P., *Beaverbrook* (London, 1972)
Taylor, H. A., *The Strange Case of Andrew Bonar Law* (London, 1932)

[17] Stanley Baldwin, *On England* (London, 1926), p. 169.

14

STANLEY BALDWIN

BY

KEITH MIDDLEMAS

Stanley Baldwin, created Earl Baldwin of Bewdley, 1937. Born 3 August 1867, son of Alfred Baldwin, ironmaster, and Louise Macdonald, one of four sisters, the others marrying Edward Burne-Jones, Lockwood Kipling and Edward Poynter. Educated at Harrow and Trinity College, Cambridge. Joined the family business. Married Lucy Ridsdale 1892; two sons and four daughters. MP for Bewdley 1908 in succession to his father; private secretary to Bonar Law and Financial Secretary to the Treasury under the Lloyd George Coalition Government. President of the Board of Trade 1921; took the initiative in the revolt of junior ministers which resulted in the fall of the Government. Chancellor of the Exchequer 1922–23; Prime Minister in preference to Curzon 1923; leader of the Opposition 1924; Prime Minister 1924–29; consented to serve in MacDonald's 'National' Government of 1931; Prime Minister 1935–1937 (retired). Died December 1947.

STANLEY BALDWIN

A well-tried story of the early 1920s had Churchill, playing chess with Asquith, urge his opponent to open up the field – 'Get out your Baldwins' (pawns). Yet, twenty-five years later, when Baldwin's Worcestershire memorial was dedicated at a dismal, sparsely attended ceremony in 1948, Churchill, alone of the ministers of the inter-war years, came down and spoke: 'He was the most formidable politician I have ever known in public life.' Rarely has the reputation of a prime minister in modern history fluctuated so violently as did Baldwin's, between public ignorance after the First World War and extravagant vituperation in the middle of the Second, adulation on his retirement in 1937 and cautious reappraisal in more recent years.

To many of those who in May 1923 queried why the self-effacing Chancellor of the Exchequer should have been preferred as Prime Minister to Lord Curzon, glittering ex-Viceroy of India and ex-Foreign Secretary, it seemed that Baldwin was indeed Churchill's 'pawn' and that Curzon's failings were alone responsible – his notorious antipathy to the nascent Labour party, and the fact that he could never take a seat in the House of Commons. Until the beginning of his longest term of office, in 1925, Baldwin's public presence, and the observations of many of his Cabinet colleagues, still echoed Curzon's disdain at being rejected for such a man. As Thomas Jones wrote, in friendly disparagement, after his first acquaintance with the family in 1923, 'I am never sure whether the PM is thinking at all or simply wool-gathering. Here in his rural home one feels the old England of the villages is getting a bit of its own back in the person of S.B.'[1]

Political observers found it more than strange that a man who had spent his first eight years in the House of Commons as an orthodox backbencher should after another seven take the highest office. It was a shorter parliamentary career than that of any politician since the growth of national parties in the nineteenth century, but, in sharp contrast to the youthful leaders such as Rosebery and Gaitskell, Baldwin did not

[1] R. K. Middlemas (ed.), *Thomas Jones: Whitehall Diary* (3 vols, London, 1969–71), i, 256.

even become an MP until he was forty-one. The nearest parallel is Campbell-Bannerman, Prime Minister at sixty-nine; but he died two years after, whereas Baldwin's three terms spanned nearly the whole inter-war period.

The view of him as a compromise candidate put up by the Conservative managers to calm the rough tides of opinion in the party after the fall of Lloyd George's Coalition drew some colour from Baldwin's resemblance to familiar Tory stereotypes: the successful businessman turned politician, expert in a narrow field, like the men Lloyd George had relied on in the war, such as Lords Weir and Cowdray; or the magnate with wide influence in the countryside and on the 1900 Committee, such as Baldwin's real political friends, William Bridgeman and Edward Wood (Lord Halifax). For his achievements appeared modest. His successful industrial experience, at work, first for his ironmaster father, and then after 1908 as financial director of Baldwin & Sons, was recognised by Bonar Law, and then by Lloyd George who made him Financial Secretary to the Treasury in 1916. Here, in what was one of the more important posts outside the Cabinet, and as deputy to Bonar Law, Leader of the House, he acquired the political standing he had lacked and significant acquaintance with Whitehall and the mandarins of the Treasury. But he accepted the prevailing financial orthodoxy and he could be found, as the war ended, urging the need for retrenchment and economy in order to face what he, like most ministers, feared would be a peacetime slump. His famous gesture after the Armistice, in which he donated one-fifth of his total fortune (£120,000) to the nation 'as a thank-offering in the firm conviction that never again shall we have such a chance of giving our country that form of help which is so vital at the present time',[2] was made anonymously, and signed simply 'F.S.T.'. In the post-war euphoria scarcely anyone emulated his example.

Later, as President of the Board of Trade, he was responsible for such undramatic but useful measures as the Safeguarding of Industries Act, and for the extension of government authority in the fields of statistical information, standardisation and merchandise marks. In a still unprofessional age, his influence, like that of A. J. Balfour and Lord Haldane, was directed towards making the sphere of government administration, vastly extended as a result of the war, both effective and efficient.

[2] *The Times*, 24 June 1919.

There was nothing here, except a notable Cabinet dispute over tariffs, under the Safeguarding Act (of all things, centred on the duty on fabric gloves), to turn Baldwin against the leadership of Lloyd George, which the chiefs of the Conservative party, Law, Birkenhead and Austen Chamberlain, seemed likely to endorse in perpetuity. His reasons were private, though only partly personal. He believed in what he called 'the morally disintegrating effect of Lloyd George on all whom he had to deal with', whether MPs, Civil Servants, trade unionists or the public; and he regarded Lloyd George's relations with the press barons, Lords Northcliffe, Beaverbrook and Rothermere, as a close conspiracy alien to the proprieties of Cabinet government. Like his close friend, J. C. C. Davidson, he knew enough of the world of Maundy Gregory, where honours were traded, like groceries, with the prices clearly marked, to feel that 'the system was poisoning the whole atmosphere of public life'.

He felt the political decay of the Coalition even more keenly. Lloyd George was a parliamentary middleman, a broker who, in order to contain a 'ministry of all the talents', could destroy the two-party system by eviscerating both Liberals and Conservatives. Baldwin might have used Disraeli's words on Peel to describe him: 'He is so vain that he wants to figure in history as the settler of all the great questions; but a parliamentary constitution is not favourable to such ambitions; things must be done by parties, not by persons using parties as tools.'[3] Wedded unquestioningly to party politics, Baldwin was to see a supreme need after 1922 'to restore and maintain the unity of the party' – not least because, looking across the Channel, he saw only the weakness of the Weimar Constitution, and the shifting, corrupt alliances of the Fourth Republic in France. These feelings sustained a hostility to Lloyd George which lasted into the 1930s.

Of course when Baldwin, appalled at the Chanak affair and at the bellicose stand against Turkey made in defence of his pro-Greek policy by Lloyd George, decided in October 1922 to resign from the Cabinet in protest and stand as a free Conservative, he did not break up the Coalition single-handed. That needed a majority of junior ministers, who had watched anxiously Lloyd George's manoeuvrings for a general election on the Coalition platform, dissident Cabinet ministers, Sir George Younger, the party Chairman, and the Chief Whip, as well as the cumulative pressure of party agents and the press; and finally,

[3] Robert Blake, *Disraeli* (London, 1966), p. 223.

decisively, the presence of Bonar Law at the Carlton Club meeting on 19 October. It needed the external decay of the Coalition, the ruin of Lloyd George's European policy after the break-up of the Genoa Conference, the grave estrangement of the Dominions after Chanak, and the spectre of mass unemployment at home.

Yet the role of catalyst is not insignificant. Baldwin saw clearly what he was doing and he carried weight, though not in terms of public affiliations. His speech at the Carlton Club, with its mordant phrases – 'The Prime Minister is a dynamic force and it is from that very fact that our troubles arise. . . . It is owing to that dynamic force that the Liberal party has been smashed to pieces. . . . I think that, if the present association is continued, you will see the process go on inevitably until the old Conservative party is lost in ruins' – was second in effect only to Bonar Law's. He lacked, of course, the political birthright of a Chamberlain or a Churchill and at that time he lacked Cabinet presence. Tom Jones wrote in 1921 of 'the long silences of S.B.'. But he represented the party, pillaged of its leaders by Lloyd George and vulnerable in the constituencies to the threat of a politically mature Labour party. He also had won the high esteem of powerful Civil Servants, Sir Norman Warren Fisher, the Head of the Treasury, Sir Maurice Hankey, Secretary of the Cabinet, and Treasury officials such as Bradbury, Leith-Ross, Niemeyer; even of Maynard Keynes, who looked to him to help solve the intricate problems of the post-war European economy. His party political base, built up during the war, when he played host to the Tory opponents of Asquith, was only enhanced by the break from Lloyd George. He was respected in the City and in business circles and, as Chancellor, was favoured by Montagu Norman, Governor of the Bank of England.

A man for the post-war Establishment, then, and a fit heir for Bonar Law, since his record on the crucial post-war issues was impeccable, in the party sense. Baldwin had stood to the right over the Irish Treaty, though not with the diehards against it. He had advocated economy and retrenchment in 1919, yet dissociated himself (in his own famous phrase) from 'the hard-faced men who looked as if they had done well out of the war'. His speeches on social policy since 1908 had been humane and liberal, his record as an employer was outstanding by pre-war standards, and (unlike Lloyd George) he was respected by trade unionist MPs and by the Labour party as a whole. He believed, as did most men in government, in the need to restore the international trading network, and the Gold Standard at the pre-war parity. Unlike many of his colleagues, he was familiar with the Continent from pre-war experience. He spoke French fluently, and a little German, and, like MacDonald in 1924, found no difficult in casting his policy in a European mould.

Above all, Baldwin claimed to stand for well-tried things and traditional remedies, at a time of intense Conservative sensitivity to the dangers threatening the social framework. Revolution in Russia and Germany, inflation across Europe, war in Ireland, thunderous discontent at home, had left even the Cabinet unsure whether peace could ever wholly be restored. Beside the paladins surrounding Lloyd George, he seemed mundane; a sound family man, a good churchman, a lover of the country, a speaker who could distil the quintessence of English history into words and talk openly about 'the things that strike down into the very depths of our nature, and touch chords that go back to the beginning of time and the human race'. The public picture of affable sympathy, as it became known through columnists and cartoonists, ignored both his classical literacy and the high degree of nervous tension which enjoined frequent rest and travel abroad, but it was not unrecognisable. When Baldwin explained the results of the election that returned Bonar Law as Prime Minister, he quoted Lloyd George's disparaging phrase that Law was 'honest to the point of simplicity'; 'By God,' he went on, 'that is what we have been looking for.'[4] He might have been speaking of himself.

Law made him Chancellor of the Exchequer. In the six months at the Treasury, he had to cope principally with the intractable problem of the British war debt to the United States which, four years after the Armistice, had become a festering sore. The Americans contended that Britain was wholly responsible, while the terms of the Balfour Note, suggesting the general trading-off of all inter-allied debts, amounted, as Baldwin told a City friend, to the jibe, 'We will pay you if we must, but you will be cads if you ask us to do so'. Baldwin went to Washington in January 1923 and after tough but amicable talks with the American Treasury, the Commission on the Debt, and East Coast bankers, reached an agreement which provided for annual payments of $161m for ten years and $184m for a further fifty-two, harsh in comparison with British aspirations but generous in relation to American. Law objected and was furious when discussion was effectively pre-empted

[4] *Whitehall Diary*, i, 241.

by the unguarded remarks Baldwin made to journalists on his arrival at Southampton. In Cabinet, however, the Prime Minister was isolated, and upset so greatly that his close friend Lord Beaverbrook believed the episode hastened his premature death.

That he risked such political conflict with his leader, and a public outcry in the press, can be explained by Baldwin's synoptic approach to the problem not only of inter-allied debts, especially those of France to Britain, but of German reparations, unpaid since the end of 1921, the spiralling inflation of both German and French currencies, and the disastrous outcome of the French military occupation of the Ruhr (the attempt 'to dig out coal with bayonets') early in 1923. As Chancellor and later Prime Minister, Baldwin saw the absolute need to re-establish the European exchange rates and normal trading relations, if British industry were to be able to recover. Thus the results of the debt settlement – an improvement of the pound against the dollar, and a warmer American attitude towards Europe's financial troubles – must be seen together with the long, tortuous bargaining to get France out of the Ruhr, and the personal confrontation between Baldwin and the French premier Raymond Poincaré, in September 1923. The lines came together with the *entente* between the two new Prime Ministers, Herriot and MacDonald, in 1924 and the first sensible settlement of reparations by the committee headed by an American, General Dawes. For this and the changed climate, for the brief golden years after Locarno, Baldwin deserves some credit.

During the intricate king-making of May 1923, at least four participants could claim to have influenced the choice, yet in the end, with his accustomed shrewd common sense (and against the urging of Lord Stamfordham, his private secretary) King George V made his own choice. Baldwin took his elevation with a mixture of wry humour, humility and religious dedication. Meanwhile the Central Office set the press to make him more widely known; the story of F.S.T. was leaked, and one sardonic observer wrote: 'All of us are astonished at the swiftness of his ascent. . . . A plain man, domesticated like B.L., fond of books and music and walks in the country. Nothing like B.L.'s brain – much slower, and always eager to consult one or two others; but stands by his decisions, once taken.'[5]

Passive expectation was belied. Baldwin had been a protectionist since 1903 when his father followed Joseph Chamberlain's original

[5] *Whitehall Diary*, i, 237.

Tariff Campaign. He became convinced, during his summer holiday at Aix-les-Bains, that protection was the only remaining cure for unemployment, then totalling $1\frac{1}{2}$ million, or 10 per cent of the (insured) working population. There were also other reasons; strong pressure had built up in the Cabinet in preceding months, much of it the result of clamour by interested groups of industrialists. The Prime Ministers of South Africa, Australia and New Zealand made keen bids for quotas and tariff agreements at the Imperial Conference in October; and there was a chance of splitting off the remaining Tory coalitionists, Austen Chamberlain, Birkenhead and their followers, and perhaps even the Liberal, Churchill, from Lloyd George.

Unfortunately, Bonar Law had left the damaging heritage of a promise of no major fiscal change without a general election. The 1923 tariff policy did not touch corn, but it did represent the reversal of a century of British policy. Although Baldwin, in an exercise of almost presidential power, pushed it through Cabinet in a single meeting, he was constrained by party divisions, chiefly between the Cecils and the Chamberlains, and by the fear that Lloyd George himself might switch from free trade, to exempt food and call a general election. At its best, his policy stood for help to the declining staple industries where unemployment was heaviest, and for the development of reciprocal trade with the Empire; but during the campaign the message bore all the signs of the confusion that was still endemic in the party. Against the old cry of 'dear food' raised by the Liberals, who united under Lloyd George and Asquith for the first time since 1916, it was not enough. Against the Conservatives' 257 seats, the Liberals held 158, Labour 191, and by courtesy of Asquith, the first Labour Government took office.

The *cognoscenti* expected Baldwin to fall and be forgotten. He had indeed to eat humble pie: the Lancashire interest and Austen Chamberlain exacted a pledge not to reintroduce a tariff without clear proof of a change in public opinion. There were attempts to enforce his resignation. But they failed; and as 1924 passed, sweeping MacDonald away on a tide of anti-Russian sentiment, Baldwin and the party were strengthened precisely because of the way party politics had been polarised. The Coalition Conservatives came into the fold; and Churchill also – though not without a storm which led Baldwin to write, 'Leading the party is like driving pigs to market'. Meanwhile Lloyd George, by his own choice shackled to the increasingly obsolete doctrine of free trade, and cut off again from Asquith, was reduced over the next decade to offering himself, his brilliant schemes, and his fund, to the highest bidder in what had become again, and despite his efforts, a two-party system.

During his time in opposition, Baldwin began the long process of party reform. With Neville Chamberlain as his instrument, a new manifesto, *Aims and Principles*, was published; the Shadow Cabinet was formalised for the first time, and a series of party committees set up, responsible to the leader rather than to Central Office. In the summer of 1924, in a series of major speeches, Baldwin launched what came to be called the 'New Conservatism'. It was his only populist experiment, but it was successful in the hardest task of an opposition, which is to capture attention in the teeth of the reigning government. Many of the themes of the next decade were already evident: the needs of Imperial defence, despite arms limitation; independence for India; peace in industry, and schemes for housing and social welfare. Out of 1923 Baldwin had also learnt the value of political education. In future, over industrial strife, India and rearmament, he was to wait, some thought too long, until the electorate had been taught to accept what his governments proposed. Deductions from one episode reinforced his natural caution and became a cardinal rule of democracy. So, as Lord Haldane wrote, 'Baldwin has established himself. He is out to develop a democratic Conservatism – and he has a great deal of sympathy with the aspirations of Labour'.[6]

Before the election of 1929, Baldwin chose not to issue a manifesto but to fight on his Government's record and to attack the manifestos of his opponents. Conservative spokesmen claimed that record could stand beside the Governments of Disraeli or Gladstone or of 1906. Although historians, counting the total of the unemployed, have on the whole been less flattering, by most political standards it was a great reforming ministry.

The Conservatives began with one of their two absolute majorities in this century, with over 50 per cent of the vote in contested seats, and 415 MPs against 152 Labour and only 42 Liberals. Whatever the effect of the 'red scare' and the Zinoviev letter, this result suggested that 1923 had been only a momentary revival in the prolonged death of Liberal England. The Cabinet Baldwin chose was as formidable as the majority in the House of Commons, for it included Curzon, Balfour, Churchill, Hailsham, Salisbury, Austen and Neville Chamberlain, Birkenhead,

6 Baldwin papers.

Steel-Maitland, Hoare, Amery and Cunliffe-Lister. It was more difficult, however, to lead than to choose such a *galerie* of talent. Many of them, in their letters and memoirs, suggested that Baldwin, like a Disraeli in carpet slippers, had led from behind, and that successes accrued to them as individuals – particularly the Chamberlains and the Chancellor of the Exchequer, Churchill. Yet most contemporaries had to conclude that, despite their achievements, it was a *Baldwin* Cabinet.

Baldwin had a great capacity for taking advice, from Civil Servants, private secretaries, party officials, journalists and friends; but since he was a competent broker of ideas, as well as a ruminant and original thinker, few others branded him with theirs. The secret of his style of leadership lay in the creation of a supportive environment in which others could work. To the creative minds, Chamberlain with his long list of Bills and Churchill with his 'hundred horsepower brain', he gave freedom from irksome restraints and petty control; to others, like Austen Chamberlain before Locarno, he gave private help and asked no credit. Lord Eustace Percy, Minister of Education, saw that 'his support contributed more to their very solid achievements than any attempt he could have made to alloy their policies with bright ideas of his own in the Lloyd George manner'.[7] Again, the contrast with his predecessor was marked. Unlike Lloyd George or Neville Chamberlain, Baldwin never tried to be senior partner in each department as well as president of the Cabinet. His style was similar to Disraeli's, and Churchill commented, 'He was singularly adroit in letting events work for him and capable of seizing the right moment when it came.'[8] Birkenhead used to say, wisely, 'He takes a leap in the dark; looks round – and takes another'.

To those obsessed with the paraphernalia of red boxes, he appeared idle; but rather he was a reflective, indulgent chairman of Cabinets. Davidson saw that 'he intervened rarely with a definite conclusion of his own, yet when he did so, his mastery was complete'.[9] Thus he spoke out, decisively, against the Tory attempt to change the basis of the trade union political levy by McQuisten's Private Members Bill in 1925, in a famous speech which ended with the appeal; 'Give us peace in our time, O Lord.' A year later he forced through a reluctant party the

[7] Lord Eustace Percy, *Some Memories* (London, 1952), p. 128.
[8] Winston Churchill, *The Second World War*, i, 'The Gathering Storm' (London, 1959), p. 202.
[9] Viscount Davidson, Draft Memoirs (Davidson papers).

reorganisation of the electricity supply in the first Conservative essay in state capitalism. Above all, he made it possible for his ministers to speak out freely in Cabinet and yet listen to each other; and he created an environment in which men whose stature and wills could not easily be contained around a table found easy access, a sense of place, and a corporate aim. Samuel Hoare noted the contrast after Baldwin retired in 1937; 'Chamberlain seemed at once to crystallise all the fluid forces in the Cabinet. His clear-cut mind and concrete outlook had an astringent effect upon opinions and preferences that had hitherto been only sentiments and impressions. As soon as he succeeded Baldwin, I became increasingly conscious of two distinct points of view in the Cabinet.'[10] With this talent went a rare mastery of the House of Commons and of his backbenchers which rested on patience, infinite tact, and the acceptance of the art of the possible. As he once told a dinner of Royal Academicians; 'Your instruments, by which you work, are dumb – pencils and paints. Ours are neither dumb nor inert. I often think we rather resemble Alice in Wonderland, who tried to play croquet with a flamingo instead of a mallet.'

Between 1925 and 1929 Baldwin's direct influence is to be found principally in economic and foreign policy, rather than in social reform. In that sphere, given his head, Chamberlain ran remorselessly through a tide of legislation culminating in the Local Government Act of 1929 and the administrative foundations of the Welfare State. Meanwhile, Baldwin broke slowly through the carapace of his years at the Treasury. In his only Budget speech, in 1923, he had called for 'an avowed and sustained programme of debt reduction from revenue'. Such orthodoxy underlay his own and the Labour Government's approaches to what the Treasury called 'the Departmental Problem' until interest rates finally fell in 1932. His essay in Protection can, however, be seen as an attempt to escape from the remorseless logic of deflation and return, at the old parity, to the Gold Standard as the only cure for the overriding questions of unemployment and industrial stagnation. After the loss of that hope in the 1923 election, Baldwin had reluctantly to accept the consequences, and take over where the Labour Government and Snowden had left off. Despite the fulminations of Keynes, he supported Churchill in returning to gold in 1925. It was not then clear that the pre-war standard had worked, not of its own momentum, but because the Bank of England made it work. But in the later 1920s it proved impossible to

[10] Lord Templewood, *Nine Troubled Years* (London, 1954), p. 257.

build up strong enough reserves, in relation to Paris and New York, to support such a role again, while high interest rates made the conversion of the wartime National Debt impossible and impeded the flow of capital for industrial investment.

For these reasons, and despite his pledge against tariffs, Baldwin was tempted to use the Safeguarding procedure as a means to help industries threatened by excessive competition and dumping. Sadly, he allowed himself to be restrained by Churchill's threat to resign over the test case of iron and steel. Some ways *were* found to help industry; Baldwin was instrumental in the formation of the Lancashire Cotton and English Steel Corporations, and he urged the Bank of England to take the first steps in what became in 1929 the Bankers Industrial Development Corporation. Some government facilities were provided via the Industrial Transference Board for unemployed men to change jobs; and industry was relieved of the burden of rates. These were not insignificant measures in the 'rationalisation' period after 1927, which saw the creation of great combines such as ICI and British Oxygen. But, like all his ministers, Baldwin accepted the Treasury arguments against the use of government funds on any large scale to propagate employment by public works. Retrenchment was still valued as the classic remedy, while deficit financing was repelled, together with Lloyd George's brilliant programmes set out in the Yellow Book and *We can conquer unemployment*. In a dubious precedent, Baldwin asked the Treasury to prepare an antidote to the latter, for public consumption – and this negative response proved to be the only real Conservative manifesto for 1929.

Industrial discontent and the General Strike were seen through a similarly clouded glass. Baldwin stood for a world of free bargaining, in which a government's duty was to hold the ring and protect the weak, without going so far as to coerce the strong. It was not an easy line to maintain in the 1920s, given the rapid decline of the coal industry, working-class insecurity in the face of unemployment, and the desperate struggles of employers' organisations to recapture markets and profits which led to the widespread attempts to lower wages in 1925–6. Since 1910, and particularly under Lloyd George, governments had committed themselves further and further to intervention in major strikes. However Conservatives might deplore the trade union expectations to which this gave rise, they could not easily ignore them. Each special circumstance thus became a test case.

Baldwin intervened, personally, on 'Red Friday' in July 1925, to extend the government subsidy to the coal industry, despite warnings of Conservative economists and mine-owners, because he believed that the public was not then ready for a showdown over the issue of reducing wages. Yet he believed wages were generally too high in the declining staple industries for Britain to recapture her export markets in coal, iron and steel, cotton and the rest. In his view, rationalisation of the mines, as expressed in the Samuel Report, was the correct approach; streamlining would make them profitable, and profitability would, in time, restore wages. Nationalisation was not an answer nor (and here there was a good deal of ambivalence) was state capitalism, even though that had already been acceptable when applied in the case of the Central Electricity Board.

The Government prepared for the General Strike with considerably more resolution than the TUC, and its organisation included not only the civilian volunteer brigade but a highly efficient deployment of paramilitary strength. The evidence of the negotiations in the fortnight before the Strike shows that Baldwin went well beyond the majority of his Cabinet in his attempts to agree on a formula with the trade union negotiating committee; but he would not use government authority to coerce the mine-owners, and when the talks broke down he took a high 'constitutional' stand – against the day when government would become, irrevocably, third party to any major dispute. The Government won, but for the last time; and as the coal strike dragged on, in desperate misery, into the winter, Baldwin and Churchill attempted to pick up the pieces. They were only partly successful. Despite Baldwin's broadcast 'our business is not to triumph over those who have failed in a mistaken attempt', he was unable to prevent widespread victimisation of strikers, many of whom lost seniority and pension rights.

Baldwin had been known as an unusually humane, if paternalistic, employer. He knew well and valued what he regarded as the moderate trade union leaders, Pugh, Hodges, Hicks, Bevin or Citrine, but he eschewed the Communist party and the Minority Movement. Hence his support for the 1927 Trades Disputes Act, intended as an occasion to define picketing, bring in a secret ballot and restore what Conservatives considered the imbalance of 1906 Act. Even when it was distorted by violent pressures from the party Conference into a vindictive and legally absurd reprisal, he did not dissent. Conservative policy towards industry was still inchoate. Without the aid of Protection or state control, there was perhaps no way to create a 'national' coal industry to satisfy both owners and miners. Instead, after the men returned, beaten, to district agreements and longer hours, Baldwin, working through Lord Weir, discreetly set the stage for the Mond-Turner 'peace in industry' talks which took place in 1928. As the number of strikes fell sharply, and as real wages for those in work rose slowly, the methods of round table bargaining came to appear successful and desirable in contrast to the open warfare of the 1920s. By the 1930s, what had been only tentative ideas of state interference and regulation had become, in Baldwin's third term of office, acceptable and even rooted in Conservative dogma. Against the charge that these years were wasted in sterile strife, it is fair to say that the period 1921–6 was exceptional: militancy and working-class solidarity were a response to the last major assault by employers' associations against trade union rights and established wage levels. Without the strife, Baldwin might not have been able after the General Strike to forecast a new *entente* between government and TUC, and certainly not one that lasted for forty years.

In foreign affairs, Baldwin's policy was in the long term equally definitive for his party and for the National Government of the 1930s. He took the chair at the Committee of Imperial Defence regularly after Curzon's death in 1925, believing (as he said when he opposed the creation of a separate Ministry of Defence) that the Prime Minister himself must have full knowledge of grand strategy and the means to control it. As Chairman, he instituted the Joint Planning Committee and the Chiefs of Staff annual review of defence, and did much to whittle down inter-service rivalry. But in defining the balance between defence requirements and the claims of the peacetime Budget, he had to contend with Churchill's restless search for economy, the assault on the naval estimates, and the 'cruiser crisis' of 1925 – perhaps the nearest his Government came to breaking up, and on lines of the old division between Coalition and Baldwin devotees.

Towards the League of Nations Baldwin showed a sympathetic scepticism. While he mortified League supporters by abandoning the Geneva Protocol, he gave Lord Robert Cecil (and, by association, the League of Nations Union) a place in the Cabinet and put up with his harangues because he represented to the public all the emotional and political capital vested in the concept of collective security. Nevertheless, Baldwin gave priority to old-style diplomacy and to the balance of power in Europe. Sensitive to the economic strength of Stresemann's

Germany, he was in the 1920s isolationist in the sense that Lord Salisbury had been – so long as the winds across the Channel were fair. Mistrustful of Russia and the subversive work of the Comintern, he also turned against the United States because of the aggressive role of the 'big Navyites' and the American attack on British cruiser ratios at the Geneva Disarmament Conference in 1927. Chamberlain noted: 'S.B. says he has got to loathe Americans so much he hates meeting them.'[11] This sharp contrast with 1923 reflected his disappointment at the American failure to live up to role of arbiter in European affairs. The mood did not last and amity was restored in Roosevelt's day, but by then, after the Depression, American isolationism was firmly anchored in public policy. This was the price of Baldwin's perception of the incompatibility of American ambitions and British Imperial defence.

No prime minister can emerge from a five-year term with his old vitality intact. Baldwin, once a competent skier and still a prodigious walker, had been exceptionally fit, but by 1929 he was suffering from diminishing returns even from his lengthy holidays abroad. The nervous weakness of his childhood returned, especially in the months after the General Strike. Family discontents dogged him: his eldest son lived with another man, and for a while, until their reconciliation, as a Labour MP taunted his father from the opposite benches of the House of Commons. Steel shares plummeted in the 1920s and diminished income brought Baldwin a series of debilitating worries. Astley was run on a pittance and the house in Eaton Square had to be sold. Much of his former lightness vanished, and his quips – about Lloyd George ('he who lies in the bosom of the Goat spends his remaining days plucking out the fleas'), or Curzon ('I met Curzon in Downing Street, from whom I got the sort of greeting a corpse would give to an undertaker') – were heard more rarely. His acquaintances noted an increasing deafness. He was, after all, 62.

There is no need to look to the leader alone for the loss of the 1929 election. Abroad, the Depression was gathering; at home, rising unemployment. The memory of the slack years 1927–8, the fitful attacks of the press, and the behaviour of the lunatic fringe of the party, all contributed, while Labour and Liberals made steady gains in local politics and by-elections. But against the vivid promises of the Liberal programme and *Labour and the Nation*, both of which urged vast

11 Neville Chamberlain papers.

extension of state authority, Baldwin could only proclaim bleakly that there was no easy substitute for the long road of economic reconstruction, by what now seemed a scarcely credible private enterprise.

For this reason, the attacks on his leadership revived when the results (Conservatives 261, Labour 287, Liberal 59) were known. His failure was doubly exposed because many had predicted astonishing success for Lloyd George, and when that too was denied, they blamed Baldwin's torpor for the Labour gains. In 1924, reprisals had come chiefly from the press lords, Beaverbrook and Rothermere, but in the two years after 1929, it was more broadly based and the rebels found two great causes, Empire free trade and the 'defence' of India against independence. In retrospect, given Baldwin's experience of Dominion protectionism at the Ottawa Economic Conference in 1932, Empire free trade was a decade late and slightly absurd. But both causes appealed to deeply felt Tory traditions, the more so since this time the dissidents had a Crown Prince in Neville Chamberlain. Against what Bridgeman called 'a display of the worst qualities of the Party under the effects of defeat',[12] Baldwin retreated steadily. The campaign enforced the resignation of his close friend J. C. C. Davidson as chairman of the party, and over India Churchill, 'once more the subaltern of Hussars of '96', retired to the back benches. Yet it was only when the Principal Agent defected, in February 1931, that Baldwin seriously considered resignation. He was instead induced to test his popularity at the by-election at St George's, Westminster, where Duff Cooper agreed to act as his champion. During the campaign, which Cooper won spectacularly, Baldwin worked off a lifetime's anger against irresponsible Fleet Street political demands: 'What the proprietorship of these papers is aiming at is power, and power without responsibility – the prerogative of the harlot throughout the ages.'

Beaverbrook said afterwards: 'He always won – the toughest and most unscrupulous politician you could find – cold, merciless in his dislikes.'[13] For once in his lifetime this was true of Baldwin; and his fury was enhanced by a sense of time slipping by. His recapture of the political limelight was overdue, for the Labour Government was manifestly tottering. In the subsequent months, some of the ground of attack against MacDonald was fair – the failure even to contain unemployment after the promises of 1929, and the refusal to consider a

[12] Lord Bridgeman, Political Notes II (Bridgeman papers).
[13] Sir John Elliott papers.

tariff (now firm Conservative policy); but some was less so, for it was questionable for an ex-Prime Minister, who in his own time had accepted the bankruptcy of the Unemployment Insurance Fund, to damn Labour's borrowing from future taxation as 'unsound finance'. Overtures from MacDonald in the summer of 1931 were rejected: and when the storm broke in August, Baldwin held firmly that if the Government resigned, the Conservatives should reign instead. Sympathy for the Labour party did not extend as far as support for its incompetence. He resisted Neville Chamberlain's blandishments to join a National Government and wrote to him: 'I think in the long view it is all to the good that the Government have to look after their own chickens as they come home to roost, and get a lot of the dirt cleared up before we come in. To have the consequence of their finances exposed – and acknowledged to the world – within four months of their budget, would be a wonderful lesson.'[14]

Nevertheless, Baldwin obeyed when the King asked him, as Conservative leader, to join the National Government under MacDonald. He did respect the Labour leader, and he accepted the need, then and later, to contain Liberal support in face of the world crisis. Party duty was served by ensuring fair shares in the election of 1931 – an often vindictive affair in which Baldwin, more than most, restrained himself from throwing mud at the Labour party MacDonald had left. He contented himself with talk of 'sound, clean, honourable finance' and 'the acid test of democracy', and many who had voted Labour for a generation abstained or even swelled the massive National gains, like Thomas Jones, who 'voted Conservative for the first time in my life . . . we had to do it. . . . we could not trust them with the Bank of England – just yet. But that too will come.'[15] In the aftermath, with his sense of the absolute need for a two-party system, and his fear of what Jones called 'parliamentary dictatorship,' Baldwin may have helped to accomplish the latter. He never denied the moral challenge of socialism. He admired Lansbury's courageous leadership of the denuded Labour party in the 1930s, and in ways both open and obscure he tried to keep open the parliamentary stage for its revival after 1935. What he despised were 'economic dons who were using the working man as a tool for trying their intellectual experiments on England', and he deplored the attempts of the ILP, the Communist party and the Socialist League to drag

[14] Neville Chamberlain papers.
[15] Thomas Jones, *Diary with Letters* (London, 1953), p. 20.

politics out of the House of Commons onto the platform of populist revolution.

The fact that Baldwin was only Prime Minister again between June 1935 and June 1937 is significant: he allowed the compact with Mac-Donald to run for four years, despite the enormous preponderence of Conservatives in the Coalition. As Lord President of the Council, Baldwin had a brief to interest himself in whatever issues he chose. Others took the great offices – Neville Chamberlain the Exchequer, Simon the Foreign Office. Like Balfour after 1904, Baldwin became an elder statesman above the ordinary rut of party warfare. To a large extent as a result of his work, the Conservatives had emerged from their half-way house of 1929 into acceptance of the tariff, low interest rates, a managed currency and abandonment of the fixed parity with the dollar. They would not yet face up to the problem of the depressed areas, nor Keynesian economics, but these were not the issues Baldwin chose in the 1930s. Instead he took India, his preoccupation since his choice of Edward Wood (Lord Irwin, later Lord Halifax) as Viceroy in 1926. To bring the subcontinent nearer to independent status seemed the climax of his career, an achievement for which he would have been happy even to split his party. Discord was inevitable, whether the rebels were led by Churchill or not. After the Irwin Declaration which he supported, though doubtful about the specific promise of Dominion status, Baldwin was unable to smooth over the jagged conflicts of Conservative opinion. During what he called 'the year my party tried to get rid of me', he identified his opponents and sought instead to smash them. In the debate on the Round Table Conference in 1931, he said of Churchill's intemperate language: 'I felt that if George III had been endowed with the tongue of Edmund Burke, he might have made such a speech.' Uneasy parallels with the tragic dealings with Irish nationalism recurred, through four years of strife, through the next Conference, the Commissions of Inquiry, and the elephantine progress of the Government of India Act, until its conclusion in 1935. As Party leader, he sustained the filibustering of the diehards of the India Defence League which reached its climax at the 1934 Party Conference when the platform survived by a meagre 17 votes – 540 to 523 – the nearest a Conservative leader has come to public defeat in recent times.

Baldwin made India an issue of confidence in his own leadership, and although it is arguable that he knew little of the real India and could not hope to see it through Indian eyes, he saw clearly that the debate lay with the British Parliament, which alone could grant political freedom. In one of his finest speeches he graduated from his traditional concept of Empire to a truly modern stance: 'There is a wind of nationalism and freedom blowing round the world, and blowing as strongly in Asia as anywhere. . . . What have we taught India for a century? We have preached English institutions and democracy and all the rest of it. We have taught her the lesson and she wants us to pay the bill. . . . And are we less true Conservatives because we say: "The time has now come"?'[16]

Many of his arguments for Indian independence were strategic. Just as with India, so with Egypt and the Suez Canal: it was time to settle before Britain's standing in the world was challenged too sharply. Since his first concentration on European problems in 1923, Baldwin had brooded on the terms for British survival in a world in which she was no longer more than one great power amongst five others – the United States, Russia, Japan, Germany and France. Unlike these, as he found from bitter experience, Britain had permanent commitments and liabilities across a world Empire, from which she drew little practical support. Hence his opposition to the scaling down of the cruiser ratio at the London Naval Conference in 1931 and his sensibility to the aggressive designs of Japan in the Far East. During the Shanghai crisis, in January 1932, Baldwin foresaw the depth of Britain's weakness and her inability to defend her interests in China, Singapore, even Australia and New Zealand. He threw his weight behind the demands of the Chiefs of Staff for abrogation of the Ten Year Rule, but the point at which he finally abandoned the MacDonald Government's quest for disarmament came when the report of the Defence Requirements Committee of the CID, in February 1934, defined Japan as the immediate but lesser threat; 'We take Germany as the ultimate potential enemy, against whom our "long range" defence policy must be directed.'[17]

During 1934, and at the heart of government policy-making committees, Baldwin strove to put that warning into practice, through new priorities of allocation within the defence budget, and by radically revised forward planning In March 1934 he defined his argument in the House of Commons: 'In air strength and air power, this country shall no longer be in a position inferior to any country within striking distance

[16] Speech to the Conservative Central Council, 4 December 1934.
[17] CAB 50/51.

of our shores'.[18] But this policy led to a sharp division in the Cabinet. It took shape in a confrontation with Neville Chamberlain over the defence estimates in June 1934, but personal differences only masked the contrast between two views of overall foreign policy, both of which superseded the search for disarmament. Chamberlain stood for limited liability, for a withdrawal from European commitments, in particular the promise of a field force to France, for concentration on air defence rather than on offensive bomber capacity, and for an accommodation with Japan in the Far East. Against this, Baldwin advocated the view that whatever the white Dominions might demand, it was impossible to withdraw Britain from the European context. Because Baldwin won, overall, the field force was retained as a pledge to the defence of north-western France and Belgium; and the Locarno provisions were tacitly extended to Holland. The Navy was set to maintain the ratio of its lead over Germany – a policy that gave rise to the bitterly disputed Anglo-German Naval Treaty – and the mammoth base at Singapore was begun as a counter to Japanese expansion. The prime aim was the creation of a bomber deterrent, backed up by fast fighters and radar, to restrain Germany from aggression (much as the atomic bomb has been used in diplomacy since 1945) and to bring the Nazi regime to terms before it was too late.

Baldwin's standpoint was Eurocentric; and risked grave Dominion fears of exposure, because he declined to come to terms with Japan at the price of alienating the United States, for whose aid, in a European conflict, he still hoped. Over the next three years this policy encouraged a remarkable improvement in the Air Force: Scheme F, adopted in January 1936, added over three years 8,000 new aircraft of the latest types, including Hurricanes, Spitfires and Blenheims. Great risks were taken, the Hampdens and Wellingtons were ordered before prototypes had been tested, and the Bristol Beaufort went into production straight off the drawing-board. They were successful and Baldwin has a good claim to the Air Force that contained the German attacks in 1940. But rearmament conflicted with the popular mood – and it had only mixed results abroad.

In spite of his many speeches on rearmament in the 1930s, Baldwin found the process of public political education as hard to achieve as Churchill did in a hostile House of Commons. One of his potent warnings, 'The bomber will always get through', aimed at the unpreparedness

[18] Hansard 286 co. 2078.

of 1932, proved a two-edged phrase, and in later years was used to defend appeasement, while his pledge to the pacifists of 'no great armaments', rather than rebutting accusations of a renewed arms race, stuck in the public memory as pledge against any rearmament. The tide of pacifism ran high, and not merely in the millions of signatures on the Peace Ballot. Sensitive to electoral vagaries, Baldwin watched swings of 20–25 per cent against the National Government in nearly every by-election from summer 1933 to summer 1935, of which Fulham East was only one amongst fifteen seats lost to a Labour party wedded blindly to disarmament. When he became Prime Minister, he was able to redress the balance by the cautious timing of the general election in November 1935 where he won a guarded mandate to rearm. This he preferred to Churchill's autocratic advice: 'There need be no talk of working up public opinion – you must not go and ask the public what they think about this'.[19]

Considering the broad support for war in 1939 it is likely that Baldwin was right. But the rearmament programme ran into severe difficulties in 1936, into bottlenecks of production, shortages of skilled labour, factory space, machine tools, and above all, into a debate in which the National Government and the parties refused to accept the logic of war demands on peacetime 'normal' economy. Worse, in 1935–6 the deterrent failed to deter. If Baldwin had been Prime Minister, or if he had gone to Stresa in April 1935, to try to ram home the disadvantage of Germany when faced by the other Locarno powers, there might perhaps have been hope for a European *détente*. In the event, Hitler refused to be tied to arms limitation, used the British Defence White Paper of 1935 as justification, and claimed 'absolute equality of status'. Anglo-French accord dissolved, over the Franco-Soviet Treaty and the Anglo-German Naval Treaty, even before the Italian invasion of Abyssinia. The attempts of Laval and Hoare to settle Mussolini's demands at the expense of Abyssinia and the League brought particular personal shame for Baldwin who, though largely ignorant of his Foreign Secretary's commitment, was forced by public clamour to sack him, and then stand penitent before an angry House of Commons. In the wake, Germany reoccupied the Rhineland and Britain proved militarily, and France politically, incapable of enforcing the Treaty of Versailles. The 'Subterranean Stage' of German recovery was complete.

Baldwin was urged by such powerful friends as Geoffrey Dawson,

[19] Hansard, 8 Nov. 1934.

Editor of *The Times*, to take advantage of Hitler's promises which accompanied the militarisation of the Rhineland in April 1936. Then, as in 1933, he refused to meet Hitler personally, fearing to commit the country as Chamberlain was later to do before Munich. Instead, Baldwin hung, doggedly, to the French *entente*; and it can be argued that, until the end of 1936, the Baldwin-Eden line of 'keeping Germany guessing' (what Vansittart called 'cunctation') while catching up in armaments had been, in terms of relative strength, a success. But in 1937 Belgium withdrew into neutrality and the Spanish Civil War focused attention on the growing weaknesses of France.

Supporters of the deterrent policy wavered, even before Chamberlain came to power bearing fixed ideas of limited liability. Some saw Britain's role in a form of Atlanticism, or as part of an Imperial aggregate; others looked to a more direct deal with Germany over African colonies; and this wave swept away the restraints, into the full flood of appeasement in 1938. Baldwin could not withstand it. He had already collapsed from overstrain in the summer of 1936, leaving Eden to cope with the Spanish Civil War – and he would almost certainly have retired that year if it had not been for the Abdication crisis.

Much of the attention focused on that dramatic and romantic episode has detracted from the reasons why Baldwin judged it so seriously. Long before the King's attachment to Mrs Simpson was known in Whitehall, he had been worried by what he had seen of the King's cursory attitude to his duties as monarch, and his pro-German sympathies. Baldwin hoped that the former might, with time, approximate more to the dignified version demanded by an Empire opinion which was in many ways decades behind British attitudes. The latter was more serious, given the Government's conclusion that Germany was the enemy against whom Britain should rearm. But Baldwin did not submit to the demands of several ministers and senior Civil Servants that the King's desire to marry Mrs Simpson should be used as a pretext to replace him. Only Edward VIII's firm will, and the Dominion reactions to it, made abdication inevitable.

Baldwin's handling of the crisis – his tact and the manner in which he ensured a dignified conclusion – was greatly praised at the time, as the supreme act of his political career. He himself attached more importance to the warnings he gave, after he had begun to hand over defence policy to Neville Chamberlain, and before his actual retirement in June 1937: such as that to the House of Commons in February 1937: 'We shall neither assure our safety and that of the Empire, nor play our part in securing the peace of the world, unless we bring our forces up to the necessary standard. Deterrence is our object . . . ineffective deterrence is worse than useless.'

Within weeks of that speech, Chamberlain had begun to recast defence priorities to the exclusion of deterrence. The new order led directly into the appeasement policy which culminated in the Munich 'settlement' of 1938. With that, Baldwin disagreed, and for a while he became the focus of the Tory opposition to Chamberlain. But he was nearly seventy then, and he preferred to abstain from active politics, propagating instead, in lecture tours in Britain and America, his distilled opinions about the value of democracy and the evils of totalitarian authority. The hyperbolic praise showered on him in 1937 soon dissolved, and the war brought obloquy and splenetic denunciation for his alleged failure to rearm. A sustained assault against his reputation was mounted, by sections of the press, the authors of *Guilty Men*, and a number of private individuals whose letters penetrated, unfailingly, to Astley, where he spent his retirement. He bore them in public silence. Privately he came near to despair and found pleasure only in his friends, and in his honorific duties as Chancellor of Cambridge University. Restricted by ill health, he walked with difficulty; afflicted by the public clamour over the requisitioning of his garden gates for scrap, he seems to have accepted the role of scapegoat and sought comfort in his High Anglican faith. His wife died first, leaving him bewildered and lonely: he followed in 1947.

It was not a time for praising the great men of the inter-war years, and Baldwin suffered posthumously in the account of his unwilling first biographer. Criticism was directed, ironically, to rearmament, an issue where his record was impeccable, and the equally important work of the 1920s was ignored. Now, half a century has passed since he became Prime Minister and his achievements can be seen in the mainstream of British Conservatism, which he did more than most twentieth-century party leaders to shape. His public persona, remembered through his mastery of the political platform, the House of Commons, and broadcasting, coloured two decades – the Baldwin Age. His phrases and images became clichés from constant repetition. By giving illustration and substance to the concepts of party, democracy, freedom, he welded his own particular vision into a public consciousness and ensured that the result reflected a wholly 'English' tint. In this he fulfilled Hegel's dictum: 'The great man of the age is the one who can put into words the will of his age, tell his age what its will is, and accomplish it.'[20] His definition of politics lay midway between nineteenth-century paternalism and the as yet unsolved search for popular participation. As he told Halifax in 1928, 'Democracy has arrived at a gallop in England and I feel all the time that it is a race for life; can we educate them before the crash comes?'[21]

The 'civilisation' he spoke of frequently, defended, and feared to see destroyed in war with Germany, was, properly, European from before the 1914 deluge; it was restricted by certain standards but was not exclusive, nor wholly class-based. He would quote approvingly the words of Colonel Rainboro, who put the case for the Army in the Putney debates of 1647: 'Really, I think the poorest he that is in England hath a life to live as the richest he.' Baldwin's creed was that of individual responsibility through political commitment. Hard as it was for him to understand the dictators, he did not make the mistake of underestimating them or the ideology they represented. He defended democracy to a Canadian audience in 1927: 'How often has mankind travelled on the circumference of a wheel, working its way to a point that you could call democracy. Go but a little further, and democracy becomes licence, licence becomes anarchy, and the wheel goes full circle and anarchy comes back to tyranny, and man has to fight his way back out of tyranny once again.'

BIBLIOGRAPHY

Baldwin, A. W., *My Father: The True Story* (London, 1955); *The Macdonald Sisters* (London, 1960)
Hyde, H. Montgomery, *Baldwin, the Unexpected Prime Minister* (London, 1973)
Middlemas, R. K. and Barnes, A. J., *Baldwin: A Political Biography* (London, 1969)
Young, G. M., *Stanley Baldwin* (London, 1952)

[20] Hegel, *Philosophy of Right* (London, 1942), p. 295.
[21] Halifax papers.

15

JAMES RAMSAY MACDONALD

BY

KEITH ROBBINS

James Ramsay MacDonald, PC (1924), FRS (1930); Hon LLD (Wales, Glasgow, Edinburgh, Oxford, McGill), JP. Born 12 October 1866, son of J. MacDonald of Lossiemouth, and educated at a board school. Secretary, Labour Party 1900–12; Treasurer 1912–24; Chairman, Independent Labour Party 1906–09; Leader of the Labour Party 1911–14; member LLC 1901–04. Sometime editor of Socialist Library *and the* Socialist Review. *Contested (Lab.) Southampton (1895), Leicester (1900), W. Leicester (1918), E. Woolwich (1921). MP (Lab.) Leicester 1906–18, Aberavon 1922–29, Seaham 1929–31, Seaham (Nat. Lab.) 1931–35, Scottish Universities 1936–37. Chairman of Parliamentary Labour Party and Leader of the Opposition 1922; Prime Minister and First Lord of the Treasury, Foreign Secretary 1924; Leader of the Opposition 1925–29; Prime Minister and First Lord of the Treasury 1929–35; Lord President of the Council 1935–37. Married 1896 Margaret Ethel, daughter of Dr J. H. Gladstone, FRS; two sons, three daughters. Died 9 November 1937. Author of* Socialism and Society, Labour and the Empire, Socialism and Government, Margaret Ethel MacDonald – a Memoir, Social Unrest, The Government of India, Parliament and Revolution, *etc.*

JAMES RAMSAY MACDONALD

The early twenties in Britain witnessed a glut of prime ministers. Lloyd George, the man who had won the war, struggled in vain to keep his peacetime Coalition together. When it collapsed, in October 1922, few supposed that he would not be back. Bonar Law then formed a 'pure' Conservative administration. Within six months cancer was diagnosed and he died shortly afterwards. Then came the amiable ordinary Stanley Baldwin and it seemed that the country was about to settle down. Nevertheless, before the end of the year, despite his parliamentary majority, Baldwin declared that he could not fight unemployment unless he had a free hand to introduce Protection. That free hand was not vouchsafed. Both opposition parties gained ground but Labour was the larger. Free trade prevented a Conservative-Liberal coalition. Since prime ministers were on short service commission, Asquith may have supposed that soon, when Labour had failed, he would be called upon once more.

It was, therefore, a novel group of politicians who visited their rather puzzled monarch at Buckingham Palace in January 1924. For the most part quaintly attired, and looking somewhat embarrassed, they kissed hands on appointment as Ministers of the Crown. Having resumed their normal dress, the new Cabinet posed for a photograph. With one exception, the social origins of the members stood out – gentlemen and players rubbed shoulders uneasily on the road to Jerusalem. The exception was the new Prime Minister. Ramsay MacDonald faced the camera with resolute assurance, his features displaying neither humour nor amazement. He contrived to make the occasion seem perfectly natural. Nothing in his manner or appearance betrayed the fact that at his birth, fifty-seven years earlier, the suggestion that he would be a future Prime Minister would have been deservedly derided, for he was the product of a passing liaison between a ploughman and a serving-girl, both living in the north of Scotland.

At this juncture, MacDonald was the most remarkable man in British public life. He had not been to public school or university. He had not distinguished himself in commerce or in a profession. Yet he had broken through from obscurity to the highest office in the land. Lloyd George apart, he was unique among prime ministers. He knew in his own life the reality of deprivation and poverty. Mindful of this fact, there were those who believed that his first act would be to drag the mighty from their seats. Few could have predicted the course MacDonald did follow over the next decade.

The fears gained strength from the fact that it was Labour that was in office for the first time. In January 1924 new man and new party came together. The King could not recall an occasion when his first minister had to be sworn of the Privy Council before accepting office. Nevertheless, he thought the Socialists ought to be treated fairly and given a chance. The coincidence was indeed highly significant, though the relationship between leader and party was more complex than it would appear to indicate. Neither gloating over his origins nor denying them, MacDonald had changed in the course of his long journey from Lossiemouth. He did not forget the past, indeed he regularly returned to the scenes of his upbringing, yet its inheritance was ambiguous. He wanted the circumstances of the masses to change, as his had changed, but at the same time was there not something striking about his own achievement which marked him off from the masses?

MacDonald's strict Scottish education gave him a taste for reading and study. His matriarchal home encouraged the belief that he was rather out of the ordinary. Perhaps taunts about his illegitimacy spurred him to outstrip those who taunted. He came to England, first in 1884 and then, in 1886, to stay. He took clerical jobs, working hard and studying in the evenings. He did some occasional journalism. Politics already attracted him – he had latterly become private secretary to a Liberal candidate. MacDonald was sober, industrious, intelligent and eloquent. If he could wait, some Liberal association might adopt him as a candidate.

About this time, 1893, the Independent Labour Party was formed in Bradford. Its leading light was Keir Hardie. MacDonald had already corresponded with him, but delayed a year before applying for membership. He stated that he had hitherto placed his trust in Liberalism but he now encountered a disturbing hostility to Labour. MacDonald's decision was a bold one. The future of the new party was very uncertain and metropolitan intellectual circles tended to look down on this provincial creation. Undeterred, he campaigned up and down the country and became a member of the ILP's national council. His marriage, in

1895, to Margaret Gladstone, daughter of a distinguished scientific family, did not impede this activity. She shared his interests and their home became a place where Socialists visiting London frequently called. His wife's private income helped him to fit into the intellectual middle class. He may have lacked an extensive formal education but he gave the appearance of being thoroughly at ease in discussing the scientific and social questions of the day.

The Labour Representation Committee was formed in 1900 and MacDonald became its unpaid secretary. Its purpose was to co-ordinate the activities of the existing Socialist societies and the trade unions. An independent Labour group in Parliament was the aim. He excelled in this post. He negotiated a secret agreement with the Liberals whereby the two bodies agreed to give each other a clear run in certain constituencies. Under this arrangement, MacDonald himself entered the House of Commons in 1906. There were those who saw the twenty-nine 'Labour' MPs so returned as the advance guard of what would prove in a short time to be a mighty army. Looking at his colleagues, MacDonald was more sceptical.

The basic problem that confronted the Labour party, as it now called itself, was one of ideology. How wide should its net be thrown? Should it embrace all supporters of 'Labour', confine itself to trade unionists or restrict membership to Socialists? MacDonald's role in these debates was of fundamental importance. In a series of books, *Socialism and Society* (1905), *Socialism* (1907), *Socialism and Government* (1909), *The Socialist Movement* (1911), *Syndicalism* (1912) and *The Social Unrest* (1913), he made a decisive contribution to the party's thinking. In this decade his own outlook was settled. His prose style may not excite universal admiration. He is both pretentious and, at times, vague, yet the basic argument he presented was serious and his ability to interest his readers cannot be disputed. He was neither a Marxist nor a Utopian but he believed, nevertheless, that he was a Socialist. His critique of the existing capitalist system was a moral one. 'In every workman's heart,' he wrote 'there is a dim perception of a social order based upon the instinct of human equality and justice.' In time, expediency and business advantage would yield before this perception. The resulting 'society of human order' was what he called Socialism, and until it came there would be 'an agitating ferment in all other social forms'. The Co-operative movement, social welfare measures and agencies, profit-sharing, were all good in themselves but they only represented stations along the road to freedom. The time had now come to nationalise the land, the mines and the railways.

MacDonald did not doubt that it would be difficult to achieve this new order. Society could not be magically transformed overnight. However, he claimed that the Socialist method was the Darwinian method. Socialism was the logical culmination of Liberalism, not its antithesis. It wanted to extend not to restrict human liberty, but only where there was proper organisation and control could individual liberty flourish. He therefore worked for what he called 'organic transformation'. He despised what he termed the 'wild ravings' of Syndicalists and others who thought that they had found a short-cut to the future, by-passing Parliament. In his view, the nation was not a mere abstraction but rather a real community which transformed itself in the light of its past. The clamour in some quarters for a 'thorough' Socialist party was a mere apeing of methods proper to countries not endowed with a functioning parliamentary system. He went even further. Socialism was more likely to come about through a 'socialistic' party than through a Socialist one. A pure Socialist party would be tempted to believe that it could ignore the methods by which a society evolved, but that would be a profound mistake. It was also wishful thinking to believe that the assumption of governing authority by the people would make the State redundant. The object of government, he concluded, was not to enlighten the individual to do without government, but to enlighten him so as to co-operate with it.

MacDonald was Chairman of the ILP from 1906–1909, and it is not difficult to understand why he did not have an easy time keeping the party together. When he became Chairman of the Labour party in 1911 his problems were even greater. There was little parliamentary discipline and on a number of important occasions members opposed each other in the lobbies. The idea of a distinct Labour party did indeed make some progress but, in a period of social and industrial unrest, many felt that it should have been faster. Since MacDonald was, for most of the time, in one or other position of leadership, the criticism fell upon him. Personal relations with his colleagues deteriorated, particularly with Henderson and Snowden. MacDonald became introspective and acerbic. His wife died at the end of 1911 and he brooded long over his loss. For a time he talked of giving up politics altogether. His colleagues did not seem to realise how fortunate they were to have him.

The proper course for Labour to follow was still being debated when war broke out in 1914. The conflict split the party on new lines. Mac-Donald condemned British intervention, but after the invasion of Belgium most of his colleagues supported it. Probably with relief, he resigned the chairmanship, though he retained the post of Treasurer. His personal attitude towards the war was very complex, not to say contradictory. His statements are carefully qualified, if not deliberately ambiguous, and this has prompted the supposition that he hoped to emerge at a later stage in the conflict as the man to negotiate peace. He associated with dissident Liberals in the newly formed Union of Democratic Control though he was sceptical of some of its leading ideas. Yet, whatever the subtlety of his views, he was branded as a pacifist and the full welter of patriotic fury fell upon him. The personal slights he believed he received during these years left a permanent mark.

Throughout the war MacDonald firmly denied that he wanted a German victory, but he considered that it would be possible to arrange a reasonable negotiated peace. A penal settlement imposed as a result of outright victory would have disastrous consequences. He hoped that the growing confidence of international Socialism would mean that there would be a much greater sense of community among nations. He welcomed the revolutions in Russia in 1917 and his commitment to peaceful evolution seemed momentarily to waver. His popularity in the ILP reached levels never attained in the past. Yet this reputation for Radicalism did not mean that MacDonald was losing touch with the solid centre of the party. After Henderson resigned from the Cabinet in 1917, the way was open for a reconciliation between 'pro-war' and 'anti-war' factions. In any case disagreement on the war had not impaired co-operation on other issues. The days of a 'progressive alliance' with the Liberals were over. Labour was increasing in confidence and it was time to consolidate the party organisation and prepare for peace.

In the general election of December 1918, MacDonald's lonely wartime stand brought him scant reward. He lost his seat at Leicester and other 'pacifists' also fared badly. Labour emerged with a mere sixty-three seats, an improvement on 1910, but a figure that seemed insignificant beside the massive support for the Coalition. The idea that five years later Labour would take office and that the spurned candidate for Leicester would be Prime Minister seemed far-fetched. Labour's position was in fact stronger than its meagre representation seemed to suggest. It was equipped with a new constitution and a new programme. The wartime split in the Liberal party provided an opportunity for advance. Even in 1918, Labour was stronger than the non-Coalition Liberals and was, in effect, the Opposition. This status would be lost if the Liberals succeeded in coming together again as a united political force, but it was questionable whether this would happen. The leaders of the other parties were more worried by the advance of Labour than they allowed to appear.

MacDonald was bitter about his defeat at Leicester. He raged against the 'unregenerated villadom' and the 'darkened slumdom' to whom he attributed his defeat. His strength lay with 'the intelligent artisan and the intellectual well-to-do', but that had not been sufficient. Despite his anger with the obtuse democracy he refused to abandon his faith in open elections and the parliamentary process. Many around him were doing so. The post-war world hardly offered the peace and security that had been promised. Labour condemned the treatment of Germany in the peace settlement. Domestically, there was disillusion and industrial unrest. The example of the Soviet Union was contagious in some circles. 'Direct action' was in the air. MacDonald sharpened his criticism of government policy but he did not change his fundamental standpoint. In *Parliament and Revolution* (1919), he deprecated slavish imitation of the Soviet Union. Revolution would only create more problems in Britain than it would solve. Parliament was still essential and what was needed to make it more effective was better political education of the people. He was anxious to make it clear that opposition to intervention in the Soviet Union did not mean acceptance of Communism. His influence was critical in preventing the ILP from joining the Communist International and he worked hard to revive the Second International. In *Socialism: Critical and Constructive* (1921), he again stressed that Socialism could only move men 'by education and moral idealism . . . it takes no part in a purely horizontal tug of war between the working and the capitalist class, but is a Plutonic force beneath both heaving them upwards'.

The verdict of the general election in November 1922 seemed to show that Pluto was pushing to some effect. The Conservatives gained a clear majority but Labour had more seats than the still divided Liberals. MacDonald had tried to return to the House of Commons in the Woolwich by-election in 1921. Will Crooks's old seat was won by a VC who made free use of MacDonald's wartime position. In the general election he came back as member for Aberavon and within a few weeks was once again elected Chairman of the Labour party. The circumstances in which, a year later, he became Prime Minister, have already been described.

The mature MacDonald of 1924 was Labour's greatest asset. In the ten years since he had last been Chairman of the party there were a number of occasions when his career had seemed in ruins. The experiences toughened him but they also accentuated his tendency to rely exclusively on his own judgement. His stature both as a speaker and as a writer was invaluable. The poor performance of the Labour party in the post-war House of Commons in his absence seemed to show that his ability as a tactician was sorely needed. Henderson may have been a better organiser, Snowden a more electric orator, Clynes a solider worker, but in sum their qualities could not compete with the new Prime Minister. In this respect, the narrowness of the majority by which he had been elected leader was no real reflection of his stature in the party. There were the usual mutterings from Lansbury and others that MacDonald's Socialism was not their idea of Socialism, but they were discounted. MacDonald seemed to have sufficient support from all sections of the party to see him through.

Loneliness in high office is inescapable. It brought no new terror to MacDonald. From the very beginning, from the way in which the Cabinet was chosen, it was made clear that authority rested with the Prime Minister. He had no hesitation about appointing men who had little connection with Labour if their services were needed, though there were more working men than in any previous Cabinet. He made himself Foreign Secretary, believing, rightly, that no one else had a superior claim. He ruled the Cabinet firmly from the outset as if he had been sitting in the Cabinet room all his life. His less confident colleagues were both impressed and alarmed. They were pleased that MacDonald could hold his own with his predecessors, yet this very success meant that he would be unlikely to inaugurate a new style of government. A Labour prime minister seemed to be like any other prime minister. It also began to look as though a Labour government was like any other government.

MacDonald was not worried by these criticisms. He had early decided that it would be better if Labour did very little. It was in office, not in power. The Liberals were watching and waiting. Once they sensed that the Government was conducting itself incompetently, or that it was stepping ahead of what would be electorally popular, they would bring it down. Since there was a good chance that his colleagues would prove incompetent, it was best not to allow them to parade this publicly. Only in two areas, housing and education, did Labour strike a new note. The Housing Minister, Wheatley, was the only newcomer to make a name for himself. Local authorities were encouraged to increase their house-building for rent by an increased subsidy. The building industry was encouraged to gear itself for higher levels of activity by the prospect that this would continue for many years.

MacDonald himself was chiefly occupied with foreign affairs. The situation in the Ruhr, following the French occupation in 1923, had reached the stage where both France and Germany might be prepared to accept a settlement. He persuaded both countries to agree to fresh proposals for settling the reparations question drawn up by a committee under the American General Dawes. The result pleased the Prime Minister. He had demonstrated to France and Germany that Britain would act as a detached conciliator in Europe. The French connection, which he had so much disliked before 1914, was undermined and the Germans were encouraged.

In other respects, MacDonald was less 'successful'. Although personally not very enthusiastic about the League of Nations, it was expected that he should support it. He even appeared at Geneva. The great project of the time was the 'Protocol' which was supposed to strengthen and clarify the founding Covenant of the League. However, the employment of 'sanctions' – which could include the use of force – divided the Labour party. MacDonald gave his blessing to the plan, but in so qualified a form that it is likely that Labour would have rejected it in the end. That task was bequeathed to its successors.

The Prime Minister was also cautious in his dealings with the Soviet Union. On coming into office, he recognised the Soviet Government but the slogan 'friendship on the Left' had little appeal for him. He took a firm line in the negotiations with the Russians on questions of war debts, loans and trade. It was probably pressure from the back benches, led by E. D. Morel, that eased the path to the agreement. The fact that a treaty was eventually concluded led to criticism from the Conservatives and the Liberals. It seemed that the Cabinet was susceptible to 'pro-Communist' activity. When, shortly afterwards, the Government decided not to prefer charges against the Communist J. R. Campbell, accused of incitement to mutiny, the opposition parties saw their opportunity. MacDonald refused to accept a Liberal amendment – calling for a select committee investigation – to a Conservative motion of censure. The Conservatives then voted for the amendment and the first Labour Government was over. It had lasted less than a year.

In the general election of 1924 the Conservatives gained a comfortable majority over both opposition parties. It was a vigorous contest, made sensational by the release of the 'Zinoviev' letter purporting to urge British Communists to embark on a campaign of disruption. Labour lost seats but increased its vote substantially. The Liberals slumped badly. Inevitably, the record of the Labour Government was criticised within the party. Some now believed that Labour should never have accepted office in circumstances in which it could not carry out Socialist policies. There were over a million unemployed and the Government had made little contribution to solving the problem.

MacDonald seemed unperturbed. He had demonstrated to the country that Labour could be trusted to govern. Patience was needed and in due course the party would be given power, not merely office. The left growled angrily and the ILP went off in search of 'Socialism in our Time'. MacDonald refused to follow. Even though the general Strike in 1926 could have provided an opportunity to sharpen the class-consciousness of the Labour party, he would not be drawn. MacDonald reverted to his earlier conviction that Socialism was more likely to be achieved by a party that was not 'pure' in its Socialism. There was no evidence that the nation as a whole wanted Socialism and it was, to him, a contradiction in terms to talk of imposing it on the people. Socialism was a matter of intellectual and moral conviction which the community as a whole had to be persuaded to adopt. Time had to pass so that the appeal to 'Labour and the Nation' could be consolidated.

MacDonald never had enough time. At the general election in May 1929 Labour became the largest single party in the House of Commons. Nearly as many voted Labour as voted Conservative. The Liberal vote increased substantially but it was not reflected in additional seats. Nevertheless, the Liberals still held the balance, though they were in a weaker position than in 1924. MacDonald was at last near to that moral consensus of the nation which he so much prized. He anticipated that the Government would have a long life since the Liberals would be unwilling to expose themselves to a fresh election. This time the situation seemed much more propitious for Labour.

The Prime Minister seemed in a confident mood. He was even prepared to allow Arthur Henderson to become Foreign Secretary. George Lansbury became First Commissioner of Works. Philip Snowden resumed as Chancellor of the Exchequer. A million workers were still unemployed, but the industrial outlook seemed brighter and Labour was confident that the figure could be reduced. A modest degree of public expenditure would suffice, if the Chancellor could be persuaded to agree. As far as international policy was concerned, it was hoped that Henderson could settle the outstanding German grievances, mollify French anxieties, strengthen the League of Nations and bring about general peace and disarmament.

It is conceivable that all of these desirable ends could have been accomplished had it not been for the Great Depression which began in the United States in October 1929. Within a year the number unemployed had doubled and there were fears that the total would go on rising inexorably. The crisis was of a proportion beyond all calculation in May 1929. It was, at last, the crisis of capitalism, so long expected and so eagerly anticipated in Socialist circles. Eager anticipation did not characterise the reactions of the Labour Government. The Prime Minister told the Labour Party Conference in 1930 that 'the system' had broken down everywhere, as it was bound to do. The difficulty for MacDonald, however, was that it had apparently broken down under a Labour government. Labour would have relished the collapse if it had occurred under a Conservative government, but now it had an unwelcome degree of responsibility. MacDonald found himself entangled in the vagueness of his own rhetoric. What exactly was this 'system' that had broken down? Was it really 'capitalism' that was on trial?

The simplest solution to the difficulties was apparently to move directly to Socialism. There would not even be any need for a revolution. The Prime Minister could carry through the necessary changes under the rubric of his beloved 'organic transformation'. Yet, with the road so unexpectedly open, the Prime Minister suddenly found that he could not see the details of the Socialist city ahead. Twenty years earlier he had written of the seaman who steered by certain marks and then, as appropriate, altered course and followed new marks when the old could lead him no further. 'So', he had concluded, 'with Socialism.' The Socialist method was the 'organic and experimental one of relieving immediate and pressing difficulties on a certain plan, and in accordance with a certain scheme of organisation.' In the second Labour Government, MacDonald had no 'certain plan', though the difficulties were immediate and pressing. He had run out of metaphors and the limitations of his economic judgement were exposed. There was little openness towards new ideas and policies.

The Prime Minister no longer even seemed efficient and confident. He could derive no encouragement from his colleagues and could not share his own problems with them. Only in matters of foreign policy did he show any of his old vigour and spark. His visit to the United States in October 1929 was regarded as a personal triumph and put an end to a period of Anglo-American tension. It paved the way for the London Naval Conference of 1930-1 at which again MacDonald played a leading role. He seemed to revel in these occasions and foreigners still found his personality impressive. It was understood that the Prime Minister would deal personally with Anglo-American relations but in fact he did not confine himself to this sphere. He constantly expressed views on relations with France and Germany, on the League, on disarmament and on the Soviet Union which frequently clashed with those of Henderson, the Foreign Secretary. Their personal relations deteriorated and on several occasions it seemed possible that Henderson would resign. MacDonald's views deserve respect, but the extent of his supervision and intervention was inevitably irksome. It was symptomatic of his loss of confidence in other matters that he turned to the one field of policy where he felt at home.

It was, however, impossible to ignore the effects of the Great Crash. All sorts of unorthodox ideas for dealing with the crisis were being canvassed. The Liberals under Lloyd George had fought the election with ambitious schemes of public works – roads, houses, telephones, power stations – which would mop up unemployment. MacDonald was suspicious both of Lloyd George and the scale of the programme. However, he did appoint J. H. Thomas as minister with special responsibility for employment, assisted by Lansbury, Mosley and Johnston. It did not take long for the limits of Thomas's understanding and energy to be revealed. In January 1930 the Prime Minister announced the creation of the Economic Advisory Council composed of economists, businessmen and trade unionists. He chaired these sessions but little seemed to emerge from them. The energetic young Mosley became impatient and drew up a memorandum urging action over a wide front. His proposals included public control of industry, increased pensions and allowances and the public control of banking to finance development. However, he also proposed Protection for the home market. The Chancellor of the Exchequer was not moved. He adhered rigidly to free trade and to the balanced budget. MacDonald may have had some sympathy for Mosley's proposals but he had no stomach for a struggle with Snowden. Mosley resigned and Thomas went to the Dominions Office. MacDonald announced that he was taking personal responsibility for the fight against unemployment.

This announcement made little difference. The number out of work reached $2\frac{1}{2}$ million in December 1930 and the future of the Government began to look uncertain. It was unlikely that the Liberals, internally divided as they were, would continue to support it. The Prime Minister's hold on the party was not in danger – Mosley had made little impression – but the crisis only deepened. The Conservatives criticised the wasteful policies of the administration. A committee was appointed to investigate the position and reported at the end of July. It drew a most gloomy picture and recommended increased taxation and economies, particularly in unemployment expenditure. Three weeks later, the Labour Government was over. What began as a financial crisis turned into a political battle. In the end the figure of a 10 per cent cut in the dole proved the stumbling-block. Although the Cabinet contained a majority of one in favour of the proposal, the size and stature of the minority made the continuance of the Government impossible. MacDonald asked his colleagues for their resignations and they were offered.

Next day he returned to tell them that he had accepted the King's commission to head a 'National' Government and that Baldwin and Samuel had agreed to serve. He invited their co-operation in what would be a temporary expedient to resolve the financial crisis but only Snowden, Thomas and Sankey gave him their support. In due course the political parties involved would resume their respective positions.

In the event, something rather different happened. Despite its protestations to the contrary, the new Government took Britain off the Gold Standard. Shortly afterwards, MacDonald received his 'doctor's mandate' from the electorate with a massive majority. He remained Prime Minister until 1935 when he exchanged places with Baldwin and became Lord President. He resigned with Baldwin in 1937 and later the same year died at sea on a cruise to South Africa.

It was a quiet end to a stormy career. It would be a slight exaggeration to describe MacDonald as a mere figurehead in his final term as Prime Minister. For good or ill he maintained an interest in defence and foreign policy. Yet he was inevitably isolated, surrounded by the Conservatives and ultimately powerless to resist their wishes. 'National

Labour' never amounted to anything substantial. He had made his decision in 1931 and for the remainder of his life could never escape from its consequences. The Labour party expelled him, attacked him and did its best to humiliate him. It had not occurred to MacDonald that men who would have been prepared to accept the cuts would round on him so fiercely. On the other hand, it was alleged that MacDonald had betrayed the party and had been plotting this course for some time. A great deal was made of MacDonald's supposed weakness for aristocratic company. Historians since have agreed that the most satisfactory explanation for his conduct is that he was the outsider who longed to be inside. There is always room for theories of this kind. Yet, with justice, MacDonald did not see himself as being inconsistent in his actions. He had been committed to the remoulding of the nation, not the emancipation of one particular class. He had failed. Even in his failure, however, he remains the most remarkable Labour Prime Minister, the only one to have come from the working class, the only one to have learnt his lessons in the 'school of life'. It is, no doubt, a sad commentary on this experience that Labour has since come to expect its salvation from the University of Oxford.

BIBLIOGRAPHY

Barker, B., *Ramsay MacDonald's Political Writings* (London, 1972)
Bassett, R., *1931: Political Crisis* (London, 1958)
Elton, Lord, *Life of James Ramsay MacDonald (1866–1919)* (London, 1939)
Mowat, C. L., 'Ramsay MacDonald and the Labour Party', in A. Briggs and J. Saville (eds), *Essays in Labour History 1886–1927* (London, 1971)
Skidelsky, R., *Politicians and the Slump: The Labour Government of 1929–31* (London, 1967)

16

NEVILLE CHAMBERLAIN

BY

CHRISTOPHER COOK

Arthur Neville Chamberlain, PC (1922), FRS (1938). Born 18 March 1869, second son of the Rt Hon Joseph Chamberlain, and educated at Rugby and Mason College, Birmingham. Hon LLD (Birmingham, Cambridge, Bristol, and Leeds); Hon DCL (Oxford); Hon DLitt (Reading). Resided in the West Indies 1890–97. Birmingham City Council 1911; Alderman 1914; Lord Mayor of Birmingham 1915–16; Director-General of National Service 1916–17; MP (Unionist) Birmingham (Ladywood) 1918–29, Edgbaston 1929–40; Postmaster-General 1922–28; Paymaster-General 1928; Minister of Health 1923, 1924–29, 1931; Chancellor of the Exchequer 1923–24, 1931–37; Prime Minister and First Lord of the Treasury 1937–40. Married 1911 Annie Vere, daughter of Major W. V. Cole; one son, one daughter. Died 9 November 1940. Author of The Struggle for Peace, *1939.*

NEVILLE CHAMBERLAIN

Despite the fact that Neville Chamberlain was Prime Minister for only three years, from May 1937 to May 1940, his premiership has proved to be one of the most controversial in modern British history. Perhaps in compensation for Chamberlain's failure to 'sell himself' while he was alive, he was very fortunate to have as his official biographer Sir Keith Feiling. Feiling published a large and judicious defence of his subject six years after the latter's death in 1940; but, apart from this 'Academy portrait' and one or two apologias from his ministerial colleagues, Chamberlain found few writers in the post-war decade who would defend his policy of appeasement, which had so manifestly failed. For a long time, it was virtually historical orthodoxy that Neville Chamberlain was probably the most naive, vain and pusillanimous Prime Minister Britain had ever suffered; not only had he repeatedly given way in the face of the armed might of the dictators, but he had wantonly obstructed measures to augment British strength to face further confrontations. It is only really since the arrival of the horrible possibility of a nuclear holocaust and the failure of the British venture in Suez in 1956, which made clear the dangers of the cavalier alternative to the kind of policy Chamberlain and others were pursuing during the 1930s, that there has been a serious revision of the over-facile condemnation of the 'appeasers'.[1] With the opening of the relevant Cabinet papers after 1967, the whole controversy has been rekindled, and it is, perhaps, ironical that the first scholarly book to appear on Chamberlain's premiership, using the new Cabinet material, is written by an anti-appeaser of the late 1930s, Ian Colvin, and published by Victor Gollancz, arch-critic of appeasement.[2] Colvin's book attempts a real body-blow to the revisionist school because it argues that the Cabinet documents do not, in fact, vindicate Chamberlain's policy, but make it even more certain that Chamberlain even undermined democratic government by making certain vital decisions without first consulting

[1] See Donald C. Watt, 'Appeasement: The Rise of a Revisionist School', *Political Quarterly*, vol. 36, no. 2 (April–June 1965).
[2] Ian Colvin, *The Chamberlain Cabinet* (London, 1971).

the Cabinet. Colvin's indictment of Chamberlain has been somewhat tempered by his reviewers and subsequent narrative accounts, but a full-length reply to Colvin's charges is still awaited.

Despite Chamberlain's predictable and easy succession to Stanley Baldwin in May 1937, there was a touch of controversy about even in the early phase of the new Government. Chamberlain had been a most orthodox Chancellor since the formation of the National Government in November 1931, and had religiously maintained Birmingham's eleventh commandment, that one should balance one's books. However, he somewhat departed from peacetime orthodoxy in his last Budget (April 1937), in which he levied a special tax, the National Defence Contribution, on those who were making a profit from manufacturing arms. There was such an outcry against the new tax on the privately owned arms industry (which the Chamberlain family had been so involved with), that Chamberlain was forced to withdraw the tax and replace it with a straight 5 per cent tax on all profits. Although this return to financial orthodoxy was typical of the future Chamberlain policy (until March 1938), it was a very rare example of Chamberlain giving way to outside pressure and admitting that he was wrong. Stubborness and righteousness were the key-notes of Chamberlain's character.

Neville Chamberlain, despite his age (he was sixty-eight), was the obvious successor to Stanley Baldwin, for whom he had already deputised during the latter's illness. Churchill later admitted that 'there was no doubt who his [Baldwin's] successor should be. Mr Neville Chamberlain had, as Chancellor of the Exchequer, not only done the main work of the Government for the five years past, but was the ablest and most forceful Minister, with high abilities and an historic name.'[3]

Three days after being made Prime Minister, Chamberlain was elected Tory leader, and with a wider electoral basis than the party had previously been used to. Chamberlain received particular support from those Conservatives who desired a more active leadership than Baldwin had provided. In so many ways, Baldwin and Chamberlain, though loyal to each other, were complete opposites. A. J. P. Taylor has pithily described the differences between the two men: 'The two were yokefellows rather than partners, bound together by dislike of Lloyd George and by little else. Chamberlain was harsher than Baldwin, more im-

[3] Winston Churchill, *The Second World War*, i, 172. Quoted in Robert McKenzie, *British Political Parties* 2nd edn (London, 1963), p. 45.

patient with criticism and with events. He antagonised where Baldwin conciliated. He was also more practical and eager to get things done. He had a zest for administrative reform.'[4] Chamberlain, like Baldwin, was a Midlands businessman, though not a very successful one; he had spent seven years vainly trying to make a profitable venture out of his father's sisal plantation in the Bahamas. On his return to England, Neville went into the copper-brass business but found his real niche in Birmingham city politics, where he became Mayor in 1915 and founded the first and only municipal bank in England. In December 1916, Lloyd George made him Director-General of National Service, giving him responsibility but insufficient powers to fulfil the job properly. The appointment was disastrous and lasted only seven months, but it left Neville Chamberlain with a hatred of Lloyd George that lasted a lifetime. Chamberlain was a most energetic administrator but an inexperienced politician, who compensated with a stubborn, self-righteous integrity. All his life he mistrusted the flamboyant rhetoricians – men like Disraeli, Lloyd George and Churchill.

Chamberlain made his reputation as Minister of Health during the second half of the 1920s. Keith Feiling describes the Chamberlain achievement in stark statistics: 'He was free from the elections [of 1924] on October 30th; on November 7th he set his office to work on a four-year plan, and on the 19th laid before the Cabinet a list of twenty-five measures which he desired to pass. Of these, twenty-one became law before he left the ministry, the remainder were incorporated in later legislation. . . .'[5] This same penchant for detailed planning and forceful execution marked Chamberlain's chancellorship and his prime ministership.

It was Chamberlain's great misfortune that during his tenure of the premiership, foreign affairs and not domestic issues overwhelmingly occupied the Cabinet's attention; for Chamberlain's forte was in domestic concerns and in peacetime preoccupations, such as recovery from the slump and rehousing. He was not the ignoramus in foreign affairs that some historians have made him out to be, by taking seriously a joke that Austen Chamberlain aimed at his brother. However, he approached foreign policy with too many mental blank spots. For instance he mistrusted Russia and had the same dislike of Eastern European affairs that had marked his brother's regime at the Foreign

[4] A. J. P. Taylor, *English History, 1914–45* (Oxford, 1965), pp. 205–6.
[5] Keith Feiling, *The Life of Neville Chamberlain* (London, 1946), p. 129.

Office. Chamberlain did not trust the diplomats, whose methods he found cumbersome and contorted, and decided to undertake his own personal brand of diplomacy, which would bypass the Foreign Office. Unfortunately, he did not possess the subtlety or the mental agility or the skilled subterfuge required of the successful diplomat. Because of his integrity he could not hide his knowledge, and as his biographer admitted, 'His mental definitions were black or white, he distrusted neutral greys'.[6] Furthermore, Chamberlain decided on a dual policy of appeasement of the dictators and rearmament, which required more tact and subtlety than he possessed.

Such was the strength of Chamberlain's character and will that he managed affairs so that Treasury thinking dominated the issue of re-armament and in consequence, to some extent, foreign policy; while the Home Civil Service, in the guise of Sir Horace Wilson and Sir Warren Fisher, provided much of his advice on foreign policy. Anthony Eden, at the Foreign Office, had initially welcomed Chamberlain as Prime Minister, expecting to benefit from a man who was interested in and would support his foreign policy. It was not long, however, before the two men clashed over the direction of foreign policy. In September 1937 Eden learnt that the Prime Minister wished to speak in public on foreign policy the following month but was embarrassed that Eden had arranged to make one of his rare speeches only three days later. If this was a disconcerting omen of the dominant role the Prime Minister wished to play in foreign affairs, there were other more solid issues on which the two men disagreed. In January 1938, while Eden was abroad, Chamberlain personally replied to an American 'feeler' for a plan to launch a world discussion on the underlying causes of present discontents. Roosevelt required a swift reply and received it in the form of a chilly communiqué that American plans were cutting across British plans to discuss the *de jure* recognition of Abyssinia with the French and the Italians. Eden favoured outright acceptance of Roosevelt's proposals but returned home too late to participate in drafting the reply. Eden could not agree with Chamberlain's efforts to override the dictators by making terms with Italy, especially as the Prime Minister conducted this particular piece of overseas wooing through his sister-in-law, Lady Austen Chamberlain, who happened to be wintering in Rome. It is important to note that Chamberlain did, in fact, agree to stop using Lady Chamberlain as his contact with Mussolini when Eden

[6] Feiling, op. cit., p. 122.

objected, and that he almost reversed his policy in the Cabinet on the matter of the Roosevelt plan in order to pacify Eden. As it happened, the President's plan came to nothing, whereas the issue of *de jure* recognition to Abyssinia was to provide the immediate cause of Eden's resignation in February 1938. It is not true that Eden resigned over Central European appeasement, or because he objected to the Prime Minister's dictatorial takeover of foreign policy; the two men differed about the method of dealing with the dictators, but the important fact is that Eden failed to convince the majority of the Cabinet that his was the correct policy. Eden's private secretary, Oliver Harvey, realised this fact in his diary entry for 3 November 1937: 'His [Eden's] supporters in the Cabinet are flabby or unassertive, i.e. Stanley, MacDonald, Elliot, De La Warr; his opponents, Simon, Sam Hoare, Kingsley Wood, Swinton, Hailsham, are important and effective.'[7]

Eden was replaced by Halifax as surely as the fashionable Edenesque Homburg hat was replaced in government circles by the more traditional bowler. The 'Glamour Boys' were defeated and the 'Old Gang' were surely entrenched. Sir Robert Vansittart, Permanent Under-Secretary at the Foreign Office and a staunch opponent of Germany, had already been 'kicked upstairs' to become the rarely consulted (and never listened to) Chief Diplomatic Adviser to the Government. There is much truth in the accusation that Chamberlain surrounded himself with advisers who already agreed with his line of thought, but there is no truth in Colvin's allegation that he undermined democratic government by making important decisions without consulting the Cabinet. Several critics of Chamberlain have accused him of using an 'inner Cabinet' of four, which included himself, Halifax and two former Foreign Secretaries, Hoare and Simon, to make major foreign policy decisions. Colvin itemises the shifts of personnel that took place in the Chamberlain Cabinet and concludes that

'the Cabinet composition in May 1937 contained a wider range of minds than the Cabinet that faced the war crisis of 1939 . . . of the twenty-three Ministers whose opinions and responsibility were necessary to the decisions on war and peace in August 1939, eighteen Ministers were so like-minded with the Prime Minister as to preclude a real sifting of policy. Only MacDonald, Elliot, Oliver Stanley, Hore-Belisha provided

[7] John Harvey (ed.), *The Diplomatic Diaries of Oliver Harvey* (London, 1970), p. 56.

a little leaven to the debate. This had become a Cabinet of nonentities, presided by one magisterial personality.'[8]

Colvin exaggerates the measure of agreement within the Cabinet and understimates the divergency of the opinions that were put forward by the Foreign Office and the Defence ministries. If Chamberlain had his way in the Cabinet, it was because of the sharp rationality of his arguments, not because he browbeat the opposition. Chamberlain reflected the pessimism of the Chiefs of Staff about the ability of Britain and France to face the military strength of the Dictators; his policy of negotiation with the Dictators received overwhelming public support.[9]

Chamberlain based his policy on an utter hatred of war, a deep desire for social reform (which excessive arms expenditure would have made impossible), a mistrust of diplomatic entanglements, a realisation of the military weakness of Britain, the unlikelihood of Dominion support in a European war, a belief in personal diplomacy, and a feeling that the Dictators had genuine grievances, which, if met, would re-establish peace in Europe. The so-called 'inner Cabinet' was basically in complete agreement with Chamberlain over his policy. Samuel Hoare was much keener on a Soviet alliance than his colleagues, and Halifax had serious qualms about Munich, but these differences were subsumed and the inner Cabinet had a unanimity that allowed the Prime Minister to achieve speedy assent for most of his plans in full Cabinet session. The Cabinet was always consulted on major issues, though sometimes only after an urgent decision had already been taken. There was nothing unusual in this – Lloyd George had relied on a much smaller group of confidants, while each Labour government of this century has had its own informal inner Cabinet.

Chamberlain's mistakes in foreign policy stem not from a lack of good advice, but from his own belief in rationality. A. J. P. Taylor has written of Chamberlain's agreement with Southern Ireland that 'he [Chamberlain] did not appreciate that practical grievances, though real, were often the cover for deeper sentiment, which could not be so easily satisfied'.[10] De Valera would ultimately be content with nothing less

[8] Colvin, *The Chamberlain Cabinet*, pp. 261–2.
[9] A Mass Observation survey of September 1938 showed that 70 per cent of those questioned favoured Chamberlain's decision to go to Germany and to try to negotiate a settlement of the Czech crisis.
[10] Taylor, *English History* . . ., p. 406.

than Irish reunification, the negotiations were payment on account, as far as he was concerned, whilst Chamberlain regarded them as a final settlement. Hitler would not be limited to expansion in German populated areas as Chamberlain hoped. Perhaps Chamberlain's political security at home made him underestimate the forces of political unrest in Germany which provided both the impetus and the Achilles' heel of Hitler's regime. There can be little doubt that Chamberlain (and others) overestimated the armed strength of Germany and, in particular, that country's unity.

As far as Colvin and other critics of Chamberlain are concerned, he stands condemned at the bar of history for three main reasons. Firstly, for failing to rearm in time; secondly, for surrending in Czechoslovakia in 1938 when he need not have done; and, thirdly, for failing to achieve an alliance with Russia. None of these charges stands too deep an investigation. There can be few historians left who still regard Chamberlain as a simple opponent of rearmament. Chamberlain's role in the mid-1930s was that of Chancellor of the Exchequer, faced with an up-hill economic recovery from the slump, whose job it was to fight large demands for the armed services from scarce economic resources. Naturally, the Chancellor protected his own field, but there was more to it than that. Chamberlain and the Treasury regarded a strong national financial position as being an indispensable weapon in a long war. Thus, when Prime Minister, Chamberlain aimed at limiting defence expenditure over the next four years to £1,500 million, to maintain balanced budgets, and to concentrate on defensive arms expenditure, rather than offensive. Under the last heading, Chamberlain switched resources from the building of bomber aeroplanes to that of fighters and attained agreement in the Cabinet to concentrate on imperial defence rather than on maintaining a sizable army available for immediate use on the Continent. Chamberlain's rearmament policy fitted in logically with other plans he had; by limiting arms expenditure he hoped that social reforms could be continued; by restricting offensive arms expenditure he hoped that Hitler would feel less threatened and therefore be more amenable.

Chamberlain's policy of 'business as usual' only ended after Hitler had incorporated Austria in the Reich in March 1938. Chamberlain then cancelled the policy adopted in 1934, that rearmament should only be undertaken on the understanding that it did not interfere with normal foreign trade or alter the industrial capacity of the nation in any marked way.

The policy adopted at Munich and Chamberlain's rearmament policy stand or fall together, as they formed part of the same plan. It is a fact that Chamberlain's personal diplomacy failed, but it is not at all clear that any alternative policy would have fared better (unless one accepts the very dubious argument that war in 1938 would have been better than war a year later). Chamberlain followed the lessons of Canning's diplomacy, that to threaten without the means or the will to execute your threats is a fatal form of diplomacy. He tried to come to terms with what he regarded as legitimate German grievances, whilst at the same time trying to limit further German aggression and, incidentally, placing British reasonableness in the face of American opinion. The policy was a failure, but it was neither indefensible nor irresponsible.

Although Chamberlain was probably prejudiced against Russia, he cannot be blamed for failing to secure a Russian alliance in 1939. A Russian alliance would have defeated the whole purpose of his diplomacy, which was to convince Hitler that there was no attempt to encircle him, and to maintain the utmost diplomatic flexibility. As it happened, Russia put forward terms that were unacceptable to the British. It is important not to exaggerate Chamberlain's control of events; an expert on Britain's inter-war foreign policy, Professor Medlicott, concludes that it cannot be shown 'that he took the conduct of foreign affairs into his own hands or peregrinated abroad to anything like the same extent as Lloyd George, or Churchill, or even Disraeli, or MacDonald or Macmillan did on occasion'.[11] In fact, Chamberlain revived the Cabinet foreign policy committee and presided over at least fifty of its meetings between 1937 and 1939.

The real basis of criticism of Chamberlain's premiership does not lie in his broad strategy but rather in his faults of manner and tactics. Chamberlain lacked the ability to 'sell himself'; he could not inspire others. He was a very poor war premier, probably worse than Asquith. Chamberlain's paternalism, his firm belief in free enterprise, and his acerbic debating tongue, did not win him the support of Labour leaders, who were eventually responsible for his overthrow in May 1940. His policy of 'business as usual' could never have been less apposite – his Government completely failed to exploit the national mood.

Significantly, Chamberlain stayed on as party leader after he had resigned the premiership. He had been Chairman of the Conservative

[11] W. H. Medlicott, *Contemporary England 1914-64* (London, 1967), pp. 357-8.

party at the turn of the decade and as Premier had done much to inject party solidarity into the nominally National Government of the 1930s. However, the historian of the Conservative party, Lord Blake, has argued that Chamberlain's attitude and policies hardened the divisions within the Conservative party and made them much worse than they had been under Baldwin: 'They left a lasting mark on the party, not wholly obliterated even as late as 1957.'[12] Twenty Conservative MPs abstained in the vote after Eden's resignation and between twenty-five and thirty abstained over Munich later in the year. Chamberlain was finally ousted on a vote of censure in which his majority dropped from 200 to 80. He made the mistake of identifying his party with appeasement; he would have been much wiser to spread the responsibility for unpopular but necessary decisions by widening his Government during 1939 to include the Labour party.

Neville Chamberlain died only months after leaving office. There can have been few more luckless politicians. Perhaps his worst misfortune was being born too late! One feels he would have made an eminently successful Prime Minister in the age of *Pax Britannica*, whereas he appears lost in the world of *Blitzkrieg*.

[12] Robert Blake, *The Conservative Party from Peel to Churchill*, paperback edn (London, 1972), pp. 238, 240.

[297]

17

SIR WINSTON CHURCHILL

BY

M. R. D. FOOT

Sir Winston Leonard Spencer Churchill, born at Blenheim on 30 November 1874, elder son of Lord Randolph Churchill, third son of the 7th Duke of Marlborough, and Jennie, second daughter of Leonard Jerome of New York. Educated at Harrow and Sandhurst. Served in the 4th Hussars in Cuba, Malakand, Tirah and Soudan 1895–98. War correspondent in South Africa 1899–1900; captured and escaped. MP (Cons) for Oldham 1900–05; (Lib) N.W. Manchester 1906–08; (Lib and Co-Lib) Dundee 1908–22; (Cons) Epping 1924–45; Woodford 1945–65. Married 1908 Clementine, daughter of Colonel Sir H. M. Hozier and Lady Blanche Ogilvy; one son, three daughters. Under-Secretary of State for Colonies 1906–08; President of the Board of Trade 1908–10; Home Secretary 1910–11; First Lord of the Admiralty 1911–15; Chancellor of the Duchy of Lancaster 1915; commanded 6th Royal Scots Fusiliers 1916; Minister of Munitions 1917; Secretary of State for War 1919–21; Secretary of State for Colonies 1921–22; Chancellor of the Exchequer 1924–29; First Lord of the Admiralty 1939–40; Prime Minister and Minister of Defence 1940–45; Leader of the Opposition 1945–51; Prime Minister 1951–55, and Minister of Defence 1951–52. PC 1907, CH 1922, OM 1946, KG 1953. Hon. DCL (Oxford; Rochester, USA); Hon. LLD (Belfast, Bristol, Harvard, McGill, Brussels, Louvain, Miami, Columbia, Aberdeen, St Andrews, Liverpool); D. Litt. (London); etc. Died 24 January 1965. Author of The River War, *1899;* The World Crisis *(5 vols), 1923–31;* Marlborough *(4 vols), 1933–38;* The Second World War *(6 vols), 1948–54;* A History of the English-Speaking Peoples *(4 vols), 1956–58; etc, etc. Nobel Prize for Literature 1953.*

SIR WINSTON CHURCHILL

Churchill's ancestry and character provide the keys to understanding his achievement; before we can consider what he did, we must remember who he was. He never forgot that on his father's side his roots lay in the western English countryside, that his people had long been of tremendous social standing, and that his forbears included one of the greatest captains of all known time. His father, a political comet that for a moment outshone even Gladstone in the bright sky of the mid-eighties, rose to great but not to the greatest heights in Conservative politics; fell correspondingly fast and far; and died, mad, when his elder son was barely twenty. His mother, still bewitchingly lovely, remarried five years later. By the social conventions of the day, he and she could not see a great deal of each other, even when he was an infant. But the practical, inventive Jerome strain in him was strong – stronger, some close friends thought, than the somewhat etiolated strain of the Churchills.

From his ducal descent he derived the hauteur of his manner. Though never as insolent as his father had been, he was often grumpy or downright rude; his scowl was notorious, and he was not an easy man to work for at close quarters. On the other hand, he was a good diner-out if he got a chance to talk, and liked to scintillate among cronies. Beneath the abrasive social manner, common in the upper class into which he was born, lay a much more formidable strength: a tough tenacity, a refusal to be overwhelmed by adversities, for which his half-American birth bears some responsibility.

His tenacity and resilience, almost as well known as his super-abundant energy, hardly need recall to a readership whose fathers at least knew him. He inherited another quality, that was reinforced by his upbringing, and is rare enough in politics to deserve remark: generosity. Gentlemen, he learnt in boyhood, ought never to be mean; and in later life he seldom was. It is almost impossible for a prime minister to avoid occasional touches of the appearance, at least, of meanness; public life is notoriously a hard taskmaster. But Churchill carried over into his principles of grand strategy the line of generous conduct he was taught to approve in the nursery. This may not always have been wise; at least it was not mean.

Again, he shared with the polo-playing and fox-hunting companions of his youth the quality of courage; gentlemen no more flinch than they are mean. As a subaltern, he rode without a tremor in the lancers' charge at Omdurman; saying afterwards that his time was so taken up with sheathing his sword and drawing his pistol at the gallop, that he had no time for alarm. A couple of years later, he spent over an hour under fire, trying to shift a derailed armoured train in South Africa; to the warm admiration of those who saw him. His months in the trenches in France in 1916 left him equally unperturbed. And as an old man, during the bombardment of London, he said simply to Pile, the anti-aircraft commander, 'I love the bangs!'

This brings out an unexpected quality in any prime minister, particularly in one who did not attain the post till he was sixty-five: boyishness. A strong streak of the schoolboy remained near the surface of his character, long after it had been suppressed in his staider contemporaries and in many younger people with whom he had to work. This was not naughty-boyishness, but impishness without malice; what his age called cheek. With it went a delight in gadgets, codes, covers, minor and major mysteries, and a robust sense of humour. This made him original, rather than reliable, as a leader in difficult times.

From an early age he had had dinned into him that deadly text round which the nineteenth-century public schools revolved: 'Unto whomsoever much is given, of him shall be much required.'[1] His parents were not wealthy, his mother had sore financial troubles after his father's early death, and one of his own main reasons for writing was to make money; but he always believed that he was one on whom fortune had smiled, and that his birth had given him a flying start in life. He was aware that he had powers, and determined in due course to exercise them; he had ambition to match his energy, which was well beyond the common run. Where did it lead him?

He did badly at Harrow, and only scraped into Sandhurst; he understood that his father thought him a fool, and had to make clear to himself at least that Lord Randolph had been wrong. He was indeed a late and slow developer intellectually. 'I knew nothing of science,' he once said, nor was he a linguist. But he absorbed a lot of history, and formed himself a distinct and characteristic style, both for writing and for speak-

[1] Luke xii: 48.

ing. He conflated Gibbon, Macaulay, and the necessary brevities of campaign life to produce English that was always vigorous, sometimes racy, and usually clear.

As he was his father's son, and as he became a newspaper correspondent in the intervals of regimental duty, he attracted publicity; but he was not merely a newspaperman's hero. He was not too proud to write for a paper that would pay him a decent fee, but he did not envisage a career in Fleet Street; any more than he fancied one in Grub Street. He was too disdainful of journalists and of the public they served.

His personal life was of course hedged round, as closely as his professional life in the Army or in politics, by rules about how one should behave. At the fourth attempt, he was accepted in marriage – in August 1908 – by the beautiful Clementine Hozier, whom he married the following month. This gave him a perfectly firm personal base for the rest of his long life; she still survives him. As his future mother-in-law remarked at the time, 'He is gentle and tender, affectionate to those he loves, much hated by those who have not come under his personal charm.'[2] His great gifts for making enemies, as well as friends, need to be remembered: they were among the brakes on his action, when he reached the summit and before.

Two important enemies were obstacles to him in the Army. Neither Roberts nor Kitchener had wished to forward his military career, and each felt himself offended when Churchill outflanked him, got to a scene of action, and started writing to the newspapers about it. He resigned his commission early in 1899; the South African war provided him with the opportunity he eagerly sought, to enter Parliament. He won Oldham, which had rejected him at a by-election in July 1899, at the khaki election of 1900; having meanwhile been out to the Front, been captured, and escaped. Thereafter he rose like a cork. He was just under twenty-five when he went to Westminster; elected as a Conservative, he went as a Free Trader to sit on the Liberal benches in May 1904. He had just turned 31 when he entered Campbell-Bannerman's ministry, as Under-secretary for the Colonies, at the end of 1905. Asquith brought him into the Cabinet at 33, as President of the Board of Trade, and moved him before he was 35 to the Home Office, traditionally one of the three or four topmost posts in the government. But it was over thirty years more before he reached the summit.

[2] Lady Blanche Hozier to W. S. Blunt, in R. S. Churchill, *Winston S. Churchill* (London, 1969), ii, 268–9.

What happened in those thirty years could not help affecting the way he behaved then, and deserves a moment's attention from us now.

At the Colonial Office he learnt how the Civil Service works, and how to speak for a department in the Commons; but had no time to make any mark on colonial policy. At the Board of Trade, under the guidance of his predecessor Lloyd George – with whom he began a close friendship at this time – he carried on with the origins of the mid-century Welfare State: labour exchanges and unemployment insurance. At the Home Office, he was able to do something to soften the harsh regime in prisons; though a single episode from his spell there is more generally remembered. When a small murder gang barricaded themselves in Sidney Street, Stepney, and fired on the police, his adventurous and boyish streak surfaced: he went down to the East End to watch the shooting. Oddly enough, this scuffle is better known than all the rest of his eighteen months' work at the Home Office put together; save for the legend that he sent troops to put down a riot at Tonypandy, which is pure fiction.

In October 1911 Asquith sent him to the Admiralty, where for the first time he made an impact of first-class importance on the nation's life. He turned out an admirable continuator of the work of the recently retired Admiral Fisher. Fisher and Churchill had been on opposite sides in the controversy over the naval estimates for 1909;[3] but Churchill as usual came fast under the influence of his technical advisers, formed a warm friendship with Fisher, and carried Fisher's reforms further. He made the Dreadnoughts of 1906 obsolete with the Queen Elizabeth class of fast super-Dreadnoughts; he began the naval air service; still more important, he began the conversion of the whole fleet from coal to oil fuel, a conversion that made a mark on British foreign policy that lasts to this day. In short, he maintained continuous pressure for reform on a traditionally conservative and slow-moving service. As a result, the outbreak of war in 1914 found much the world's strongest fleet fully mobilised at its war stations, and able to exercise an international impact which, over four and a quarter years, proved decisive. This impact was as much Fisher's achievement as Churchill's, but neither could have done as much as he did without the other.

During the Great War, Churchill at first played a, but not *the*, leading part in forming British strategy. As Liddell Hart has observed, his activities outside the German far right had a perceptible influence on

[3] cp. p. 174 above.

the battle of the Marne;[4] and he was one of the three people who influenced the development of the tank, the weapon that broke the deadlock on the Western Front that derived from the Marne. The other two, Swinton and Hankey, were probably more important; but Churchill's help here was critical.

His other principal contribution to the conduct of the war was his sponsorship of the Dardanelles expedition. There is no point in stirring the still glowing embers of that controversy here. Instead, let us look at his retrospect:

'. . . power in a national crisis, when a man believes he knows what orders should be given, is a blessing. In any sphere of action there can be no comparison between the positions of number one and numbers two, three, or four. The duties and the problems of all persons other than number one are quite different and in many ways more difficult. It is always a misfortune when number two or three has to initiate a dominant plan or policy. He has to consider not only the merits of the policy, but the mind of his chief; not only what to advise, but what it is proper for him in his station to advise; not only what to do, but how to get it agreed, and how to get it done. Moreover, number two or three will have to reckon with numbers four, five, and six, or maybe some bright outsider, number twenty. . . . I was ruined for the time being in 1915 over the Dardanelles, and a supreme enterprise was cast away, through my trying to carry out a major and cardinal operation of war from a subordinate position.'[5]

The strategy was sound, the execution was weak: he could not get the best men to help him carry it out. In his own Admiralty headquarters, he had brought Fisher back as First Sea Lord when an absurd press campaign drove out Prince Louis of Battenberg; the strain was too much for the termagant old man. 'Fisher went mad', as Churchill put it succinctly, and flounced out in May 1915. The Conservatives heard of this, and moved in to evict Churchill, whom they detested.

They did not only hate him as a renegade; the black core in the party had never forgiven him for ordering a battle squadron to Lamlash, in the Isle of Arran, during the Ulster crisis in March 1914.[6] (Lady

[4] In A. J. P. Taylor *et al.*, *Churchill: Four Faces and the Man* (London, 1969), pp. 165–8.
[5] Winston Churchill, *The Second World War* (London, 1959), ii, 14–15.
[6] See A. T. Q. Stewart, *The Ulster Crisis* (London, 1967), pp. 148 ff., 163.

Milner held forth to the present writer at length about the unforgivable enormity of this order, thirty-five years after the event. The fact that no ship in the squadron then got nearer to Lamlash than the Scillies made her no less angry.) Mean revengers made sure that he left the Admiralty; as Chancellor of the Duchy of Lancaster he found that he had no real hand in running the war.

So he went to France, to command an infantry battalion at the Front. This places him in a special category of prime ministers, in which Wellington is his only predecessor. Several others had heard shots fired in anger: Liverpool at the taking of the Bastille, Russell as a tourist in the Peninsula, Asquith and Lloyd George as visitors to quiet corners of the Western Front; Aberdeen had ridden over the battlefield of Leipzig, and could still hear the cries of the wounded forty years later; Canning had fought a duel. But only Wellington, till Churchill, had been resident in danger; had been personally a target for enemy fire, for a living, for months on end. This brings a real grasp of what war is like, though it does not always bring steady judgement. Attlee, Eden, Heath, and Macmillan have gone through the same mill; Wilson and Home have been bombarded from the air, which is not exactly the same.

Soon after Lloyd George replaced Asquith, he recalled Churchill from France, to take over the Ministry of Munitions; where Churchill made no particular mark. In the winter of 1918–19 he moved on to a pair of secretaryships of state, for war and air, where he had more influence. On the air side, he accepted Treasury advice and was sorely cramped in the peacetime RAF; on the military, he handled demobilisation sensibly, but then got entangled in the Russian revolutionary civil war.

'The foul baboonery of Bolshevism', one of his more memorable phrases, revolted him, and all through 1919 and 1920 he urged his colleagues to adopt a resolute policy of intervention against it: in vain.[7] Intervention had begun in 1918 as an anti-German measure – originally, at the Bolsheviks' own request. Churchill tried to turn it into a successful anti-Bolshevik war, and failed; made no secret of his efforts; and was widely mistrusted on their account by those of the British working classes who felt instinctive sympathy with their Russian opposite numbers.

This mistrust helped to lose him his seat at Dundee in 1922, and was

[7] See R. H. Ullman, *Britain and the Russian Civil War* (Princeton, 1968), especially pp. 298–304.

strengthened during the General Strike of 1926. Unexpectedly made Chancellor of the Exchequer by Baldwin, he played a prominent part in the counter measures mounted against the strike as editor of the *British Gazette*, which strikers found provocative. As Chancellor, he put Great Britain back on the Gold Standard, at the pre-war parity of £1 = $5, a measure that boded little good to British industry; and, prisoner as before of departmental views, he severely pruned the service estimates. Much of the Grand Fleet he had built up in 1911–14 was broken up, as a result of his financial stringency, in 1924–9: with bitter consequences arising from British impotence later.

Soon after the end of the Great War, he had begun to assemble material for a history of it; as a friend said, 'Winston has written an enormous book about himself and called it *The World Crisis*.' He wrote most of it when out of Parliament in 1922–4, and had much more leisure to write in his ten years out of office, from 1929 to 1939. Delving deep, with professional help, in the papers at Blenheim, he wrote a detailed life of his direct ancestor, the great Duke of Marlborough; the task gave him leisure to reflect on the problems of coalition warfare, and so had an importance for history as well as for literature. Much of his time in Parliament was taken up with a struggle against the extension of Indian powers of self-government; he still saw India through the eyes of a cavalry subaltern of the nineties.

This shows how far he was out on the margin of politics. Shades of Lamlash for the few, of Gallipoli and Murmansk for the many, overlay his reputation; he was thought restless, excitable, bellicose, unreliable. In the second half of the thirties, he gathered round him a group of well-informed backbenchers, who preached danger from Hitler to deaf ears. Churchill knew a tyrant when he saw one, and was not afraid to say so; saying so did not make him more popular with an electorate and a ruling class that disliked excitement and suspected 'cleverness'. He tried to form a 'King's party' during the Abdication crisis of 1936, but Edward VIII's established enemies were too nimble for him: again, he seemed a rogue elephant.

When his preachings turned out true and war began again, in September 1939, he returned to the Admiralty. In his eight months there, he galvanised the entire naval service with inquiries, investigations, ideas; few of the ideas came to much in the short run. One of them, the Naval Wire Barrage (known afloat as the Pig Trough), an anti-aircraft rocket device adopted at the behest of Churchill's scientific adviser F. A. Lindemann, may have destroyed *Hood* in the spring of 1941.[8] But he woke everybody up, and stretched everybody to his limit: an enormous achievement in wartime.

He did the same for the whole nation when he became Prime Minister, at one of the darkest moments in England's history, on 10 May 1940. He was more nearly lost at once than is generally recalled. On 12 June, on his way back from an attempt to stiffen the faltering French Government at Briare, the crew of his unarmed and unescorted airliner had 'seen two German aircraft below us firing at fishing-boats. We were lucky that their pilots did not look upward.'[9] So were we all. He has already been quoted on the advantages of being in command. The passage goes on:

'At the top there are great simplifications. An accepted leader has only to be sure of what it is best to do, or at least to have made up his mind about it. The loyalties which centre upon number one are enormous. If he trips he must be sustained. If he makes mistakes they must be covered. If he sleeps he must not be wantonly disturbed. If he is no good he must be pole-axed.'[10]

There was talk of pole-axing him in the spring of 1941, when the war was going poorly, and again in the summer of 1942, when things seemed worse still; but there was no one, absolutely no one, to match him in powers of leadership, at home or abroad. It is certainly true that he sustained, it is hardly too much to claim that he saved the country in the summer crisis of 1940. His gifts of oratory may in the end have bored sophisticated MPs,[11] but the age of broadcasting had now begun, and he continued to delight a listening public, both sides of the Channel. Had those two German pilots looked up and seen his Flamingo – but speculation is supposed to be unhistorical. He survived; the country survived. Our least passionate historian ends a biographical thumbnail sketch of him with the words 'the saviour of his country'.[12]

The heart of his war policy was to act. He knew that indecision, Asquith's bane, is the one catastrophic vice in a war leader. He often

[8] A. J. Marder in *English Historical Review*, supplement 5 (1972), pp. 9–10.
[9] *The Second World War*, ii, 141.
[10] ibid., p. 15.
[11] R. R. James (ed.), *Chips* (Penguin edn, 1970), pp. 375, 378, 388–9.
[12] A. J. P. Taylor, *English History 1914–1945* (Penguin edn, 1970), p. 29n.

acted wrongly; but even acting wrongly was as a rule better than not acting at all. Most military, like most political, choices are between two evils, and in wartime people hardly ever had enough data before them to be quite sure that they were always quite right. Churchill was ready to undertake the responsibility of being wrong; he preferred doing that to doing nothing.

To uphold Great Britain against Germany was no mean achievement. To uphold her against Germany, Italy, and Japan combined turned out to be possible, but fatal to her greatness. Many detailed, technical criticisms are made of Churchill as a war leader. As research on the recently opened war archives gets under way, there will be more pieces of tactic or branches of strategy to deplore; some of these attacks will be sound. The grand fact remains as Taylor states it. Yet in saving England he ruined her: because he could not bear to be mean.

When Japan entered the war, in December 1941, British resources in men and women, in machines, in foreign reserves, were already nearing exhaustion. The prudent course would have been to retire from the war as far as possible, or even altogether; leaving it to Germany and Japan to wear themselves out eventually against the superior wealth of the United States and the superior manpower of the Soviet Union. Churchill would have none of this: the only decent, honourable course was to fight on, however ruinous that course might prove. 'We shall go on to the end . . . we shall never surrender', he had said in one of his most famous and most electrifying speeches;[13] was he the prisoner of his own rhetoric? No: he meant what he said. If he was a prisoner, it was of his own upbringing.

That upbringing led him never to say 'I told you so' to those who had derided him in the days before the war when he had spoken of a German danger and opposed 'appeasement'. The attitude, again, is creditable to him, and was appreciated by public and private figures alike. He has been reproached for not perceiving, or rather for not preventing, the rise to world power status of Soviet Russia; a task beyond any Englishman's capacities. To have upheld the free world was a feat: wherever the free world may have gone since. The current (summer 1973) scandals on both sides of the Atlantic are nasty enough; but they are not nasty in the way that Himmler's camps were nasty. To resist Himmler, Hitler, and their friends with all one's force was wise and

[13] House of Commons, 4 June 1940; reprinted in *Blood, Sweat and Tears* (New York, 1941), p. 297.

humane; even if it meant making friends, when they changed sides, with Stalin and Beria, whose camps were not much more fragrant. Nor is it clear how Stalin's rise to world power could have been checked, unless by making friends with people who were even fiercer and more treacherous than he.

In occupied Europe, Churchill's name carried weight; more in some countries even than Stalin's or Roosevelt's. Millions of people looked to him, for he saw – even foresaw – resistance as the means by which they would recover their own moral balance after the shock of defeat, and throw the Nazis out; and he at least was a man who had never succumbed to any of Hitler's blandishments. Through Churchill, and SOE which Churchill created and supported, and through the RAF, a vast reserve of pro-British goodwill was built up in the western half of Europe; most of it squandered, it is true, by subsequent British policies, some of them Churchill's.

In home affairs his touch was much less sure than in foreign. They interested him little, and he left them to his able coalition assistants, Anderson, Bevin and Morrison. The achievement of a coalition, at a moment of intense crisis, appeared a personal triumph for him; he was in fact sustained, much as Lloyd George had been in 1916, by the anxiety of politicians to forget old scores and get on with the war. He has himself testified to the sloth of the Conservative party in welcoming him as its leader: indeed he did not formally take up that position till October 1940, shortly before Chamberlain's death.[14] The Labour party, which supported him against Chamberlain, did not support him against itself; as the war went on, and Labour ministers – Bevin particularly – proved their worth in office, the Labour politicians drew somewhat away from him. They held off from his offer of a renewed coalition after the defeat of Germany.

His 'caretaker' Government, purely Conservative, only made one decision of importance: 'unanimous, automatic, unquestioned agreement' to the use of atomic weapons on Japan.[15]

In the general election campaign of June and July 1945, he made a tour of the industrial Midlands. Wherever he went, crowds turned out to see him. He was not often punctual, nor always visibly sober, on this trip; and the map of election results showed a swathe of labour gains across the country, following roughly in his track. It was not that the

14 *The Second World War*, ii, 8–9, 211, 438–9.
15 ibid., vi, 553.

electors were ungrateful to him for rescuing them; but they felt that his tremendous gifts as a war leader fitted him less well for the tasks of reconstruction and social reform than did those of his wartime deputy, the meticulous Attlee.

He had a quiet six years in opposition. We need only note his speech in 1946 at Fulton, Missouri, on the Russian danger, which gave currency to the phrase 'iron curtain'. He was of course a cold warrior *par excellence*, as he had been a hot one, and a strong supporter of NATO. Now that the cold war appears to be over, we need not be too hasty in assuming it was a mistake to wage it.

He came back to power in October 1951, having only missed it by half a dozen seats eighteen months earlier, but his parliamentary majority was only seventeen, and the total of votes cast in the country showed a majority for Labour of some 200,000. So, the steel industry apart, his Government left most of their predecessors' socialising reforms alone; and he kept up his own interests in strategy and foreign affairs. He continued the production of British atomic weapons, and did his best to foster the European Defence Community. It was approved in 1952, but two years later the French Assembly refused to ratify it, and it never came into actual being. He did approve, in 1954, the withdrawal of British troops from Egypt, a decision his successor tried with unfortunate results to reverse soon afterwards. For he was very old; by 1955 even his walk was tottery, and he was persuaded it was time to go. He settled down to publish a history of the English-speaking peoples and to die with dignity; a process drawn out for nearly ten years more, till the seventieth anniversary of Lord Randolph's death.

When he died, his body lay in state in Westminster Hall, as Gladstone's alone among commoners had done before him. Many scores of thousands of people, most of them too young to recall him at his zenith, queued for long hours – a wait in the snow from two to six a.m. was common – to file past. At his funeral, which began in St Paul's, grown men were weeping in the streets; and every crane driver in the Pool of London dipped his crane in salute when the coffin appeared at the water's edge on its last journey, carrying him back to the graveyard in north Oxfordshire where his father's body lies.

Whatever else he did, he left a mark on his day; he was much hated, but he was also much loved. Of him it can be said by every Englishman now alive – and of no one else in this book is this true – 'Had it not been for him, I should not now be here.'

[311]

BIBLIOGRAPHY

Churchill wrote several volumes of autobiography. A monumental life of him, begun by his son Randolph, who died in 1968, is being completed by Martin Gilbert. Three volumes, accompanied by five volumes of supporting texts, have so far appeared (1966–72); they advance the life to 1916. Two other posthumous books and a short monograph deserve note: Lady Violet Bonham Carter's *Winston Churchill as I Knew Him* (London, 1965), A. J. P. Taylor and others, *Churchill: Four Faces and the Man* (London, 1969), and A. J. Marder, 'Winston is Back: Churchill at the Admiralty 1939–40', *English Historical Review*, supplement 5 (1972).

18

CLEMENT ATTLEE

BY

RICHARD ROSE

Clement Richard Attlee, created 1st Earl Attlee 1955. KG (1966), PC (1935), OM (1951) CH (1945) FRS (1947). Born at Putney 3 January 1883 and educated at Haileybury College and University College, Oxford (MA, Hon. Fellow 1942). Called to the Bar 1906. Secretary Toynbee Hall 1910; Lecturer Ruskin College 1911; Tutor and Lecturer, London School of Economics 1913–23; served in Gallipoli, Mesopotamia and France 1914–19; Major 1917; Mayor of Stepney 1919, 1920; MP (Lab.) Limehouse 1922–50, W. Walthamstow 1950–55; Under-Secretary of State for War 1924; Chancellor of the Duchy of Lancaster 1930–31; Postmaster-General 1931; Deputy Leader of the Labour Party in the Commons 1931–35; Leader of the Opposition 1935–40; Lord Privy Seal 1940–42; Secretary of State for Dominions Affairs 1942–43; Lord President of the Council 1943–45; Deputy Prime Minister 1942–45; Prime Minister and First Lord of the Treasury 1945–51; Minister of Defence 1945–46; Leader of the Opposition 1951–55. Attended San Francisco and Potsdam Conferences 1945; Leader of UK Delegation to the General Assembly of the UN 1946; led the UK Delegation to the Paris Peace Conference 1946. Hon. DCL (Oxford), Hon. LLD (Cambridge, London, Wales, Glasgow, Nottingham, Aberdeen, etc.), Hon. DLitt (Reading), Hon. FRIBA. Hon. Fellow Queen Mary College (London), London School of Economics. Married 1922 Violet Helen, daughter of H. E. Millar; one son, three daughters. Died 8 October 1967. Author of The Social Worker, The Town Councillor, The Will and the Way to Socialism, The Labour Party in Perspective, As It Happened, *etc.*

CLEMENT ATTLEE

The political career of Clement Attlee challenges many preconceptions about political leadership. Attlee did not stand out among his contemporaries as a forceful orator or as a man of magnetic personality. Nor did he stand out as an original thinker, or a proponent of a particular brand of Socialism. He did not dominate the organisational life of the Labour party, nor was he the head of a powerful trade union. Yet among twentieth-century party leaders, Clement Attlee ranks first, if the test of political leadership is survival; his twenty-year tenure of the leadership of the Labour party is unrivalled in any party. Moreover, his experience as deputy Prime Minister in the wartime coalition of 1940–5, followed by six years as Prime Minister, put him at the centre of power longer than any other prime minister of this century, with the exception of Stanley Baldwin.

The question arises: why? Unlike other little men, physically and politically (Harry Truman is a good example), Clement Attlee did not compensate for his stature by a pugnacious manner, or self-assertiveness. Instead, his political style matched his physical demeanour: short, unprepossessing statements, delivered in a clipped manner without much argument. These are the mannerisms one might expect of a City solicitor advising a client, rather than the mannerisms of the leader of the Labour party in its most challenging and successful decades.

The distinctive feature of Clement Attlee's style of leadership is carefulness. He was cautious when confronted with political problems; yet cautiousness did not make him timorous. Once sure of political support, he could act swiftly, even ruthlessly. He was solicitous of the feelings and opinions of political colleagues; he never claimed to have discovered the one true path to socialism. Attlee was fond of quoting the remark of a Labour MP of the inter-war years, Tom Shaw: 'When I was young I was always talking about my conscience. When I grew older, I discovered it was just my blooming conceit.' Care also showed in the economical use of words; one was employed where other politicians would use a dozen. The words chosen were sometimes opaque and often vague, or harmless. When doctrinaire colleagues waged battle

[315]

about the meaning of Socialism, Clement Attlee was careful to avoid inflaming others, or entangling himself in their controversies.

Not least, Clement Attlee was full of care for the conditions of ordinary Englishmen, most of whom had been born and raised in conditions far less comfortable than his own. He did not enter politics to seek fame, power or money. The impulse that led him into politics was moral and philosophical; it was a decision, based on first-hand experience of social work in the East End of London, that 'the economic and ethical basis of society was wrong'.

In the course of a political career that almost exactly spanned the first half-century of the Labour party, Clement Attlee developed personally as the party itself grew. The party reached national prominence before the man. The man grew into authority as a servant of the party rather than as a creator of the party, as did Ramsay MacDonald. The career of the man cannot be understood apart from the life of the party. Nor did the man himself see the situation otherwise. His long innings as leader resulted from an ability to assess carefully the state of opinion and the balance of power within the party, never acting outside these constraints, while promptly acting when the exigencies or evolution of events gave an opening to take a major decision.

The upbringing of Clement Attlee was, in his own words, that of 'a typical family of the professional class brought up in the atmosphere of Victorian England'. His father was a successful City of London solicitor: uncles and great-uncles were millers, brewers, farmers, doctors and an occasional clergyman. The Attlees were established in Surrey centuries before the county became part of commuters' London. The family home at Putney was still surrounded with fields, farms and country pubs when Clement Attlee was growing up in the final decades of Victoria's reign. A half-century after the event he could write of the news of Queen Victoria's death as 'a tremendous shock'.

There was nothing in this upbringing to make Clement Attlee particularly conscious of the conditions in which millions of people were then living 'In Darkest England'. His family and residence left him remote from industrial life. Nor was there anything in this upbringing to make a career in Parliament seem either likely or desirable. The family were predominantly Conservative, strictly sabbatarian supporters of the Church of England. They were not politically active.

The education of Clement Attlee was for service, not leadership. By coincidence, his sisters' governess had also been governess to Winston Churchill. The young Churchill, grandson of a Duke, could be imperious even when young; once he rang a bell and, when a maidservant appeared, announced that the governess should be taken away, as she was very cross. This could not have happened in the more modest Attlee household.

At public school, Haileybury, the dominant ethos was service in the Army or in India. The school's imperialist tradition emphasised service in the officer class, but not aspiration to a field-marshal's rank or the eminence of a viceroy. As a Commoner at University College, Oxford, Attlee did not seek the limelight. He read history and poetry for pleasure, and was too shy to attempt speaking in the Oxford Union. In politics, he held to the family's Conservatism, affecting a worldliness above concern with great religious or social questions. In 1904, Attlee went down to London to begin studying for the Bar, a career chosen less from a desire to shine as a barrister, than from its obvious appropriateness to family circumstances.

Neither calculation nor ambition started Clement Attlee on the trail that led to Downing Street. Instead, it was the strong tradition of social service, inspired by church, school and family. In October 1905, Attlee began going one night a week to Haileybury House, a boys' club in Stepney, one of the poorest parts of the East End of London. In 1907 he became the club's manager, and moved from Putney to begin a fourteen-year residence in the East End. In the same year he became a Socialist, joining the Independent Labour Party; he preferred its religious and ethical approach to social problems to the dogmatic Marxism of the Social Democratic Federation, or the pragmatic gradualism of the Fabian Society. Until the outbreak of the First World War, Attlee was a Socialist propagandist and held a variety of positions in the East End concerned with social betterment. This gave him great first-hand knowledge of the conditions and attitudes of ordinary working-class people. In later years Attlee was careful not to deduce their attitudes from theories of class conflict, but to argue them from this inductive knowledge.

The outbreak of the First World War united the country politically, except for the Labour movement. Unlike some members of the ILP (and some well-born, well-educated Radicals in the Liberal party), Clement Attlee responded to the call of patriotism. Just as boys from the East End joined the ranks and became NCOs, Attlee entered as an officer in the South Lancashire Regiment, and ended a Major; he served at Gallipoli and in the trenches in France, and was wounded in action. Service as a soldier appears to have confirmed Attlee's early patriotism. It also gave him a keen interest in military affairs. As he later recalled, 'Many Labour people in fact seemed to be of the opinion that an inefficient army was less wicked than an efficient one. Having served in the First World War, I did not share that view'.

The first political office that Clement Attlee ever held was Mayor of Stepney. He was co-opted to the borough council after Labour gained power there for the first time with a spate of inexperienced candidates in the local elections of 1919. He held the post for two years, and served as a Stepney alderman for eight. These offices brought him first-hand experience of local government possessed by very few twentieth-century prime ministers, except Neville Chamberlain. In 1922 marriage to Violet Millar, daughter of an old family friend, led Attlee to leave his East End residence for suburban Essex, and then move to Middlesex. But his political connections there were lifelong, for he sat in Parliament from 1922 to 1950 for Limehouse, and from 1950 to his retirement in 1955 for West Walthamstow.

There was no glamour and little publicity in the offices Attlee held during the 1920s. But the man was not a seeker of the spotlight, nor did his personality invest his every activity with the aura of importance, or attract press publicity. The platform speaking of pre-war days, useful in overcoming shyness and as preparation for the rough-and-tumble of parliamentary debate, was not his natural role. Nor did his lecturing post at the London School of Economics imply academic brilliance; he held a post in social administration because of his practical knowledge of social conditions.

In the period up to the 1931 Labour collapse, Clement Attlee established himself as a respected member of the Parliamentary Labour Party. By virtue of his class and educational background, he was more at home with the printed word and the intricacies of legislation and administration than many Labour MPs who had come from the work-benches or the pits to Parliament. By the same token, the emotionally charged (but administratively hollow) rhetoric that marked the leading working-class orators was alien to him. Nor did he seek to compensate for his background by becoming, like Sir Oswald Mosley or John Strachey, a spokesman for extremist views.

Service as parliamentary private secretary to Ramsay MacDonald when MacDonald was leader of Labour in opposition, 1922–3, was followed by an Under-secretaryship in the War Office in the first Labour Government. In the late 1920s Attlee gained experience of overseas affairs as a member of Sir John Simon's Indian Statutory Commission. When Labour returned to office in June 1929, Attlee was not offered a ministerial post. When the post of Chancellor of the Duchy of Lancaster became vacant in May 1930, he moved there from the back benches. When H. B. Lees-Smith was moved up to a Cabinet post in March 1931, Attlee became Postmaster-General. None of these appointments brought Cabinet rank. Retrospectively, these varied tasks can be seen as useful background for a person required to assume general oversight of policy as Prime Minister. At the time, they were no more than way stations along a path that was not meant to lead to any eminence.

Events, not personality, catapulted Clement Attlee forward as a Labour leader. The general election of October 1931, held after Ramsay MacDonald left the party to become Prime Minister in a National Coalition, removed nearly all senior Labour politicians from the House of Commons, as well as creating a vacancy for the post of leader. Attlee was fortunate in scraping back at Limehouse with a majority of 551 votes. The Parliamentary Labour Party of less than fifty was short of men of experience. George Lansbury was elected leader of the Parliamentary Labour Party and Attlee was elected deputy leader without opposition. Together with a new recruit to Labour's cause, Sir Stafford Cripps, they shared the burden of leading the party through hopeless years of opposition.

With the great fall in Labour's numbers, the work load of individual Labour MPs rose. Attlee suddenly found himself pushed into the position of responsible spokesman for the party in many fields. From 1931 to 1935 his routine was to leave home at 9 a.m. and not return until near midnight on days when the House of Commons was sitting. In his second year as deputy leader, he filled more columns of Hansard than any other MP, not because of garrulousness but because of the party's need for a man who could speak and speak reliably on many subjects. By contrast, Sir Stafford Cripps was suspect for lack of judgement, and George Lansbury was ageing and unsuited to debating the details of legislation. In 1934 Lansbury was in hospital for months, thus placing Attlee in the post of acting leader of the Labour party.

Events again favoured Attlee when the leadership of the Labour party unexpectedly fell vacant before the 1935 general election. He was the only candidate for the post at that time, but the choice was seen as temporary. The 1935 election trebled the size of the Parliamentary Labour Party. The new MPs, including men who had been senior to Attlee in the party prior to the 1931 débâcle, were offered three candidates for the leadership: Attlee, Arthur Greenwood and Herbert Morrison. On the first ballot, Attlee received 58 out of 135 votes. He gained the leadership because Greenwood's supporters swung almost *en bloc* to his side. The narrowness of Attlee's victory rankled for years with Herbert Morrison, who periodically sought to displace him. It seemed to have little effect on Attlee's self-confidence. He had gained his eminence by acting as the spokesman for the majority of opinion in the party. He saw his new role as remaining the careful articulator of the views of the party. This role was in keeping not only with his temperament and aptitudes, but also with the temper of the times: Ramsay MacDonald and Sir Oswald Mosley had frightened Labour by first swaying opinion within the party and then deserting it.

The first four years of Attlee's leadership were the most difficult for the party, but less so for the man on top. While debates raged within the party between proponents and opponents of rearmament, Attlee carefully stayed on middle ground. When the issue of collaboration with Communists or Liberals came forward, Attlee avoided encouraging such alliances; he also remained aloof from the intense controversy required to defend the party's *status quo*. When left-wing Socialists thundered about the extremist measures that might be required to build Socialism in Britain, Attlee sympathised with many of their aspirations, but refused to endorse methods alien to parliamentary traditions. In one respect he did take the initiative: he used his position and European Socialist contacts to travel widely on the Continent, meeting a variety of political leaders and becoming familiar with the threat of totalitarianism at first hand.

In 1937 Clement Attlee published *The Labour Party in Perspective*, an exposition of his political ideas. At a time of great ideological strife between and within parties, the author characteristically concentrated upon a few things of general importance and general agreement. The book was self-consciously ethical and undoctrinaire. Notwithstanding support of the League of Nations, it was also patriotic, presenting the Labour party as 'typically British' and Socialism as 'a characteristic example of British methods, and as the outcome of British political instincts'. It was gradualist in temper and recommendations. Yet there was no attempt to be all things to all men. In the 1930s there was not enough common ground among the electorate (let alone among MPs) to permit a party leader to avoid commitment to distinctive party principles. Attlee's characteristic mixture of ethical and Socialist concerns is epitomised in the objectives he defined for the party: freedom, economic security, equality, democracy, common ownership of the land and major industries, beauty and internationalism.

The realisation of many of the ideals expressed in Attlee's pre-war writings and speeches was made possible in the aftermath of the Second World War. It was not made inevitable. If Attlee's wartime colleagues deserve some of the credit for anticipating actions undertaken by the post-war Cabinet he headed, so it might be claimed that Attlee himself deserved credit for actions undertaken by the War Cabinet in which he was important.

When the downfall of Neville Chamberlain as Prime Minister was imminent, Attlee was not prominent in the negotiations that dislodged Chamberlain and brought in Churchill in his stead. Attlee concentrated upon two points: the need to create a coalition government with the will and means to pursue the nation's defence; and, by acting carefully and correctly according to the party constitution, to ensure that the Labour party was united behind those invited to sit in Cabinet with such old enemies as Churchill and Lord Halifax. Fortuitously, the occurrence of the party's annual conference during delicate negotiations concerning the Coalition enabled Attlee to enter government with the expressed support of the whole party.

Initially, the Labour leader was appointed Lord Privy Seal, and awarded residence at 11 Downing Street. Attlee was effectively deputy Prime Minister, a title granted formally in 1942. He was vice-chairman of the Defence Committee of Cabinet and latterly became head of the Cabinet's Committee on the Home Front. In the Commons as well as in Cabinet, he acted as Prime Minister when Churchill was abroad.

The contribution of Clement Attlee to Britain's war effort was general, rather than specific. He neither directed grand strategy like Churchill, nor did he carry diplomatic responsibilities, like the Prime Minister and his Foreign Secretary, Sir Anthony Eden. On the domestic front, Herbert Morrison as Home Secretary and Ernest Bevin as Minister of Labour respectively organised civil defence and the massive mobilisation of labour. Sir Stafford Cripps re-emerged as a responsible political figure within the Labour movement as Ambassador to the Soviet Union and then Minister of Aircraft Production.

Attlee's role was to hold the party together; by doing this, he enabled the Coalition Government itself to hold together. The intrigues and political disruption of the First World War provided cautionary tales of what could happen if party leaders quarrelled about the spoils of office in the midst of the havoc of war. In demeanour as in political objectives, Attlee was an exemplary foil for Churchill. He was careful not to insist upon party claims at a time when wartime mobilisation was leading the country's diplomatic, economic and social policy along lines he had long urged: an international alliance to secure collective security; full employment and state direction of the economy; and 'fair shares' rationing of food and other resources, based upon need rather than wealth.

When the war in Europe ended in May 1945, Attlee once again carefully consulted colleagues before departing from the Coalition. If Labour was to suffer defeat, the leader wished to assure that all were equally implicated. The Conservative terms for continuing the Coalition were unacceptable to the party's National Executive Committee; a general election was held forthwith. The result was victory for the Labour party by a landslide margin that surprised Attlee by its extent. At the age of sixty-two, Clement Attlee became Prime Minister, notwithstanding last-minute efforts by a small clique to substitute Herbert Morrison in his place.

Clement Attlee entered 10 Downing Street with great political advantages. He was careful to maintain them, as far as possible, during his six years in office. He knew how to manage the House of Commons, a skill acquired in the early 1930s; and how to conduct Cabinet business, learned on the job as Deputy Prime Minister. Experience had given first-hand familiarity with political problems at every level from local government to international diplomacy. In addition, he could call upon the talents of experienced and able Labour politicians from all wings of the party. Men of the calibre of Ernest Bevin, Herbert Morrison, Hugh Dalton and Sir Stafford Cripps greatly strengthened the effectiveness of the 1945–51 Labour Government. Its aims could not be achieved by the efforts of a single man. For every major task, Attlee had a man with the ability and experience to do the job. As long as the Cabinet held together, Attlee was proof against rebellion in the House of Commons. The Cabinet held together not only out of regard for their chairman, but also because they disagreed bitterly about who should inherit his position, if and when he left. Ernest Bevin's consistent support of Attlee and refusal to allow his own name to go forward as a replacement gave the Labour Prime Minister great security against the intrigues that inevitably arise when a government goes through an unpopular period.

The achievements of the 1945–51 Labour Government were far greater than the accomplishments of any single individual. The Government introduced the National Health Service and a national insurance scheme that abolished the old means test; it also sustained full employment in peacetime. Coal, gas, electricity, the railways and the steel industry were nationalised. Food subsidies and rationing were continued to prevent inflation and allocate basic goods by reference to need, not income. A new Representation of the People Act established the principle 'one man, one vote'; the delaying powers of the House of Lords were also reduced. The post-war demobilisation of the wartime fighting services was carried out satisfactorily. All of these measures were measures that the Prime Minister, as well as many rank-and-file members of the Labour party, had long advocated. They were thus a collective achievement; as leader of a team, Attlee deserved the credit due to a successful captain.

In international affairs, Clement Attlee could claim personal credit for effecting the transition from Empire to Commonwealth. This change was forced forward by the granting of independence to India and Pakistan in 1947. Difficult decisions were required before this could be achieved. In the transition from war to peace, Attlee was also personally concerned with the decision to build British atomic weapons, following the breakdown of Anglo-American wartime co-operation. Most foreign affairs achievements of the 1945–51 Labour Government reflected the efforts of his Foreign Secretary for almost six years, Ernest Bevin. In Attlee's own words: '"If you have a good dog, don't bark yourself" is a good proverb, and in Ernest Bevin I had an exceptionally good dog.' These two Englishmen, one a trade unionist raised in rural poverty and the other a social worker with a private income, had a common view of the realities of the post-war world. Collaborating closely with the American Government of President Truman, the Labour Government transferred its responsibilities for the defence of Greece and Turkey to the United States in 1946, participated in the establishment of the

Marshall Plan for the post-war economic recovery of Europe, the airlift to counteract the Berlin blockade, the establishment of the North Atlantic Treaty Organisation for the defence of Europe, and, after the outbreak of the Korean War in 1950, commenced rearmament against a potential Russian threat.

The acts of omission are fewer and more controversial. The Government turned down continental requests to join a nascent European Coal and Steel Community, withdrew troops from Palestine rather than mediate indefinitely between Jews and Arabs, and withdrew from the oilfields of Iran, rather than intervene with troops following the nationalisation of British oil interests there in 1951.

The great personal contribution of Clement Attlee was to ensure that the disparate talents and interests of the members of his Government were concentrated upon common goals. Success was gained by carefully calculating the tolerances of different individuals and groups within the Labour movement. By meeting party expectations in domestic policy, credit was gained within the party, useful to offset frustrations arising from the inability to meet expectations in the rapidly changing currents of foreign affairs.

That success was due to the skilful management of political forces, rather than to a compelling personality, was clearly demonstrated by the record of Attlee's last five years as Labour leader. Prior to the election of 1950, divisions were beginning to show within the party between those who wished to carry out more Socialist policies, and those who wished to consolidate legislation realising the promises of a generation. The election result left Labour with a precarious overall majority of five. The failing health of Bevin and Sir Stafford Cripps deprived Attlee of two great stalwarts in Cabinet. The claims of rearmament upon domestic resources triggered off a battle in Cabinet, climaxing in the resignation of Aneurin Bevan and Harold Wilson in April 1951. Herbert Morrison proved unable to carry the full responsibilities of the Foreign Office at a time when foreign affairs and defence were of great urgency. The Prime Minister's health suffered, requiring hospital treatment for a duodenal ulcer and eczema. Uncertain of support, uncertain of direction and uncertain of the men needed to share the burdens, Attlee called a general election in October 1951. A small Labour majority was turned into a slightly larger Conservative majority.

Out of office, Clement Attlee showed once again the care with which he led the Labour party. In a very different political situation –

personally as well as in party terms – he avoided fully committing himself on divisive issues. For three years a great debate raged within the party about the propriety of rearming Germany. With it were linked disputes about the furtherance or consolidation of nationalisation. Aneurin Bevan and the *Tribune* group of MPs used rank-and-file antipathy towards Germany to advance a broad left-wing attack on the party's programme. Herbert Morrison and Hugh Gaitskell defended the position of the second Labour Government. As in the late 1930s, Attlee saw his role as reflecting the balance of power in the party, rather than as an active determinant. When the crucial vote on German rearmament was taken in the House of Commons, he recommended that Labour MPs abstain.

Unlike most prime ministers, Attlee retired from politics in good health, and with the praise of the nation. The controversies within the Labour party made it inopportune for MPs to choose a new Labour leader before the May 1955 general election could be held. In December 1955 the 72-year-old Attlee announced his retirement. The Queen conferred an earldom. The ex-Prime Minister retired to the Lords, appearing from time to time in print, television, or on the lecture circuit with his reminiscences, but rarely entering party controversy. Uncharacteristically, he did allow his name to be used as Honorary Chairman of the moderate Campaign for Democratic Socialism when it was founded in 1961 to defend Hugh Gaitskell from the left-wing critics who had also harassed Attlee. Advancing years gradually restricted his movements, prior to his death on 8 October 1967.

If not one of the very greatest prime ministers, Clement Attlee was, at the least, a very good prime minister. He was less the cause of events than the means by which great events came to pass. He spoke little, but when he spoke it was to the point. He usually did not speak until and unless he was sure he could speak with good effect. In foreign affairs he played a weak hand, but he played it well. In domestic affairs, the actions of his Government, rather than the phrases of its leader, are memorable. The statute books from 1945 to 1951 are a memorial of his work, and more than that. The achievements of that Government were also the achievements of tens of thousands in the Labour movement who committed themselves to Socialism in times and places as inauspicious as that chosen by the youthful Attlee. If fortune or events had taken a different turn at any number of points in his political career, Attlee's name would be little more familiar than the names of his Stepney comrades, or of his comrades in the pathetic battles in opposition in the early 1930s. There is no doubt that he, like them, would have been satisfied enough by collective success, without personal fame.

While Clement Attlee was a dedicated Socialist during his half-century in politics, he was throughout his life an Englishman, dedicated to maintaining and advancing all that he thought best in a land that has a Radical as well as a Tory tradition, and respect for social service as well as deference in its culture. In the final paragraph of his autobiographical memoir, Clement Attlee succinctly sums up what he saw as the chief features of his life: 'I have been a very happy and fortunate man in having lived so long in the greatest country in the world, in having a happy family life, and in having been given the opportunity of serving in a state of life to which I had never expected to be called.'

BIBLIOGRAPHY

Writings by Clement Attlee
As It Happened (London, 1954)
Empire into Commonwealth (London, 1961)
The Labour Party in Perspective (London, 1937)
A Prime Minister Remembers (by Francis Williams, based on the private papers and a series of recorded conversations) (London, 1961)
Purpose and Policy: Selected Speeches (London, 1947)
The Social Worker (London, 1920)
The Town Councillor (co-author W. A. Robson) (London, 1925)
War Comes to Britain (speeches) (London, 1940)
The Will and the Way to Socialism (London, 1935)

Books about Clement Attlee
Jenkins, Roy H., *Mr Attlee: An Interim Biography* (London, 1948)
Murphy, John T., *Labour's Big Three* (London, 1948)

19

SIR ANTHONY EDEN

BY

ANTHONY NUTTING

Anthony Eden, created Earl of Avon 1961. Hon. DCL (Oxford and Durham); Hon. LLD (Birmingham, Bristol, Cambridge, Leeds, Sheffield, Belfast, etc). Born 12 June 1897, son of Sir William Eden, Bart. Educated at Eton and Christ Church, Oxford (BA 1922). Served in the European War 1915–19; Bde Major (MC). Contested (Con.) Spennymoor 1922; MP for Warwick and Leamington 1923–57. Parliamentary Private Secretary to Sir Austen Chamberlain (Foreign Office) 1926–29; Parliamentary Under-secretary for Foreign Affairs 1931–34; Lord Privy Seal and Minister for League of Nations Affairs 1934–35; Foreign Secretary 1935–38; Dominions Secretary 1939–40; Secretary of State for War 1940; Foreign Secretary 1940–45; Leader of the House of Commons 1942–45; Deputy Leader of the Opposition 1945–51; Foreign Secretary and Deputy Prime Minister 1951–55; Prime Minister and First Lord of the Treasury 1955–57. Chairman of the OEEC 1952–54; Trustee of the National Gallery 1935–49; Chancellor of the University of Birmingham 1945; President of the Royal Shakespeare Theatre 1958–66. Married (1) 1923 Beatrice Helen Beckett, one surviving son (one son killed on active service); (2) Clarissa Anne Churchill. Author of Places in the Sun, Freedom and Order, Days for Decision, The Eden Memoirs, *etc.*

SIR ANTHONY EDEN

After the 1955 general election a friend of mine in the Labour party told me that what clinched the victory for the Tories was a poster which appeared on almost every hoarding in Britain depicting Anthony Eden's face with the brief and simple slogan underneath, 'Working for Peace'. If there had ever been any chance of Labour regaining power, 'that poster', said my friend, 'finally disposed of it'.

As one of Eden's ministers especially deputed to speak on foreign affairs during that election campaign, I know just how true this was. For one thing the poster reminded the electors of the Prime Minister's reputation as a master practitioner of international negotiation. More important still, it emphasised how, largely due to his personal and prodigious efforts as Churchill's Foreign Secretary over the previous three and a half years, most of the conflicts across the world which the Tories had inherited from the Labour Government in 1951 had been peaceably resolved; and at that moment in time there was no actual war in progress anywhere on the surface of the earth.

Consequently the 1955 election not only gave Eden, as Churchill's successor, a renewed mandate to carry on the Conservative Government and to continue 'working for peace'; it also gave him a majority in the new Parliament more than three times that which his illustrious predecessor had gained at the previous contest in 1951. Those middle-of-the-road voters who had earlier felt a certain anxiety at the thought of Sir Winston with his bulldog image leading the nation at a time when world peace seemed to hang in the balance, had no such qualms about Anthony Eden. To them the new Prime Minister epitomised their idea of the perfect peace-maker – a man who had been instrumental in halting the war in Korea and bringing about a ceasefire in Indo-China, who had resolved Britain's disputes with Persia and Egypt and who had initiated the first tentative steps towards ending the Cold War between the West and the Communist bloc. And with the first post-war Summit Conference between the leaders of America, Russia, Britain and France about to take place, it seemed inconceivable that the search for peace should be entrusted to anyone but the man who had brought about this remarkable sequence of settlements.

Indeed seldom has any Prime Minister of Britain taken office under more auspicious circumstances or with a greater fund of goodwill at home and abroad, in Parliament and in the councils of the world outside. Yet within less than two years, Eden was to throw that goodwill away and to bring about his own downfall by plunging into a conflict that was as unnecessary as its outcome was mortifying for him and for the nation he aspired to lead. By one of the most tragic paradoxes of modern times, after the 'belligerent bulldog' Churchill had retired, leaving behind him a long line of peaceful arrangements, the deft diplomatist who had been the principal architect of these settlements was to bequeath to his successor a legacy of war, humiliation and confusion. In so doing, he lost not only his reputation as a peace-maker *par excellence* but also the premiership for which he had worked and waited for so long. And whereas his record as Foreign Secretary was studded with one brilliant success after another, his brief reign as Prime Minister will be remembered only for the titanic disaster of Suez.

To understand how so experienced and pre-eminent a statesman as Eden came to break all the rules that had hitherto governed his political career it is necessary to turn the pages of history back to the time when he first took over the office of Foreign Secretary at the end of 1935 at the tender age of thirty-eight. In a brilliant personal portrait Lord Vansittart, then the permanent head of the Foreign Office, described how his political chief rose to such dizzy heights at so early an age:

'Young Eden, straight from charm school, omitted nothing to deserve his promotion. . . . His appearance went far to ensure that he would get what he wanted, and that was a lot. . . . Zealous, affable, intelligent . . . he possessed early the makings of a good House of Commons manner. Desirous and deserving of praise, he avoided suspicions of brilliance or originality [and] he said the right thing so often that he seemed incapable of saying anything else. . . . In three years he was Lord Privy Seal, in four Foreign Secretary. It all seemed probable.'

During these formative years it was for the most part plain sailing for 'young Eden'. Always a glutton for work, he revelled in the activity of international conferences and parliamentary debates. Both in the

House of Commons, where he served his apprenticeship as Under-secretary of State for Foreign Affairs, and then as Britain's spokesman in the League of Nations, he quickly established himself as a most skilful parliamentarian and negotiator. True, when Mussolini set the pattern of Fascist aggression in the thirties by attacking Abyssinia, Eden failed to mobilise sufficient international support for effective sanctions against the aggressor. Yet it was generally recognised that this was not for want of trying on his part. Hence he personally bore no share of blame for the failure of the sanctions policy. Even the scandal of the Hoare-Laval plan for buying off Mussolini, by awarding him a substantial portion of Abyssinian territory, had no adverse effects on Eden who, together with the Prime Minister, Stanley Baldwin, and the rest of the Cabinet, contrived to dissociate himself from what the Foreign Secretary had agreed with his French opposite number. And when Hoare, finding himself disowned by his colleagues and pilloried by the press, resigned from the Foreign Secretaryship, Eden was, despite his youth, the natural and inevitable successor.

However, within three months of his succession, his days of plain sailing were brought to an abrupt stop and the first major crisis of his political life burst upon him, which no amount of 'charm school' train-ing could help him to surmount and which was to scar him for all the rest of his political life. In March 1936 Hitler tore up the Versailles peace settlement and the Locarno treaty by sending German troops to reoccupy the Rhineland, which Germany had agreed under both of these treaties should remain demilitarised.

Up to this point Eden's aim had been to do all in his power to avert a second war with Germany, to which end he was, as he told his Cabinet colleagues, fully prepared to make 'concessions of value to her as part of a final settlement. . . .' Although the Germans had announced in March 1935 that, contrary to the Versailles terms, they already possessed an air force and would shortly have a conscript army of thirty-six divisions, Eden continued to regard Mussolini rather than Hitler as the principal villain of Europe and to contend that a settlement with Germany would be possible if only she would play her part in the League of Nations and sign a disarmament treaty.

Hitler's reoccupation of the Rhineland should therefore have come as a serious setback to such hopes. Yet, far from abandoning his appease-ment policy, Eden's reaction was to persist in his search for an accom-modation with Nazi Germany. Brazen though it was, he told his colleagues, Hitler's move had been most skilfully contrived. And while it might now be clear that the German leader would repudiate any treaty if convenient, the Government could not ignore the fact that 'not one in a thousand Englishmen' was prepared to resist the reoccupation of the Rhineland by force of arms. British public opinion, along with most of the Cabinet, felt that Germany had a right to send troops into a piece of her own territory. And a lot of people thought that there was something to be said for Hitler's argument that France had been the first to break at least the spirit of the Locarno treaty by her recent alliance with Russia, which had effectively encircled Germany. Moreover, the Government had also to take into account that, even as his army marched into the Rhineland, Hitler had offered a new European settlement which included the creation of a demilitarised zone on both sides of Germany's frontiers with France and Belgium.

It was all very well, Eden contended, for the French to call for a military showdown with Germany on this issue. But Laval's recent attempt to inveigle Britain into betraying Abyssinia and the League scarcely suggested that French counter action would in practice be more than a bluff which Hitler would be certain to call. Therefore he suggested, to the infinite relief of the Cabinet, that in view of 'Germany's growing strength and power of mischief', Britain should continue to seek 'as enduring a settlement as possible while Hitler is in the mood to do so'. And since there was no alternative but to submit to the reoccupation of the Rhineland, it would be preferable for Britain to persuade France to accept the *fait accompli* 'while surrender still has a bargaining value'. All that Eden asked of Hitler was that, to show good faith, the Germans should withdraw all but a token force from the former demilitarised zone while the proposed new treaty was being negotiated. And when the answer came that Germany could only guarantee not to increase the existing occupation army, his sole practical riposte was to announce that France had been invited to join in staff talks in London.

As a result the Germans got what they wanted over the Rhineland without being obliged even to spell out their proposals for a new Locarno, let alone to enter into any fresh engagements. Yet, as late as the end of 1937, only a few weeks before he resigned from Neville Chamberlain's Government, Eden was still talking of the need for a settlement with Hitler. Harold Nicolson records that, at a meeting of Tory MPs, Eden asserted that there was no imminent likelihood of war.

Despite Hitler's repudiation of the peace settlement, he told them that there was now a better than ever prospect for a policy of appeasement and that Britain should seize the opportunity to reach a general settlement with Germany. Moreover, in order to clear the decks for the appeasement approach, Eden had shunted the resolutely anti-Nazi Vansittart from the post of Permanent Under-Secretary at the Foreign Office into a sinecure assignment whence he could exercise no effective influence on policy. And even although his attitude towards Hitler hardened somewhat after his resignation and more especially after Munich, he steadfastly refused to join in any backbench campaign to stiffen the Government's resistance to the Nazi menace.

It would, of course, be grossly unfair to say, with the advantage of hindsight, that Eden ought to have acceded to French demands for joint military action in March 1936 and that, when his colleagues rejected such counsels, he should have resigned. Although the French persisted in saying so, nobody could then have been certain – as we are now from the German documents which have since come to light – that Hitler would have backed down, if he had been confronted by an Anglo-French show of force. But it was because Eden knew, on reflection, that he had been responsible for what Sir Alexander Cadogan afterwards called this 'great and tragic appeasement', that he himself was to state in his own memoirs that Britain and France 'should have attempted the impossible' and braved the public outcry against forcing Germany to withdraw her armies from the Rhineland. And to a former private secretary, Sir Pierson Dixon, he confided some twenty years later that if Britain had resisted Hitler in 1936, the Second World War might have been avoided, in which case 'millions of lives would have been saved'.

Thus it is clear that, for all the rest of his most distinguished political career, Eden was scarred by a feeling of guilt for his inaction over the Rhineland. Yet far from suffering any censure for his tame surrender, his reputation as Foreign Secretary went from strength to strength. And when he finally resigned early in 1938, having found that he could no longer work with his Prime Minister, Neville Chamberlain, he was revered by all those who opposed appeasement as a man of conscience and courage who wanted to stand up to the European dictators, Hitler as well as Mussolini.

In fact Eden's resignation, when it came, had nothing to do with Hitler and, so far as it concerned the Government's attitude towards Mussolini, it turned on an issue more of procedure and timing than of principle. Whereas Baldwin had been largely uninterested in international affairs and so had left his Foreign Secretary a very free hand, Chamberlain, deeming it his duty to pacify the situation in Europe, intervened constantly in the conduct of foreign policy after he succeeded to the premiership in 1937. Being essentially more vain than most politicians, Eden soon came to resent such interference after the relative freedom of action he had enjoyed under Baldwin. And although, to begin with, Eden told a close friend that Chamberlain had the makings of a great Prime Minister, within a very few months his opinion of his chief underwent a drastic change. In January 1938, President Roosevelt proposed to Britain a conference of the major European powers and the United States to discuss and, if possible, settle outstanding international problems. The Foreign Secretary was abroad at the time on a brief spell of leave and, as if deliberately taking advantage of his absence, Chamberlain dashed off a damping reply saying that he was hoping to reach a settlement with Hitler and Mussolini and that he did not want any crossing of wires at this delicate juncture.

Eden exploded with rage when he learnt of this, and on his return to London promptly sent Roosevelt a message designed to mitigate the Prime Minister's negative response. After a week of arguing he prevailed on Chamberlain to cable the President that he warmly welcomed his initiative and would support it whenever he decided to launch it. But although Roosevelt replied that he was deeply gratified by the Prime Minister's second message, the damage had been done and nothing more was heard of the President's project.

Convinced that Chamberlain had torpedoed the best, if not the only, hope of the Americans throwing their weight behind the European democracies' search for peace, Eden now began to realise that he would never be able to work harmoniously with his Prime Minister. And when Chamberlain insisted on holding formal discussions for a settlement with Mussolini, based on Britain's *de jure* recognition of the Italian conquest of Abyssinia, he argued strongly that only informal talks should take place unless and until the Italian dictator made some gesture of good faith, such as withdrawing the troops he had sent to fight for General Franco in the current Spanish Civil War. Various attempts were made by Eden's friends in the Cabinet to draw up a compromise formula on which both the Prime Minister and the Foreign Secretary could agree. But to no avail. Chamberlain was no less delighted to get rid of Eden than Eden was determined to stick to his guns. And in February 1938 the two men formally parted company.

However, after an interval of less than two years during which, to the dismay of his supporters in Parliament and the press, he preserved an uncritical silence on foreign policy issues, Eden returned to Chamberlain's Government as Dominions Secretary following the outbreak of World War II. In this capacity he chafed at the relative inactivity and it was with the greatest enthusiasm that he took over the War Office when Churchill was precipitated into the premiership in the spring of 1940. Churchill had long been an admirer of Eden, who he thought was by far the best member of those governments of the 1930s from which he himself had been excluded. And when Eden had resigned, he described how for once sleep deserted him: 'From midnight till dawn I lay in my bed consumed by emotions of sorrow and fear. There seemed one strong young figure standing up against long, dismal, drawling tides of drift and surrender. . . . Now he was gone. I watched the daylight slowly creep in through the windows and saw before me in mental gaze the vision of death.'

Not surprisingly therefore, when Lord Halifax, who had succeeded to the Foreign Office in 1938, was appointed as Ambassador to Washington three years later, it was Eden whom Churchill chose as Foreign Secretary. With his customary love of hard work, Eden once more plunged into the direction of British foreign policy and soon became, along with Lord Beaverbrook and Field-Marshal Smuts, a member of the most intimate circle of Churchill's friends. And although Churchill interfered constantly in foreign policy matters, any differences between the two men were mostly of method only and, more often than not, Churchill would be able to charm his lieutenant into agreement. Indeed one of Churchill's private secretaries has stated that only on one occasion did he ever witness an open disagreement between Eden and his Prime Minister in all the five years in which they worked together during the war.

So great was the harmony of this partnership that Churchill very soon nominated Eden as his successor over the heads of several senior ministerial colleagues and in 1942 asked him to take on the task of leading the House of Commons in addition to his Foreign Office responsibilities. Realising that the intention was to groom him for the eventual succession to the premiership, Eden accepted these additional burdens with alacrity. And although his Foreign Office advisers complained that he henceforth became more than ever what Cadogan called 'a cat on hot bricks', and never had enough time to discuss foreign policy, his three years' spell as Leader of the House was a brilliant success, from which he emerged as a parliamentarian of the very highest order.

However the burden of combining these two jobs, with the Commons then sitting morning and afternoon, eventually undermined his health, and just before the 1945 general election he was stricken with a virulent jaundice which effectively prevented him from any participation in the campaign. This was the first warning that physically he was no superman, however much he might rely on his abundant store of nervous energy to get him through his work. But Eden refused to admit the fact, and after he became Foreign Secretary for the third time when the Tories were returned to office in 1951, he would take elaborate steps to demonstrate his physical fitness to the world and to conceal from all but his closest advisers that he could be laid low by so much as a head-cold. Working from before breakfast to the early hours of the next morning his day was a non-stop series of Cabinet meetings, conferences and interviews, with questions or debates in Parliament to answer at least once a week. Never able to be alone for more than a few minutes at a time, he loved to preside over large gatherings of ministers and Foreign Office officials. And on these occasions he would more often than not put on the kind of performance that prompted Anthony Quayle, who met him during the war, to remark that he seemed like some actor playing the part of Eden. To save time, meetings with his closest advisers would frequently take place with him in bed, sun-bathing on a terrace or dressing for dinner – and occasionally even in the bath-tub. Indeed, except for his few hours of sleep, there was never one moment in the day or night when he ever seemed to want to relax.

Inevitably the strain of such working hours was to take its toll and early in 1953 he was wheeled off to hospital to have his gall-bladder removed. Then, as ill luck would have it, he suffered a serious relapse due to trouble with the bile-duct, the exhaust-pipe of the human system, from which he was never to recover fully and which kept him away from the conduct of foreign affairs for the next months.

Nevertheless, despite this setback, there can be no doubt that the third spell as Foreign Secretary marked the high point of Eden's political career. Taking over at the height of the Cold War between the West and the Soviet bloc, he set about trying to reduce international tensions and to substitute discussion for diatribe as the means of diplomatic communication. When he took office, in addition to the overriding problems of the Cold War with Russia, the armistice talks in Korea were deadlocked, the Communists were threatening to take over all Indo-China, British oilmen had been thrown out of Persia, relations with Egypt were in a state of undeclared war over the presence of the British bases on the Suez Canal and, for good measure, Italy and Yugoslavia were at odds over the future of Trieste. Yet when he succeeded to the premiership three and a half years afterwards, all these critical issues had been settled, largely, and in some cases entirely, due to his persistent diplomacy; and relations with Russia had improved to the point where the first post-war Summit Meeting was about to be held in Geneva. Seldom in history has Britain and a British Foreign Secretary been so highly revered in the councils of the world.

Well might two of his senior Foreign Office advisers, Cadogan and Lord Strang, say of Eden in their memoirs that no other Foreign Secretary whom they served could excel him in finesse as a negotiator or in a sense of international relationships. Nobody appreciated this better than Churchill who, even as he formed his last Government at the age of seventy-six, was thinking of retiring in the near future. But after Eden's grave illness in 1953, Churchill began to wonder if his chosen successor was physically and mentally strong enough to take over as Prime Minister. At the same time, he was determined that no one else should succeed him and so, although he himself suffered a serious stroke in 1953, he held on to the premiership hoping that the interval would give Eden the necessary time to recoup his strength. Nevertheless Churchill's puckish sense of humour could not resist the occasional opportunity to tease his successor, as happened when he announced, during a visit from Dean Acheson, the American Secretary of State, that he intended to cut down the trees in the Downing Street garden. Eden protested that he had no right to do so. Living at No. 10 did not mean that he owned the place. 'I see what you mean,' Churchill replied with a mischievous twinkle, 'I'm only the life tenant, you're the remainder-man.'

But Eden could not understand why Churchill continually postponed his retirement and he persisted, with more petulance than discretion, in telling his friends and colleagues that the 'old man' was playing cat and mouse with him. For, sad to say, he never really reciprocated Churchill's feelings of real affection for him. Indeed he was sometimes extremely jealous of his chief. Dixon cited an instance in his diary when, after the Yalta Conference in 1945, Eden became furious with Churchill for insisting on accompanying him on a visit to newly liberated Athens where he had hoped to have all the limelight. The Prime Minister's decision, Dixon recorded, 'reduced Eden to such a state of exasperation that he sulked all the afternoon, refused to look at any work and then complained . . . when he did read some telegrams that matters of importance had been kept from him'

What is more Churchill was not the only object of Eden's jealousy. During the war he resented the independent status Harold Macmillan enjoyed as Minister Resident in North Africa and Italy, and wanted him to be subordinate to his orders as Foreign Secretary. Then, when he himself became Prime Minister, he very soon realised that Macmillan, whom he first appointed to the Foreign Office, was too strong a character to work as a subordinate in the sphere of foreign affairs, where he intended as Prime Minister to exercise no less paramount an influence than before. Not only had the new Foreign Secretary gained the credit and distinction of signing the long delayed Austrian peace treaty, but he had also shown a far greater understanding of the Greek Government's attitude in the Cyprus dispute than Eden was prepared to concede. Consequently, at the first available opportunity in the late autumn of 1955, Macmillan was transferred to the home front as Chancellor of the Exchequer in place of Rab Butler who was in need of a change after four anxious years at the Treasury.

Not surprisingly such jealousy towards his political contemporaries made it extremely difficult for Eden to give his friendship wholeheartedly to any of his senior colleagues. Consequently he was a very lonely man, and although he made sure that he was seldom without company, his choice of companions generally fell on men much younger than himself who could not possibly represent any threat to his supremacy and who, as Dixon once described them to me, were more like 'buddies' than real and enduring friends.

Nor were these egocentric susceptibilities confined to personal relationships. As Butler wrote in his autobiography, Eden was extremely sensitive to criticism, especially in the press. Many is the time that he called me at home before breakfast to complain bitterly about some editorial which was not to his liking. Occasionally he would hit back justifiably, as happened when the *Sunday Express* once launched a most unjust attack on a senior Foreign Office official who had no right to reply for himself. But, less wisely, he would all too often allow himself to be goaded by some personal criticism into an outburst of rage reminiscent no doubt of his father, an irascible baronet who, when a downpour of rain ruined a day's partridge shooting, is alleged to have beaten with his fists on the drawing-room window shouting, 'Oh! God, how like You!'

As Eden climbed to the top of the political ladder, these quirks of his character seemed to grow rather than to diminish. In part this could be attributed to the debilitating after-effects of his illness in 1953. But aside from that, he found himself altogether too isolated as Prime Minister. Unlike the Foreign Office where he was constantly surrounded by hordes of experts and officials, No. 10 was a very lonely pinnacle. And Eden compensated for this loneliness by continually intervening in the work of his ministers, especially those at the Foreign Office, even to the point of sometimes countermanding decisions which, although they conformed to established policy, had not been specifically referred to him for approval. As Butler put it, the Prime Minister was driven to making 'innumerable telephone calls on every day of the week and every hour of the day which characterised his conscientious but highly strung supervision of our affairs'. And as one who was frequently at the receiving end of those calls, I can honestly say that Eden in his days as Foreign Secretary could never have suffered more interference from his various chiefs than Selwyn Lloyd and I endured during his brief premiership.

As this interference increased so a sense of frustration and distrust began to pervade the atmosphere of Whitehall which did not take long to communicate itself to Fleet Street. And before Eden had been in office for six months, the press began to attack him for lack of effective leadership. Inevitably comparisons were made between him and his predecessor from which he emerged dwarfed by the mantle of Churchill. And as if this were not hurtful enough to his vanity, a scathing attack appeared in an editorial in that archetypal Tory newspaper, the *Daily Telegraph*. Describing how, when making a speech, Eden would often stress a point by putting the clenched fist of one hand into the palm of the other, the editor commented, 'But the smack is seldom heard', and he went on to say that it was high time that the smack of firm government was heard from No. 10.

Eden had never been exactly the darling of the Conservative right who had consistently opposed him and supported Chamberlain's policies in the late thirties. Also, during his last spell as Foreign Secretary, they had bitterly criticised him for tamely giving way to nationalist pressures from Nasser's Egypt and agreeing to remove the British bases from the Suez Canal Zone. Being as always highly sensitive to criticism from the press and now nagged by deteriorating health, he responded to the *Daily Telegraph* editorial like a kicking mule. Instead of following his own natural bent as a deft diplomat and negotiator *par excellence*, he decided totally out of character to show his critics that he was the strong man who could wear Churchill's mantle without being bowed down by it. Talleyrand was to play the part of Napoleon. Eden was to silence his critics of the right by joining them.

Thus when, two months later, King Hussein of Jordan dismissed his British Commander-in-Chief, General Glubb, at twenty-four hours' notice, Eden reacted violently. Instead of taking care to discover what motives lay behind this sudden action, he immediately concluded that it was Nasser's doing. Gone was the desire to get on terms with the new Egypt which, as Foreign Secretary, he had expressed to me when Nasser and I signed the agreement about the British bases less than two years before. Arab nationalism, which had earlier been a legitimate aspiration in his sight, had become what he termed a 'bacillus' which had to be exterminated. As he now told me, Nasser must be destroyed and it was only a matter of waiting for a suitable pretext to do so.

From that moment onwards, therefore, Eden declared a personal war on Egypt's ruler. Nasser, he asserted, was the sworn enemy of Britain throughout the Middle East. Not satisfied with getting the British to remove their troops from Egyptian territory, he was engaged in a conspiracy with Arab nationalist forces everywhere to destroy all British influence and interests in the Arab world. And as he pondered how best to kill this mad dog before every other Arab was bitten and infected by its rabid poison, the memory of 1936 came back to haunt him. World War II might not have happened, he told himself, if Britain and France had stopped Hitler when he marched into the Rhineland; and he felt that he bore a major share of the responsibility for their failure to do so. Now, twenty years later, he felt he had the chance to expiate his inaction at that fatal turning-point in history. Come what might, he would not be found wanting a second time.

To compare Nasser with Hitler, or even Mussolini, was of course grossly to misread his motives and even to exaggerate his power to challenge Britain's position in the Middle East. For Egypt had neither the strength nor the intention to remove more than Britain's military presence from Arab soil. Yet when Nasser nationalised the Suez Canal

Company in the following July, Eden contended that his action was proof of his implacable hostility to every British interest in the area and of the need to crush him without delay.

In the event, such was Nasser's skill in avoiding any open collision with British interests, following the nationalisation of the Canal Company, that Eden was obliged to wait until he could concoct with the French and the Israelis the necessary pretext to destroy his enemy by force of arms. And when, as was inevitable, the pressures of world opinion, led by America and Russia, brought about the withdrawal of the Anglo-French force that had been sent to seize the Suez Canal, the Prime Minister's strong-arm policy lay in ruins. Britain and France, together with Israel, had been branded throughout the world as aggressors for their gunboat diplomacy and were obliged to withdraw without achieving any of their objectives. Not surprisingly in a sick man, a total breakdown of Eden's health now followed, as the fevers induced by the damaged bile-duct became more frequent and violent with the nervous strain of those last terrible weeks. And when the doctors told him that he could not carry on, he had no alternative but to tender his resignation to the Queen.

In one way, perhaps, the fates were kinder than they seemed when they decreed that Eden should retire for reasons of health. For it is hard to see how he could have carried on as Prime Minister after the sordid fiasco he had brought about. Indeed, from his performance throughout his twenty-one nervous months at No. 10, it is more than likely that, even if Nasser and Suez had never happened, he would not have been able to hold down the premiership for very long. Brilliant diplomatist and parliamentarian that he was, when put to the test he did not have the right temperament for the tasks involved.

If the premiership were merely a prize for diligence and hard work, no one ever earned it more than Eden. But, as it turned out, he had neither the confidence in himself nor the trust in others to fulfil the expectations of his admirers. When things went wrong he answered his critics from an injured vanity rather than a sense of purpose. In part, this was because he had for too long been the Golden Boy of the Tory party, the glamorous Crown Prince awaiting the summons to mount the throne in place of the ageing Emperor. This inevitably made it that much harder for him to rise above the criticisms that descended upon his head once he had reached the summit. In part also his failure was due to his inability to think and plan strategically. Consummate tactician that he was, both in diplomacy and politics, he lacked the strategist's sense of direction and, when blown off course, his helmsmanship degenerated into a series of reckless manoeuvres designed to court an ephemeral popularity and so undermined still further that sense of confidence among his colleagues which is quintessential to a successful premiership.

Would that Eden had heeded the lines of the poet Longfellow:

> 'Not in the clamour of the crowded street,
> Not in the shouts and plaudits of the throng,
> But in ourselves are triumph and defeat.'

For if only he could have accepted ultimately to be judged on his own real merits and achievements, he would not have needed to seek 'the shouts and plaudits' of a fickle public.

But it was not to be so. Unable to be true to his own nature, on the morrow of his greatest diplomatic triumphs, he plunged into a suicidal and ignominious defeat. That Eden should have failed so miserably in the office for which he had waited for so long was tragic indeed. Yet more tragic still was the fact that in those last few disastrous months of his career, he destroyed so much of the respect and esteem which he had earlier won for himself and for Britain among the nations of the world.

BIBLIOGRAPHY

Acheson, Dean, *Present at the Creation* (London, 1970)

Avon, Lord, Eden Memoirs: *Facing the Dictators* (London, 1962); *Full Circle* (London, 1960)

Butler, Lord, *The Art of the Possible* (London, 1971)

Cadogan, Sir Alexander, *Diaries 1938–45* (London, 1971)

Churchill, Sir Winston, *The Second World War*, vol. i, 'The Gathering Storm' (London, 1959)

Cook, Don, *Floodtide in Europe* (New York, 1965)

Cooper, Duff, *Old Men Forget* (London, 1953)

Dixon, Pierson, *Double Diploma* (London, 1968)

Harvey, Lord, *Diplomatic Diaries of Oliver Harvey 1937–40* (London, 1970)

Johnson, Alan Campbell, *Viscount Halifax* (London, 1941)

Macmillan, Harold, *Riding the Storm* (London, 1971)

Murphy, Robert, *Diplomat among Warriors* (London, 1964)

Nicolson, Harold, *Diaries and Letters 1930–9* (London, 1956)

Normanbrook, Lord, and Colville, John, *Action This Day* (London, 1968)
Nutting, Anthony, *No End of a Lesson* (London, 1967)
Strang, Lord, *Home and Abroad* (London, 1956)
Taylor, A. J. P., *English History 1914–45* (Oxford, 1965)
Trevelyan, Lord, *Worlds Apart* (London, 1971)
Sherwood, Robert, *White House Papers of Harry L. Hopkins*, vol. ii (London, 1949)
Vansittart, Lord, *The Mist Procession* (London, 1958)

20

HAROLD MACMILLAN

BY

DUNCAN CROW

Maurice Harold Macmillan, PC (1942), FRS (1962). Born 10
February 1894. Educated at Eton and Balliol College, Oxford.
Served in the Grenadier Guards 1914–18. Married Lady Dorothy
Evelyn Cavendish, one son, two daughters. ADC to the Governor-
General of Canada 1919–20. MP for Stockton 1924–29 and 1931–
45, for Bromley 1945–64. Parliamentary Secretary to the Ministry
of Supply 1940–42; Parliamentary Under-Secretary of State for
the Colonies 1942; Minister Resident at Allied HQ in North-
West Africa 1942–45; Secretary for Air 1945; Minister of Hous-
ing and Local Government 1951–54; Minister of Defence 1954–
55; Secretary of State for Foreign Affairs 1955; Chancellor of the
Exchequer 1955–57; Prime Minister and First Lord of the Treasury
1957–63. Chancellor of the University of Oxford from 1960;
President, Macmillan (Holdings). Hon. DCL (Oxford) 1958,
LLD (Cambridge) 1961, (Sussex) 1963. Author of (Memoirs):
Winds of Change, *1966;* The Blast of War, *1967;* Tides of
Fortune, *1969;* Riding the Storm, *1971;* Pointing the Way,
1972; At the End of the Day, *1973. Also* Reconstruction; A
Plea for a National Policy, *1933;* Planning for Employment,
1935; The Middle Way, *1938; etc.*

HAROLD MACMILLAN

EARLY POLITICAL CAREER

Maurice Harold Macmillan was born in London on 10 February 1894, the youngest of the three sons of Maurice Crawford Macmillan and Helen *née* Belles, the daughter of Dr Joshua Tarleton Belles of Spencer, Indiana, USA. His paternal grandfather, Daniel Macmillan, and Daniel's brother Alexander, who were brought up in extreme poverty in the west of Scotland, founded the family's publishing house of Macmillan. In 1855 they published their first best-seller, Charles Kingsley's *Westward Ho*! One of Daniel Macmillan's greatest friends was another Christian Socialist, the Reverend Frederick Denison Maurice. The admiration he felt for Maurice was perpetuated in the name of one of his sons, Harold's father, who carried on the link, as indeed did Harold himself in his turn.

Harold Macmillan was educated at Summerfields (a preparatory school in Oxford), Eton (where he was a Scholar and which he had to leave prematurely because of ill health), and Oxford (Balliol as an Exhibitioner), 1912–14 (a First in Classic Moderations). During the period between Eton and Oxford he had a series of tutors including Ronald Knox who, he wrote later, 'had a profound influence upon me, both then and afterwards'.

He was commissioned in the King's Royal Rifle Corps in 1914, then transferred to the Grenadier Guards in which he subsequently became a captain. He was wounded at the battle of Loos in 1915, and on the Somme in September 1916. This latter wound shattered his pelvis, keeping him out of action and mostly in hospital for the rest of the war. Not until 1920 did the wound finally heal.

In 1919 he went to Canada as ADC to the Governor-General, the ninth Duke of Devonshire. He became engaged to the Duke's daughter, Lady Dorothy Cavendish, returned to England with her in January 1920, and was married at St Margaret's, Westminster, three months later. Soon afterwards he joined the family publishing firm.

His political career began at the general election in December 1923 when he stood as Conservative candidate for the north of England industrial constituency of Stockton-on-Tees. In a three-cornered fight he lost to the Liberal by 73 votes with the Labour candidate 1,042 behind in third place. At the next general election, in October 1924, he won Stockton by 3,215 votes from the Labour candidate with the Liberal third. He made his maiden speech in the Budget debate on 30 April 1925.

Macmillan was MP for Stockton from 1924 to May 1929 when he lost the seat to Labour by 2,389 votes with the Liberal again third. In the October 1931 election he beat the Labour candidate by 11,031 votes in a straight fight. He retained the seat in the November 1935 election with a 4,068 majority over Labour, the Liberal losing his deposit, and continued as Conservative Member for Stockton-on-Tees until he was defeated in the July 1945 election.

Macmillan, who had great ability and was deeply interested in politics, was nevertheless much neglected during his years in Parliament before the outbreak of World War II. He earned for himself the reputation of a rebel. When he entered the House of Commons in 1924 he gravitated towards the left wing of his party and was one of a group who were nicknamed 'The YMCA' – as opposed to another section of the Conservative party called by their opponents 'The Forty Thieves'. The young enthusiasts of 'The YMCA' were keen advocates of social reform and of a planned economy. In 1927, with Robert Boothby, John Loder and Oliver Stanley, Macmillan published *Industry and the State*, which was regarded as a manifesto of the progressive Conservatives. From then until the outbreak of war he continued to write books and pamphlets (*The State and Industry* 1932, *The Next Step* 1932, *Reconstruction* 1933, *Planning for Employment* 1935 (joint author), *The Next Five Years* 1935 (joint author), *The Middle Way* 1938, *The Price of Peace* 1938, *Economic Aspects of Defence* 1939), which propounded his unorthodox Conservative views.

For Macmillan the stimulus for planning and reform was the constituency he represented, acting on an awakened social conscience that had been stirred by his experiences in the trenches. Stockton-on-Tees was one of many depressed areas where widespread unemployment that went on year after year made a mockery of 'the land fit for heroes' that had been promised to the returning soldiers of the 1914–18 war. This dreadful evidence of human waste that surrounded him in his constituency affected Macmillan throughout his political career – as indeed it lingered with anyone who saw the hopeless street-corner groups of unwanted men that haunted Britain in the years between the two world wars.

Although Macmillan still maintained a close interest in social and economic questions, after 1935 he began to turn his attention more and more to foreign affairs and to defence. The *Zeitgeist* was changing. Abyssinia, Hitler, and the Spanish Civil War were beginning to over-shadow Jarrow and the hunger marchers. When sanctions against Italy were abandoned in 1936 he was one of only two Conservatives to vote with the Labour Opposition against the Government on a three-line Whip, supporting the motion 'That His Majesty's Government by their lack of a resolute and straightforward foreign policy, have lowered the prestige of the country, weakened the League of Nations, imperilled peace and thereby forfeited the confidence of this House'. Immediately after this act of open mutiny he resigned the party Whip, on 29 June, and remained as an Independent Conservative until 27 July 1937, when he wrote to Chamberlain, who had succeeded Baldwin as Prime Minister, asking for re-admission to the Whip. His return to the ranks of Conservative respectability was hardly wholehearted. In October 1938 he supported the Independent Socialist candidate, Dr A. D. Lindsay (later Lord Lindsay of Birker), against the official Conservative candidate, Quintin Hogg (later Lord Hailsham), in the Oxford City by-election. Macmillan, like Lindsay, was opposed to Chamberlain's Munich policy. There was now no chance of his getting office under Chamberlain. Not until the premiership passed to Churchill, whose firm supporter he was, did Macmillan at last get office. He was forty-six.

On 15 May 1940 Churchill gave him his first ministerial appointment as Parliamentary Secretary to the Ministry of Supply. Up till then his sole job connected with the war had been as a member of a committee set up to organise aid for the Finns in their Winter War against the Russians, and as a representative of that committee he had visited Finland in February. He remained at the Ministry of Supply under three successive ministers (Herbert Morrison, Sir Andrew Duncan, and Lord Beaverbrook) until 4 February 1942, when he became Parliamentary Under-secretary at the Colonial Office under Lord Cranborne (later Lord Salisbury). Neither of these positions was of any great consequence in the hierarchy of political power and they brought him to the brink of resignation. Then all at once he came to the top. At the end of December 1942 Churchill appointed him Minister Resident at Allied Force Head-quarters in North-west Africa and he became a member of the Cabinet (though not of the War Cabinet) with direct access to the Prime Minister.

Macmillan held this office for thirty months, during which its title changed slightly as AFHQ moved to Italy and General Maitland Wilson succeeded General Eisenhower as Supreme Commander for the Mediterranean. It was a position of immense importance and immense power. It demanded a quite remarkable ability for its success. As the course of the war brought the Allies to North-west Africa and then to Italy the political problems that emerged, and which had a profound effect on the military campaign, had to be solved in concert by the Americans and the British in relation to those factions of the French and Italian schisms that could wield significant power. And after French North Africa and the new government in Italy came the attempted Communist takeover of Greece and the Yugoslavian Communist irredentism under Tito. In all these affairs of nations Macmillan played a dominant role in his three-cornered hat as British Resident Minister in the Mediterranean, Political Adviser to the Supreme Allied Commander, and Acting President of the Allied Commission for Italy.

Macmillan's Mediterranean duties came to an end on 26 May 1945 and he returned to the United Kingdom. From his heights of power as virtual Viceroy of the Mediterranean he, like others in his party, went into the wilderness of political frustration. After two months as Secretary for Air in the Caretaker Government he lost his seat at Stockton in the general election of July 1945 by 8,664 votes to the Labour candidate, with the Liberal nowhere.

His absence from Parliament was, however, brief. In August 1945 he was adopted as Conservative candidate for Bromley, and at a by-election on 16 November 1945 he won a three-cornered fight with a majority of 5,557. He retained the seat at the general elections of February 1950 and October 1951 with majorities of 10,688 and 12,125 respectively. Macmillan was not enthralled by opposition work and the return to power of a Conservative Government under Churchill in October 1951 seemed to augur well for his own return to a Cabinet post of significant power. But Churchill offered him the Ministry of Housing.

After the years in the Mediterranean and the discreet wielding of great power in the councils of nations it was hardly an appointment to enthuse him. Even in the years of opposition he had, at Churchill's request, taken a considerable part in the European movement and had been a delegate to the Council of Europe. From this to building houses, even for the former Member for Stockton-on-Tees, was surely a political backwater of dreadful stagnancy. It would, said Churchill, make or mar his political career, and he pressed him with tears and Victorian mottoes ('Every humble home will bless your name'). Macmillan took time to decide. Then he accepted – and succeeded in building the number of houses promised. He established a reputation as a man 'who could get things done' and was consequently the darling of the 1952 Conservative Party Conference.

After three years at Housing ('three of the happiest years of my life') Macmillan succeeded his friend and wartime Mediterranean colleague Earl Alexander of Tunis as Minister of Defence in a Cabinet reshuffle on 18 October 1954. He held that office for six months. On 6 April 1955 Eden succeeded Churchill as Prime Minister and the following day Macmillan became Foreign Secretary. Once again it was a short tenure. Reluctantly he left the Foreign Office on 20 December 1955 (where he was succeeded by Selwyn Lloyd) and went to the Treasury as Chancellor of the Exchequer in succession to R. A. Butler. His time at the Foreign Office included the Austrian peace treaty in May, the first Summit Meeting at Geneva in July (and the subsequent Foreign Ministers' Conference there in October–November), and the defection of Burgess and Maclean in November. At the Treasury he introduced one Budget only, which included the starting of Premium Bonds. By the time the next year's Budget was due he was no longer at the Treasury but found himself, almost unbelievably it might seem to those who had studied his earlier political life, in No. 10 Downing Street as Prime Minister.

PRIME MINISTER

Harold Macmillan's appointment was only the second occasion this century on which the Crown exercised its prerogative in choosing the Prime Minister. The first was in 1923 when Baldwin was preferred to Curzon on the resignation of Bonar Law through ill health. With the resignation of Eden, also through ill health, on 9 January 1957, there were again two contenders: Macmillan and R. A. (later Lord) Butler.

Eden held his last Cabinet at five o'clock on the day of his resignation. After it was over Macmillan and Butler left separately, while the remaining ministers were asked to see Lord Salisbury (the Lord President), who was the senior Cabinet minister, and Lord Kilmuir (the Lord

Chancellor), one by one in the Lord President's room in the Privy Council offices, which could be reached without leaving the building. As each came in he was asked by Salisbury, 'Well, which is it, Wab or Hawold?' Kilmuir and Salisbury also consulted the Chief Whip, Edward Heath, and the Chairman of the Conservative party, Oliver (later Lord) Poole. The Chairman of the Conservative backbenchers' 1922 Committee gave his opinion. 'An overwhelming majority of Cabinet Ministers were in favour of Macmillan as Eden's successor, and back-bench opinion, as reported to us,' wrote Lord Kilmuir in his memoirs, 'strongly endorsed this view'.

Usually the choice of the next Prime Minister is so clear that there is no need for the Crown to take advice. In this case, because of the doubt, the Queen, on the following morning, consulted some of the 'old Tory hands'. These were: Lord Salisbury (who simply conveyed the general view in the party as gleaned from his canvass with Lord Kilmuir); Lord Waverley (better known in public life as Sir John Anderson); Lord Chandos (Oliver Lyttelton); and Sir Winston Churchill. The answer of all four was 'Macmillan'. Eden was not asked for his advice, nor did he volunteer it.

At 2 p.m. on that same day, 10 January, the Queen received Harold Macmillan and asked him to form a government. However long she may have expected it to last, neither Macmillan himself nor the generality of politicians expected it to be more than a stopgap. They could hardly have been more wrong – just as the generality of political journalists could hardly have been more wrong in prognosticating that the Queen would choose Butler. Only Randolph Churchill in the *Evening Standard* got the right answer.

When Lord Melbourne was offered the premiership in 1834 it is said that he was at first reluctant to accept it on the grounds that it was a 'damned bore'. But a friend pointed out that such a position was never held by any Greek or Roman and that even if it only lasted three months it would be 'worth while to have been Prime Minister of England'. Although Harold Macmillan showed no reluctance and required no friendly persuasion, his own estimate of how long his new Government would last was only half that 'worth while' period. He told the Queen that he doubted if it would last six weeks. Six years later, when he was still Prime Minister, she reminded him of his pessimism. Indeed, despite the rickety foundations on which it was built his premiership lasted for six years nine months, the longest unbroken term since Asquith's.

The reason for his initial pessimism was not that he had any doubts about his ability to discharge the duties of Prime Minister – indeed his American mother had always spurred his ambition to that end and he himself had always been confident of his ability. His feelings of imminent mortality for his Government were caused by the political circumstances in which he found himself. To his old friend and colleague Lord Salisbury, when Salisbury resigned from his Cabinet on 29 March 1957 over the decision to release Archbishop Makarios from his sequestration in the Seychelles, Macmillan wrote that he deeply regretted the resignation because he had 'taken on a very difficult job in circumstances almost unparalleled in political history', and he wished that Salisbury could have stayed with him to see it through.

Before examining those circumstances it is worth commenting on Macmillan's generalisation that they were almost unparalleled. His great relaxation was reading and one of his foremost traits was his knowledge of history. His conversation, wrote Sir Robert Menzies, was 'garnished with analogies from the European past', and 'had he not chosen the more arduous paths of political service, [he] would have made a professor of Modern History whose classes would have been thronged with delighted students'. Another friend and Cabinet colleague told me: 'If you got him on the day something happened – and this was before he flowered with the responsibility of the premiership – his opinion was one of the best I know. Leave him for half a dozen days and it was one of the worst. This was because he saw everything very much against a historical background.'

That Macmillan was faced with a task of great difficulty, even if not unparalleled, is without question. He took office in the bitter aftermath of Suez when his party was in disarray and the country was still in a fury of frustration and recrimination. For Britain the Suez operation had the same shatteringly divisive effect as the Dreyfus case had had on France at the turn of the century. This deep division in the instincts of the nation was caused because on the one hand there were many who felt that Britain should never have embarked on the operation at all, and on the other there were perhaps just as many who felt that having done so it should have been carried through to a successful conclusion and should not have ended in the bitter demonstration that Britain was no longer a Colossus that bestrode the world but was only a small island on the shoulder of Europe. It was the unwelcome proof that an era had ended.

Surveying the range of his immediate problems on taking office Macmillan listed six main ones.[1] 'The first need was to restore the confidence of the people in their Government and in themselves. . . . The fact that France and Britain, even acting together, could no longer impose their will was alarming. Never before in history had Western Europe proved so weak.' Secondly there were the practical problems of reopening the Suez Canal, ensuring the flow of oil, and getting compensation for losses to British subjects as a result of Nasser's actions – all of which would no doubt involve the imposition of indignities 'which we must struggle to resist'. Thirdly there was the United States. Suez had destroyed the alliance that had begun in World War II. How could that alliance 'which I knew to be essential in the modern world', be re-established? Fourthly there was the economic situation. Having just spent a year as Chancellor of the Exchequer Macmillan was well aware of the great difficulties involved in maintaining the British economy at the correct level between inflation and deflation. The fifth problem was defence, including the true value of Cyprus as a base in Britain's defence pattern. Finally there was the future of the Commonwealth: was Macmillan 'destined to be the remodeller or the liquidator of Empire'?

If we add two further problems to the above list we have a broad appreciation of the main themes in Macmillan's premiership. These two additional problems were the East-West split across the Iron Curtain, and the relations between Britain and Europe.

The solution of the first problem was not achieved overnight; but it was achieved. At the parliamentary level the fact that the Government had a majority of forty-nine after the final debate on the aftermath of Suez on 15 and 16 May 1957 was generally regarded as proof of this. As to the restoration of confidence in the country at large Macmillan had certainly achieved this in sufficient measure by October 1959 to give his Government a substantially increased majority at the general election, an election in which Suez played no significant part. By that time indeed even the financial negotiations with Egypt had been concluded, the oil was flowing, and the Canal had been reopened – only to be closed again for a much longer period after the Arab-Israeli Six Day War of 1967. In 1967, however, the fleet of giant tankers that was gradually taking over so much of oil transportation, and the dominance of the aeroplane over the ship, were both turning the Suez Canal into a stretch of industrial archaeology.

[1] Harold Macmillan, *Riding the Storm 1956–9* (London, 1971), pp. 198–200.

[354]

While the aftermath of Suez was taking its course Macmillan was already in the thick of the other immediate problems. His most urgent task, as he saw it, was to repair the breach with Washington. Closely linked to this was Britain's defence situation. Was Britain to rely on the nuclear deterrent, as a White Paper published when Macmillan was Minister of Defence had suggested? If so, the Americans must be persuaded to repeal the McMahon Act which prevented the sharing of American nuclear information.

At President Eisenhower's suggestion Macmillan went to Bermuda in March 1957, taking with him Selwyn Lloyd, the Foreign Secretary. There they met the President and the Secretary of State, John Foster Dulles. Although, as Macmillan wrote in his autobiography, neither he nor his colleagues were prepared 'to appear in a white sheet' because they felt that they had been 'let down, if not betrayed, by the vacillating and delaying tactics which Dulles had pursued in the earlier stages of the Suez crisis and by the viciousness with which he and his subordinates had attacked us after the launching of the Anglo-French operation', and although for their part, Eisenhower and Dulles, as the President recorded, found it difficult at first 'to talk constructively with our British colleagues about Suez because of the blinding bitterness they felt towards Nasser', the Bermuda Conference nevertheless succeeded in its object: the alliance was re-established and Macmillan and Eisenhower, already old friends from the days of AFHQ, instituted a system of constant and frank communication that lasted throughout Eisenhower's presidency and was continued throughout Kennedy's. The renewal of close relations was such that when menacing issues arose, as for example they did in 1958 over Jordan and the Lebanon and over the off-shore islands and Formosa, and in 1962 over Cuba, there was no question of Britain's view being ignored. 'Our relations with America were so good,' wrote Macmillan, 'that our influence could during my term of office be exerted to the full.'[2] This did not mean, however, as has sometimes been suggested, that Macmillan put Britain in America's pocket. A clear example was over Indo-China. Macmillan was determined that Britain should not get involved in any military commitment in that area. When Kennedy asked for British help there, Macmillan refused.

There were three specific agreements reached at Bermuda. The first was that the United States would join in the work of the Baghdad Pact's

[2] *Winds of Change 1914–39* (London, 1966), p. 28.

Military Committee; the second, that the United States would supply Britain with guided missiles; and the third, that both countries would continue with nuclear tests. Also arising out of the Conference was the release of Makarios from the Seychelles. This was something that Eisenhower wanted, that Macmillan agreed to, and that Lord Salisbury resigned over. His resignation without any shattering effect on the Government was the first sign of Macmillan's growing political strength. Two years later, in February 1959, the Cyprus agreement was signed, and on 16 August 1960 Cyprus became an independent republic under the presidency of Makarios.

Consequent on the agreements reached at Bermuda the final revision was made to a British Defence White Paper. It was a drastic document. It announced the end of conscription. It announced the reduction of the armed forces from 690,000 to 375,000 in five years. And it announced the reliance on nuclear forces as Britain's main means of defence. The following month, on 15 May, the first British H-bomb was exploded.

Looking back on this 1957 Defence White Paper in the fifth volume of his autobiography, Macmillan wrote that 'for good or ill' it marked a new era.

'Our decision to develop and maintain an effective nuclear deterrent had important consequences both internationally and nationally. It involved the British Government in the problem of convincing our NATO allies both of its wisdom and its consistence with the theme of interdependence which I had agreed with President Eisenhower and preached in and out of season as a sound basis for the effective defence of the non-Communist world. Equally it engaged Britain, as one of three nuclear powers, in the long arguments on tests and negotiations for their restriction or abolition. It may indeed be claimed that our determination, in spite of heavy expense and many technical difficulties, to remain in the nuclear club at least allowed us to play an important and perhaps decisive part in the negotiations which finally led to the abandonment by the Three Powers of all atmospheric tests.'[3]

The Test Ban Treaty was eventually ratified on 8 October 1963, at the very end of Macmillan's premiership. It was one of his greatest triumphs.

The visit to Bermuda was the first of many journeys that Macmillan made and visits that he received from other national leaders during his

[3] *Pointing the Way 1959–61* (London, 1972), p. 249.

years as Prime Minister. Outstanding among these journeys was his visit to Russia in February 1959, a year after Krushchev had become Premier of the Soviet Union. The visit arose out of an invitation that had been given to Eden as Prime Minister when Krushchev and Bulganin visited Britain in April 1956. This was not Macmillan's first visit to Russia. He had previously been there in 1932. This new 'Voyage of Discovery', as he called it in his memoirs, was not an unqualified success at the time; snubs punctuated the cordiality. But it achieved Macmillan's object, which was to lessen the tension in East-West relations that had reached danger point as a result of Krushchev's ultimatum over Berlin the previous November, and to make some progress, however slight, towards a nuclear test ban treaty. The visit also helped to make possible the ill-fated Summit Meeting in Paris in May 1960. That this took place at all was the result of Macmillan's perseverance, and when it was broken off because of the shooting down of an American U2 aircraft over Russia his disappointment amounted 'almost to despair – so much attempted, so little achieved'. The unresolved problem of Berlin 'hung over the whole world, like a dark cloud' throughout the rest of his premiership and beyond.

As well as his frequent meetings with the American Presidents, Eisenhower and Kennedy, and his repeated exchange of visits with the French and German leaders, Macmillan kept his personal links with the Commonwealth as close as possible. During his premiership there were Commonwealth Prime Ministers' Conferences in 1957, 1960, 1961, and 1962, and he himself made two Commonwealth tours – the first in January-February 1958 to India, Pakistan, Ceylon, Australia and New Zealand; the second, exactly two years later, to Africa, where he visited Ghana, Nigeria, Rhodesia, and South Africa. It was on this second tour that on two occasions, once in Accra on 9 January 1960 and the second time in Cape Town on 3 February, he used the phrase 'the wind of change'. On the first occasion it passed unnoticed in the world press; the second time it echoed round the world:

'The most striking of all the impressions I have formed since I left London a month ago is of the strength of this African national consciousness. In different places it may take different forms, but it is happening everywhere. The wind of change is blowing through the continent. Whether we like it or not, this growth of national consciousness is a political fact. We must all accept it as a fact.'

The wind of change blew the British Colonial Empire out of existence, and especially out of Africa. It did this mainly during Macmillan's premiership, so that whether or not time will show that he did any remodelling of the Empire it is already clear that he liquidated it. Nor was this liquidation carried out without grave difficulties. In particular, 'the complications, confusions and conflicts of Central Africa seemed never to be absent from our minds' throughout the whole of his time as Prime Minister. And in place of a Colonial Empire overseas the British got the Empire in their back garden through immigration. This was not to the taste of the whole community and in August 1958 there were race riots in Nottingham and Notting Hill.

These journeys and meetings of Macmillan's were part of a new pattern of international practice, especially between the major powers, which he largely created. To some extent, it is true, he inherited the 'summit idea' from Churchill, but more than that his experiences as 'Viceroy of the Mediterranean' had shown him what the personal touch could achieve in international affairs. Only a few months after he became Prime Minister the first sputnik went into orbit. His whole approach to the overriding problem of East-West relations was a complete acceptance of the technology the sputnik and the H-bomb represented. This in a way was curious because his intellectual background, his distaste for any aspect of the 'permissive society', and his manner of an 'unflappable' Edwardian gentleman to whom politics was simply 'fun' would suggest that he would have been unwilling, or at least would have found it difficult, to accept the realities of the space age. Not a bit of it. He adapted the technique of the Field of the Cloth of Gold to the era of the jet aircraft, and he did this as far as the public was concerned with a panache and insouciance which, at any rate in the first years of his premiership, made Bevan's jibe and Vicky's cartoon character into complimentary realities. Macwonder and Supermac were just what he was, not only because of his skill in international negotiations but because of the boom that came to Britain in the early years of his premiership.

Economically the Britain of 1957 was very different from the Britain of twenty and thirty years earlier. To a politician like Macmillan who had represented Stockton-on-Tees throughout its years of misery, the face of Britain when he became Prime Minister was so changed that it seemed as if only a miracle could have wrought the transformation. It was with this in mind that he told an audience at Bedford on 20 July

1957, 'Let's be frank about it; most of our people have never had it so good. Go around the country, go to the industrial towns, go to the farms, and you will see a state of prosperity such as we have never had in my lifetime – nor indeed ever in the history of this country.' But, he went on,

'What is beginning to worry some of us is "Is it too good to be true?", or perhaps I should say, "Is it too good to last?" For, amidst all this prosperity, there is one problem that has troubled us – in one way or another – ever since the war. Its the problem of rising prices. Our constant concern today is – can prices be steadied while at the same time we maintain full employment in an expanding economy? Can we control inflation? This is the problem of our time.'

The problem was still there long after Macmillan's departure from office. Many attempts were made by his and subsequent Governments to solve it. None appeared to succeed. The first of these attempts was debated in the House of Commons five days after Macmillan's Bedford speech. This was the Government's decision to set up an independent Council on Prices, Productivity and Incomes – 'The Three Wise Men'. The Prime Minister repeated his 'Never had it so good' phrase; but he repeated it in its context, as an achievement and again as a preface to a warning, not as a boast. A third time he used it, on another occasion, and the phrase began to assume an individual existence as the slogan for Macmillan's administration and of the boom that was taking tele-vision sets and washing-machines into millions of homes and was chang-ing the stream of bicycles that emerged from factory gates at the end of the day's work into a stream of cars bought on hire-purchase.

Not that the boom was without its setbacks. There was a cut-back in government spending and a 2 per cent rise in Bank Rate to 7 per cent in September 1957. Macmillan was not prepared to accept a continuing policy of deflation, however. In January 1958 the Chancellor, Thorney-croft, and his political lieutenants at the Treasury resigned rather than approve estimates for increased government expenditure in the follow-ing year. Macmillan was on the eve of departing on his first Common-wealth tour. He referred to the resignations in press and television interviews as 'little local difficulties' compared to the wider vision of the Commonwealth. The phrase became part of his image. He was the man who 'played it cool'. This in itself contributed importantly to the restora-tion of national confidence.

Macmillan's calm was something new in his political career. Lack of power had made him extremely restless, and even when he held a senior position in the Cabinet the restlessness was still there. This stemmed from his feeling that a full use was not being made of his unusually complete personality. He seemed to at least one of his friends to be 'much in touch with the press and apt to inspire rumours that stirred things up a bit'. He had considered resigning from the Colonial Office in November 1942 because his career seemed to be reaching a dead end; he was even closer to resignation from the Chancellorship of the Exchequer in February 1956 over his determination to remove subsidies from bread and milk. Unlike Thorneycroft's disagreement with his colleagues, Macmillan's was eventually resolved by compromise. Both could have brought down the Government.

When he became Prime Minister all this changed almost literally overnight. The restlessness disappeared. So too did the intriguing. It was no good intriguing for anything more. You were Prime Minister and, for better or for worse, that was it! Greater even than Viceroy of the Mediterranean, you were now Prime Minister of the United Kingdom – 'worth while', as Melbourne acknowledged, if only for a few months. And so the restlessness disappeared and in its place – and it was a curious transformation to those who watched it – there emerged a great calmness which was characterised in the press as 'unflappability'. Harold Macmillan, whose mother had insisted on his becoming a French linguist, believed with the French that '*on ne règne sur les âmes que par le calme*'. Indeed, though it may have been his instinctive formula for exercising power, it was also a conscious attitude. On No. 10 Downing Street notepaper, in his own hand, he wrote out a text from *The Gondoliers* for his aides in his private office and the Cabinet room: 'Quiet, calm deliberation disentangles every knot. H.M.' Sometimes, it is true, the calmness was only skin-deep. At the time of the landings by British and American troops in Jordan and Lebanon in July 1958 he wrote in his diary of 'trying to . . . hide his sickening anxiety'. Outwardly, however, the resignations of three ministers from the Treasury in January 1958 were 'little local difficulties'.

Thorneycroft was replaced as Chancellor of the Exchequer by Heathcoat Amory. When signs of a slump appeared later in 1958 measures were taken to reflate the economy. The 1959 Budget was expansionist. This cannot have been without its effect on the result of the general election in October that year. It had been a glorious summer, the economy was booming, the Conservatives increased their majority over all other parties to 100. Macmillan himself, whose majority in the 1955 election had been up by 1,014, was now returned with an even larger majority.

It was held against Macmillan by many, including Archbishop Fisher of Canterbury, that his Bedford phrase, 'Never had it so good', was a reprehensible slogan of out-and-out materialism. Lord Salisbury, too, took him to task for its sentiment. Later, in a speech in November 1961, Macmillan tried to put across the fact that the phrase, now become notorious, had continually been used out of context and had in the process totally lost the import he had intended. He reminded his audience that the phrase had been embedded in a paragraph that was far from hubristic. But the attempt to repaint the phrase in its true colours was totally unsuccessful. Like Asquith's 'Wait and see' (the parallel with which Macmillan drew in his autobiography), 'Never had it so good' was given a lasting life in a sense that was never intended. None the less, as a straight statement of fact it was incontrovertible. The outstanding domestic phenomena of Macmillan's years as Prime Minister were the multiple signs of what was being called the Affluent Society. The British people had only recently been totally rid of the austerities of rationing. It was hardly surprising that the demand for consumer goods welled up and that the drab macintosh days of post-war Britain gave place to the cheerful fashions of a new age.

Admittedly there were grim black clouds mounting above the economic horizon. Their message read, 'Is it too good to last?' Selwyn Lloyd, who replaced Heathcoat Amory as Chancellor in July 1960 and whose Budget in April 1961 continued the expansionist theme, was forced to introduce a 'Little Budget' on 25 July 1961 because of a full-scale sterling crisis. It included a 'pay pause' to stop spiralling wages. 'Though clumsily enforced, and very badly presented', wrote one of Macmillan's biographers, 'it represented the first serious attempt towards an incomes policy, which five years later was to be far more widely accepted.'[4]

In an endeavour to run the economy in a manner that would allow expansion without an unacceptable level of inflation, Macmillan made planning a respectable part of Conservative orthodoxy: 'Neddy' (National Economic Development Council) was set up in 1961, 'Nicky'

[4] Anthony Sampson, *Macmillan: A Study in Antiquity* (Harmondsworth, 1967), p. 198.

(National Incomes Commission) in 1962. But neither the pay pause nor the credit squeeze did anything to endear the Prime Minister or his party to the electorate. Nor did mounting unemployment. The days of Supermac were over. The by-elections of March 1962, especially the one at Orpington, proved the point.

Throughout Macmillan's premiership the economic position of Britain steadily declined. Partially this was because her competitive power in world markets deteriorated; partially because she could not face the challenge of the European Economic Community. Macmillan, with the experience of two wars behind him, had always been in favour of a closer unity in Europe. He had helped in the formation of the European movement. But he had not gone against the tide when the Treasury, the Foreign Office, the Board of Trade, and many of his Cabinet colleagues in the post-war Conservative governments, had been opposed to Britain's taking any part in the budding Common Market. Later he recognised his mistake, for which, he wrote in the Prologue to his autobiography, published in 1966, 'I shall never cease to blame myself'.

Scrambling along behind the increasingly powerful EEC Britain in November 1959, having failed to inveigle the Common Market countries into a wider free trade area, signed the European Free Trade Agreement with the other countries of the 'Outer Seven'. This too proved insufficient to solve the market problems of British industry. At last, on 10 August 1961, Britain applied to join the EEC. The negotiations were begun under the leadership of Edward Heath. They continued throughout 1962. But de Gaulle was not disposed to accept this British 'Johnny-come-lately' with its schizophrenic ambivalence between Europe and the Commonwealth. On 14 January 1963 he gave a press conference. France would impose her veto. Britain was to be shut out of Europe.

As Macmillan wisely foresaw in the Prologue to his autobiography de Gaulle's veto proved to be only the end of a chapter, not the end of the story. The successful outcome of that story was to belong to the man who had led the negotiations in 1961–3 and who had staked his career on Britain's joining the Common Market. But the veto in January 1963 emphasised the change that had taken place in Macmillan's image with the public and in Parliament. Little was going right. In July 1962, in response to growing unrest in the party that resulted from continuing evidence of the Conservatives' unpopularity in the country, he had dramatically reconstructed the Cabinet, replacing Selwyn Lloyd by

Maudling at the Treasury, making Butler Deputy Prime Minister and First Secretary of State, Brooke Home Secretary, Manningham-Buller Lord Chancellor in place of Kilmuir, Thorneycroft Minister of Defence, and introducing seven new men into the Cabinet (including Thorney-croft). At the end of the year the Radcliffe Tribunal on the Vassall case resulted in journalists being sent to prison for refusing to disclose the sources of their allegations. This caused bitter resentment in the press, which was to stand Macmillan in no good stead when the Profumo scandal broke about his head the following summer. The British public was in one of its periodical fits of morality, egged on by a Fleet Street that was thirsting for revenge over the Radcliffe Tribunal. His enemies saw the perfect chance to get rid of him. He himself was undecided. He survived the Profumo debate on 17 June – the fourth time in eighty years that British political life had been rocked to its foundations be-cause of a woman – but he wondered whether he should resign. The decision was taken out of his hands. On 8 October he went into hospital for an operation on his prostate gland. The following day he announced his intention to resign. His intention was read out to the Conservative Party Conference at Blackpool by Lord Home, who eventually proved to be his successor. On 19 October Macmillan sent his resignation to the Queen.

Macmillan has often been characterised as 'The Old Entertainer' or criticised as an 'actor-manager'. In the present-day world this is more a compliment than a criticism as far as a prime minister is concerned. Macmillan's flamboyance, which so irritated his political opponent Hugh Gaitskell, was only his public face; privately, and especially in Cabinet and in committee, the casual, colourful approach disappeared and he was master of the table, brilliantly in command.

When he resigned he accepted none of the honours traditionally bestowed on departing prime ministers; neither an earldom, nor the Garter, nor even one of the life peerages that had been introduced under his aegis in 1958. He resigned as Prime Minister of the United Kingdom, but remained Chancellor of Oxford University, which he had been since 1960, another 'worth-while' office for an old Balliol Exhibitioner.

BIBLIOGRAPHY

Macmillan's Memoirs, 6 volumes, 1966–73
Winds of Change (London, 1966); *The Blast of War* (London, 1967); *Tides of Fortune*

(London, 1969); *Riding the Storm* (London, 1971); *Pointing the Way* (London, 1972); *At the End of the Day* (London, 1973)

Egremont, Lord, *Wyndham and Children First* (London, 1968)
Hughes, Emrys, *Macmillan: Portrait of a Politician* (London, 1962)
Sampson, Anthony, *Macmillan: A Study in Ambiguity* (London, 1962)

21

SIR ALEC DOUGLAS-HOME

BY

IAIN SPROAT

Sir Alec Douglas-Home, Born 2 July 1903, eldest son of the 13th Earl of Home. Succeeded his father in 1951 but disclaimed his peerage for life 23 October 1963. Educated at Eton and Christ Church, Oxford. Married 1936 Elizabeth Hester Alington; one son, three daughters. MP (South Lanark) 1931–45, Lanark division of Lanarkshire (1950–51), Kinross & W. Perth (1963–). Parliamentary Private Secretary to the Prime Minister 1937–40; Joint Parliamentary Under-Secretary, Foreign Office, 1945; Minister of State, Scottish Office, 1951–55; Secretary of State for Commonwealth Relations, 1955–60; Deputy Leader of the House of Lords 1956–57; Leader of the House of Lords and Lord President of the Council 1957–60; Foreign Secretary 1960–63; Prime Minister and First Lord of the Treasury 1963–64; Leader of the Opposition, 1964–65. Hon. DCL (Oxford); Hon. LLD (Harvard, Edinburgh, Aberdeen, Liverpool, St Andrews); Hon. Master of the Bench, Inner Temple. Foreign Secretary 1970–74.

SIR ALEC DOUGLAS-HOME

The Earl of Home became Prime Minister on 19 October 1963 when the fortunes of the Conservative Government were at a very low ebb, and, as Sir Alec Douglas-Home, left that office on 16 October 1964. Within that short period he came within a hair's breadth of achieving what no British prime minister has ever achieved for his party: the winning of a fourth general election in a row.

This feat was the more remarkable in that Sir Alec had to overcome a series of obstacles dauntingly numerous and varied. In October 1963 the Conservative Government was still tainted by scandal from the Profumo and Vassall affairs. After twelve years the Cabinet was in grave danger of becoming stale, of losing intellectual and political dynamic. Sir Alec himself had been absent from the rough-and-tumble of Commons debate – so different from the more courteous and leisurely attitude of the Lords – since he became the Earl of Home in 1951, and the troops on the Conservative benches behind wanted, as always, a leader who could raise their morale by patently and decisively crushing Labour spokesmen. Harold Wilson was a formidable opposition leader, with a ready debating wit and a command of economic fact and jargon, which was far from being Sir Alec's strength.

The Tory ranks in the Commons were in disarray, with memories of Harold Macmillan's wholesale Cabinet sackings of July 1962 still smouldering. Even more importantly, two able and respected ministers of long experience, Iain Macleod and Enoch Powell, refused to serve in Sir Alec's Cabinet. This disarray in the House of Commons was reflected, if not so strongly, in the Tory ranks in the country. And in addition to all this, there were growing economic difficulties; there was a yawning gap in policy left by the failure of the Common Market talks the year before; there had been morale-sapping by-election defeats; there was the charge, difficult to counter, that after twelve years it was 'time for a change'. Above all, there was an acute shortage of time, and the concomitant factor that Sir Alec must fight with a Cabinet largely not of his own choosing.

All these factors Sir Alec had to overcome before a general election in November 1964 at the latest.

There were, of course, advantages also to hand. Although the team was mainly Macmillan's, it contained men of outstanding calibre and experience like Edward Heath, R. A. Butler and Reginald Maudling. Sir Alec could rely confidently on these ministers to pursue government policies with sense and vigour without interference from No. 10. This left the new Prime Minister able to concentrate on what was virtually twelve months of non-stop electioneering.

Furthermore, Sir Alec could call on what Lord Kilmuir, Macmillan's last Lord Chancellor but one, described as the Tories' secret weapon: loyalty. In spite of many media prophecies to the contrary, the passing over of the vastly experienced Butler, and the resignation of Macleod and Powell, caused no major splits within the party in the country. A strain on loyalty, some disgruntlement, and even the odd resignation in constituency associations, there certainly were; but there was never the slightest question, when it came to the crunch, that the Tories would develop and nourish a Butlerite faction, as the Labour party so disastrously had earlier a Bevanite; and the personality of the new Prime Minister, and the natural inclinations of his supporters, effected an almost solid closing of the party ranks long before the election came. The only initiative of the Home Government to operate against Conservative unity, in any major way, was that on the abolition of Resale Price Maintenance, which considerably angered small Tory shopkeepers. For this reason Sir Alec was much less keen to push the measure through than Heath, who as the minister involved, was convinced of its importance.

But in addition to the ability of his colleagues and the traditional loyalty of the Conservative party to its leader, there was another factor which accounted greatly for the astonishing proximity to electoral success that Sir Alec achieved – astonishing, that is, to most of the media, who consistently underrated him – and that was the particular, if elusive, indeed deceptive, personality of the man.

The deceptive aspect of Sir Alec's character was that, unusual in anyone who has climbed to the top of the political ladder, it was strong without many of the normal outer signs of strength, decisive without the usual trappings of decisiveness. Sir Alec was not arrogant, bullying, abrupt, ruthless, cold, egocentric or determinedly charismatic; he did not parade himself as a great orator. On the contrary, he was amiable –

a virtue which, perhaps significantly, Jane Austen once wrote of as especially British – approachable, and unfailingly courteous, whether to opponents or to the least important of his party's supporters. Tory audiences loved him; they loved his straightforwardness, his manner that was both gentle and crisp; they warmed to him – as they never warmed to one of his chief rivals for the premiership, R. A. Butler, although Butler had given unparalleled service to the Tory party for a generation. Among Tory audiences there was an affection for Sir Alec, which his rivals, Butler, Hailsham, Macleod or Maudling, could not command, however much respect, admiration or even fervour they could evoke. In 1964 the British public still loved, if less a lord, then certainly a 'gentleman', and whatever precise definition of gentleman you preferred, Sir Alec looked like, acted like, and indubitably was a 'gentleman'. Sir Alec's own party, and indeed the country at large, could recognise in him a disinterestedness in personal ends. When, for example, Iain Macleod, that politician of brilliance, tragically never destined to fulfil his great potential, dazzled a conference by his oratory, there was always a thought that he was delighting in the personal impression he was making; that he was tacitly asking the audience to mark what an exceptional fellow he was. That was never so with Sir Alec: he made a speech because he quite simply wanted to communicate what he considered an important message, divorced from personalities. He was obviously not ambitious for himself. He was born with social position; he was born rich; he had already achieved high office: it was clear to even his bitterest opponent that he accepted the office of prime minister because – rightly or wrongly – he believed it to be his duty to his country. All this gave Sir Alec a moral stature which no other politician of the day could match.

Much of the strength of Sir Alec's character sprang from an ultimate confidence in his own beliefs. Behind his agreeable manner, he hid a number of steely convictions, much tougher, in fact, than those held by many of his apparently more abrasive colleagues. It was the confidence of someone born well socially at a time when such birth still meant much; the confidence of someone of great inherited wealth; the confidence of someone whose natural abilities and apparently languid charm had shielded him from most of those vicissitudes, at school and at university, to which his money and station might still have left him vulnerable. Sir Alec could have possessed all these attributes, and still done little with them; but in fact they did give him a solid bed-rock of confidence, which an agreeable diffidence of manner might sometimes conceal, but never erode.

Sir Alec also possessed a moral certainty that sprang from the strength of his religious convictions. During his time as Prime Minister, he was perhaps the only important figure in political life who regularly worked into his speeches references to Christianity in a manner acceptable to his audience. Not, of course, that he was the only man in politics to hold such convictions. But where others were content to omit references to them, or, as in the case of Quintin Hogg, to speak of them in a manner much more high-flown, and occasionally at the risk of making some of his audience uneasy, Sir Alec did so in a matter-of-fact way that heartened those who shared, or at least inclined towards, his religious beliefs, and to many agnostics or atheists, lent him a comforting reassurance whose source they might not accept, but whose results they did.

A third factor that deepened and strengthened Sir Alec's political convictions arose from what at the time must have seemed to him the cruellest misfortune. In 1940 he aggravated an old injury, and for the next two years he was compelled to lie on his back. At that time he was thirty-seven, an age when most men in his position have reached certain conclusions about life – however inadequate those conclusions may be – and from then on they continue down their chosen paths, thinking freshly less and less and merely reacting to outside events more and more. Enforced inactivity gave Sir Alec a chance to look at himself, to examine and sift what he had learnt from life, and to remedy by study any gaps in his knowledge which such an examination might reveal. This chance he took. He read widely and deeply, and in particular he studied everything on which he could lay his hands about the theory and practice of Soviet Communism. When, later, he became Foreign Secretary, Prime Minister, and then Foreign Secretary again, he viewed the moves and counter moves of the Kremlin in a long perspective, and, it must be said, in a far more suspicious and hostile light than did many of his colleagues. During the years in hospital he reached certain sombre conclusions about the nature of Soviet ambitions, which the optimism or the wishful thinking of others in British public life never dispelled. What had largely been, during his pre-war years as an MP, the natural political instincts of someone from his particular background, now became hardened during this period into conscious, thought-out political convictions.

Nevertheless, it was not until Macmillan had made what seemed to many at the time the astonishing choice of Home as Foreign Secretary that the toughness and the independence of his mind made much public impact. But thereafter he soon developed an individual manner of speech which endeared him at first to Tory audiences, and, as it turned out, later to a wider section of the public. He spoke more directly, more clearly, and more forcefully than was usual in Foreign Secretaries. He had no constituents to worry about; he was not made cautious by amibition. For example, in April 1963 he was speaking of the H-bomb in these terms: 'The great advantage of the nuclear bomb is that at last ordinary decent men have been given a weapon which can stop the wicked from achieving their ends by war.' There was a *simpliste* note about that, combining the words of politics with those of morality, that many found appealing. Again, there was his famous, or infamous, speech at Berwick-on-Tweed in December 1961, in which, although he came down in favour of retaining the United Nations, he refused to indulge in the fashionable hypocrisy about its virtues and attacked it for irresponsibility; and publicly said that the barbaric chaos in the Congo had been the result of that country's getting its independence too soon. That was strong meat from a British Foreign Secretary.

This political confidence and outspokenness in Sir Alec were a late flowering, and a long way from the politician of whom Winston Churchill remarked, when he was recommended by the then Chief Whip, James Stuart, as Minister of State at the Scottish Office in 1951: 'Never heard of him.'

Naturally, there were those to whom Sir Alec's views and outspokenness as Foreign Secretary were abhorrent. When he became Prime Minister, however, the main matters upon which the Opposition sought to blacken him in the eyes of public opinion were different.

The first of these was the charge that Sir Alec knew nothing of domestic matters, and, in particular, was spectacularly ignorant of even the rudiments of economics. This was at a time when it was a maxim of accepted wisdom that 'Politics is Economics'. Sir Alec had added fuel to the these flames by saying in an interview that when he opened a newspaper he turned to the sporting pages first, and that he liked to use a box of matchsticks to help him in his economic calculations. Harold Wilson thereafter made much of scathing references to 'matchsticks'. It was at this time that Wilson was successfully developing his theme of harnessing science to Socialism, and he would contrast the future possibilities for Britain in the 'white heat of the technological revolution' with the supposed economic and technological illiteracy of Sir Alec. In fact, this campaign by Wilson may have slightly back-fired with the wider public, as there was in Sir Alec's approach something that appealed to the traditional British love of the amateur.

Labour's second main charge against Sir Alec was connected with the first; it was, quite simply, that he was an aristocrat, a fourteenth Earl, and thus out of touch with the ordinary man, with the modern world, and was indeed a living symbol of the reactionary, old-fashioned order that Labour was pledged to sweep away in every field. It was a charge that found a responsive echo in the minds and hearts of those to whom the theme of harnessing science to Socialism most appealed. There was no doubt that Sir Alec was vulnerable to both charges, but the second, the charge of being 'the fourteenth Earl', he neutralised to a considerable extent by pointing out good-naturedly that 'if you came to think about it', Mr Wilson was presumably 'the fourteenth Mr Wilson'. None the less, behind the specific charge lay a general feeling in the country – rightly or wrongly – that it was time for thrusting new measures, and Sir Alec had difficulty in projecting himself to the dynamic young executive – a much quoted and appealed-to figure at the time – as the man best suited to bring such measures about. Of course, he could point to abrasive and dynamic figures under his command in the Government, like Heath. If anyone said he himself was far removed from the world of young executives, he could point out the fallacy, which Dr Johnson's ridicule first demolished in the famous remark, 'Who drives fat oxen must himself be fat'. He could try to convince the public that unless the defence of the country was guaranteed, nothing else mattered, and that Labour, with their pacifist and extreme left-wing factions, were tragically ill suited to dealing with defence and foreign policy matters. He could project himself as an honest, reliable man above political ambition.

All of this Sir Alec did in the year of his premiership; but it was an uphill struggle. Except on defence matters, it was nearly always Wilson on the attack – although, of course, the electorate often found Sir Alec's defences more convincing than Wilson's attacks. Ridiculous as it seems in the light of subsequent events, Wilson sought to attach to himself some of the glamorous dynamic which at that time adhered to President Kennedy, and was not unsuccessful in the attempt. Kennedy-

Wilson's supposed youthful drive was contrasted with Sir Alec's supposed reactionary irrelevancy to the twentieth century.

During his brief twelve months as Prime Minister, Sir Alec was acting against a background of difficulty simply in presiding over the tail of twelve years of Conservative government. This meant not only that there was a genuine danger of the Cabinet's running out of steam; not only that there was little, if any, time for fresh political initiative to capture the support of the electorate; but also, so long was it since Labour were last in power, that there was almost no problem facing the country for which Harold Wilson could not attempt to pin blame on the Tories. Slum housing, poor schools, the plight of old age pensioners, low wages, industrial unrest, poor road and rail communications, inadequate hospitals, scandal in high places, low investment, falling production – everything was grist to Labour's mill.

But there was a deeper background of difficulty than this against which Sir Alec must act. In 1963, Britain was still on the path of retreat from world possession and power. Empire had been largely turned into Commonwealth. Macmillan's concept of being the 'honest broker' between the United States and the Soviet Union, diminished a role as that was, was now the maximum to which Britain could aspire: very useful, but ultimately not crucial. World markets had long since ceased to be the easy targets they had once been for British manufacturers. The people of the United Kingdom were uneasily aware that they were being steadily overhauled by their erstwhile enemies, Germany and Japan, whom less than twenty years before they had seen crushed in ruin. In national terms, it seemed a time of running downhill, of contraction all round. Actually, the wonder was that the retreat from Empire, and all that meant, caused as few socio-political traumas as it did, that the British remained as sane and tolerant as they did in the face of their vastly altered world position.

Sir Alec, therefore, knew that he was facing a holding position not only with regard to winning a new term of office for the Conservative party, but on a more important level waiting for the opportune moment to start negotiations again for the entry of the United Kingdom into Europe, which alone, he believed, would halt and reverse the retreat and contraction.

In Sir Alec's mind the priority was clear from the moment he succeeded Macmillan. As he put it to a Conservative audience in November 1963: 'From this moment on, the fact that there is a general election

[373]

ahead of us must never be out of our minds.' And during the by-election at Kinross to get him into the House of Commons, after he had re-nounced his peerage, he already appeared to be electioneering for the national campaign that was to come, rather than the one he was then fighting. He promised 400,000 houses a year, £350 million a year for higher education, £800 million a year for hospital building, £100 million a year for roads by 1969, and £400 million a year for schools by 1968. At the end of 1963, he accepted the recommendations of the Robbins Report for vast increases in university education: the doubling of higher education places by 1973, and concomitant capital expendi-ture.

During what, therefore, amounted to a year of almost continuous election campaigning, Sir Alec personally concentrated on getting him-self more widely known to the public. He initiated no unexpected new major policy decisions, but restored drive and gloss to what was already under way. He envisaged fighting on a variant of Macmillan's success-ful domestic maxim of 1959, 'You've never had it so good', combined with his own personal stature as Foreign Secretary, and such govern-ment foreign affairs successes as the Test Ban Treaty, signed in Moscow in the summer of 1963. Even when the Conservatives were trailing to the Socialists in the polls in every other aspect of policy – the balance of payments, which became a serious issue from February 1964, house prices and mortgages, technological advance – the Government were always ahead in questions of foreign policy.

Sir Alec's major tactical decision was when to call the election. At the time, there were Tory voices calling for a June poll. This was mainly because, in spite of some serious by-election swings against the Govern-ment in May 1964, it was believed that the economic situation was deteriorating fast, and that it would certainly be worse in the autumn than it was in the summer. The first major shock had been in February, when the very day after Sir Alec had claimed in a television interview that the economy was extremely healthy – as indeed in a long-term prospect it was – trade figures were released showing an alarming deficit in the balance of payments. Furthermore, no government likes to be pushed right up against the final time limit for holding an election, with no room for manoeuvre. Nevertheless, Sir Alec took the decision to go to October; and almost certainly, on balance, he was right, for although the economic situation did indeed deteriorate as Maudling, the Chancellor of the Exchequer, had predicted, the extra months were needed for the consolidation of Sir Alec as leader, for allowing the public time to forget the distasteful Profumo scandal of the previous year, and for the party to recover from the strain of Macmillan's resignation and the consequent jockeying for position between Home, Butler, Macleod and Powell. Indeed, there were many in October 1964 who believed that had Krushchev fallen a day or two before the election, instead of just after, the Conservatives might have won because of the greater public confidence in the Tories to deal with an uncertain foreign situation.

Conducting what, therefore, was essentially a holding operation, Sir Alec was obliged to make the difficult choice between, on the one hand, taking few major policy initiatives, and thus opening his Government to a charge of inertia from a vociferous Opposition already in full cry against thirteen 'stagnant' years, and on the other hand, risking upsetting his own ranks or the uncommitted electorate by introducing controversial measures. Such latter considerations affected his postponement of plans to make labour contracts legally binding, but did not prevent the courageous decision to abolish Resale Price Maintenance, a policy relentlessly pushed through by Heath although deeply resented at the time by small shopkeepers.

During the election campaign itself, Sir Alec pressed strongly on the issue of nuclear defence in almost every major speech he made: his theme was the necessity for the United Kingdom to retain her own independent deterrent. This policy was very much a part of Sir Alec's personal political thinking, as opposed to those other Tory policies with which, to be sure, he did not disagree, but which lay in fields, such as economics, where he had little expertise. And because of the strength of his own feeling on this matter, he commanded a fluency, a comprehensiveness, and a conviction that he was not always able to display elsewhere. On this and on foreign policy, he was most himself and most successful. Particularly on these issues, Sir Alec possessed an air of statesmanship to which Wilson, whatever his other considerable skills, could not aspire. Furthermore, not only was Sir Alec at his best, but Labour were at their weakest: they could not disguise entirely from the British electorate that they had a considerable, pacifist and far left wing, which had always been antipathetic to the mainstream of political tradition in this country. It must be said, however, that apart from the staunchest Tory newspapers, Sir Alec did not receive much support in the media: fashionable thinking was largely opposed to his nuclear concepts, even derisive. Nevertheless, probably in strategic terms, certainly in political terms, Sir Alec's personal judgement was right in that these concepts undoubtedly found an echo not only in nearly all Tory hearts, but also in Labour ones – not among Labour's articulate intellectuals but among its many traditional supporters, who, for example, had taken no little semi-jingoistic satisfaction in the Suez operation. And in the event, Wilson in office was to adopt a nuclear policy not much different in practice.

Sir Alec Douglas-Home was not Prime Minister for long enough to fashion fresh Conservative policies after his own philosophy. What he was required to do was to restore the assurance of integrity in high places, to unite a battered party both at Westminster and in the country, and to win the fourth general election running for his party. He succeeded wholly in the first; he succeeded largely in the second – with the exceptions of Macleod and Powell at Westminster, and none of significance in the country outside; and came within a hair's breadth of the third. It was an astonishing achievement. It was Sir Alec's fortune that the diffident, if crisp, manner by which he did this caused others to underestimate the magnitude of his achievement. It was his happier fortune that circumstances contrived to return him to office as Foreign Secretary in the Heath administration of 1970, where he exerted a profoundly formative and significant influence at a watershed in British history, in taking the United Kingdom into the European Economic Community.

No prime minister in modern times achieved his office with so little seeking of it. No leader of the Conservative party so gracefully relinquished that post, as did Sir Alec in 1965. In the regions of high office, Sir Alec's was a unique character.

BIBLIOGRAPHY

Brittan, Samuel, *The Treasury under the Tories, 1951–64* (London, 1965)
Butler, D. E. and King, A., *The British General Election of 1964* (London, 1965)
Churchill, Randolph, *The Fight for the Tory Leadership*, 2nd edn (London, 1964)
Dickie, J., *The Uncommon Commoner: Sir Alec Douglas-Home* (London, 1964)
Eden, Sir Anthony, *Memoirs: Full Circle* (London, 1960)
Macmillan, Harold, *Tides of Fortune* (London, 1969); *Riding the Storm* (London, 1971); *Pointing the Way* (London, 1972)
Taylor, A. J. P., *Oxford English History, 1914–45* (Oxford, 1965)
Thomas, Hugh, *The Suez Affair* (London, 1967)
Young, Kenneth, *Sir Alec Douglas-Home* (London, 1970)

22

HAROLD WILSON

BY

GERARD NOEL

*James Harold Wilson, PC, CBE, FRS, born 11 March 1916 and
educated at Wirral Grammar School and Jesus College, Oxford.
Lecturer in Economics, New College, Oxford, 1937; Fellow of
University College, Oxford, 1938; Praelector in Economics 1945;
Director of Economics and Statistics, Ministry of Fuel and Power
1943–44; MP for Ormskirk 1945–50; Parliamentary Secretary,
Ministry of Works, 1945–47; Secretary for Overseas Trade 1947;
President of the Board of Trade 1947–51; MP for Huyton
1950– ; Chairman, Labour Party Executive Committee, 1961–
62; Chairman, Public Accounts Committee, 1959–63; Prime
Minister 1964–70; Leader of the Opposition 1970–74; Prime
Minister 1974– ; President of the Royal Statistical Society
1972– ; Hon. Fellow of Jesus and University Colleges, Oxford;
Hon. LLD (Lancaster, Liverpool, Nottingham, Sussex); Hon.
DCL (Oxford); Hon. DTech. (Bradford and Essex). Married;
two sons. Author of* New Deal for Coal, *1947;* In Place of
Dollars, *1952;* The War on World Poverty, *1953;* The Rele-
vance of British Socialism, *1964;* Purpose in Politics, *1964;*
The Labour Government, 1964–70, *1971; etc.*

HAROLD WILSON

It is impossible to assess the distinctive contribution of Harold Wilson as Prime Minister to British political history without a fairly intimate familiarity with the history of British Socialism. And the soul of such Socialism is unknowable to anyone mystified by such names and phrases as Robert Owen, Cold Bath Fields, Chartism, Tolpuddle, Taff Vale, Hyndman, Conrad Noel and the Bridlington Rules. The examples spring readily to the pen and are written down almost at random; but one of them is particularly important: Bridlington Rules. Did these – do they yet – mean much to those who felt (and still feel) that the Government's 1969 'showdown' with the trade unions was actually a surrender? It is the sort of question that must be borne in mind when considering that particular, and very revealing, example of Wilsonism in action at 10 Downing Street.

It is equally impossible to have a full understanding of Harold Wilson without an authentic insight into the world where Socialism is anathematised with as much fervour as elsewhere it is professed. And one is speaking of nothing as nebulous as the 'middle' and professional strata of society in general but of that rarefied upper-class enclave, that inaccessible holy of holies which is fully comprehensible only from within. This resilient citadel still exercises immense if almost wholly unsuspected influence, and its often invisible power operates at every level of British life. The infinitely complex socio-industrial network through which it works – greatly helped by the struggle in each generation to climb the social scale – had, *until Wilson's day*, made Conservative government the natural kind for Britain, and Socialist government the exception.

Wilson's whole career, however, has been inordinately overshadowed by this circumstance of power-from-the-top. He has always been acutely sensitive to its subtle but formidable strength, and has often over-reacted against it. Though far too intelligent to suffer from the inferiority complex of lesser Socialists, he has detonated so many depth-charges in the wells of power as to bring to the surface a bitter personal animosity against him experienced by very few of his Downing Street predecessors. Wilson has thus paid a high price in personal terms for a

[379]

political achievement that has outstripped that of former Labour Prime Ministers. For if Ramsay MacDonald made Labour government possible, and Clement Attlee made it respectable, it is Harold Wilson who has made it successful; and the assumption that this success had been permanently curtailed by the setback of 1970 was rudely displaced by the shock defeat of an over-confident Conservative Party in February 1974. But his very success, considerable if unfinished, and his relentless pursuit thereof at every stage, have provoked an implacable hostility that has had the twofold effect of damaging his image and, at the same time, spurring him on to greater efforts, by similar means, in pursuit of yet further successes. In this sense Wilson, so far anyway, has been imprisoned in a sort of vicious circle; his future fortunes may well depend on the extent to which he has now escaped.

Well known by now is the saga of progress from staunchly Congregationalist lower-middle-class Yorkshire surroundings, via great brilliance at pre-war Oxford; vital and formative, if underestimated, wartime civil service; and post-war political high-flying, to ultimate tenure of 10 Downing Street. It represented not only a remarkable personal triumph but also a long-delayed one for the Dissenting Radicalism that had inspired even the High Church Gladstone in the eighteen-seventies and Lloyd George in the Edwardian era; only now did it find its natural home in the Labour Party.[1] But Wilson has not always seen Socialism as necessarily the only vehicle capable of forwarding the great Radical dream; he is not only extremely cautious by nature, but, with the razor-sharp instincts of the thoroughbred political animal, he has never ignored the vital role of balance in the affairs of the body politic.

He flirted with Liberalism at Oxford, when Gladstone was still his principal hero. But the decision to become a practising Socialist was a case of unambiguous commitment. To Wilson Socialism is unquestionably 'a moral crusade'. 'But his socialism is fundamental; it is the dropped clue in the common interpretation of him and his work that causes

---

[1] Wilson's religious convictions – very strong and notably different from those of either Ramsay MacDonald or Clement Attlee – made him the first Nonconformist Labour Prime Minister. See *The Churches and the Labour Movement*, by Stephen Mayor (Independent Press, 1967), which remarks (p. 382) on the 'extraordinary feature of English life that the Socialist movement, to which Marxian – and Owenite – sceptics and Secularists had contributed so much, produced as its first three premiers a sincere if obscure Theist, a solid Anglican, and a representative Noncomformist'.

criticism to miss its mark. It is, as he has said, not "a revealed dogma, but a spirit and a tendency": *it is a principle at once of efficiency and of service*.[2] These words were originally written of Ramsay MacDonald.[3] They are of interest because of the uncanny degree to which they apply also to Harold Wilson, for whom 'British Socialism is essentially democratic and evolutionary'.[4] One phrase is italicised as being particularly applicable to the present Labour leader for whom ideological advance (in education, social security, welfare, etc.) is inseparable from economic expansion, greater dynamism in industry and, in fact, a fundamental scientific revolution. His view of Socialism, in other words, is an 'essentially pragmatic conception, related to the age in which we live'.[5]

If efficiency and service are thus quintessential in this context, Wilson has always possessed in addition the prowess to will the means as well as the end. This has involved a principle at all times central to his political thinking, namely party unity. He has long realised that if this is lacking all is lost, not least because of his ever-present awareness of the strength of opposition – social, psychological, personal and political – to his aims and methods. Wilson's approach to party unity involves assessment of where the ideologically true centre of gravity is – *or should be* – at any given moment; and this often involves support for minority as opposed to majority views, so as not to upset that over-all 'balance' previously referred to. It is thus a mistake to suppose that Wilson has made a point of favouring popular causes; the opposite has more often been the case, particularly between 1951 and 1962.

After his legendary rise to Cabinet rank in the late nineteen-forties – when he himself was just over thirty – Wilson suddenly resigned, in 1951, from the Presidency of the Board of Trade. For reasons vital to an understanding of his political make-up this resignation did not, *in the long run*, damage either party unity or his own future career. The issue concerned Hugh Gaitskell's proposed £4,700 million arms programme which would have involved an expenditure cut in the social services. Aneurin Bevan resigned on principle because 'his' Health Service would be the prime sufferer. Wilson, helped by his experiences at the Ministry

[2] Italics added.
[3] By Mary Agnes Hamilton in *The Book of the Labour Party*, ed. Herbert Tracy (Caxton, 1926), iii, 141.
[4] cf. Harold Wilson, *The Relevance of British Socialism* (Weidenfeld & Nicolson, 1964), p. 2.
[5] cf. Harold Wilson, *Purpose in Politics* (Weidenfeld & Nicolson, 1964), p. 270.

of Supply in 1940, resigned because he was convinced that the proposed programme could not be fulfilled in the time stated and that it was unnecessary and wrong to attempt to finance an unrealistic arms programme by the measures proposed. Bevans's resignation was entirely dogmatic. Wilson's was guided by greater sensitivity to reality and the future as well as to the fundamentals of Socialism; by a principle, that is, 'at once of efficiency and service'. Wilson turned out to be right, though the subsequent arms cut-back was, ironically, made by a Conservative government. It is important to recall, meanwhile, that Wilson was never a 'Bevanite', and even remarked that there was never really any such thing as 'Bevanism'. Wilson, in other words, has never looked on Socialism as a theory to be molly-coddled in a vacuum; still less has he ever expected it to flourish in a Labour movement damaged by its age-old proneness to internal division. It was thus that Wilson took his stand on the twin pillars of party unity, as against Bevan in 1954, and fundamental Socialist ideology, as against Gaitskell in 1960.[6]

On the former occasion Bevan resigned from the Shadow Cabinet, and Wilson, being next in line, was automatically deemed the man to replace him. As he wrote, however, to the Secretary of the Parliamentary Labour Party: 'I am in entire agreement, as the Party know, with Aneurin Bevan on the policy issues involved – on the dangers not only of Mr Dulles's policies in South-east Asia but also of German rearmament. Obviously, therefore, it is extremely difficult to accept cooption to a vacancy caused by his resignation. Nevertheless what matters in the last resort is the unity and strength of the Party.'

The latter situation came about through the new line taken (in 1960) by party leader Hugh Gaitskell who regarded Clause Four, the main plank of Labour policy since 1918, as ripe for immediate scrapping. But within the context of evolutionary Socialism, the very vagueness of this Clause – the product of Sidney Webb's fertile brain – with its demand for the common ownership of the means of production, distribution and exchange, was its strength, for it permitted flexibility in any Labour programme. To Wilson it seemed a grave error to delete, by a stroke of the pen, so basic an article of Socialist faith when the question of nationalisation had, in any event, to be decided on the individual merits of each particular case. In fact Gaitskell's defeat over Clause Four at the next conference was not as serious for him as the defeat of the Executive (at the same conference) on the question of defence, when a

6 cf. Gerard Noel, *Harold Wilson* (Victor Gollancz, 1964), p. 119.

resolution for unilateral disarmament was carried by a small majority.

It was this (not the Clause Four battle) that originated Gaitskell's famous phrase that he would 'Fight, fight and fight again' to ensure that the decision was reversed. Wilson was no unilateralist but he did differ from Gaitskell as to the means of achieving a similar aim. He wished, in fact (and in a manner typical of him) to retain the basis of the official defence statement without condemning the wishes of the party conference.

With Hugh Gaitskell's untimely death (early in 1963) Wilson inherited the leadership of a party whose new-found unity owed more to himself than any other individual. During his first administration (1964–6) such unity was not likely to be seriously threatened because of the razor-thin majority secured by Labour in the 1964 general election.[7]

The scene was wholly different in the late sixties when the mammoth battle to restore the balance of payments was finally won but only at the cost of much extremely unpopular legislation. Party unity moreover – inevitably vulnerable during the false security of a substantial parliamentary majority – faced a crucial test at this time on the question of industrial relations. It was a question of party unity, not alone but in conjunction, as invariably with Wilsonian political philosophy, (and the pattern in this regard is remarkably consistent) with national efficiency and basic ideologies. In April 1969 legislation on prices and incomes was being phased out in favour of a voluntary incomes policy; at the same time the Chancellor of the Exchequer, Roy Jenkins, was to announce in his Budget speech the decision to introduce an interim Industrial Relations Bill. One of the main purposes of this Bill was to curb unconstitutional and unofficial strikes. Its passage was considered by the Prime Minister[8] to be essential to the Government's continuance in office *unless* the TUC came forward – as they had been invited to do – with equally effective alternative proposals. With the threat of legislation in the background it was, in the event, such very alternative proposals that were finally adopted. They took the form of a 'binding agreement', that is a 'rule of Congress' similar to the Bridlington Rules of 1939; and the latter, which governed inter-union relations, were the most binding Congress had ever imposed. Without some knowledge of what this implies in trade union parlance, one may well be as sceptical

[7] In this election, held on 15 October 1964, the final figures were: Labour 317; Conservative 303; Liberal 9; the Retiring Speaker 1.

[8] In a speech outlining the proposals to the weekly party meeting on 17 April 1969.

as to the obligations involved as foreigners have often been about the Englishman's interpretation of a 'gentleman's agreement'.

It is difficult, in summing up the net result of the whole incident, to improve on the candour of Wilson's own description:

'The issues posed in Barbara Castle's White Paper *In Place of Strife* had therefore been settled by a decision to introduce legislation to enact the positive provisions of the Donovan Report, and by our decision of 18th June to follow Donovan in not proceeding with punitive legislation. For good or ill, we had accepted the views of the TUC, but only because under the catalytic action of our legislative proposals, they had "moved forward forty years in a month". . . . The advance we had won was the unanimous decision of the TUC to use its powers both in inter-union and in unofficial disputes. Although there would be cases that neither it nor any other agency could hope to settle, there would also be a large number of cases where none but the TUC would have the authority or power to settle.'[9]

Whether Wilson was wise to overemphasise, as he seemed (intentionally?) to be doing, the dependence of the Government's continuance on the 'passage of this Bill' is a very different matter. Knowing as he did the strength of the opposition press – and all that this implies in terms of power-from-above – he took what one can only call an uncalculated (or perhaps miscalculated) risk. He was and is entirely satisfied himself that the operative words were fully qualified by others used in the same speech, and that the overall context of his message was quite clear – as indeed it appears when the whole speech is read with care in the cold light of day. But he might well have anticipated that his opponents would champion a different interpretation. The net upshot of the whole affair was that Wilson got what he wanted in the national interest by methods favourable to both party unity and Socialist philosophy; but he paid a heavy price for his victory, for at that moment a new anti-Wilson legend was born and subsequently nurtured with dedication and skill.

Perhaps the most important of the test cases whereby Wilson, as a political thinker-cum-practical politician may be judged, is his stance on the European Economic Community. Its consideration, however,

[9] Harold Wilson, *The Labour Government 1964–70. A Personal Record* (Weidenfeld & Nicolson and Michael Joseph, 1971), p. 662.

should come at the end of the essay, both chronologically and logically, in view of its on-going relevance to Britain's present and future political scene. The title of this book moreover implies that final judgement on the men in question must be attempted primarily on the basis of their actual performance while holding the highest office in the land.

No Prime Minister in history had, so soon after going back into opposition, more painstakingly provided as much and as revealing information about himself while in power as did Harold Wilson in 1971. Nothing, least of all so brief a summary as the present one, can replace the massive 'Apologia' contained in his *Personal Record*. Its close study is indispensable for any clear understanding of Wilson as British Premier. It is better than any of the many books written *about* him, particularly those written with supposedly intimate knowledge but providing only the most superficial of analyses. Indeed it reveals even more of the subject than probably the author himself intended.

It portrays a man almost obsessively preoccupied with the minutiae as well as the memorabilia of prime ministerial responsibility; with the paraphernalia as much as with the potentialities of power: but aware throughout of the humbling no less than the exhilarating effects of high office. It remains true, more than ten years after his becoming party leader, that Wilson is, as he was then, 'indefinably but distinctly modest, though in no way self-effacing or retiring', while Sir Alec Douglas-Home is 'retiring and self-effacing but not particularly modest'.[10] But one might bring the generalisation up to date by saying that Sir Alec was fairly sure of himself even when he was wrong (and never felt the need for elaborate self-justification); while Wilson is not always completely sure of himself even when he is right. This, at least, is the impression that emerges strongly from his own devastatingly detailed account of his first six years of power – the sort of book, incidentally, that Sir Alec would never think of writing.

The very preoccupation with minutiae enhances rather than deprecates the overall picture of Wilson as Prime Minister: his life at Downing Street and Chequers exhibits none of the hauteur of incumbents affecting concern only with the great moments of history.[11] Apart from

10 Gerard Noel, *Harold Wilson*, p. 35.
11 As he wrote in 1964: 'What one learns in British politics, and in my case, this realisation has inevitably been more forcefully expressed since I was elected Leader of my Party, is the essential unity of the problems we are facing, the need for

anything else, Wilson enjoys his work at Downing Street far too much not to be a glutton for even some of its most extreme demands. He is conscientious to a fault in matters of protocol, procedure and preparation. During the sometimes feverish activity between 1964 and 1970 he managed almost always to remain, at least outwardly, calm. The actual volume of mental and physical exertion he expended was phenomenal, almost incredible; and there are constant reminders – with little relaxation allowed during plane, train and even car journeys – of a maxim he had devised himself when collaborating with Beveridge before and during the war, namely that there is no substitute for self-executed work. Thus, behind the hazy impression most people have of Wilson the Prime Minister – headline-hunter, hustler, traveller, debater, memory man, reparteeist, negotiator, media master, 'starring' here, 'flopping' there – there is the hidden reality of Wilson the footnote-fiend, drafting for himself his own most important speeches and statements, revelling in rather than retreating from tight corners and hostile crowds, and never – but never – neglecting his endless 'homework'.

One naturally reads and re-reads his remarkable personal narrative with constant 'interlinear' reference to the other written records of the period. By doing this and by letting Harold Wilson speak for himself, as I have done, in private question-and-answer session, one feels that one has got as close to Britain's present Prime Minister as is practical for the purposes of writing a realistic short essay about him. Anyone with more intimate knowledge would probably be 'too near' for this purpose; but neither is anyone who has not pored over the hundreds of thousands of words written by and about him likely to be very close to the mark in summing him up.

Personal diplomacy was, above all, what gave flesh to the basic bone structure of Wilson's tenure of prime ministerial office between 1964 and 1970; a distinctive style was strikingly evidenced by the encounters and relationships with world figures no less than in direct interventions (fewer than often imagined) in industrial disputes.

During his five and a half years as Premier, Wilson intervened directly in only five disputes. The first intervention was just before the 1966

harmony and integration between domestic and overseas affairs. This is why I have more than once described the task of a party leader, be he Leader of the Opposition or Prime Minister, as essentially that of conducting a mighty orchestra. One false note, one badly scored part, can destroy the unity of the whole.' *Purpose in Politics,* p. viii.

general election and ended the railway dispute; but the net effect of this on electioneering was negligible. If domestic affairs dominated this election, the most prominent of other issues during the campaign was that of the Common Market. Wilson, during a speech at Bristol shortly before polling day, said: '. . . given a fair wind, we will negotiate our way into the Common Market, head held high, not crawl in. And we shall go in if the conditions are right. . . . Negotiations? Yes. Unconditional acceptance of whatever terms we are offered? No. We believe that given the right conditions it would be possible and right to join the EEC.'[12]

With supreme irony, as it turned out, Wilson's fifth prime ministerial intervention into an industrial dispute came just before the 1970 election and broke the deadlock that had caused all national newspapers to suspend publication. Wilson thus, in the cause of free and full comment on the issues before voters, enabled two newspapers in particular to unleash attacks of unprecedented ferocity against him. His intervention, in fact, virtually lost him the election, though one Conservative paper paid handsome tribute to him for enabling the papers to resume publication. The article containing the tribute, however, did not appear until after polling day.

Personal diplomacy with regard to world figures, however, was probably the most fascinating single aspect of the Wilson years from 1964 to 1970. It deserves a whole book to itself. The passages in the *Personal Record* that touch on it stand apart, to a great extent, from the rest of the narrative; they have a more intimate and informal, but at the same time even more urgent, tone, exhibiting both spontaneous personality interaction and a sense of achievement that was extra-dimensional to orthodox politics. And this indeed was what actually happened, to the extent, for example, that peace in Vietnam (on terms better than those settled for in 1973) came within a hair's breadth of resulting from the cliff-hanging Wilson-Kosygin London talks in early 1967. The killing of the plan in Washington was a historic if tragic turning-point; but the whole episode makes gripping 'personality-politics' reading.

If this particular diplomatic exercise was the most dramatic of those engaged in by Wilson, the saving of the critical 1969 Commonwealth Conference, and the attempts on *Tiger* and *Fearless* to negotiate

[12] The state of the parties after this general election (held on 31 March 1966) was: Labour 363; Conservatives 253; Liberals 12; Republican Labour (N. Ireland) 1; the Speaker 1; Labour majority over Conservatives 110, overall 97.

[387]

meaningfully with Rhodesia's mercurial Ian Smith, do not rank far behind. But the same note of urgency and total immersion – and almost always of remarkable *rapport* even in the most unpropitious circumstances – emerges in varying degrees from all such Wilsonian encounters: with Lyndon Johnson, de Gaulle, Terence O'Neill, Kenyatta, Kaunda, Nkrumah, Pompidou, Moro, Gowon and many others.

Few reminders are needed that, on the home front, Wilson's first administration inherited an unprecedented adverse balance of some £800 million. It was not generally anticipated in the 'money' world that – in his second administration – this would be put right; but it was. And Wilson thus came within an ace of being the first man in history to be elected Prime Minister three times running. But his departure from Downing Street in 1970 turned out to be only a temporary separation.

Harold Wilson's initial overall achievement as Prime Minister went, of course, far beyond the mere balancing of Britain's books. The pace he set himself and sustained to the bitter end (future historians may judge this to have been a mistake) was flat out from the word go. An almost immediate decision was made to proceed as if there were a majority not of five but of a hundred. This was to establish the paramountcy of long-term aims in contrast to the atmosphere of electioneering that had been going on for the previous year and a half. The international financial position was the first priority. The principal weapon adopted with a minimum of delay was a 15 per cent surcharge on all imports except food, tobacco and raw materials. And the pattern for the early days of Britain's first Labour Government for thirteen years was then outlined in the Queen's Speech: in overseas affairs emphasis was laid on interdependence, on nuclear questions and on the United Nations and its agencies; at home, principal stress was on economic strength and social progress, with special provision for regional planning and the development areas.

The deficit inherited in 1964 has been played up and played down for purposes of party propaganda. (And when the Labour leader returned to Downing Street in March 1974, the balance of payments position was no less than five times worse than it had been ten years earlier.) Some have felt that Wilson allowed himself to become disproportionately influenced by this problem in the late sixties and almost obsessively preoccupied by its solution. The decision to impose surcharges had been preceded by a fateful decision by the new Prime Minister, during the first weekend, not to devalue sterling. To do so, within twenty-four hours of taking office, would have been politically tempting; but the temptation was resisted. When, three years later, devaluation was forced on the Government, it was at least recognised (and internationally backed) as an economic necessity rather than a political expedient.

Wilson will long be remembered for his immense energy, unremitting attention to detail and almost incredible resilience in times of adversity. All three qualities were much in evidence during his celebrated 'first hundred days' of office. The quality of resilience was particularly needed after a shock defeat in a by-election at Leyton in January 1965, when Patrick Gordon Walker narrowly lost to the Conservatives.[13] This reduced the Government's majority from five to three. Lord Longford (Lord Privy Seal) could hardly believe how outwardly unconcerned Wilson seemed when discussing routine business with him within hours of so unnerving a development. But Wilson is very good (perhaps too good) at hiding his acute sensitivity; though inwardly shaken he not only refused to bow to the inevitable feeling around him that the end was nigh, but became more determined than ever to govern according to mandate. His approach to this task was characteristic; for the extent to which Wilson (and even his rivals are quick to confirm it) stays near to people is remarkable. Even at the busiest moments he has never neglected close personal contact with constituents and other voters. At the beginning of 1965 it seemed clear to the Prime Minister that his ministers were operating, however conscientiously, at one step's remove from the party in the country as a whole. A back-to-the-grass-roots process was set in motion by the Premier himself; very possibly it was this, more than anything else, that enabled him to survive for another year before having to call a general election.

Before 1965 was out the worst financial implications of the balance of payments deficit had been blunted, and the distinctive hand of Wilson had been imprinted on the foreign field as well: what he referred to as the 'pretence' of nuclear independence had been ended, as had the controversial 'Multilateral Force'. Wilson's Scarborough philosophy on technology[14] was beginning to bear fruit in terms of acceptance by

13 Patrick Gordon Walker had been Wilson's first choice as Foreign Secretary but he had been defeated at Smethwick at the general election. The by-election at Leyton, made possible by the elevation of Frank Bowles to the Lords, was won by the Conservatives by a majority of 205.

14 As set out in his speech to the Labour Party Conference of 1963.

British industry, and the new corporation and capital gains taxes had inaugurated a virtual fiscal revolution. The size and scope, in fact, of the new Government's legislative programme up to that time exceeded any two legislative sessions between 1951 and 1963. With hardly a pause for breath the programme for the next session seemed even more ambitious, foreshadowing, as it did, the Prices and Incomes Bill among its most important provisions.

What stands out sharply, however, from the mass of detailed history for this period, is the driving force of the Prime Minister himself. It was almost entirely due to this that, in the country at large, confidence in the Government was increasing. This meant that an election was not vital; but for the sake of a more clear-cut mandate it seemed eminently desirable, being held, and triumphantly won, on the last day of March, 1966. The victory had important personal effects for Wilson. He became freer to spend more time in different parts of the country, something he was always very anxious to do. He had the welcome opportunity of looking for himself at housing progress and other social problems, and for visiting industrial organisations, research stations and trade union conferences. And as 1966 went on it became clear that the trade deficit had been forced back to a point almost of balance. From now on the Prime Minister could address himself to his favourite themes of social reform, and a more human future for ordinary people, from a position of economic strength. Had it not been for a prolonged and somewhat shattering seamen's strike during the summer of that year, a sort of economic-social miracle might have been in embryo. As it was the strike proved an acid test of government determination to preserve the criteria laid down for an incomes policy. The test was passed, but at heavy cost. The earlier advances – the first fruits of Wilson's personal dynamism – began to be counterbalanced. The Prime Minister, in a doughty, dogged style now becoming familiar to viewers and voters, hit out not only at the employers, but also, on the union side, at 'pressures which are anything but democratic'. This was an obvious reference to the notorious fact of Communist or near-Communist terrorising tactics against moderate members of the seamen's Executive. Wilson did not hesitate to name names when challenged to produce evidence for his charges.

All of this helped to highlight the difficulty of retaining as Minister of Technology (an entirely new creation under Wilson) a man, namely Frank Cousins, who was at the same time General Secretary of the

Transport and General Workers' Union. The appointment – a typical example of Wilsonian *penchant* for balance and consensus thinking – had worked well to begin with. But a tougher incomes policy – as foreshadowed by the Queen's Speech following the 1966 election – had practical implications which Cousins could not conscientiously accept. He was replaced at this (by now greatly enlarged) Ministry by Tony Benn, hitherto a highly successful technological Postmaster General and, though often misunderstood, already looked on by many as a possible future prime minister.

Wilson's astonishing resilience was never more needed than in the grim period between the summer of 1966 and the end of the following year. The damaging seamen's strike turned out to be the first in a series of fortuitous economic setbacks. Stringent economic measures and a prolonged wage freeze postponed but could not prevent the need to devalue the pound in November 1967. There was evidence, however, that Wilson's personal magic *vis-à-vis* ordinary people was still working behind an economic screen now in need of more armour plating. The wage freeze, though total, was honoured without exception. The only major dispute during its six-month duration (October 1966–April 1967) was a strike against redundancies in BMC's radiator factory at Oxford.

Devaluation when it came occasioned one of Harold Wilson's major mistakes while in office. The actual decision to devalue was made imperative not by any failure of the policies which had in fact already turned the famous deficit into a surplus. The decisive factors were the consequences of the crisis in the Near East – notably the closure of the Suez Canal – combined, at home, with dock strikes in Liverpool and London, followed by financial manoeuvring within the Common Market (then generally referred to as 'the Six'). Wilson's mistake was in not presenting devaluation to the nation as a reverse of fortune, although this had been his original intention. He was persuaded by others, notably Richard Crossman, to describe it in more euphoric terms. This marked a psychological turning-point in Wilson's premiership. Having played down defeat in 1967, he was unable, in 1970, to extract full electoral mileage from what was in fact an immense personal triumph: his holding together of a notoriously divisible party through the six most momentous and difficult years of its history, while simultaneously winning the battles for solvency and his concept of a Socialist New Britain.

[391]

His tactical error did not, of course, prevent his exploiting, with the plentitude of his political and economic expertise, the full potentialities of devaluation. By the end of 1969 he could make a 'look around' speech at the party conference at Brighton which, with justification, painted a rosy picture. A man with less steel-like political nerves might well have been got down by the Opposition's supreme confidence that neither he nor any other Socialist leader could get the economic situation right. But he had done so, and by early 1970 opinion polls were showing a marked trend toward Labour. The gap in Wilson's favour appeared to widen into a chasm, and there was talk of a possible Labour landslide. But there is often talk of landslides, which seldom happen; and anyone over-confident of a Labour victory was reckoning without the expensive and formidable machinery of Conservative organisation, especially in such moments of supreme emergency. To the computerised strength of Central Office moreover were allied strong, silent armies of Conservative ladies in town and hamlet: an example of power-from-above at its most intangible and most intense. Wilson was defeated by it in June 1970.

Though, in his *Personal Record*, he disclaims having been certain of winning this election, he clearly expected to do so. The aftermath of defeat was traumatic for such a personality as Harold Wilson as he looked back in anguish during the months that followed. Then came the pouring out onto paper of the chronicle of his years of office; and the very method, apart from the content, of this chronicle greatly helps to fix Wilson's 'place' among the prime ministers. For he worked on the book not only at home with all records of events readily available, but with equal speed during odd hours and in all sorts of different places while travelling around, relying for the most part on his remarkable facility for total recall. This precious inheritance from a very gifted father enabled him to put a personal stamp on his premiership in a manner equalled by few if any other prime ministers. But it was a weakness as well as a strength. For it was linked to something first acquired during a key wartime job involving familiarity with the Civil Service and then, after the war, as Parliamentary Secretary at the Ministry of Works: intimate practical acquaintance – the salient facts never being forgotten – with every single ministerial department. As a consequent perfectionist and demon for detail, this led Wilson, the possessor of a prodigious memory, to enunciate a highly individualistic view of a premier's function:

'Every Prime Minister's style of government must be different, but I find it hard to resist the view that a modern head of government must be the managing director as well as chairman of his team, and this means that he must be completely *au fait* not only with the developments in the work of all main departments, including the particular responsibility of No. 10, but also with every short-run occurrence of political importance. And all he does, and says, must be part of a coherent political strategy.'[15]

This has been a source of immense strength at most times, particularly when things were going really well. It has enabled him to take a broad and long-term view, to be a step ahead of others, and – because of his memory, grasp of detail and late-flowering dialectic skill – to sparkle in debates and interviews. (Not the least considerable of Wilson's personal triumphs was to graduate from being considered, in the late forties, one of the dullest and flattest orators in the House, to dominating its proceedings, both in Opposition and as Prime Minister, through most of the sixties.) But the very breadth of his strategic concept can be a cause of weakness in times of adversity; for it necessarily involves, at all stages, the provision of alternative policies ('leaving the options open'). And although these are invariably adverted to in advance by Wilson, they usually come under the heading of 'small print' as far as the general public (to say nothing of the Opposition) are concerned. And when options left open have finally had to be exercised, Wilson has come to be looked on by many as a short-term tactician rather than a long-term strategist. To make matters worse for his 'image' he has, despite his basic cautiousness, an inclination to live dangerously in certain directions, generally reserving, for example, his criticisms of trade unionists for trade union conferences and those of speculative excesses and unpatriotic attacks on sterling for City audiences. Those who have, year after year, worked very closely with Wilson laugh at the description of his being wily and devious. They know him to be neither. But it may be that the outward appearance of one or the other has, at times, been an unconscious cover for acute sensitivity to criticism.

He was naturally apprehensive of an overdose of this on the morrow of his 1970 electoral defeat. Little consolation, at that moment, were certain undisputed facts: the beginnings of his 'New Britain' with sweeping reforms in the realms of education, social security, welfare,

[15] *Personal Record*, p. 45.

transport, taxation, and the mining and the other industries. And this had been achieved not at the cost of bankrupting Britain, but simultaneously with turning the unprecedented deficit into a large surplus. The cost was of a different kind. It was a cost as personal to Wilson as was the degree of his own responsibility for the achievement involved. And this was considerable. But of the many mistakes inevitably made in the course of its pursuance, perhaps the greatest was allowing an aura of infallibility to grow up around Downing Street, thus obscuring the true Wilson: a genuine man of the people who, idealistic and supremely talented, had got to the top in a pitilessly competitive world.

At the moment of electoral defeat in June 1970, Wilson remarked, in answer to a journalist's question:

'No incoming Prime Minister, if Mr Heath takes over, in living memory has taken over a stronger economic situation. I wanted to use that as we have never been able to, in the past five or six years, to use the economic situation for building on what we have done, for example in the social services, health and education and social security and housing – to accelerate what we have been doing, to intensify and develop it. Now we hand over the means to do that, to somebody else.'

The strong economic position inherited by the incoming Prime Minister would be of particular significance in the attempt to enter the EEC 'from a position of strength'. The Labour Government's application for EEC membership came at a time when sterling was strong and Britain's economic position improving; it was endorsed in Parliament by a vote of 488 to 62.

In 1972, on the other hand, legislation to enable Britain to join the EEC at the end of the year was subject to certain crucial divisions in the House of Commons. That the Government's majority was on occasion down to a single figure was due not to the fact that Wilson, now in opposition, had changed his mind on the whole issue, but to the fact that he hadn't. His most succinct statement on the matter had been made as far back as 1962, when he said, 'Our position is that if we can get the terms, then we go in.'[16] Despite the millions of words and thou-

[16] House of Commons debate, 8 November 1962. The sentence quoted above was immediately preceded by the following passage: 'The third thing I must say – and

sands of negotiating man-hours that have been devoted to this subject in the interim, there has never been any change in this basic Wilsonian stance as regards the EEC; but there is of course a considerable differ-ence between the circumstances wherein entry was being sought in 1967 and those wherein it was actually achieved in 1972. The 1972–3 terms were not 'the terms the Labour Government told Europe in 1967 would be necessary for British entry'.[17] And in addressing the Socialist International Congress in Vienna in June 1972, Wilson reminded his audience: 'The decision, of Conference and of the Parliamentary Party, has not changed. The policy of the British Labour Party is one of opposition to the terms negotiated by the Conservative Government, not to the principle of entry on the right terms'.[18]

In other words, the lapse of six years, during which so many changes had occurred, had convinced Wilson – rightly or wrongly – that the terms felt acceptable by the Government in 1972 for EEC entry would, mainly through the heavy demands of the Common Agricultural Policy, produce disadvantages – particularly in terms of rising prices at home – insufficiently counterbalanced by the advantages envisaged. Soon after Wilson had become Prime Minister again in 1974, the first steps were taken by the new Foreign Secretary, James Callaghan, towards re-negotiating the terms of British EEC membership.

Light is above all shed on Wilson's political approach to such major problems by his personal-cum-parliamentary diplomacy during the early seventies. It was in a sense the supreme test for his leadership, certain to have similar but ever-further-reaching effects on his own future and that of his party than his actions in the early fifties. In 1971–2, with the two main parties divided on the Common Market issue, the task of both party leaders was delicate. Fortunately for Mr Heath, Conservative anti-Marketeers were unwilling to push their opposition

---

it is perhaps a pity that I need to say it, but our position has been misrepresented so much – is that our attitude is not based on national sovereignty. We are not clinging like woad-painted aboriginal Britons to outmoded concepts of national sovereignty. In our first debate in August 1961, I said: "The question is not whether sovereignty remains absolute or not, but in what way one is prepared to sacrifice sovereignty, to whom and for what purpose. That is the real issue before us. . . ." That has been our attitude right through.'

[17] Wilson's speech to the Labour Party Conference, Blackpool, 1972. The speech is important as containing detailed examples of respects in which conditions for EEC entry as insisted on in 1967 differed from those accepted in 1972.

[18] Labour Party Information Department, *News Release* S. 153/72.

to European entry to the point of bringing down the Government. Wilson's problem, meanwhile, was to pilot the official Labour policy of 'entry on the right terms' as between the Jenkins line of accepting the terms then offered and views of those (a much smaller group) opposing entry altogether.

The climax came at the 1972 Labour Party Conference where the spirit of tolerance overcame any tendency toward a major split. Veteran politicians could recall the contrast with 1939 when Cripps, Bevan and Strauss were expelled from the party for opposing official Labour policy with their demand for a popular front against the appeasement of the Chamberlain Government. Though unity was restored under Clement Attlee, it was lost again in the days of Gaitskell, who, with all his virtues, seemed powerless to prevent deep bitterness between himself and other leading party members. Such bitterness came to an end with Wilson. Preservation of party unity has been his special achievement and was a key factor in winning the general elections of February and October 1974.

Historical parallels, if seldom wholly exact, are invariably helpful, for example Asquith with Burleigh, Macmillan with Walpole, Churchill with the Elder Pitt, Heath with Peel. But particularly useful is the comparison between Wilson and George Savile, Marquis of Halifax, provided one makes full allowance for the changed interpretation, during three centuries, of the word 'Trimmer'. For Halifax, a key political figure in the reign of Charles II, the word signified 'no more than this, that if men are together in a boat, and one part of the company would weigh it down on one side, another would make it lean as much to the contrary'.[19] Macaulay says of him:

'He was the chief of those politicians whom the two great parties contemptuously called Trimmers. Instead of quarrelling with this nickname, he assumed it as a title of honour, and vindicated with great vivacity the dignity of the appellation. Every good thing, he said, trims between extremes. The temperate zone trims between the climate in which men are roasted and the climate in which they are frozen. . . .

Thus Halifax was a Trimmer on principle. He was also a Trimmer by the constitution both of his head and of his heart.'[20]

[19] H. C. Foxcroft, *Character of the Trimmer* (Cambridge, 1946).
[20] Macaulay's *History of England*, i, chap. 2.

The application of such principles, duly brought up to date, has obvious relevance to the Labour Party of today, never more so than during the run-up to the general election of February 1974; and the state of the parties after all the votes had been counted[21] made another election inevitable in the near future. But it was with characteristic determination and confidence that Harold Wilson, in March 1974, kissed hands for the third time as Prime Minister, to become head of the first minority government of recent years. It was a dramatic and historic moment with nothing but imponderables and uncertainties lying ahead. Wilson, however, applied himself to the land's highest office with his customary energy and dynamism, now tempered by a concern to delegate more authority to others and to mastermind affairs from what he called a 'half-back' position. His interesting choice for the key post of Secretary of State for Employment was the colourful veteran parliamentarian Michael Foot; and his concept of a new 'social compact' to govern industrial relations found favour with voters in the General Election of 10 October 1974. Harold Wilson was on this date returned to prime ministerial office for the fourth time in a victory which was more impressive than at first appeared from the final state of the parties.[22] For the same forces – unknown to any computer – that had defeated Labour in June 1970 were strongly at work in marginal constituencies in October 1974;[23] and the same prior presumption of overwhelming Labour success had sprung from yet another opinion poll miscalculation. Wilson nevertheless achieved a majority over all the other parties of an unprecedently fragmented 'opposition', and the Conservatives received the lowest percentage of popular votes recorded this century. Short of extreme partisanship there was no belittling this triumph for a Labour leadership whose mantle now appeared more likely than ever to fall eventually on Anthony Wedgwood Benn, a politician with the advantageous distinction once enjoyed by Wilson of being exaggeratedly attacked and complacently underestimated by his opponents.

To none, perhaps, more than to observers belonging, like myself, to no political party, did October 1974 seem to portend a major turning point in British political history. For the Labour Party now began to

[21] Labour: 301; Conservative: 296; Liberal: 14; Others: 23.
[22] Labour: 319; Conservative: 276; Liberal: 13; Scottish Nationalist: 11; United Ulster Unionist: 10; Plaid Cymru: 3; Others: 3.
[23] See page 392.

look unmistakably like becoming – in fulfilment of Wilson's great ambition – the normal governing party of the future. And the man who had kept this party united as well as inspired had simultaneously set his seal on the most successful peacetime premiership of modern times. Described, on the day after the election, by so leading a conservative as Edward du Cann as 'the most accomplished politician of our generation', Harold Wilson had already staked a claim to ultimate recognition as one of the greatest of all the Prime Ministers.

BIBLIOGRAPHY

Books by Harold Wilson
New Deal for Coal (London, 1945)
War on World Poverty (London, 1953)
Purpose in Politics (London, 1964)
The Relevance of British Socialism (London, 1964)
The Labour Government 1964–70. A Personal Record (London, 1971)

Foot, Michael, *Harold Wilson. A Pictorial Biography* (London, 1964)
Noel, Gerard, *Harold Wilson. A Political Biography* (London, 1964); *The New Britain and Harold Wilson* (London, 1966)
Smith, Leslie, *Harold Wilson* (London, 1964)

23

EDWARD HEATH

BY

ANDREW ROTH

Edward Richard George Heath, PC, MBE, born 9 July 1916 and educated at Chatham House School, Ramsgate, and Balliol College, Oxford. Served in France, Belgium, Holland and Germany 1940–46; Major, 1945; Lieut-Col. commanding 2nd Reg HAC (TA) 1947–51. MP (Cons) for Bexley 1950–74, Sidcup 1974–   ; Assistant Whip, February 1951; Lord Commissioner of the Treasury, November 1951; Joint Deputy Chief Whip 1953–55; Parliamentary Secretary to the Treasury and Chief Whip 1955–59; Minister of Labour 1959–60; Lord Privy Seal 1960–63; Prime Minister, 1970–74; Chairman, Commonwealth Parliamentary Association, 1970–   ; Member of the Council of the Royal College of Music 1961; Chairman, London Symphony Orchestra Trust 1963–70; Vice-Pres., Bach Choir 1970–   ; Fellow of Nuffield College, Oxford, 1962–70; Hon. Fellow 1970. Co-author of One Nation, a Tory Approach to Social Problems, *1950; author* Old World, New Horizons, *1970.*

EDWARD HEATH

'None goes so far as he who knows not
whither he is going.' Oliver Cromwell

Edward Heath's narrow defeat in the February 1974 general election
only began the process of a bipartisan assessment of his three and a half
years in office. Initially, his defeat partly freed the voices of Tory backbenchers. Their criticisms of his style of leadership while in government
had been muted previously, out of both loyalty and self-interest. But
they soon began to make known their dissatisfaction when he changed
tactics without consulting backbenchers soon after Harold Wilson
had replaced him. But the narrowness of the Conservative defeat, and
uncertainty of when the next election would be held, did not free the
tongues of front bench Conservatives who had observed him more
closely from within his Cabinet. Since he might soon again be Prime
Minister, with the power to distribute Cabinet posts, this reticence was
understandable. It did, however, inhibit the judgement of political
historians anxious to fill out an assessment of where Mr Heath stands in
the parade of British prime ministers.

Partly because of his spasmodic interest in the 'One Nation' Group,
Edward Heath has been attracted by the figure of Disraeli, who started
as an 'outsider' but came to dominate Toryism. If comparisons are to
be made, however, Heath has a greater resemblance to the man Disraeli
destroyed: Robert Peel.

Robert Peel, the son of a Lancashire calico-printer, was also an
'outsider' in a party dominated by the landed gentry. He, too, had been
a 'gentlemanly commoner' at Oxford. Pushed by his party because they
thought him an efficient servant, he turned out to be a tough-minded
master. With a shy and secretive manner, he refused to take the Conservative rank and file into his confidence. His smile, said Daniel
O'Connell, 'was like a silver plate on a coffin'. Peel, too, despised the
'narrow representation' of interests on the benches behind him. Returned
by the squires to protect the Corn Laws which ensured high prices for
their produce, he became a convert to free trade in corn even before the

[401]

Irish potato blight and a poor English harvest gave power to his aboli-
tionist elbow. Mr Heath has applauded Mr Peel's decision to put 'the
national interest' before 'the landowning interest'.

It is difficult to assess whether Mr Heath will split the Tories as badly
as Peel while he is still in mid-stride. Nor is it easy to assess in which
direction he now faces (summer 1974). Prime ministers are often 'blown
off course', but few have put about as dramatically, or as secretively,
as Mr Heath. The inside story of the dramatic change from an almost
pre-war right-wing Conservatism to a very left-wing Keynsian pump-
priming was long one of the best-kept secrets of any post-war regime.
The proposal for naval co-operation with the South Africans with
which the Heath Government was launched was soon sunk without
trace. Detested offspring of the Wilson Government – boards to control
prices and incomes and government investment in industry – were
first buried with relish only to be dug up with life blown into them under
different names.

This Heathian ability to change his mind did not disturb the inner
core of his Cabinet – Whitelaw, Carrington, Barber, Carr. They saw
him not as a fancy-talking philosopher, but as a resolute man of decision. They saw him as capable of keeping his eye on the target and
persevering in that direction when all but him have lost heart and courage. His lieutenants have fought willingly by his side because they
have found in him a command quality and daring rarely seen among
post-war politicians. They felt that nobody else would have kept believing he could win the 1970 election. Nobody else, they feel, would have
pushed through the Industrial Relations Act, despite the opposition of
Labour and the trade unions and the thinly concealed scepticism of
industrialists. Only Heath, they feel, could have secured Britain's entry
into the EEC by January 1973, in the face of Labour opposition, a
divided Tory party and the drag of traditionalism and chauvinism. Who
but Heath, they insisted, could have jettisoned his long-standing opposition to a prices and incomes policy to claim as a revelation and a revolution a version of President Nixon's three-phase fight against inflation?

It was difficult to arouse similar enthusiasm among backbenchers
and activists in the country. Darting raids in different directions are
suitable for a small, mobile commando. But it is difficult for a large and
traditional army of politicians organised for set-piece confrontations.
It was difficult for an ordinary Tory MP, elected on a 1970 platform
favouring slashed government spending, to defend overnight the July

1971 decision to spend £4,000 million on 'pump-priming' to escape 'stagflation'.

Mr Heath's Cabinet lieutenants and activists in the country have largely kept their safety belts fastened and their mouths shut because of the evident risks of going 'hell for broke', as Anthony Barber described it. But by the end of 1972 the desired 5 per cent growth target had been reached, although the 1971 favourable balance of £1,000 million had been completely erased. The pound sterling continued to float, although this proposal had been rejected when Enoch Powell had proposed it and it was continued long after January 1973, when Britain had committed itself to anchor its currency. His lieutenants continued to have faith that the economy would be riding high in the autumn of 1974, the target date for a general election.

This inflationary 'gamble on growth' was overtaken in the autumn of 1973 by the worldwide inflation in raw material costs, spearheaded by skyrocketing oil prices. On top of this came the strike of the coalminers at the end of 1973. Mr Heath had never forgotten his humiliating defeat by the miners two years before. It was largely to avoid another similar capitulation he had erected his elaborate three-phase prices and incomes policy. He was willing to make the miners the most generous offers possible within his policy of dictating the limits of prices and incomes increases. But he was not willing to buy the miners off with the extra two or three pounds beyond Phase Three which would have avoided the miners' strike. Once the strike was on, his Government broadened the confrontation by imposing a three-day week. Mr Heath initially resisted the argument from Conservative Central Office and the bulk of his Cabinet colleagues that he should go for an early election. This was based on the assumption that the bulk of the middle class would vote Conservative rather than give the victory to the miners. Another assumption was that the economy would get much worse later in the year. Mr Heath delayed for three weeks before agreeing to hold a general election. In the event enough of the middle class voted Liberal to allow Labour to gain a five-seat plurality of seats. For a few days Mr Heath tried to hold on to Number Ten by offering the Liberals a coalition before handing over to Labour.

Mr Heath's willingness to take chances almost of a swashbuckling quality owes little to a background more suitable for a suburban architect or insurance executive. He was born in the middle-class seaside town of Broadstairs, Kent, on 9 July 1916, into the family of Will Heath, then a carpenter and later a small builder, and the former Edith Annie Pantony, the daughter of a poor and illiterate farmworker who had been a domestic. If, as psychologists suggest, being the indisputable favourite of your mother gives you the feeling of a conqueror, then young Ted had early reason for his obsessional drive. 'She worshipped him,' recalled a family friend. His mother gave him not only every opportunity the family could afford, but also the upward-looking aspirations and puritanical inhibitions that one would expect of an ambitious, respectable, churchgoing Victorian mother.

The mother-encouraged hard work of a bright young boy enabled him to get his foot on the crucial rungs of the musical and educational ladders. First was the best local grammar school, Chatham House School in Ramsgate down the coast. He spent nine years there, with his eye on a scholarship to Balliol College, Oxford. He failed his scholarship examination in French. But a loan from Kent County Council and his mother's willingness to pledge another £120 a year secured him entry; it was only after entry that he won the needed organ scholarship.

'Balliol opened all the doors for me,' Heath has said. Under A. D. (later Lord) Lindsay, Balliol had been broadening its intake to produce a more encompassing 'democratic aristocracy'. With a pleasant but inexorable drive, which a contemporary *Isis* compared to that of a tank, Heath made his mark across the whole range of Oxford activity. He formed the Balliol Choir, joined the Oxford Union and the Oxford University Conservative Association. Although his political ambitions were strongly evident during his four years at Oxford, so was his loathing for the dominant Chamberlain appeasers. After a trip to Spain, he was the leading anti-Franco young Tory at Oxford. He won the presidency of the OUCA against a pro-Franco Tory. He campaigned alongside Harold Macmillan against Quintin Hogg, the pro-Chamberlain Tory in the Oxford by-election. He won the presidency of the Union as an anti-Fascist candidate. His Union activity enabled him to join in a debating tour of the United States, where he warmed to 'the social freedom, the classlessness . . .'.

Heath spent six formative years, 1940–6, in the Royal Artillery, largely as Adjutant of the 107th Heavy Anti-Aircraft Regiment. As a person he was a 'loner', avoiding drinking with brother officers and regarding women as plague-bearers. As an officer he was enormously hard-working and efficient, even if given to over-documentation. His unit was the second into liberated Antwerp in September 1944. His band played at a 'liberation dance', but Captain Heath spent most of the night doing paperwork in his makeshift office. A Major in command of his own battery in January 1945, he was transferred to the 86th HAA Regiment of the Honourable Artillery Company only after the war was over. His rank of Lieutenant-Colonel was acquired in 1947 when he reformed a Territorial HAA regiment for the HAC. This led to his becoming Master Gunner within the Tower, 1951-4.

THE NEW MEMBER

By this time Heath was already a new Conservative MP for Bexley, in south-east London's Kentish suburbs. Like many another politically ambitious Tory returned officer, he had had difficulties in finding both employment and a winnable seat in the Labour-governed Britain to which he returned. After passing out joint top for his age in the Civil Service examination, he was assigned to the Ministry of Civil Aviation's Directorate of Long-Term Planning under Peter Masefield. But he did not find this congenial and was not sorry to resign on being adopted for Bexley in October 1947.

Even that marginal seat was hard to find. He had been beaten at Ashford by William Deedes, a descendant of local squires. He was beaten for East Fulham. He was beaten again for Sevenoaks. He struck it lucky at Bexley, partly because his witty friend, Ian Harvey, had been placed the week before at Harrow East. This made it easier for local activists who wanted a local boy from an ordinary family. But he had to disarm local women with 'I have no prejudice against matrimony. I just think it is not a matter that should be rushed.'

Over the next two years Heath worked very hard, attacking the 'specious promises' and 'lack of leadership' of the Attlee Government. Meanwhile, he supported himself first, unhappily, as well-paid news editor of the *Church Times*. Then, more happily but at a third of the pay, he became a trainee in the City merchant bank, Brown, Shipley. Finally, in February 1950, his gamble paid off: he was elected by a majority of 133 votes in a four-way contest in which a Communist took almost four times that margin from the Labour candidate.

Heath, already greying and plump, was one of a hundred new Tory MPs in the famous 'Class of '50', which included other ex-officer newcomers like Powell, Maudling and Macleod. They demonstrated that the domination of Old Etonians, squires and business magnates was being assaulted by professionals. Despite this, Heath had a social identity problem in what remained a class-conscious political community. He saw no point in identifying with fellow ESBs (elementary school boys), preferring to emphasise that he was a Balliol man, the Lieutenant-Colonel of an HAC regiment and a 'City banker' (at £200 a year).

Heath made a number of shrewd initial decisions. He joined the 'One Nation' Group with Angus Maude, Robert Carr, Iain Macleod and Enoch Powell. He made an impressive maiden speech in June 1950 urging European unity. He accepted in 1951 an invitation from Patrick Buchan-Hepburn to join the Whips' Office. It was as an extremely efficient, flexible and rapidly promoted member of that Praetorian Guard to successive Tory prime ministers that Heath made his mark, particularly after succeeding Buchan-Hepburn as Chief Whip in December 1955. His great achievement was in holding the Tories together in the wrenching days after the collapse of Sir Anthony Eden's Suez intervention in 1956. But Heath only came to public attention in January 1957 when the press discovered him celebrating Harold Macmillan's victory over R. A. Butler with oysters, game pie and champagne. A fellow Balliol man who had campaigned with Macmillan against Quintin Hogg in the 1938 Oxford by-election, Heath was very much a 'Macmillan man' from the outset and was trusted and consulted as such.

Heath's first chance as a minister was in Labour, beginning in 1960. His brief, nine-month role there was played very much in the pacifying Monckton tradition, very different from the part he sought to play a half-dozen years later. He was plucked out of this obscurity to make his reputation as Mr Macmillan's 'Mr Europe' and No. 2 to Lord Home at the Foreign Office, beginning in 1961. Over the next eighteen months Heath flew 100,000 miles in pursuit of terms for EEC entry that would satisfy both a divided Cabinet and a President de Gaulle mordantly suspicious of Britain as America's 'Trojan Horse'. When de Gaulle slammed the door on Britain in January 1963, he made Heath the beneficiary of popular sympathy and his own prediction: 'The Labour Party will come to power for a short and disastrous period, to be followed by the Conservatives, with Heath at their head. It is he who will enable Britain to enter Europe.'

Initially, de Gaulle's prediction seemed a nonsense. When Macmillan's prostate enabled him to throw in the towel at the Conservatives' turbulent October 1963 Blackpool conference, Butler and Hailsham were the leading contenders for the succession. Only Maudling among Heath's contemporaries had a chance. After Hailsham threw away his chance to lead the 'stop Butler' movement, on Macmillan's advice Heath threw in his lot with Lord Home to enable him to buy time to overtake Maudling.

Heath's reward was the Board of Trade, with his title upgraded at his request to 'Secretary of State for Industry, Trade and Regional Development and President of the Board of Trade'. With typical dynamism, he chose to make his mark in the year left before the general election with an attack on Resale Price Maintenance. This aroused Cabinet dissension because it was seen as divisive and a provocation to the Tory shopkeepers. But he got his legislation – and the subsequent credit for it.

Heath was deeply shocked by Labour's narrow victory in October 1964 because he could not hide his contempt for Labour as a ruling party. Sir Alec Douglas-Home named Maudling his deputy, but gave Heath the pace-setting job of policy planner and economic spokesman. While Maudling devoted much of his time to his City directorships, Heath (with only a Brown, Shipley directorship) was in command of the assault on Callaghan's mammoth 1965 Budget, with the aid of lieutenants like Anthony Barber and Peter Walker. When it became clear he was running neck-and-neck with Maudling, Heath discreetly supported the 'Alec Must Go!' campaign launched by PEST.

When Sir Alec unexpectedly decided to step down in July 1965, an over-confident Maudling confided his campaign to a diffident aristocrat, Lord Lambton, while Heath put his in the hands of efficient, thrusting Peter Walker. *The Economist* thought him more 'abrasive' and a 'riskier choice,' but he had the better record on EEC entry and the encouragement of competition. He was 'the cannon' who would 'batter down the walls'. Heath had the majority of the press, Maudling most of the Tories outside. In the Conservatives' first democratic election for leader, Heath secured 150, Maudling 133 and Powell 15.

From the outset the Heath-Wilson battle more resembled a Sicilian vendetta than Britain's normal gentlemanly politicians' rivalry. Wilson, who preferred Maudling, tried to destroy Heath by splitting the Tories three ways over Rhodesia. Heath regarded Wilson as a tricky opportunist, willing to sacrifice the national interest for party advantage. Heath surprised even enthusiasts like *The Economist* by how far right he went as Opposition leader. He ridiculed Wilson's prices and incomes policy as threatening a 'totalitarian society'. When he lost the March 1966 general election by a hundred-seat majority, Heath survived because he had performed creditably as a campaigner and because the Tories had no heart for another leadership struggle.

Heath tried to keep party unity behind him by setting a fast attacking pace led by younger men. He shelved veterans Selwyn Lloyd, Duncan Sandys and John Boyd-Carpenter and promoted younger 'Heathmen' from modest backgrounds like Geoffrey Rippon and Peter Walker. He urged party Chairman Edward du Cann to purge elderly squires from the candidates' list.

Heath made his comeback through Wilson's economic difficulties after July 1966. He attacked Wilson for devaluing in November 1967. He profited from Wilson's unpopularity as a result of post-devaluation economy measures like prescription charges. He began to win safe Labour seats in by-election swings of over 20 per cent.

Heath kept burnished his links with de Gaulle. He spoke vaguely of Anglo-French nuclear collaboration. He demanded Wilson disavow his Defence Secretary, Denis Healey, for attacking de Gaulle as a 'bad ally'. 'A Europe without France in the long run makes as little sense as a Europe without Britain,' he told a Hague meeting.

Unlike de Gaulle, Heath remained a strong defender of the United States role in Vietnam after his 1965 visit. He attacked Wilson for dissociating the Labour Government from the US bombing near Hanoi and Haiphong. In private he argued strongly with his Defence spokesman, Enoch Powell, also a critic of the Americans in Vietnam.

Although Powell made a lot of guerrilla raids on fellow Tory frontbenchers' ideological positions, he decided to commit himself most heavily on race. After some weeks of heightening attacks, Heath sacked Powell after his explosive April 1968 Birmingham speech, which he thought 'racialist' in tone. This dismissal produced widespread pro-Powell demonstration, including a march on Parliament by Fascist-led Smithfield porters and dockers. Heath had the support of the establishment, Powell of the back-street Tories. When Powell turned against EEC entry in March 1969 it was clear he was trying to destroy Heath as the young Disraeli had destroyed Peel.

Heath was furious at these stabs in the back just when the Tories were poised on the brink of victory on a rather right-wing platform, as unveiled at the Selsdon Park Hotel in January–February 1970. A strengthened police force and a stronger law on trespass was promised to block unruly pickets and anti-Apartheid demonstrators. Direct taxation would be cut. Agreements with trade unions would be made legally binding. Immigration controls would be tightened. Heath also swung rightwards on education by dropping his liberal friend Sir Edward Boyle and replacing him with a grocer's more right-wing daughter, Mrs Margaret Thatcher.

Suddenly Tory confidence plummeted at the end of April 1970 when the Harris Poll and Marplan both showed Labour in the lead for the first time since 1967. Wilson called for a general election. Leading Tories, who had hoped that Heath's attractiveness had been enhanced by his winning the Australian ocean yacht races, resumed their conviction that he was the party's albatross, to be jettisoned as soon as the election was over. Only Anthony Barber and Lord Aldington shared Heath's unbending self-confidence. In fact, the tide shifted in the last week. Tory market researchers had discovered that their best hope was to persuade working-class housewives that they could curb price rises. Heath resisted, but on 15 June a monthly trade deficit of £31 million was announced. Next day reporters were given a statement signed by him that tax cuts and curbs on nationalised industries' prices 'would, at a stroke, reduce the rise in prices', while Labour might bring in another devaluation.

When Edward Heath became Britain's unexpected Prime Minister in June 1970, he had 'made it on his own', owing little to anyone else. Most of his Cabinet appointments – Maudling (Home Office), Macleod (Treasury), Sir Alec (Foreign Office), Carrington (Defence) – were predictable. Some – Prior (Agriculture) and Peter Thomas (Wales *and* party Chairman) – owed more to loyalty than to proven ability. His exclusions – particularly of Powell and du Cann – showed how strong could be his pique.

His initial policies were right wing enough to be almost pre-war in quality. He told the October 1970 Blackpool conference he was trying to persuade 'our fellow citizens to recognise that they must be responsible for the consequences of their own actions'. His Minister of Technology, John Davies, predicted that 'lame ducks' would be plucked. The October 1970 'mini-Budget' cut expenditures on school milk and subsidies on council houses and increased prescription charges. The interventionist Industrial Reconstruction Corporation and the Prices and Incomes Board were both wound up. Thomas Cook was tagged for denationalisation. As if to make clear that a new man was in charge who would not accept dictation from the black Commonwealth leaders, an unnecessarily exaggerated campaign was launched to announce the sale of arms to South Africa. It was 'sold' as necessary to protect the vast Indian Ocean against a massive Soviet naval influx. But in the end all that was involved was the sale of a few helicopters and frigates. It seemed hardly worthwhile souring the Singapore Commonwealth Prime Ministers' Conference in January 1971 over this.

This policy of unnecessary confrontation carried on longest with the trade unions, partly because Heath believed both in curbing trade union power and giving more incentives to entrepreneurs. He made this most evident on a *Panorama* programme on BBC-TV on 9 November 1971 when he denounced as 'blatantly nonsensical' the arguments used in the Scamp pay award of a 14 per cent increase for dustmen while applauding as 'incentives' the tax cuts promised the middle class in Anthony Barber's mini-Budget the month before. This policy of confrontation began to crumble. The Cabinet stood up to the electricity workers, but the award of the Wilberforce tribunal turned out to be an 18 per cent increase. In January 1972 Heath decided to fight it out with the miners, with the assurance that there was eight weeks' supply of coal above ground. In February, just before the country ground to a complete halt, the Government gave the miners almost exactly what they had demanded. The patent failure of confrontation made the Industrial Relations Act almost a dangerous irrelevance, which neither the Government nor industry wanted to invoke.

More fundamental was the search for a new formula for keeping the mixed industrial economy working at full stretch while making its living in an increasingly competitive world. The need to rescue Rolls-Royce airplane engines by nationalisation in February 1971 knocked off one leg of a doctrinaire approach. The need to prevent the death of ship-building on the Clyde severely damaged the other. But the very seat of Tory belt-tightening was blocked by the discovery that the policies of the outgoing Labour Chancellor, Roy Jenkins, had been much more powerful than anticipated in cutting imports while expanding money in circulation. When Heath suggested cutting the money supply to Bank of England chief Sir Leslie O'Brien, on top of his budget-cutting activities, he was warned that it would mean widespread bankruptcies and unemployment would expand far beyond the 600,000 inherited. By the late spring of 1971 this figure had expanded to 750,000, with the assurance that it would top one million by the next winter. The Cabinet faced the danger of continuing 'stagflation' and the consequent loss of by-elections at a time when the contested European Communities Bill would be wending its protracted way through a Commons, where the thirty-man Tory majority could be eroded by a score of hardline anti-Marketeers.

In July 1971 Mr Heath put the helm smartly to port, with no fanfare. His Cabinet decided to pump £1,900 million into the economy during the first year, and more in the second year, in order to go 'hell for broke' (Barber) for an annual increase in production of 5 per cent. This hope became a reality in the first quarter of 1973. By that time, unemployment, declining at 30,000 a month, had ceased to be a political problem.

The serious problem then was inflation, both international and internal. By the autumn of 1972 this threatened to become a runaway inflation. Heath tried to secure a voluntary anti-inflation agreement by negotiations with the CBI and TUC in the summer of 1972. When this failed, he took a leaf out of President Nixon's book and proclaimed a three-phase statutory control of prices and incomes, beginning in November 1972 with a standstill. Heath proclaimed this as a historic turning-point, completely ignoring the vitriol he had poured on Wilson's efforts in 1965 and 1966.

It did indeed represent a turning-point in his own attitude because he increasingly attempted to become a Peel-like Tory spokesman of the 'national interest' rather than the sectional interest. The CBI complained that the draft of the Price and Pay Code lowered the ceiling so low on possible price increases as to discourage industrial investment. The final form, which came into effect in April 1973, was slightly more flexible. But Mr Heath was still able to claim that it imposed the tightest price control since World War II, albeit without the price-reducing subsidies that had made British food prices relatively cheap before EEC entry.

As Heath entered the home stretch of his foreshortened term of office, he was much nearer the centre of the political spectrum than anyone could have anticipated at its beginning. Tories suspected him for having stirred sleeping dogs by searching for a socially just society. And trade union leaders were beginning to think that he was a man with whom they might possibly negotiate. But all that went sour with the miners' strike on which he lost the February 1974 general election.

Mr Heath's Labour opponents won a lead of only five seats over the Tories on that occasion, without an overall majority over all parties. For a weekend he remained in 10 Downing Street in the hope that his policies favouring the European Community and government-determined prices and incomes could be retained with Liberal support. But Liberal leader, Jeremy Thorpe, found it impossible to be identified with the 'architect of confrontation' unless Mr Heath could concede the proportional representation which would further enhance the Liberals but ensure that the Tories would never again win a majority on their own.

After his replacement at 10 Downing Street by Labour leader Harold Wilson, Mr Heath's bruised ego was salved by the renewal of a Chinese invitation to visit the People's Republic. When he flew to China in May, in every city he visited thousands of schoolchildren danced their welcome and tens of thousands were mobilized along the streets to demonstrate the intensity of China's official welcome. It was Chairman Mao Tse-tung's public demonstration that he preferred the pro-EEC, anti-Russian posture of the Tory leader to the anti-EEC, relatively pro-Russian attitudes of his successor, Harold Wilson. In his private conversation with Edward Heath, Chairman Mao made it clear that he hoped the Tory leader would again lead Britain and perhaps the Community into an anti-Russian position which would serve China's interest equally with that of Britain.

On his return to Britain in the summer of 1974, it became increasingly clear that Mr Heath could not escape from his winter reputation, among working people in particular, that he was the architect of confrontation and the main begetter of the winter's three-day weeks. This was not, of course, his own view. He had prided himself as being the Prime Minister who had spent more time talking to, if not listening to, trade union leaders than any of his predecessors.

When the October 1974 general election approached, he and his colleagues desperately attempted to shed the 'confrontation' image. In their manifesto they pledged themselves not to restore the union-hated Industrial Relations Act. If the Tories were returned with a majority, he promised, they would organize a government of national unity, including others besides Tory politicians – all unspecified. But the man who could not reflect in his Cabinet the broad coalition of attitudes represented in the Conservative Party found it difficult to persuade voters that he could reflect more disparate political and non-political elements. His party lost almost another score of seats, enabling Labour to emerge with a wafer-thin majority of three overall.

His loss of the third of the four general elections into which he had led the Tories opened up a new barrage of attacks on his leadership.

Even among his pro-European, pro-consensus friends there was an argument over whether they could better maintain his policies by jettisoning him. His anti-European Tory opponents wondered how they could best get rid of his policies as well as Edward Heath himself. Even among those Tory MPs who most admired his prime ministerial and parliamentary qualities, there were hardly any who thought he would be anything but a continued disadvantage at the next general election. The only questions posed when Parliament reassembled after the general election was not whether he would be deposed, but when and how.

BIBLIOGRAPHY

Roth, Andrew, *Heath and the Heathmen* (London, 1972)

NOTES ON THE AUTHORS

BLAKE, Robert Norman William, MA FBA, DLitt, FRHistS, created Lord Blake 1971. Born 1916. Lecturer at Christ Church, Oxford, 1946–47; Student of Christ Church, 1947–68; Ford Lecturer, 1967–68; member of the Oxford City Council, 1957–64; JP Oxford City, 1964. Governor of Trent College, Bradfield College, King Edward VI School (Norwich), Malvern College and St Edward's (Oxford). Provost of Queen's College, Oxford, since 1968. Married; three daughters. Publications: *The Private Papers of Douglas Haig* (ed.), 1952; *The Unknown Prime Minister, the Life and Times of Andrew Bonar Law*, 1955; *Disraeli*, 1966; *The Conservative Party from Peel to Churchill*, 1970.

COOK, Christopher. Educated St Catharine's College, Cambridge (first class honours in history). Research at Nuffield College, Oxford, under supervision of A. J. P. Taylor. Lecturer in politics at Magdalen College, Oxford; subsequently appointed Senior Research Officer at the London School of Economics. Co-editor of *Sources in British Political History, 1900–51; British Historical Facts, 1830–1900; The Decade of Disillusion; European Political Facts, 1918–73; By-Elections in British Politics.* Joint editor of Pears Encyclopedia.

CROW, Duncan. Born Aberdeen and educated in Edinburgh and London, Grenoble and the Army. Served throughout World War Two in the Royal Armoured Corps and the 'Phantom' Regiment. Author of fourteen books including *The Victorian Woman*. Television broadcaster and editor of *Armoured Fighting Vehicles of the World*.

FEUCHTWANGER, Edgar Joseph, Reader in History and Deputy Director, Department of Extra-Mural Studies, University of Southampton. MA, PhD., FRHistS. Born 1924. Married; one son, two daughters. Author of *Disraeli, Democracy and the Tory Party*, 1968; *Prussia, Myth and Reality*, 1970; *Gladstone, a Political Biography*, 1975; and contributor to various historical journals.

FOOT, Michael Richard Daniell, Professor of Modern History, University of Manchester 1967–73. MA, BLitt, FRHistS. Born 1919. Married; one son, one daughter. Formerly lecturer at Keble College, Oxford (1952–59) and Trinity College, Oxford (1956–59). Author of *Gladstone and Liberalism* (with J. L. Hammond),

1952; *British Foreign Policy since 1898*, 1956; *Men in Uniform*, 1961; *SOE in France*, 1966; editor of *The Gladstone Diaries*, 2 vols, 1968; *War and Society*, 1973.

FORREST, D. M., born Worcestershire, educated at King's School, Worcester, and King's College, London. Worked as journalist in Oxford and Birmingham. Later Assistant Editor of *The Countryman*. Freelance correspondent in Paris. Joined Tea Bureau after World War II to edit technical and historical publications and became head of the organisation; retired 1965. Author of *A Hundred Years of Ceylon Tea*, 1965; *The Oriental*, 1968; *Tiger of Mysore*, 1970–73.

GRIMOND, Joseph, PC, TD, LLD, DCL, MP. Born St Andrews 29 July 1913. Educated Eton and Balliol College, Oxford. First class honours in politics, philosophy and economics. Practised as a barrister until 1939–45 war. Served in the 2nd Fife and Forfar Yeomanry and as major on the staff of 53rd Division. MP (Liberal) for Orkney and Shetland since 1950. Liberal Whip, 1950–56. Party leader 1956–67. PC 1961. Director of the 'Manchester Guardian' and 'Evening News' since 1967. Rector of Edinburgh University 1960–63, and of Aberdeen University 1970–73, Chancellor of Kent University 1970. Broadcaster and newspaper contributor. Married; three children.

JAMES, Robert Rhodes, MA, FRSL, FRHistS. Born 10 April 1933 and educated privately in India and England, Sedbergh School and Worcester College, Oxford. Assistant Clerk of the House of Commons, 1955–1961; Senior Clerk, 1961–1964; Fellow of All Souls, Oxford, 1964–1968; Kratter Visiting Professor, Stanford University, California, 1968; Director of the Institute for the Study of International Organisation, 1968–1973; Principal Officer, Executive Office of the UN Secretary-General, 1973; UN Consultant on the Human Environment, 1971–1972; UK member, UN Human Rights Sub-Commission, 1972. Author of *Lord Randolph Churchill*, 1959; *An Introduction to the House of Commons*, 1961; *Rosebery*, 1963; *Gallipoli*, 1965; (ed.) *Chips: The Diaries of Sir Henry Channon*, 1967; *Memoirs of a Conservative* (Lord Davidson), 1968; (ed.) *The Czechoslovak Crisis, 1968*, 1969; *Britain's Role in the United Nations*, 1970; *Churchill – a Study in Failure, 1900–39*, 1970; *Staffing the United Nations Secretariat*, 1971; *Ambitions and Realities*, 1972; etc. Awarded the John Llewellyn Rhys Memorial Prize 1961; Heinemann Literary Award, 1964; FRSL, 1964; FRHistS, 1973. Married, four daughters.

LOWE, Peter Carlton, BA, PhD, FRHistS. Born 1941. Assistant Lecturer, Manchester University, 1965–68; Lecturer in History, Manchester University since 1968. Author of *Great Britain and Japan 1911–15*, 1969; 'The Rise to the Premiership, 1914–16' in *Lloyd George: Twelve Essays*, (ed.) A. J. P. Taylor, 1971; contributor to historical journals.

McCORD, Norman. Born 1930. Educated at Tynemouth High School, King's College, Newcastle and Trinity College, Cambridge. BA, PhD, FRHistS. Assistant Lecturer in History, Cardiff, 1958–60; Lecturer in History, Newcastle, 1960–69; Reader in Modern History, Newcastle, 1969–70; Reader in Economic and Social History, Newcastle since 1970. Author of *The Anti-Corn Law League*, 1958; *Free Trade*, 1970; *Industry in the Nineteenth Century*, 1971; etc., and contributor to various historical journals.

MIDDLEMAS, Robert Keith. MA (Cambridge), DPhil (Sussex). Born 1935 and educated at Stowe and Pembroke College, Cambridge (first-class Honours in history). Served for eight years as Clerk in the House of Commons. Since 1965 lecturer in modern history at the University of Sussex. Married; four children. Author of *The Clydesiders*, 1965; *Baldwin* (with A. J. L. Barnes), 1969; *Diplomacy of Illusion*, 1972; (ed.) Thomas Jones *Whitehall Diary*, published 1969–71.

NOEL, Hon. Gerard Eyre Wriothesley, son of the 4th Earl of Gainsborough. Educated at Georgetown, USA and Exeter College, Oxford. MA (Modern History). Called to the Bar, 1952. Publisher, author and journalist. Literary editor, *Catholic Times*, 1958–61; Assistant editor, *Catholic Herald*, 1968, Editor since 1971. Director, Herder Book Co., 1959–66; Chairman, Sands and Co (Publishers) Ltd, since 1967. Married; two sons and one daughter. Author of *Paul IV*, 1963; *Harold Wilson*, 1964; *Goldwater*, 1964; *The New Britain*, 1966; *The Path from Rome*, 1968; *Princess Alice*, 1974; etc.

NUTTING, Rt Hon. Sir (Harold) Anthony, Bt, PC. Born 11 January 1920, third son of Sir Harold Stansmore Nutting, 2nd Bart. Educated at Eton and Trinity College, Cambridge. Served in the Leics. Yeomanry 1939, invalided. Foreign Service 1940–45. MP (Cons) Melton, 1945–56, resigned. Chairman, Young Conservatives, 1946; National Union of Conservatives and Unionist Association, 1950; Conservative National Executive Committee, 1951; Parliamentary Under-Secretary of State for Foreign Affairs, 1951–54; Minister of State for Foreign Affairs, 1954–56, resigned; leader of UK delegation to the UN General Assembly and to UN Disarmament Commission 1954–56. Married; two sons and one daughter. Author of *Europe Will Not Wait*, 1960; *Lawrence of Arabia*, 1961; *The Arabs*, 1964; *Gordon, Martyr and Misfit*, 1966; *No End of a Lesson*, 1967; *Scramble for Africa*, 1970; *Nasser*, 1972.

PALMER, Alan Warwick, MA, BLitt. Born 1926 and educated at Bancroft's School and Oriel College, Oxford. Author of *A Dictionary of Modern History*, 1962; *Yugoslavia*, 1964; *The Garden of Salonika*, 1965; *Napoleon in Russia*, 1967; *The Laws Between*, 1970; *Metternich*, 1972; *Alexander I*, 2974.

PREST, John Michael. Born 1928 and educated at Bradfield College and King's College, Cambridge. MA Cambridge, MA Oxford. Fellow and Tutor in Modern History, Balliol College, Oxford, since 1954. Vice-Master 1971–74. Married; two sons and one daughter. Author of *Lord John Russell*, 1972; *The Industrial Revolution in Coventry*, 1959.

RAMSDEN, John. Born 1947 and educated in Sheffield and at Corpus Christi College, Oxford. Student at Nuffield College, Oxford, 1969–72; lecturer in modern history at Queen Mary College, London, since 1972. Author and co-editor of *By-elections in British Politics*, 1973. Currently engaged in research for a book on the history of the Conservative Party from 1902 till 1940.

RIDLEY, Jasper, FRSL. Born 25 May 1920 and educated at Felcourt School, the Sorbonne, and Magdalen College, Oxford. Called to the bar 1945. Member St Pancras Borough Council 1945–49. President of the Hardwicke Society, 1954–55. Contested (Labour) Winchester 1955, Westbury 1959. Married; two sons and one daughter. Author of *Thomas Cranmer*, 1962; *John Knox*, 1968; *Lord Palmerston*, 1970; etc.

ROBBINS, Keith Gilbert, MA, FRHistS. Born 1940, educated Bristol Grammar School and Magdalen College, Oxford; Gladstone Memorial Prize, 1960; first class honours modern history; Senior Scholar, St Antony's College, Oxford, 1961–63; DPhil 1964. Lecturer in History, University of York, 1963–71. Professor of History, University College of North Wales, Bangor, since 1971. Married; three sons, one daughter. Author of *Munich 1938*, 1968; *Sir Edward Grey*, 1971; contributor to historical journals. Currently engaged on a study of pacifists in the First World War and on a biography of John Bright.

ROSE, Richard, Professor of Politics, University of Strathclyde since 1966. BA DPhil. Born 1933. Married; two sons, one daughter. Formerly lecturer, Manchester University, 1961–66. President of the Scottish Political Studies Association 1967–68 and 1972–73; Secretary of the Committee on Political Sociology of the International Sociological Association; Member of the US-UK Fulbright Commission. Author of *The British General Election of 1959* (with D. E. Butler); *Must Labour Lose?* (with Mark Abrams), 1960; *Governing Without Consensus*, 1971; *Politics in England, Today*, 1974; editor of *Studies in British Politics*, 1966, and contributor to *The Times, New Society*, etc.

ROTH, Andrew. Born in New York in 1919, attended City University (BSS), Columbia University (MA), Michigan and Harvard. He was working on his PhD in Far Eastern history and teaching history in a New York secondary school when he joined the US Navy as an Intelligence officer in 1941, to be trained in Japan. Author of *Dilemma in Japan*; *Enoch Powell*; *Heath and the Heathmen*, 1972. He settled in Britain in 1950 and became a British citizen in 1965, and is the editor of *Westminster Newsletter*.

SPROAT, Iain MacDonald. Born 3 November 1938 and educated at Melrose, Winchester and Magdalen College, Oxford. MP (Cons) for Aberdeen (South) since 1970. Parliamentary Private Secretary to the Secretary of State for Scotland, 1973–74. Serving officer in the 4th (Vol.) Battalion, Royal Green Jackets, and has lectured at the Royal College of Defence Studies on guerrilla warfare. Chairman, Sproat Group of Companies.

VINCENT, John Russell, Professor of Modern History, University of Bristol. Born 1937. MA, PhD. Author of *The Formation of the Liberal Party, 1857–68*, 1966; *Pollbooks: How the Victorians Voted*, 1967; *Lord Caringford's Journal, Reflections of a Cabinet Minister*, 1971 (with A. B. Cooke); *The Governing Passion: British Cabinet Government and Party Politics 1885–86*, 1974 (with A. B. Cooke).

WILSON, The Hon John, CMG. Born 1924. Educated at Eton and King's College, Cambridge. Served in the Royal Navy in the 1939–45 war, in the Foreign Office 1944–5; as Third Secretary at Ankara, 1948, and Tel Aviv, 1950; Second Secretary at Rio de Janeiro, 1953; First Secretary at FO, 1956; Washington 1959; and at FO, 1961. Counsellor at the British Embassy in South Africa, 1965, and head of the West African Department, Foreign and Commonwealth Office, 1968. Concurrently Ambassador to Chad from 1970. Now Ambassador to Turkey. Married; two sons and one daughter. Author of *C.B., a Life of Sir Henry Campbell-Bannerman* (1973).

YOUNG, (Charles) Kenneth, FRSL. Born 27 November 1916 and educated at Queen Elizabeth's (Wakefield), Coatham School (Redcar) and Leeds University (first-class hons, English). Served 1939–45 in the Royal Corps of Signals and the Intelligence Corps, and the Foreign Office. Joined BBC European Service 1948, *Daily Mirror* 1949, *Daily Mail* 1950, *Daily Telegraph* 1952–60, and was editor of the *Yorkshire Post* 1960–64. Political and literary adviser to Beaverbrook Newspapers since 1965. Married; three sons and two daughters. Author of *John Dryden*, 1954; *A. J. Balfour*, 1963; *Churchill and Beaverbrook*, 1966; *Rhodesia and Independence*, 1967; *The Greek Passion*, 1969; *Sir Alec Douglas-Home*, 1970; (ed.) *Diaries of Sir Robert Bruce Lockhart*, Vol. I, 1973, Vol. II, 1975.